THE
GILDED LEAF

THE
GILDED LEAF

Triumph, Tragedy, and Tobacco

Three Generations of

the R. J. Reynolds Family and Fortune

BY

PATRICK REYNOLDS

AND

TOM SHACHTMAN

LITTLE, BROWN AND COMPANY

BOSTON   TORONTO   LONDON

FIRST EDITION

Library of Congress Cataloging-in-Publication Data

Reynolds, Patrick.
    The gilded leaf : triumph, tragedy, and tobacco : three
generations of the R. J. Reynolds family and fortune / by Patrick
Reynolds and Tom Shachtman. — 1st ed.
        p.   cm.
    Bibliography: p. 330
    Includes index.
    ISBN 0-316-74121-3
    1. R. J. Reynolds Tobacco Company — History.   2. Reynolds family.
3. Tobacco industry — United States — History.   I. Shachtman, Tom,
1942-   . II. Title.
HD9139.R44R47   1989
331.7′6797′0922 — dc19   88-31437
                                                               CIP

10 9 8 7 6 5 4 3 2 1

HC

*Published simultaneously in Canada
by Little, Brown & Company (Canada) Limited*

PRINTED IN THE UNITED STATES OF AMERICA

Contents

THE
GILDED LEAF

Prologue:
Sapelo, 1975

AT MUSGROVE PLANTATION on the resort island of St. Simons, off the coast of Georgia, dinner on August 6, 1975, was a strained affair. Sixty-seven-year-old Nancy Susan Reynolds, last surviving child of tobacco magnate R. J. Reynolds and one of the richest women in the world, was entertaining relatives of her late brother R. J. (Dick) Reynolds, Jr. Dick had died nearly eleven years earlier; even so, he was the focal point of the evening. The guests at the buffet included some of Dick's sons, who were Nancy's nephews, as well as Dick's fourth wife and widow, Annemarie, and Annemarie's daughter, Irene, born just thirty-six hours after Dick's death. Some of the sons had brought wives or girlfriends. One was also accompanied by his lawyer.

The dozen visitors were almost lost in the enormous living room. At 483 acres, Musgrove was the largest private plantation on St. Simons, with ten principal buildings. The drive from the front gate to the main residence, the "Boat House," was more than a mile. Two stories high, the house was built of tabby (crushed oyster shells, sand, water, and lime) and cypress; its enclosed porch fronted onto the yacht dock, while behind were formal gardens containing a maze and ancient Roman statuary. From banquettes and plaid-covered chairs, the guests looked through a glass wall at the wind-ruffled salt marshes, colored gold by the setting sun. The servants were self-effacing, the food bland, and the conversation polite, but the animosity beneath the surface was palpable.

During his lifetime, Dick Reynolds had been married four times, and the first two marriages had produced six sons, four from the first and two from the second. All six of these sons had been disinherited by Dick's last will, a consequence that had shocked them and whose effects had not disappeared more than ten years after Dick's death. Nancy had invited all of the sons to St. Simons; three of the older sons had declined to come. There that evening, having flown in from North Carolina, Florida, and California, respectively, were the youngest "first-marriage" son — Will, thirty-five, an investor and businessman — and the two "second-marriage" sons — Michael, twenty-eight, a Vietnam veteran and owner of a dinner theater, and Patrick, twenty-six, a fledgling actor. They were curious to meet their half sister, Irene, whom they had never before seen.

Long-haired Patrick was unsure what to think or feel about Irene. Her chin was dimpled, as were all of the Reynolds brothers', but otherwise she didn't resemble their dead father. She spoke mostly German, and only a few words at that, principally to her governess. She looked more like her mother, Annemarie, a plain, no-nonsense woman in her forties who had inherited Dick's estate — a fortune in the tens of millions, possibly in the hundreds of millions — after Patrick and his five brothers had been entirely cut out of their father's will.

Patrick was reeling from jet lag. Last night in Hollywood he had been out until close to dawn dancing with his girlfriend, actress Shelley Duvall. At the last minute he'd decided to take the early morning flight cross-country. Tomorrow they were all going to Sapelo, an island a few miles north of St. Simons. Sapelo had been his father's private kingdom. Most of it had been deeded to an entity Dick set up, the Sapelo Island Research Foundation; the foundation, before selling some of the furnishings of the main house to raise additional money, had suggested through Aunt Nancy that members of the family come over and bid on the items.

Patrick had had mixed emotions about coming here. He was furious at being asked to pay for the chance to own a few pieces from what he felt should have been his rightful inheritance, but he tried to conceal his emotions as he made conversation with Nancy and Annemarie. As he talked to them, or listened as they chatted with his brothers, Patrick felt coming from the women a sense that the third-generation Reynolds "boys" were not conducting their lives to the satisfaction of the wealthy aunt and widow.

When Patrick mentioned that he had appeared in minor roles in several of the films of Robert Altman, Nancy moved away from him and across the room. There was the same smug expression on Nancy's face when she talked to Michael and Will. She was cold and reserved; her demeanor became animated only when she talked about ecology. Otherwise, she was cordial and perfunctory, as if carrying out a distasteful chore with a minimum of geniality.

Annemarie said "How nice" to Patrick's descriptions of his studies with Lee Strasberg and "Isn't that interesting" to Michael's plans for his dinner theater; she smiled at the wrong moments, which gave Patrick the impression that she thought all the sons were fools. Did she imagine they didn't know about her current negotiations to sell the remaining Reynolds property on Sapelo to the state of Georgia, supposedly at Dick's request, at a fraction of what had been stipulated as its value two years before Dick's death?

The last time Patrick had been on Sapelo — and the last time he saw his father — was sixteen years earlier, when Patrick was eleven and Dick was a dying man of fifty-three. As with all of the handful of visits he'd had with his father in his life, that one had been difficult. Dick was already racked with emphysema, confined to an air-conditioned section of the mansion. Old and withered beyond his years, Dick had been an emotional weather vane, professing at one moment to love his sons, at the next sighing gratefully as he waved them away. Yes, Patrick had to go to Sapelo because he wanted to have in his home — in his life — something of his father's, but he dreaded going there because of his conflicting emotions about that same father. After all, Dick Reynolds had disinherited his sons: it was a central fact in all of their lives, one that was very hard to bear and even harder to understand.

A few months before he died, Dick had written out by hand a short will revoking all others and leaving everything to Annemarie. Almost eleven years later, that will was still being hotly contested by Dick's third wife, Muriel, and second wife, Marianne, Patrick and Michael's mother. His father's first wife, Blitz, mother of Will and the three other sons, had died in 1961.

It wasn't as if any of the six brothers were in danger of starving. Each had $2.5 million from their grandmother, Katharine Reynolds, wife and widow of R. J. This bequest Dick had been unable to take from them. Also, during Blitz's divorce she had forced Dick to set up trust funds for her sons, though Marianne hadn't managed to get the same concessions during her own divorce. In 1965, just after Dick died, Nancy and Annemarie had joined forces to offer the boys an additional half million apiece in exchange for a contractual promise that forbade them to ask questions publicly about the will or to speculate on the paternity of Irene, as two of Dick's former wives were then doing. Patrick and Michael had both been underage at the time, and there was some question as to whether their part in the deal was legal or binding. The others had signed. But why give away money if there was nothing to hide? And how cheaply had they all been bought? Patrick didn't want to fixate on the money, but its presence and absence affected his life in ways that ordinary people didn't understand. In emulation of the father he hadn't really known, he was living lavishly in the Hollywood Hills — well beyond his means, in fact — and cutting into his capital. Determined to be an actor and a filmmaker, he knew he was moving toward his goals inefficiently, not getting enough re-sults for the hundreds of hours he'd put into taking classes and making short films. Other young filmmakers took menial jobs at production companies and worked their way up; he hadn't needed a job, hadn't taken one — and hadn't progressed very far. Truth be known, his money had isolated him. Beyond that was the iso-lation that came from being fatherless. Patrick was only three when his mother and father divorced, hadn't seen his father for six years following the event, and thereafter saw him just five times before Dick died. Patrick had decided to come east to St. Simons and Sapelo because he might never have another opportunity to visit his father's sanctuary.

In the morning several planes took the group of a dozen the few miles north to Sapelo. Approached from the air, Dick's private fiefdom made Musgrove seem small. St. Simons had been com-mercialized, but Sapelo was pristine and magnificent. From above, the island was spectacular, a rectangle about twelve miles by four. Patrick could see the eight miles of untouched beach where, when he and Michael were young, they'd spent a whole fruitless day digging for Blackbeard's treasure; the trout ponds; the reflecting pool where Dick's pet goose had ruled; bird sanctuaries; marsh areas where the older sons had often come for duck, deer, and turkey hunting. You could clearly see the markings of a central swatch on which two thousand cattle had been raised, the small settlement where the island's blacks lived, the mile-long airstrip Dick had put in so he could come and go from the island with ease.

After they landed, several jeeps — Dick had bought a whole fleet of them once — took everyone over bumpy dirt roads toward the "big house." Along the jeep trail, the fragrant scents of magnolia, mimosa, and oleander hung in the hot summer air. The jeeps seemed to travel in a tunnel of shade under the stands of live oak, hung with Spanish moss, which met above the roads and gave to the paths a feeling of perpetual twilight. Suddenly there was a break in the foliage, and the jeeps burst into full sunlight shining upon a grand manicured lawn dotted with oaks and palmettos, and the clover-shaped pool with its Florentine statuary.

The very sight of South End House, with its symmetrical, elegant white-columned front and flanking wings, hit Patrick like a slap in the face: here was the home of his infancy, where once his father and mother had lived like king and queen. Even though he'd thought about seeing it again the previous night, he wasn't prepared for the rush of feelings that engulfed him now.

Walking inside, he went through the living room, turned left, and went into a study — now the province of the estate's manager — and up a back stairway to his old childhood room. Room? It was a suite of rooms where he and Michael had stayed, with their own nurse, their own kitchen and pantry and playing areas. They'd even had a miniature toilet that flushed rather than a potty. While the children's quarters were in this isolated portion of the house, the parents' bedrooms had been in another wing, down by the pool. Patrick went back into the living room and then up another set of interior stairs to the third floor, where there was a huge ballroom with a circus tent flowing from the ceiling, chandeliers of terra-cotta acrobats and jugglers. Incongruously, the furniture in here was straight-backed Victorian sofas, covered in gilt, which had come from the parlor of old R. J. Reynolds the tobacco magnate himself. Dick's father, Patrick's grandfather, was the source of all the family's wealth.

Only now was Patrick ready for what had been his parents' rooms. They were in back of the living room, near the milk-glass-domed, colonnaded indoor swimming pool, something out of a Greek or Roman fantasy, with murals of banana trees on the walls and, down by the shallow end in a recessed arch, a marble statue of Venus surrounded by ferns. To his now adult eyes, it was odd to see the pool closed off from the breakfast room by a glass partition. Dick had put up that monstrosity in the late 1950s, when emphysema had made it impossible for him to live anywhere that wasn't air-conditioned. On the air-conditioned side of the glass were the patio and separate suites for husband and wife. In the poolside drawing room and master bedroom with its marble fireplace, his father and mother had loved — and fought. In the ballroom they had been hosts at parties to which guests had been flown in by the planeload from New York and Florida, parties that sometimes went on for weeks and frequently ended in alcoholic stupor. After Dick had divorced Marianne, married Muriel, and become an invalid, he had stationed guards outside this poolside room — his sickroom — because he'd been afraid that Muriel was trying to kill him.

In the two-story-high main living room and adjacent library were actual fragments of the past. A souvenir of Dick's involvement in early aviation, which reminded Patrick that his father held a pilot's license signed by Orville Wright. A biography of Franklin Roosevelt: Dick had become treasurer of the Democratic National Committee in 1940, after munificent contributions that helped push FDR's third-term bid over the top. Hadn't his father done something similar for Truman in 1948? His mother liked to tell a story about the president telephoning Dick, who refused to take the call because he was sleeping off a hangover.

As Patrick wandered through the halls it struck him that he knew very little personally of his father. Only in the late 1950s, when he was a preadolescent, had he been allowed five visits to a remote, beleaguered, off-putting father who seemed more like a dying god than a living man. He made notes on a few things he wanted to have — two beds in which President and Mrs. Calvin Coolidge and, later, President and Mrs. Herbert Hoover had slept, arabesque columns to hold flower vases, a writing desk his father had used, some pieces his mother had loved.

"Here, Patrick, you take this," Annemarie said, pulling out of her pocket a small sterling silver wedding cup. Patrick looked at it, especially at the engraved date, August 8, 1952. Patrick knew that date. On August 7, 1952 — precisely twenty-three years ago today! — Dick had divorced his mother, Marianne, and on the eighth had married Muriel: this was Muriel's wedding cup. Annemarie repeated that he could have it. She knew it was Muriel's, not Marianne's, but didn't want to throw it away. He shrugged off the slight and put the cup in his pocket. He and Muriel had become friends; he'd send it to her. He had to stifle a bitter laugh; the bowl was a fitting symbol of the chaos left in the wake of a man married four times!

Patrick began to feel his anger rising. Had his father really wanted to abandon and disinherit his boys? Had Dick believed that the money was not good for them — or that they could escape the fate of being Reynoldses if they had less of it? Was Dick's attitude a consequence of his own childhood experience, when his own father,

R. J. Reynolds, had passed on, leaving Dick and three other children — the youngest just six — fatherless, but with an inheritance that eventually totaled $100 million and controlled all of their lives? As it was, Patrick's only real legacy from his father consisted of the Reynolds name. At auditions for acting roles being a grandson of R. J. Reynolds was a clear hindrance: jobs didn't go to people who "didn't need to work." Often he wished to change his name, forget about his patrimony.

R. J. was an enigma, too. Near leaving, Patrick caught sight of a filigreed gilt frame enclosing a portrait of R. J. Reynolds, Sr. — unsmiling, upright, remote and craggy as some Appalachian peak. This year was the one hundredth anniversary year of the founding of the R. J. Reynolds Tobacco Company. Why had a company history been commissioned and suppressed by the company for the last ten years? Why was there such a distance between the tobacco Reynoldses and the aluminum Reynoldses, when the two branches had been founded by R. J. and his elder brother, Abram? Was there any substance to the rumor — it came up at every Winston cocktail party — that in the latter part of the nineteenth century, before his marriage, R. J. had had black mistresses and sired mulatto children?

One part of Patrick wanted to chuck everything, withdraw his bids for the Sapelo furniture, go away from here, and never think about R. J. Reynolds junior — or senior — again. But he couldn't run away any longer. He entered bids on the few pieces of his heritage he was being allowed to purchase. Then he inquired about the portrait of "the founder," his grandfather R. J. Reynolds. That was not for sale. What a joke: from this morass of memories he couldn't buy a hint of a starting point, he couldn't even take home this portrait to brood upon. He'd wanted to do so because he'd realized that, despite the emotional pitfalls, he must now spend serious time and energy trying to come to terms with the conundrum of accumulation, dissipation, and fatherlessness that seemed to be the real heritage of the R. J. Reynolds tobacco family.

PART ONE

MAKING THE FORTUNE

Chapter One

Planters

IT BEGAN with a crude practical joke.

The time was 1828. In the Piedmont area of southern Virginia, among rolling fields of grain and tobacco carved from the foothills of No Business Mountain, a tall, spare eighteen-year-old boy walked along the two-wagon-wide dirt highway that went past his family's small house toward a neighbor's farm. Excess acreage there was to be auctioned off, and young Hardin Reynolds was to bid on it. He was the son of Abram and Polly Harbour Reynolds, descended from Scotch-Irish Methodist families who a generation ago had left northern Virginia and Pennsylvania to come to the edge of the wilderness. Even now, the Piedmont retained the feeling of frontier: the Cherokee and Algonquin were only slowly retreating into the westward forests; there were a plethora of bear and moose, and uncertain roads.

The owner of the extra acres was selling them either to get money to go west, as Abram's own brothers had done, or because he had had a bad harvest and couldn't afford to plant every plot he owned. Neighbors knew that Abram had been buying up property in the area for fifteen years — fifty acres here, twelve there — but that he was ill today and had sent his son in his stead. At the auction site, the rough-hewn men of the county decided to play young Hardin for a sucker. When Hardin put up his arm to bid, the other men joined in with slightly higher bids and, as he countered, kept raising theirs to spur him on. Then, when the boy was obviously far over the limit his father had set for him, the men retired from the bidding, letting the boy's high bid stand, which forced Hardin to buy the acres at an outrageous price.

Back at the Reynoldses' two-story, two-room brick house, just up from the little creek called Rock Spring, father Abram was incensed to learn of his son's purchase. He knew the value of land in Patrick and Henry counties; he also had some influence at the courthouses and might have been able to annul the transaction. However — and this was the extraordinary thing — Hardin asked his father to let his folly stand and pledged to work the place himself, if released from his filial obligation. Abram at first said no, but his wife, Polly, took Hardin's side; she was a persuasive woman. Abram gave in. Shortly, Hardin Reynolds began to raise tobacco on his own land.

As young Hardin discovered in the fall, growing and selling tobacco in backwoods Virginia in 1828 was a risky business. By his own labor a man could raise perhaps fifteen hundred pounds of tobacco, the product of two or three acres. That was the amount Hardin harvested. After the leaves were dried he prized, or stuffed, them into an enormous hogshead, or reinforced barrel. Hitching the barrel behind a horse, he rolled it along the "Norfolk" highway to Lynchburg, the nearest large town. This took several days. In the marketplace, expecting a price of five cents a pound, Hardin got three cents per — and now it was he who was incensed. Determined never again to be at the mercy of the tobacco buyers, he told his father that rather than sell raw leaf to the manufacturers, they must make and sell their own "twist" of chewing tobacco.

Again, Abram was opposed to the idea — the Reynoldses were farmers, not tradesmen or peddlers — and once more Polly convinced her chronically ill husband of Hardin's wisdom. Next year, father and son combined operations. In the front yard of the house at Rock Spring, in the crook of an already old, gnarled catalpa tree, they placed a crude press and used it to squeeze and condense the tobacco into twist. That year at Lynchburg, Hardin got ten cents a pound for his twist, enough money to pay off his entire debt on the few acres and to have some left over to buy additional land. With one masterstroke, teenager Hardin Reynolds transformed what had been a frontier farm operation, indistinguishable from a thousand others, into a goods-manufacturing, wealth-producing machine.

In the 1830s Hardin and his father dove into the new game with gusto. To supplement their own supply they bought cured tobacco leaf from other farmers, produced wagonloads of twist, and peddled them south into the Carolinas and west into Kentucky and Tennessee. They bought land and more land. Slaves to work it. Machinery. Abram became a private banker for the region, able to lend his other child, younger son David, a thousand dollars to start a trading business. David prospered, too. He went up and down the farm valleys, which had few towns or settled marketplaces, and bartered bacon and tobacco for sugar, coffee, wine, brandy, and dry goods, then resold the last for cash.

David was twenty-five and had just returned from a selling trip in 1836 when he fell ill and died. His company's clerk stole the proceeds of the trip, five hundred dollars, from his body; to recover it, father Abram and brother Hardin sued David's partner. The next year, Abram died, and Hardin became sole owner of a substantial thousand-acre estate and a thriving tobacco business.

Hardin waited five years, until he was thirty-three, to marry eighteen-year-old Nancy Jane Cox, whose family lived just on the other side of the border with North Carolina, two days' ride south of Rock Spring. The Cox family was a bit more distinguished than the Reynoldses; some of the Coxes had fought in the War for Independence and had stayed in the East to brag of it.

Now Hardin was a good, tough businessman who held deep religious convictions, but he was relatively unlettered. Nancy Jane Cox, by comparison, was better educated, knew how to write — had beautiful, clear handwriting that showed years of practice — and could sing and play the piano. She wasn't a great beauty but was well formed and sturdy; in 1844 she began to bear children, eventually giving birth to sixteen, of whom eight survived to adulthood, not an unusual ratio in those times. She had two sets of twins; one set lived only a few days, the other was born dead. As the babies died, Hardin buried them in the farm's cemetery for whites, next to father Abram and brother David; he and Nancy Jane could see the small marble markers from the window of the master bedroom, where the little ones had been birthed.

Nancy bore two girls and a boy who lived, then one of the sets of twins, and then, in 1850, another boy. This second surviving son was born soon after the death of Nancy's aged father, a conjunction that allowed her to bring into the Reynolds family a legendary good-luck totem, the Joshua Coin. It had been named for Joshua Cox, her grandfather. Red-haired, six foot six, Joshua Cox had been exiled from England in the 1750s for stealing one of the king's mistresses. During the French and Indian War he'd been captured by a native tribe but spared death because of his unusual physique. After residing with the chief for some time, Cox escaped to civilization by swimming many miles in a river, wearing little but the square Joshua Coin around his neck. The face of the coin showed the stamp of Peruvian imprint of the seventeenth century. Cox believed the coin had saved his life, and it became a totem passed down from generation to generation together with a magic phrase to be said over it.

Touched to a man's gold, the Joshua Coin would bring good fortune. However, for it to work it had to be in the possession of a son in direct descent who bore the name Joshua; if the succession were broached, woe would result. Joshua Cox married late in life, and when he died the totem passed to his son, who also married late. When that son died, the Joshua Coin was passed into the hands of Nancy Jane Cox's second surviving boy, who was probably named after his grandfather in order to receive the totem. He was Richard Joshua Reynolds.

Fifty years later, when R. J. Reynolds and his brother Abram began to amass huge fortunes, rumors spread that the Joshua Coin was one of the original thirty pieces of silver paid to Judas for his betrayal of Christ.

In the 1850s, life at Rock Spring was slow-paced and not without charm. Hardin was getting to be a wealthy man, when compared with the average Patrick County farmer, though his net worth was far less than that of the owners of the vast Tidewater coastal plantations of Virginia and Georgia. He and Nancy Jane enlarged the house, tripling its floor space. What had been the entire downstairs became just their bedroom; more bedrooms for their growing brood were added upstairs. For the first time, Nancy Jane had a dining room and living room in which to show off her collection of seashells and natural objects, and a rosewood piano. The piano was the prize of marital trading: Nancy Jane had brought with her from North Carolina a slave who didn't get along with the blacks at Rock Spring, so she agreed to send the slave back to her parents, on condition that she could purchase the piano.

Most families in Patrick County still lived in two-room homes, ate from rough plates, and slept in hard beds. Success in business allowed Hardin and Nancy Jane to expand their home, to buy good silver, a pewter tea service made in England and an étagère buffet to display it, as well as a mahogany Empire-style four-poster bed.

When the children were very young they roamed the estate's beautiful country, the mountainside, farmland, woods crisscrossed by streams, including the spring that gave the plantation its name. As with most farms in the area, the main house was for sleeping and eating. Cooking was done in a separate kitchen building; also near the main house were a granary, a smokehouse, and an icehouse, where blocks cut from the nearby creek in winter might last until midsummer. Barns used to stable horses and others for curing tobacco were ranged farther afield. The slaves lived in a "cabin row" nearer the creek and across the turnpike, closer to the mountain, in whose lee their own cemetery was located.

The day began and ended with family prayer. On Sundays, for the entire day the family attended a church at a crossroads an hour's ride away; that was also the site of a courthouse.

Both male and female little ones wore cotton checks and linsey-woolsey, slept under brilliantly colored blankets, two and three abed. In this society, when boys were about four they "dropped the slips" that they had worn, donned breeches, and began to separate themselves by behavior as well as by garments from the girls. By the late 1850s eldest son Abram, born in 1847, and R. J., born in 1850, were growing tall and handsome — the Cox blood, it would always be said. Both boys attended a small private school that Hardin supported; such farm-country schools were in session only eighty days a year, though, and took children only when they reached the age of eight.

For the children, the most exciting time of year in Patrick County was the harvest, when they attended corn-shucking parties, which proceeded evening after evening from farm to farm. For the owners of larger farms — besides Hardin there were several — there was also deer, pheasant, and fox hunting, with packs of hounds bred especially for the chase. Fox hunting was not the elegant ritual of the English gentry, but rather a pursuit of animals that stole chickens from the yard. All the game killed was eaten; it was a welcome variation on the steady diet of turnips, sweet potatoes, cabbage, and pork. The planters also liked racing on or behind horses. Hardin was one of the few men in the county wealthy enough to own a carriage.

In this relatively backward area, wealthier planters expressed their class superiority in the annual Patrick County "tournament," a hayseed version of a medieval joust. Held in an open field or on a rough riding track, it featured young men on horseback wearing colorful sashes and using wooden lances to spear metallic rings from odd places, after which they dropped the rings at the feet of their favorite young lasses. The girl with the most rings was crowned "Queen of Love and Beauty" at the grand ball — where all danced such reels as the double shuffle, the Virginia backstep, the Georgia turndown, the pigeonwing, and the chicken-in-the-bread-tray-peck-peck-peck.

The two older Reynolds girls went away to school — Mary Joyce to the Salem Female Academy in North Carolina, a Moravian boarding school that offered academic subjects as well as fine and plain needlework. Young girls would often arrive at the school accompanied by their brothers; it may have been on such a journey that young R. J. Reynolds first saw the settlement he would later help to become Winston-Salem. Not much is known about Mary Joyce or, for that matter, any of the Reynolds sisters of this generation. They neither won fortunes nor married them, though all those who survived to adulthood did marry; in the antebellum South the lives of such women were seldom memorialized in print. Girls were raised to be accommodating, while boys were brought up to be aggressive.

The major influence on Abram and R. J. Reynolds in their very young years was their mother. Historian Bertram Wyatt-Brown believes that Southern planter mothers were highly ambivalent toward their sons, sometimes smothering them with love but at other times withdrawing emotionally in ways that befuddled them and made them confused as to how to behave with women. And psychohistorian Glenn Davis, studying families of the 1850s, suggests that plantation child-rearing practices tied children very tightly to their mothers; later, as grown men, sons of the Old South professed the belief that their mothers had never shown anger or impatience. Such sons were devoted to their mothers throughout life. Abram and R. J. Reynolds revered Nancy Jane and paid court to her all their lives. In the 1880s, after Hardin's death, Abram took Nancy Jane to live with him, and in his reminiscences painted her as a saint; in the 1890s, when R. J. came into his dominance, he claimed Nancy Jane for Winston. Further, R. J. did not marry until he was fifty-four and only did so after Nancy Jane's death.

In the late 1850s, as the boys approached puberty, they passed from the domain of their mother into the realm of father Hardin. Wyatt-Brown observes that in this era, when Southern farmers emphasized patriarchy and the need for all males to work on the land, fathers were typically "close yet distant" figures, idealized by their sons even as the fathers manipulated the boys' emotions so they would follow his authoritarian dictates. The father's commands had to be followed; to rebel was wickedness incarnate. Of all the father's possible punishments, the most intimidating was shame. Abram and R. J. feared and revered their father and, from the 1850s until the ends of their own lives, followed the path Hardin set for them in the years just before the Civil War: to manufacture tobacco products and with these to garner enormous fortunes.

=

On the eve of the Civil War, Hardin Reynolds was the most successful planter in Patrick County. He owned eight thousand acres in Virginia, three thousand in North Carolina, and fifty-nine slaves. His family was among the several hundred wealthiest in the South — but unlike most of the Tidewater Southerners who unflinchingly supported the movement toward secession, Hardin and other outstanding Piedmont farmers didn't want to leave the Union. Businessmen like Hardin recognized that secession would lead to war and economic ruin. Perhaps the Southern states could reach a compromise on slavery — phase it out over time or, in return for compensation, pledge to free slaves on the death of their owner; some Virginia slaveholders were already making such pledges.

The Piedmont planters' slave ownership, writes historian J. C. Robert, was "a less formal and more patriarchal type of slavery" than that practiced farther south, where cotton was king and slavery often enforced at the point of a whip. A plantation of Hardin's size in, say, Georgia would have had five times the number of slaves — and many more problems of discipline and control. Hardin owned slaves because tobacco couldn't be grown profitably without a great many hands. It demanded attention nearly every month of the year, since there was always something to be done: fallowing, hilling, knocking the crests off the hills, planting, topping, getting rid of suckers, weeding, cutting, transplanting, harvesting, hanging plants in the barn, stripping bad leaves, taking off stems, prizing the cured leaf into hogsheads.

Hardin and his fellow planters lobbied against secession as long as they could but were outvoted. Accepting the inevitable, the large landholders of Patrick County in 1861 began to raise and outfit troops for the Confederate States of America.

Almost immediately, as the War Between the States began, Jefferson Davis's government in Richmond issued an edict that realized Hardin's worst fears. It forbade further planting of "inedibles" such as cotton and tobacco and exhorted all planters instead to raise food for themselves and for the troops. Since crops for 1861 were already in the ground, the edict would take effect in 1862. That meant Hardin had one more year in which to sell his tobacco and use the money to obtain enough supplies to last through the war.

Hardin had another problem, a hotheaded fourteen-year-old, his eldest son, Abram, who was eager to leave nearby Edgewood Academy and join the first wave of volunteers for the Confederate ranks. Father and son compromised: if Abram would do some work for the plantation, Hardin would let Abram apply for a place at the Virginia Military Institute. The work was an adventurous trip to buy "white gold" — salt, essential to preserving food in this era before refrigeration. Hardin wanted salt for the family but also to offer for sale in the small general store on his property. Because of the shortages, the price of salt had increased tenfold. Salt was already being rationed by the Confederate government. It was being produced by the Rebels at a works just above Charleston, West Virginia, which was a continual target of raids by the Union armies. At the end of September 1862, Abram set out for Charleston with some money, a four-horse team and wagon, and Bob, a black driver.

The journey was a test of character for Abram. He drove through burned-over towns, endured bad river crossings, fixed a burst wheel. There was little corn available for the horses, and the roads were infested with marauding Confederate quartermasters who ransacked many wagons. Cannily, Abram made a compact with another salt seeker to travel together; while he rode ahead and bought corn for the horses, the partner stayed with the wagons. At night they both shelled corn and fed their teams. Abram arrived home with four thousand pounds of salt and his team "fat and Slick" (as he observed in his memoir). That was enough salt to provision the Reynolds family and much of the Patrick County neighborhood throughout the war. The normally undemonstrative Hardin rejoiced so at Abram's triumph that the boy never forgot it.

Hardin gave his son a second mission: to take a wagonload of food, and some cattle, 150 miles south to Deep River, North Carolina, and exchange the beans, peas, flour, bacon, lard, and apples for spun cotton, which Hardin could stock in the store and sell to weavers. Hardin didn't want money in exchange — people were already losing faith in the Confederate currency — but he needed something to replace his losses on tobacco. This time, Abram set out on the journey with two slaves. He made good progress until, almost in sight of the seven water-operated mills of Deep River, he came to a fence and a sign that said the area beyond was quarantined because of an outbreak of smallpox. Then,

> Very quick I ordered my teemster to unhitch and feed. . . . I had determined I would not turn back with all this produce which I would be forced to take back or Sell for Confederate money just what my father Said I must not do. So I let the two negroes Sleep until mid night and wook them up & ordered them to drive on to the factory. . . . The two negro men were greatly alarmed Small pox in that day ment death I managed to get them to Stay with Cattle and wagon while I agreed to go down and interview the Superintendent. . . .

The operator of the factory must have been astounded to see the teenager and hear that he was bringing food. He praised Abram as a brave lad, assured him that the yarn was free from infection, since workers who'd contracted smallpox had been sent home, and offered liberal terms for Abram's food. Abram made the exchange and took with him, in addition to the yarn, a letter from the superintendent to three other factories, similarly quarantined. He sold more food and obtained more spun goods. After that, "I rolled for home feeling I had done the Smart thing but to my great surprise instead of my father meeting me to laugh and brag as he did when I returned with my four thousand pounds of Salt . . . he centured me very Sevierly for being So reckless Said we would bring death to my brothers and Sisters."

An anguished Hardin immediately had all the children vaccinated against smallpox. Vaccination was then a relatively new technique, and the batch used to inoculate the Reynolds children was bad. The vaccinations produced severe itching, and the older children — led by twelve-year-old R. J. — went down to Rock Spring and let the cool autumn waters wash the itch and the poison out of their arms. Younger ones, unable to do this for themselves, quickly sickened. During a terrible week at the end of October 1862, six-year-old John, three-year-old Nancy, and one-year-old Ernest all died. The bitterness of this episode scarred the entire Reynolds clan for many years to come.

Just after Christmas, 1862, Hardin kept his promise and had his wife take down in her best handwriting and spelling a letter to the Virginia Military Institute requesting admission for Abram. There was no room for him until the summer of 1863. In July of that year, the Confederacy suffered enormous losses at Vicksburg and Gettysburg; the wound to the South was mortal, but it would take the Gray armies two more years to die. Cadets continued to flock to VMI.

The school near Richmond was the citadel of Southern military tradition, with old stone buildings, constantly shined cannons, and a library of great quality. It was the South's West Point; in fact, VMI's manual had been adopted for use by West Point, and its courses were similar. VMI alumni were the mainstays of the high Confederate command structure. Abram enrolled during the 1863 summer encampment — renamed that year for recently martyred alumnus and sometime VMI professor Stonewall Jackson.

It was artillery drills and bayonet fixings from reveille at five in the morning to taps at ten at night. In their scarlet flannel shirts crossed by two white belts, long gray overcoats, and kepi caps, the young cadets toiled to make ready for war. VMI in 1863 was overflowing with cadets, many — like Abram — sent there by families who wanted to keep the boys' war lust in check behind protected walls. When not on drill the cadets lived in old dormitories, four or five to a room, with hardly enough gas in the jets to study properly at night, broken windowpanes for which the South could spare no replacements, no milk for suppers but a plethora of turnips, a vegetable often combined with fat and pigs' feet to make a much-hated dish aptly named growley.

In late August, word came to VMI of raids being conducted by Yankee commander William W. Averell to destroy the saltpeter works, cut a railroad, and harass the upper Virginia–West Virginia border area. Confederate troops were giving ground to Averell, and the VMI cadets were called out in support. Shouts went up in the ranks.

It was fortunate, however, that the cadet corps missed the actual fighting, because the boys lacked such basics as long-range rifles and a supply of ammunition and would have been easy prey for Northern sharpshooters. Disappointed, the cadets returned to start classes. In November they were called out again and this time had enough guns and bullets to go around. The cadets were used as reinforcements in the largest battle of the war in West Virginia, in which Averell defeated the Gray units at Mill Point. The cadets didn't fire a shot, but had to huddle through torrential rains, washed-out roads, and an early winter storm to return to their school. The unsuccessful pursuit of Averell was repeated in December. By

Christmas of 1863, Averell's raids had hurt the area badly, and many of the cadets yearned to leave the school and see service on the front lines.

During six months at VMI, Abram's early maturity and leadership got him elected captain of his regiment. He was also a good talker: when he received demerits for allowing his kepi to fall on the ground, he was able to convince the authorities to erase them from his record by showing them that the cap had fallen because it was too small for his head. Hardin heard of these successes and thus was astounded to have Abram return home from VMI early in 1864, saying he'd been chucked out. Hardin had Nancy Jane write to the commandant, "I was greatly surprised and mortified. . . . I would be glad if you would send me a copy of the charge which was brought against him, as he has lost the statement he had." Most likely, there was no charge; Abram merely itched to go to the front lines. In the spring of 1864, a VMI contemporary later wrote, "Good boys became bad boys for the express purpose of getting 'shipped,' parents and guardians having refused them permission to resign."

The white lie Abram told may have been occasioned by a recently passed edict that allowed boys as young as seventeen and men as old as fifty to be pressed into service. Now, instead of the planters outfitting and paying regiments they themselves led, the Confederacy was using enlistment officers to scour the counties for likely candidates. When such an officer, Captain Ridgeway, spent a night at Rock Spring in early May, he was impressed by sixteen-year-old Abram's large physique and knowledge of military matters and said he'd like to have the boy. Hardin gave his assent, perhaps even his blessing. Abram packed up and took his own horse and Squire, his own slave. Brother R. J. rubbed his square Joshua Coin against the few gold coins that Abram took with him; used in this manner, the totem was believed to pass on its good luck to someone other than the wearer.

Next day at the county courthouse a man was trying to buy the captaincy of the new recruits with a ten-gallon jug of apple brandy. Abram countered with a rousing speech promising to "drive back the Fiendish hords invading the Sacred Soil of dear old Virginia . . . [by] Valor and discretion." He was elected by overwhelming vote and became one of the youngest captains in the Confederacy.

He was as lucky as he was young. In his baptism under fire, by deploying his men around a turnpike instead of crossing it he surprised a Union contingent. After the Rebels had jumped breast-works and trenches to drive the Yankees away, Abram discovered that the powder in their old-fashioned rifles was too wet to have fired a shot. Had he been forced to fight, his troops might have been massacred.

At Newport, Tennessee, he and his men encamped with a su-perior, a Captain Poage who had been temporarily upgraded to colonel. Poage, inebriated, took umbrage at Abram and pressed disobedience charges on him for not heeding his drunken com-mands. A new and sober higher officer managed to smooth things over but transferred Abram to Danville, Virginia. The town, al-ready well known to Abram from his youth, was the site of a large Confederate prison camp under the command of medical doctor R. E. Withers, a prominent Patrick County stalwart. Abram prob-ably worked at the camp; although he doesn't mention such service in his recollections, other contemporary records show that the guarding company was composed mainly of men who, like Abram, were a bit too young for frontline duty. In any event, after dem-onstrating prowess on the drill field with another regiment, Abram was elevated to major and went back into battle.

While Abram was gone from Rock Spring, second son Richard Joshua Reynolds reached puberty, exercised some responsibility, and received a lot of affection previously directed solely toward Abram. Because of these things, he evidently did not harbor the wish to go to war.

Rock Spring felt the pinch of war even though no battles were fought on its lands. The general store across the road from the house was used occasionally as a hospital. There were chronic shortages of food, clothing, and materials. Once it had been amusing when snakes got at the eggs hens laid in the gnarled trunk of the catalpa tree in the yard; now every egg was precious. Dick hunted wild game to replace beef and pork. The family had less fuel for lamps and was thrust back into a dawn-to-dusk schedule. On such self-sufficient farms, everyday blessings were counted anew, for in the larger cities of the South, people were rioting over allotments of bread.

During this tough period, R. J. learned things from his father that weren't taught in school. Hardin was a man determined to prevail. He stocked his store with hard-to-obtain goods, rented out his thresher and his animals for stud, made tenant-farm contracts, served as a postmaster and a local militia captain. He or Nancy Jane recorded every transaction, many on the lap-box chest whose inner portion could be transformed into a small desk.

Hardin got around the edicts against planting tobacco by a common ruse — growing corn and wheat near the roads, where they could be seen, but continuing to raise his money crop on back acres. There was no lack of market: soldiers craved the stuff and complained more bitterly about its absence or poor quality than they did about the lack of alcoholic spirits. In areas where opposing pickets fraternized during lulls in skirmishes, Johnny Reb would trade his chaw of 'baccy for Billy Yank's coffee.

As spring approached in 1865, the war was working toward its end. At the Reynolds plantation, the snow and ice were clearing from the stream, melting into a "spring fresh." The great worry was the march northward through the Carolinas of Union general George Stoneman, which, as it cut a swath across the belly of the Confederacy, might soon threaten Rock Spring. Another Yankee army was threatening Lynchburg, near which city Abram lay in a hospital, gravely ill with "bloody flux" that had caused him to lose seventeen pounds in a week. At three o'clock one morning Squire roused him and got him on a train for Richmond; in the capital, he refused further hospitalization and went to a Confederate encampment, where he inhaled smoke from green pine logs, which, as he believed, soon cured his ailments.

As the elder brother recovered, Stoneman's men reached the border and crossed into southern Virginia. For three days in early April 1865, a troop under the direction of one Colonel William J. Palmer ravaged Patrick County, destroying everything in its path, burning houses and reducing them to "Sherman sentinels" — nothing standing but chimneys — and melting railroad iron into "Lincoln gimlets" — tracks twisted and bent around trees. Bridges were severed. Cattle and horses were confiscated. Fields were set afire or despoiled.

Only quick action by fifteen-year-old R. J. Reynolds saved part of Rock Spring's wealth. When word came that the raiders were near, R. J. herded the plantation's horses deep into the woods and stayed with them in hiding until the Yankees had finished with Rock Spring and passed on toward the north. Returning home, he found his boyhood home pillaged, though not burned. Food, clothing, and livestock were gone — and so were all of his father's slaves, many of whom trailed along at the rear of the Palmer troop's caravan and could be heard giving thanks for their freedom.

While this was occurring, Abram was being burned out of Richmond by another Northern army. Shortly afterward, Robert E. Lee surrendered to Ulysses Grant at Appomattox, but Jefferson Davis would not admit defeat. Abram received orders to go farther south to Danville with Davis, his cabinet, and the government's hoard of gold and silver. No sooner did the elect of the Confederacy reach Danville than they realized that Stoneman was closing in on them. Abram volunteered to help move the officials and their treasure elsewhere, but there were not enough spaces on the troop train for all those who wished to follow the Lost Cause. Abram found a horse and rode all night for home.

He arrived to find Rock Spring still standing but in despair. Of his reception, he later wrote,

> My father was a fine disciplinarian and always Kept me at a distance. . . . I never Knew he loved me until then when he saw me he ran to meet me and threw his arms around me and Said my Son the Yankees have been here and torn up Evry thing . . . but since you have Come back alive and well it is all right. . . . I was glad my father made this demonstration it made a better man of me.

R. J.'s emotions, too, ran high. In the yard, near the old catalpa tree, he noticed on the ground a Yankee rifle that a raider had left behind; he picked it up, toyed with it, planned to teach his younger brothers to shoot back at Yankees with it when they got older. He did not know that the war was already over.

As for Hardin, he believed his fortune lost: he had corn and tobacco planted but no slaves to work the crops nor wagons to haul anything to market and very few animals to pull the plows. He had his thousands of acres, but his major wealth, in the form of a total now of eighty slaves, had vanished. All that he had slowly accumulated in the past thirty years appeared worthless. He dreaded what Yankee Reconstruction would bring and feared he might have to sell land to pay for new, harsh taxes.

All this he communicated to his older sons, Abram, now eighteen, and fifteen-year-old Dick. They vowed to help — to tend and harvest the crops with their own hands, that the Reynolds family fortune, and with it the family honor, might one day be restored.

Chapter Two

R. J. and Abram

IN THE SOUTH in the postbellum period, several sets of brothers came to prominence, among them Ben, Buck, and Brodie Duke; B. F. and P. H. Hanes; Abram and R. J. Reynolds. Some were partners. Other sets were rivals, but only if there were no outsiders involved: in a phrase common to the region in that time, "My brother is my enemy, but the enemy of my brother is my enemy." This saying encapsulates the relationship of Abram and R. J. throughout their lives.

In boyhood, before the war, Abram had been the elder and lorded it over Dick. Their tussles were invariably broken up by Hardin. A Christian man, Hardin didn't like fighting and wouldn't let it continue. He insisted that Dick and Abram kiss and make up. During one such peace initiative, R. J. bit his brother's lip, for which he was severely punished but eventually had his revenge — after a later fight, R. J. muttered through clenched teeth for Abram to "come and give me a sweet kiss," then had the satisfaction of watching Abram get thrashed for refusing the embrace. Thereafter, R. J. was not bullied. It was, perhaps, the first stroke of his independence.

Just after the war, as the family tried to make up what had been lost, the lives of Abram and Dick began to diverge. The harsh economic times spawned robbers and vagabonds in the foothill country near Rock Spring, and Abram raised a company to go after the outlaws — in a sense, he attempted to re-create his earlier shining moment of wartime heroism — while R. J. put his strong teen-aged body behind the plow and, in the absence of slaves, did the physical work of tending the crops. Abram relates that R. J. helped with the raising of the small company but makes no mention of the younger brother's riding with them. The separate paths of the young men were reinforced when, in the course of a gunfight with the outlaws, Abram took a "minie ball" in the shoulder and was unable to pitch in and help R. J. with the hard labor.

Once more Hardin sent Abram on an errand, to South Carolina, where Hardin had made what he thought was a shrewd deal in 1864, trading manufactured tobacco to a man in exchange for stored cotton. After the war Hardin's bales of cotton had been pillaged by soldiers; Abram was charged with recovering the cotton or recompense in cash. The eldest son dutifully chased over three states, got a runaround from the carpetbagger governments, and came up empty. In a sense, it was the first time he had experienced failure. Years later, he waxed philosophical about the loss: "If we had got this money RJ and my self might have felt Rich and bought bay horses and top buggy and Splurged & done no good as Some of our neighbor boys did." Such an insight might have helped later generations of Reynoldses deal with the fortune that hobbled them — and with defeats in their enterprises. Abram was able to take his failure to get the cotton money in stride and go on, sustained, perhaps, by his father's faith in his potential.

Hardin had a mission: to put the family's finances back in good order. To do that, he turned in part to tenant farming. In the Reconstruction South tenant farming had official sanction as a way to get freedmen off the relief rolls. Once the Northern armies had defeated the South, there were hundreds of thousands of former slaves roaming around, looking for jobs and homes. The cities could absorb only a fraction of these, so most had to be taken care of by the government. Soon there were laws on the books that forbade blacks from migrating to the cities — laws that had the effect of forcing freed slaves back toward the fiefdoms of their former owners.

As did other large landholders in his area, Hardin let tenant-farm contracts to his former slaves and to down-at-the-heels white neighbors. He furnished land, a dwelling place, tools, seed, and sometimes work animals in return for a rent of up to half the finished crop. His tenants, like others all over the South, frequently ran up debts buying provisions at the local store — which Hardin also owned. Sometimes a tenant owed so much that after paying back the store he had barely enough money to live until the next planting season. Soon the tenant-farming system came in some ways to resemble slavery. But there were differences.

Before the war, historian Crandall A. Shifflett points out, land-holders were obligated to feed, clothe, shelter, and provide medical care for their "property"; after the war, in tenant farming, such expenditures "were no longer capital investments but instead . . . the commodity costs of labor, and the incentive was to keep them as low as possible."

Hardin Reynolds drove hard tenant bargains, and once a Freed-men's Bureau agent reprimanded him for "whitecapping" — driving a tenant from a shack right after a harvest and not allowing her to stay through the winter:

> Colored woman by the name of Ceby [who] . . . Complains of You threatening to Drive her from your plantation. I sup-pose that you are well aware wherein Freedmen have help raised a crop they are entitled to a support   You are hereby ordered to give this woman a home on your plantation or a support to her until Christmas.

On the other hand, family stories emphasize caring for former slaves such as Aunt Kitty, John Jackson, and Abram's man, Squire. Shifflett's research shows that the war undercut the financial sound-ness of tobacco plantations less than it did that of cotton and sugar fiefdoms; he concludes that tobacco farmers could recover all they had lost "as long as they were not dispossessed of their wealth and advantages in land." Hardin lost a quarter of his acres to new tax assessments but still owned thousands more — enough to provide his tobacco-manufacturing business with plenty of raw leaf. By the fall of 1866 the family was back on sound financial ground.

Things were going so well that Abram brazenly told his father he ought to pay him five hundred dollars for the risks he'd taken and the verbal abuse he'd sustained in exposing himself to smallpox, and Hardin agreed to fork over the money if Abram used it to go to college. Abram paid it as tuition and board for the Bryant and Stratton Business College in Baltimore. In this time of industrial revolution, old apprenticeship patterns no longer served the needs of young men who wanted to go into business. Education in that field was not yet common. Bryant and Stratton, early educational entrepreneurs, had started a chain of business colleges in Rochester, Buffalo, Boston, and other cities of the Northeast; Warren H. Sad-ler, expert bookkeeper and Buffalo branch graduate, became the founders' partner and opened the Baltimore branch in 1864.

By 1867, when Abram came to Baltimore as a student, Sadler

was sole owner of the branch, promulgator of a curriculum that aimed "to graduate students as fully prepared to enter upon commercial pursuits as others are in other institutions for law, medicine, clergy and the like." Sadler was the author of the most popular text, *Calculator;* and other books used in the courses dealt with business law, accounting, salesmanship, and management.

After working through the six-month course in three, Abram was recommended by Sadler himself to a local firm as a temporary bookkeeper. Abram wrote Hardin a "very Saucy letter . . . asking him if he did not think the fathers of youthful Confederate Soldiers Should free their Sons prest Lincoln had freed the Negroes and I hoped he would allow me to work for my self I had made 25 $ in three days." Abram brashly stayed on in Baltimore, though he didn't do as well as he'd hoped and could find only a stint as a teacher for eleven weeks at moderate pay. Soon he came home to be chief salesman for the family tobacco business.

In the spring of 1867 eldest child Mary Joyce Reynolds married lawyer Andrew Lybrook. One result of the wedding was to bring Lybrook into the family firm. The other was to send rambunctious kid brother R. J. to Lybrook's alma mater, Emory and Henry, a small college for gentlemen about sixty miles due west of Rock Spring. To Hardin's apparent delight, Emory and Henry prided itself on rural isolation and moral uprightness. Daguerreotypists and trinket salesmen were banned from the campus. With rhetorical thunder, the E&H catalogue wondered,

> What hindrances to the right education of the young have parents and teachers found in the little villages and average towns with their gossip, examples of idleness and stealthy allurements to vice? What is a city by day but a great workshop . . . and by night a house of pleasure where entertainments are given, a few that elevate and refine, a multitude that utterly debase and destroy?

Born of the philosophy of Swiss educator Johann Heinrich Pestalozzi, Emory and Henry emphasized practical matters over literary and artistic ones. About 175 students lived in dormitories and purchased their food from the college's own farm. Though there were hired cooks, each student was expected to chop firewood for the stoves; lads with more money paid others for that chore. Baths could be had for a small fee, but many students rose at 4:00 A.M. and walked a mile and a half to obtain a free shower.

After one semester at E&H, R. J. came home, willing to take up manual labor rather than do academics. Hardin set him to do some plowing. He did it. Hardin switched him to clearing trees and roots. Three days later he was beaten, and ready to return to more genteel pursuit of knowledge. He went back and changed dormitories, to see if that would help. It didn't. During the winter of 1869–70 he grew increasingly restless.

On the way home from a western selling trip, Abram stopped at the college to visit R. J. The younger son informed the elder that he wasn't going to complete the degree requirements. Academics was not for him. He was (Abram later said) unable to "eclipse his class in anything but mathematics, so . . . it became necessary for him to originate all of his work in arithmetic, algebra, geometry and trigonometry." That was fine with some subjects, but not all.

For many years Abram and the rest of the Reynolds clan had thought that the cause of R. J.'s educational difficulties was a defect in vision that, they believed, made it impossible for him to see more than one letter at a time. Today, the diagnosis would be dyslexia, not a disease of visual perception but a problem with language. Dyslexics shift linguistic tasks and analysis to the less appropriate left hemisphere of the brain but often excel — as R. J. did — in right-brain skills, such as mathematics and art, which require visual-spatial manipulation. R. J. stammered throughout his life and had difficulty reading more than one letter at a time, but his grasp of mathematics and marketing was broad and deep. Three well-known near-contemporaries of R. J.'s were, we now know, also dyslexic: Auguste Rodin, Albert Einstein, and Woodrow Wilson. Like him they were poor talkers before they became poor readers; they did well in developing concepts, and when they could, in later life, they controlled the circumstances of their communication.

In this college meeting R. J. told brother Abram not that he couldn't do the schoolwork but, rather, that father Hardin wished him to come into the family business now as a one-quarter partner, even though he had no capital. Abram said he didn't want another partner — but would train the upstart. He offered a deal: if R. J. would work for two years at fifty dollars a month, Abram would then sell his own shares to R. J. and induce Lybrook to do the same, an arrangement that would give R. J. control of the family business. R. J. agreed to the plan.

In 1870, then, R. J. followed the lead of Abram and Lybrook in the family business, working primarily at home. In the off-season, he retraced Abram's footsteps to Sadler's Bryant and Stratton Business College in Baltimore. What attracted him there may have been the mathematics-based curriculum, but he also responded to the lure of the biggest metropolis that he had ever seen, a Sodom of the sort against which the doyens of Emory and Henry had railed. R. J. worked hard enough to get by — and played very hard. His role as a likable rogue took on new dimension in the city, so much so that neither father nor elder brother thought very much of young R. J.'s capabilities for business. They only begrudgingly allowed the lanky, handsome young man — not yet twenty — to take his first wagonload of twist into the counties of the Blue Ridge Mountains.

This trip had the character of a setup: R. J. was plainly riding into difficulties, just as Hardin had been thrust into the midst of a backwoods practical joke more than forty years earlier. The wagonload of twist was all but unsalable because Hardin insisted that its price be high. A good citizen, Hardin had paid tax on his tobacco while other, less responsible farmers had not and so could charge less. Also, R. J. lacked enough money in his pocket to pay his road expenses. Within a few days of the trip's start, he was out of cash and feed for his horses.

It would have been humiliating to return home with his twist unsold, so he improvised. Leaving the team to graze in a field near the turnpike, R. J. went on foot to towns off the beaten path. There he talked. When he stammered — as he habitually did — he smiled until he finished his sales speech. Probably he offered samples to convince backwoods shopkeeps that his chew and twist were worth that little bit of extra money. He managed to sell enough tobacco to get money to eat, then enough to feed his team while he traveled, and, eventually, enough to make the trip profitable.

He now knew what he was: a terrific salesman.

A second selling trip provided an even greater challenge. Times were bad, and no one wanted to pay cash for R. J.'s tobacco, so he bartered his twist for other goods. All of Rock Spring must have come out to gape when he returned home, his wagon piled high with "beeswax, tallow, ginseng, cowhides, sheep-pelts, bear and wildcat skins, possum, mink and groundhog hides, carpets, knit sox, yarn and homespun of various kinds, a few valuable pieces of furniture . . . three or four horses and mules hitched on behind, and a solid gold-case watch."

Abram, who seems to have taken over direction of the family

firm from Hardin by this time, was angry at R. J. for having traded $2,000 worth of tobacco for assorted junk. But R. J. showed him up: acting as his own crier, he auctioned the livestock and the wagon's contents for $2,500 — much more than he could have gotten in cash for the tobacco. That shut up Abram for a while. It also established R. J. as more than a salesman: he was a nascent marketing genius.

=

For his selling trips westward, Abram often dressed in an old Confederate uniform with the decorations torn off. It was sometimes useful for introducing himself as "Major" Reynolds; the old uniform also served as camouflage, for every man seemed to be wearing his in the difficult economic days after the war. On one sales trip the uniformed Abram stopped his covered wagon at a general store in the rugged Allegheny Mountains of Virginia. He left the twist and plug, the sorrel Robert E. Lee, and the bay Red Rebel in the charge of black driver John Jackson. Inside the store Abram saw a set of tiny feet and well-shaped ankles; the rest of the body was concealed behind high display cases. He strained to glimpse the woman properly, but she left the store, so he asked the manager to whom the ankles belonged.

"Oh, that was the beautiful daughter of Captain Joseph Hoge of Wheatland," the man said. Abram strolled outside, asked John Jackson to saddle the bay, and hightailed it for the estate, which was in a lofty valley of the mountains. On the way, he visited the house of another veteran, Robert "Bo" Hoge, the captain's son, and was invited to ride with him to Wheatland. It was an impressive place, and Joseph Hoge was the wealthiest man in Giles County. Abram was asked to stay for supper; he did, and was polite but frustrated because the possessor of the ankles, Miss Senah Ann Hoge, was not home.

Thereafter, Abram made it a point to stop at Wheatland on every trip, and he became acquainted with Senah. She was a lovely young woman, one of ten children — large broods were a sign of wealth and status. The family traced its lineage back before the Revolutionary War to James Hoge, builder of another Giles County estate, Belle Hampton.

Abram determined to marry Senah, and her father accepted his proposal. Hardin and Nancy Jane were most likely pleased at the choice. Southern lads in this era learned that they were to defend their honor and integrity with quiet strength, to be hospitable, to keep their true feelings to themselves — and, says historian Bertram Wyatt-Brown, "paternal advice rarely excluded warnings about feminine wiles." Young men were exhorted to choose wives not on the basis of love but out of a concern for the future, to look for a girl who had a dowry and good bloodlines (as important in a wife as in a horse) but who had less social standing than themselves. Then, too, "the younger the girl, the more likely her malleability and the weaker her self-assertiveness was presumed to be," according to Wyatt-Brown. Senah met all these conditions except one: her family status was more distinguished than that of the Reynoldses. But then, thirty years earlier Nancy Jane Cox had been a bit above the station of Hardin Reynolds.

Just before the marriage, in the summer of 1872, Abram moved to the small town of Bristol, Tennessee, on the southwestern border of Virginia, 120 miles from Rock Spring. He took with him fifteen thousand dollars. This represented the proceeds of the family business over several years. With the money, he built a factory to make chewing tobacco and a home for his future family. The factory was the largest building in town, with a reception hall big enough for five hundred people.

Bristol was a small town in an interesting location — the south side of Main Street was in Tennessee, the north side in Virginia. Before the arrival of the railroad in 1858, Bristol had been a frontier outpost; the Virginia & Tennessee put the town on a direct rail route linking the Mississippi to the Eastern Seaboard, but Bristol still had only eight hundred people in 175 houses. The war destroyed the rail line. It also brought in carpetbaggers and troops, who finally went home in 1871, after the rail line was restored. At that time, interest in the property near the railroad was so keen that sellers offered lemonade to thirsty buyers and hired four boys with little flags in hand to trail behind a horse-mounted auctioneer as he marked off lots. A growth spurt began.

By the time Abram arrived, Bristol was a thriving county seat. Court was held on the second floor of a meat-market building. The town fathers passed laws against cows and pigs running loose in the streets but couldn't prevent Bristol from having an unenviable reputation as the muddiest town this side of the Mississippi River. There were no sidewalks but plenty of churches and livery stables and smithies and small shops manufacturing furniture and doing ironmongery, using products of the nearby Appalachian range.

Abram's was the first factory in town devoted to making tobacco products.

On October 1, 1872, Abram and Senah were married. Receptions followed both at Wheatland and at Rock Spring, and then the newlyweds packed up for life in Tennessee. Abram was already well respected in Bristol; the local paper obsequiously endorsed his choice of bride: "He has now married a lady worthy of the social attention of any people. . . . We are glad that Maj. Reynolds has made a selection which this journal, devoted to all which shall build, ornament, and ennoble our town can, without reservation or fear of the issue, welcome to the social circles of Bristol."

The deal that Abram had cut with R. J. was for the younger son to take over Abram's and Lybrook's shares of Hardin's business in 1872, but the sale wasn't completed until July 1, 1873, when the new firm of H. W. Reynolds and Son was legally established. As always, the father came first, even if the son was chief operating officer. Friction between R. J. and Hardin began almost immediately. One sign of the difficulties surfaced after an early selling trip. R. J. returned to Rock Spring, where Hardin invited him in to have a drink. Accepting the offer, R. J. went to the sideboard, poured a water glass full of whiskey, and downed it in a single gulp. Hardin was annoyed: that wasn't the gentlemanly way to do things, he said, and warned that he'd never ask Dick to drink with him again.

Hardin wasn't worried about Dick's drinking, only about his manners. R. J. Reynolds always could take a drink and hold his liquor; that was one of the signs of manliness in a region that outdrank, by far, every other section of the country. In the South, especially, observers always made a distinction between a man who could drink and a drunk: alcoholism was more often the fate of younger sons of families — "late baby" children whose right to follow in the family business was routinely usurped or lost. Today's social historians, looking back, find a chilling correlation between the "failed" later sons and alcoholism.

R. J. Reynolds at twenty-three may well have been too rough-cut for old Hardin, but then, they were engaged in a struggle over the direction of the family tobacco business. Times were tough in 1873: a depression was greatly affecting farmers. Manufacturing plug on an isolated farm meant continual problems finding enough men to work the crop, as well as difficulties in hauling the product to customers. What was needed, R. J. knew, was to have a factory in a city that had a rail line and was full of workers. Abram already had such a base, while R. J. was still stuck on a farm. Life was beautiful and slow at Rock Spring — but it was also stifling.

In the planter society of the South, fathers did not transfer power easily — or early — to their sons. The usual pattern was for a son to work for the old man until the father died, then take over. Abram had already gotten off that treadmill. In mid-1874, following the financial setbacks of 1873 and scarcely a year after Abram had ceded to him, R. J. sold his interest in the family firm back to his father and made plans to move away from Rock Spring forever.

At about the same time, and shortly after the birth of Abram and Senah's first child (whom they named Harden Reynolds), Abram came back to the plantation for a visit. At Rock Spring, for three days, father, mother, and eldest son talked about everything under the sun. Abram had made a canny purchase of tobacco in the leaf, which enabled him to ride out the economic storm of 1873; there was a first grandchild; he was well respected in Bristol. It was only after Abram had mounted his horse to return home that Hardin strode to him, put his hand on the young man's thigh, and said, with tears rolling down his cheeks, "My Son I have no fears for your worldly Success but how about your Spiritual Side what are you going to do about that?"

Abram wept as he rode his horse the sixty miles to the boarding point for the train to Bristol and even at home that night couldn't shake the tears. Senah comforted him. She had just returned from a revival meeting at the First Presbyterian Church in town, and she told him he ought to go. Such revivals had been annual events in East Tennessee since the first preachers had reached the frontier settlements. They served as a yearly purging of sins and an opportunity for redemption. Abram longed to go to the revival but believed, as an old sinner who had neglected religion for too many years, that he would be unacceptable to God.

Next night they both went to the meeting, and when the call went out for people to come to the Lord, Abram strode to the altar and was saved. For ten days and nights he answered the calls, even after the revival was transferred to another church. He led his family in prayers at home, resolving nevermore to run with the "Devils Crowd" and to "do like a Christian as best I Could." On the morning of the tenth day he arose to give thanks for his newly fortified conviction of the right life and experienced a moment of "witness of the Spirit," which completed his conversion. From that day on he had faith that "the blood of Jesus Christ" would allow him to enter heaven. He became a teetotaler — the only one on record in the Reynolds family.

Some of Abram's new, anti-alcohol friends remonstrated that tobacco was as great a sin as drink and wanted Abram to go into a "clean" business, but Abram told them that his father, a Christian man to the core, was also in tobacco and that if the Lord wanted Abram to give up manufacturing twist He would find a way and a time to direct Abram to do so.

In the summer of 1874 R. J. Reynolds left the columned portico of Rock Spring with a wagon, or perhaps on horseback, and headed south. Some stories suggest that he was just a rebel eager to get away from a stern father. He was more than that, and he had planned this escape carefully. He took with him between $5,000 and $10,000 dollars — approximately the proceeds of the family tobacco business for 1872–74. Though less than Abram's stake — R. J. hadn't worked with Hardin as long as Abram had — it was quite respectable, an amount equivalent to all the taxes paid by the inhabitants of Patrick County for an entire year. Some of the money came from a man who was going to remain a secret partner, brother-in-law Lybrook. The reason for the secrecy: the lawyer and the young man didn't want their business relationship too widely known within the family circle. It would have implied that Lybrook thought more highly of R. J.'s business abilities than of Abram's — a judgment counter to the then prevailing idea at Rock Spring.

After a few stops, R. J. Reynolds arrived in the small North Carolina town of Winston. North Carolina was known as the most backward and rural of states, rife with what one historian calls "ignorance, sloth and provincialism." Winston was a cluster of dwellings and shops on the outskirts of the religious center of the Moravians, Salem. The major industry was processing dried black-berries, and the area's largest employer was the maker of Nissen covered wagons. Winston had no telegraph line, no fire company, no municipal water system; visitors and their horses put up at a campground or took one of the two dozen rooms in the small hotel.

Since the completion of the railhead in late 1873, Winston had begun to change rapidly. Population had doubled, to a thousand people. Winston now had its own newspaper, a haberdashery for men and a "Temple of Fashion" for ladies, two smithies, a handful of churches, the county jail, and several establishments for the manufacture of chewing tobacco. One visitor to Winston was urged to take up residence because "times were so prosperous that roast pigs were running around the street with a knife and fork sticking in their backs, and a placard attached, inviting the hungry to come and eat."

On October 13, 1874, country boy R. J. Reynolds paid the Moravian brethren $388.50 for a hundred-foot lot (the size of a tennis court) not far from the railhead. He touched the fabled Joshua Coin to the deed and hoped that it would bring him good luck.

It was a bold purchase, and he followed it with another shrewd move: he convinced a local contractor to put up a plug factory on the lot, without immediate payment. R. J.'s interest charges would be steep, but, by avoiding advance payment for his building, he was able to retain the bulk of his cash capital to buy raw tobacco leaf, which he'd be able to turn into plug during next spring's manufacturing season. Until then he'd use the downtime to supervise the construction, look for hands, and start making his contacts for sales, some of them Baltimoreans whom he'd called on during his Saturdays off from school. Abram might have a two-year head start on him in the chewing-tobacco business, but R. J. was determined to catch up to and surpass his brother — and everyone else.

Chapter Three

On the Rise

IN THE NINETEENTH CENTURY chewing tobacco was so much a feature of the American scene that foreign observers called the United States the land of the moving jaw, and one Englishman thought we should replace our national symbol, the eagle, with the spittoon. Europeans smoked cigars and hand-rolled cigarettes; Americans chewed and spat at cuspidors.

Making and selling chewing tobacco was a rough-and-tumble industry. For R. J. Reynolds, the action began in the auction house in Winston owned by Hamilton Scales and Thomas Brown. Auction houses were the new wrinkle in an old business — great warehouses that boasted skylights, overnight facilities for drivers, and covered driveways for unloading farmers' wagons of dried leaf tobacco, samples of which were then placed directly on the floors to be inspected and bought. A manufacturer could go out and buy leaf from individual farmers, but that was a waste of time and energy, and the price would be no better than that paid in a central auction house.

During sale days, after a bugle was blown or a bell rung, quick-speaking auctioneers (who sometimes doubled as preachers in the local churches) would hawk the tobacco to potential manufacturers or middlemen. A certain skill was needed to avoid buying at too high a price, purchasing inferior tobacco, or being outbid by a pinhooker (an unscrupulous leaf buyer who bought up leaf expressly to hold it off the market and force prices higher).

R. J. had that skill. Moreover, his agility in the auction house had been a part of his decision to come to Winston. Cities that had good auction houses — such as Durham and Winston in North Carolina and Danville in Virginia — were growing, while those without were stagnating. It was because Virginia's taxes on tobacco were high and the restraints placed on the rascality of auction-house operators low that R. J. Reynolds chose to go to North Carolina rather than stay in his home state. He decided to locate in Winston rather than in Durham because he wanted to be a big fish in a small pond; in Durham, he would have had to fight "the Bull." He wasn't ready for that fight yet.

Bull Durham, manufactured by W. T. Blackwell and Julian S. Carr, was the biggest thing in tobacco in the South in 1875. It wasn't chewing tobacco, but smoking tobacco, for pipes. The Bull logo at that time desecrated one of Egypt's pyramids, the product was sold all over the world, and its big factory in Durham was the largest tobacco manufactory in existence. The town of Durham set its watches by the bellow of the Bull's come-to-work horn. Every other manufacturing unit in Durham was in the shadow of the Bull, including the combined talents of Washington, Ben, Buck, and Brodie Duke.

It was a good model for R. J. to look up to, from afar. Winston's small pack of chew makers was led by auction-house operator Scales, with a small, two-story brick factory, followed by Brown's "story and a jump high" facility and the even smaller ones run by Pleasant Henderson Hanes and his brother John Wesley Hanes. When R. J. built the wooden two-story "Old Red" building and started turning out chew, he was immediately in the middle of the pack.

Stories about the newcomer's large appetite for work, women, strong drink, and gambling started up almost immediately. He lived on the second floor of his factory, pursued a bachelor life-style, and became friendly with such close competitors as the Hanes brothers.

Unlike the sons of the old "cotton South" gentry who started cotton cloth factories in this era, the men of the tobacco industry — the Haneses, Dukes, Reynoldses, and others — came from the middle class. The split in origins was echoed in the factories: cotton-manufacturing hands were primarily white, drawn from poor farmers who didn't want to become tenant sharecroppers; tobacco's hands were mostly black. In all the factories, historian Wilbur Cash has pointed out, the pattern of the antebellum plantations was repeated; complete control over labor seemed simply to have been transferred from the old landholder to the employer.

In Winston, during the warm-weather manufacturing season and sometimes year-round, the blacks lived in shanties in "Hell's Half Acre," whose center was the intersection of "Happy Corner" and "Cash Corner." White citizens of Winston deplored the presence of liquor and the absence of morality in this slum; however, court records show that ample quantities of booze and sin were also present in white Winston.

In season there were almost as many black hands in Winston as white citizens. Half of the black workers were men over sixteen, a third were women, and the rest were children. Most made 50 cents a day, though a skilled mechanic could earn $1 a day. The $100 that a black hand took home from May to November could get him through the slack months of the year — but just barely. If, as was often the case, several members of the same family worked in the factories, there might even be enough money for a few small amenities. It was a tough life, but most workers in the tobacco factories considered it preferable to the never-ending burden of toil and debt that was the lot of the tenant farmer.

R. J. employed about thirty hands that first year and worked right alongside them. He was not a manager whose hands never touched the product. Making plug and twist was a slow and esoteric process. Hogsheads into which tobacco had been prized were hoisted to the second floor of the factory, then opened and steamed. The midrib of the leaf was removed and the leaves loaded into a furnace-heated drying room to be dehydrated. Next the leaves were dipped into a bubbling vat containing licorice or sugar and then hauled up to the roof to dry in the sun; if it rained, everyone in the factory would rush up to take in the sugary leaves. After a spell on the roof, down they went to a room kept at over 100 degrees Fahrenheit to get every last bit of moisture out. Then the leaves were sprinkled with rum or other flavorings — that's what gave each brand its "unique" taste.

Now the leaves were ready for the lumper, who worked them into a cube while, on the next bench, a stemmer removed stems from separate leaves used to wrap the lump. Lumps that looked like cakes were plug; rolled-out lumps were twist. After being hand-shaped, the lumps were put into molds and subjected to pressure. Now, finished, they were packed in sycamore cases, the cases put into wooden billies reinforced by iron bands and blessed with a tax stamp to make them ready for shipment on the railroad.

Most factories were active only six months of the year; gas lamps and heaters could extend the working time but could also start a fire and wipe out a factory overnight. It had happened to the Hanes brothers in 1873.

The 1875 manufacturing season showed R. J. to be cagey and resourceful. Even though he'd hoarded his capital by getting the contractor to put up his building on faith, it took more money than he had to buy leaf, process it, pay the hands for months, and ship 150,000 pounds of chew, then wait for payment. Realistically speaking, R. J. had fled home before accumulating a large enough stake to cover his expenses. He took his "liquidity" problems to the nearby First National Bank in Salem, which offered him the munificent sum of $500. He refused that and instead borrowed $1,500 from his father and an equal amount from Benjamin F. Parlett, an old friend of Hardin's. Parlett, who had tobacco businesses in Danville and Baltimore, knew a comer when he saw one. By 1876 a precursor of Dun and Bradstreet estimated R. J.'s worth at between $20,000 and $30,000 — not bad for a man who'd started out two years earlier with $7,500 and had had to borrow an additional $3,000. But R. J. owed money to many people: the contractor, brother-in-law Lybrook, Hardin, Parlett, and others. Paying them off and becoming truly independent took only two more years. He was doing so well in his third season of manufacturing that he doubled the size of his factory. Now it was three and a half stories, employed seventy-five hands, and had a capacity of a quarter-million pounds of chew.

This, too, was a bold move and one that R. J. knew he had to make. In a rapidly expanding industry — a dozen new chew makers opened their doors in Winston between 1874 and 1879 — it was either grow or die. He also knew that his own company's future was linked to that of Winston itself. The town was spreading by leaps and bounds; R. J. didn't have time to sit on the new board marking out school districts, but he became a major user of the newly completed telegraph link and helped lead the agitation for a new railroad.

Brother Abram, also a chewing-tobacco maker, grumbled in letters home that R. J. took too many risks. Indeed, this was the essential difference between them. In his youth Abram had taken risks but now, after his religious epiphany, the elder brother had turned cautious, anxious to lead the right sort of life and wait to be rewarded by the Lord. Since Abram was prospering moderately, he felt that this was the best path both to riches and moral perfection. R. J. didn't agree.

In the South, with its strong tradition of primogeniture, for a second son to surpass the first was always difficult. R. J. felt he had to take risks. It was a trait he shared with most of the great businessmen who came to the fore in this era: like them, at his core he was a gambler, a man who looked for the main chance, then bet heavily on it. Abram had had quite a head start — a stake double that of R. J.'s and a year's time. But by 1878, after only three seasons in business, R. J. had made up the deficit and was drawing even with his brother. Abram was the sole chew manufacturer in Bristol. R. J. was competing with a whole town of them, which helped him sense that the potential of the public demand for chewing tobacco was enormous and that the only real danger was in *not* expanding rapidly. So he kept going, always going; he never seemed to have enough money for the business, so he borrowed $3,000 here, $500 there, and enlarged his plant every two years.

It was a sign that, with other winners in the capitalist economy, R. J. shared the ability to see what was about to happen in his industry and to take advantage of his foresight. Andrew Carnegie, never really an innovator, believed in steel, bet everything he had on its future, and netted millions. Leland Stanford sensed that California real estate would double in value every few years and bought all he could. William Gibbs McAdoo knew cities would expand and draw daily commuters, and he built "tubes" from New Jersey under the Hudson River into New York City.

Studying the successful businessmen of this era, F. W. Taussig divides them into five types: those who wanted to build an industry, those whose drive was to accumulate and acquire, those who wished to dominate (the "conqueror" strain), those who wished to emulate someone (usually their father), and those whose focus was devotion to a cause. The greatest titans, like R. J. Reynolds, embodied something of all of them.

Could anyone have pegged him for the industry's future leader in those days? Picked him out of the pack of manufacturers in Winston who all seemed to board at the Merchants Hotel and gather around the potbellied stove in Robert Gray's office to talk about tobacco? Pleasant Hanes was renowned for his prize pigs, another manufacturer for his prowess in mud wrestling. R. J. was much respected for supplying friends with moonshine: with the cooperation of the owners of a local livery stable, he brought in "brandy" from farmer-distillers in the hills, at several hundred gallons per order.

R. J.'s breeding was occasionally in evidence as he squired young white women to the roller-skating rink or attended "occasions" given in a local mansion built by a decorator and festooned with murals of allegorical travels and cupids — but he was more comfortable in less refined pursuits and surroundings. He drank many of his friends and rivals under the table and was a participant in poker games that sometimes lasted day and night through entire weekends. Once a whole factory was at stake on the table. R. J. was a man who would bet on anything: whether it would rain on Tuesday, whether a young lady could be bedded. Once, a small boy in Bristol saw R. J. and Ben Parlett walking down a street and followed them. First, the men decided to flip coins, and they bet ten-dollar gold pieces. R. J. won. Continuing on, the men bet on who could pull out the longest straw from a hay wagon. Parlett won. Walking farther, they saw two blackbirds sitting on a telegraph wire and bet on which bird would leave the wire first; when both flew together, the men finally ended the betting spree.

R. J. liked fast horses and loose women. He raised what was said by contemporaries to be the finest matched pair of horses in the state, partly in order to be able to gallop them through Winston's streets and show off. To sustain his love of horse racing, he laid out a track on the outskirts of town. To tickle his lady friends — who were generally poor whites or blacks from his factories rather than the demure daughters of the prosperous — he named new brands of chew after them. Men chewed tobacco for pleasure, not out of duty.

R. J. did not lack for female companionship. He used his power as an employer to induce women from the packing floor to come to a back room with him. Often, after having sex with such a partner, he'd return to work.

It was a common practice. In this era, sex was considered necessary for a man's health, whether or not he was married. No self-respecting male was supposed to abstain, else he might become ill. Also, a long tradition in the South cast a benevolent eye on white men having intercourse with black women; such coupling and the issue from it were accepted before the war by white plantation women and after it by white townswomen. Dozens of mulatto and even some white children in Winston in the latter quarter of the nineteenth century learned at their mother's knee that they were the bastard children of R. J. Reynolds — more of them as he became wealthier. Since there are no court cases in which he was asked — as others occasionally were — to provide money to such offspring, we conclude that he took good enough care of them so they remained silent.

R. J.'s sexual proclivities caught him in a bind typical of the Victorian era. Men who led dissolute lives were reluctant to marry because of a deeply held belief that a man's bad habits before marriage, his youthful excesses, and (in the words of psychoanalytic researcher Stephen Kern) "slightest deviation from the strictest propriety would be imprinted indelibly on his children." Bad habits included not only the contracting of venereal diseases but also excessive use of tobacco and alcohol. Men like R. J. were often hesitant to marry upstanding white women of class until they had reformed and cleansed their systems so that the marriage would lead properly to the production of healthy children. Historian Robert Lacour-Gayet has concluded that Southern men's common practice of delaying marriage until their forties or even fifties was attributable to the widespread patronage of black concubines. R. J. liked his wild life — and, year after year, put off marriage.

R. J.'s former position in his father's tobacco firm had been taken over by next-youngest son Harbour Reynolds, a graduate of an agricultural college and the family clown, wit, and contender for the title of family drunkard. The fondness for drink surfaced early. Once Hardin sent him to town with money enough to buy two mules; he blew the cash on rounds of drinks for the denizens of a saloon.

By 1880 Harbour was ready to get away from the stern Methodist who wanted his children to start and end each day with a prayer. If Harbour went to Bristol to set up his own factory, teetotaler Abram (with his four children and one on the way) would be the big man, but if he went to Winston, there would be bachelor R. J. So Harbour started his factory in Winston — his Red Elephant brand featured an engraving of himself sitting atop a factory drawn by a team of eight red elephants, emblazoned with the boast "One Thousand Spits to the Chew!" He soon wrote home that brother Dick was "the biggest blood in Winston af[fo]rds more stile than any one hear."

*   *   *

In the late 1870s, as Hardin's health declined and Dick became successful, the father seems to have tilted the family more and more toward R. J. An incident: Internal Revenue agents in Lynchburg seized forty cases of Hardin's plug for nonpayment of some of his 1880 taxes. The old man journeyed to Danville and tried to rectify matters; the agents released his tobacco, but there was still an account to be settled, and it perplexed him. For help Hardin turned not to Abram, but to R. J.

Although R. J. was involved in a race for the city council — he finished eighth out of fifteen candidates — and was ill with typhoid fever, he took the matter in hand. Within weeks he was writing to Hardin, "You are now OK with Gov. up to June 1st 1881   You ought to keep coppy of all your inventories   Harber has placed to your Cr $1113 63/100 and give check for your taxes enclose tax receipt Much love to all Your son Dick."

Although Hardin sent his daughter Lucy Burroughs to Sullins College, down the road from Abram in Bristol, he pleaded with R. J. to personally take care of the two youngest sons of the family, Walter and Will, in the event of Hardin's own death. Will, nineteen, was already working during the summers with R. J., and Walter, sixteen, was still in grade school when Hardin died in 1882 at the age of seventy-two.

Nonetheless, when the family met to discuss everything, the Rock Spring business was turned over to Lucy's new husband, Patrick County neighbor Robert Critz, who would run it for Nancy Jane and her last child, twelve-year-old Nancy Kate. Walter and Will were shunted off to Bristol's Kings College, under the watchful eye of first son Abram. R. J. might be doing well, but primogeniture still demanded that the leadership of the family now be in the hands of the first son, who, everyone acknowledged, was turning out to be a Christian gentleman just like Hardin.

=

Winston in 1882 was a racing pack of two dozen chewing-tobacco manufacturers, cheek by jowl. The smell of the cured leaf, the sweet scent of the licorice, hung in the air permanently; if you didn't like tobacco, you didn't like Winston.

Brother Harbour was in the back of the pack, but R. J. had moved up to third, behind Hanes and Thomas Brown. R. J. grew a beard so he would look properly distinguished on the package of his rather oddly named best-selling brand, Our Advertiser, and,

to stay up with the leaders, consistently bought the latest techno-
logical innovations for his factory — gas-fired dryers that elimi-
nated the need to have sugar-soaked leaves on the roof, rubber
rollers to squeeze out excess licorice, steam-powered engines to
press the tobacco. He joined with other manufacturers to build a
new auction house, rented the local skating rink in which to store
his extra tobacco, finally put up his own warehouse, and built
a new factory ten times larger than his original one. His work-
places were declared the cleanest in town in an issue of the *Southern
Tobacco Journal*. Wholesalers liked this because it meant that his
products were not contaminated (as others' were) with horse
manure.

R. J. took on management help: Thomas L. Farrow rose from
tobacco tagger to head of the prize room, while telegrapher Henry
Roan, who began as a part-time night bookkeeper, came aboard as
full-time guardian of the ledgers.

In 1884, after stints at Kings and Trinity colleges, younger brother
William Neal Reynolds, now twenty-one, officially joined the company. A year later, attending an auction sale with R. J., Will jumped
in and made a bid; initially alarmed, R. J. then saw that the batch
was good and the price reasonable. Soon thereafter, Will had total
charge of buying more than a million pounds of raw leaf each year.
A big, beefy man, Will took part in wrestling exhibitions and employed his skills of bluff, control, and pace in the high-stakes card
games of Winston. Will soon started courting Miss Kate Bitting,
daughter of a Winston banker and widely considered the most
eligible young woman in town.

Among R. J.'s new products was a plug called Snaps. Some
labels for it were received at the factory with the name misspelled
as Schnapps; R. J. was furious until told that this was the name of
a popular German spirit. He shipped the product with the mislet-
tered labels. People liked it. Most of the manufacturers didn't yet
understand the power of advertising, but R. J. knew he had hold
of a good thing and promoted it incessantly. He gave wholesalers
special discounts on the brand and capitalized on Schnapps with
an unforgettable advertising point-of-sale gimmick: a countertop
machine that featured a man who'd been slow to try Schnapps in
the process of kicking himself for his stupidity. It was just the thing
to appeal to the true consumer of plug, a backwoods, farm-grown
man. Retailers' requests for the machines soon outran the supply.
To reinforce name recognition of the product, R. J. began having

wall, fence, and billboard signs put up throughout the South for Schnapps, "the sad man's cordial."

In the mid-1880s, when he was in his thirties, the legend of R. J. Reynolds began to cohere. People forgot about his stuttering and slow speech. To Winstonians, he was "Rollax," a dashing knight of St. Patrick in an 1884 parade; he was main fiddler of three at a Mother Goose dance; he paid taxes for farmers to have the privilege of shooting quail from the skies above their lands; he was never seen walking — he ran. R. J. led the list in an article on Winston's eligible bachelors, described as handsome, "with a roseate bloom on his cheeks that never dyes. Has an eye for the main chance, a penchant for widows and would like for it to be known [that] he is the proud owner of a span of blacks [horses] that will be at the widow's disposal, at her proposal. Satisfaction guaranteed."

In the 1884 council election he garnered three times the number of votes he'd gotten in 1879, and won. He became chairman of the sanitation and fire committees. Many of the town's factories had open privies that drained into ravines and were, an observer wrote, "in such foul condition and so offensive that [the observer] was not scholar enough to describe it." Under R. J.'s chairmanship the city planned a sewer system and bought a modern hook-and-ladder engine for fires. In 1885 he helped found a chamber of commerce to bring a second railroad to Winston.

Winston existed at the end of a small spur of the Richmond & Danville, and the chewing-tobacco manufacturers had to pay whatever rate the line wished to charge or have no way of shipping out their products. The new buyer of the R&D, the Pennsylvania system, was so determined to milk the line that it raised its freight rates to double and triple the prices paid on other railroads in the region.

R. J. helped finance the start of a rival venture. It was to be a spur on the Virginia Midland (owned by the Baltimore & Ohio) that would also connect Winston with the rest of the world. Before that spur could be built, the R&D announced it would build a similar spur, and this announcement dried up the Midland's attempted bond sale. Then the Pennsy quickly bought the Virginia Midland and refused to complete either spur. The problems worsened when the Pennsy sold the entire R&D system to a New York group that seemed more bent on stock manipulation than on running the railroad.

Trying desperately to get that second line to make them independent of the R&D, in 1886 R. J. and other Winstonians tried to finance connections to yet another line, the Norfolk & Western. R. J. became a stockholder and director of the new line, called the Roanoke & Southern, and lobbied assiduously for bond issues to finance it to completion. He even went so far as to do something heretofore uncharacteristic — speak out on the issue in public, an activity he had earlier avoided because of his lifelong stutter. According to the local paper, his argument for the bond sale was this:

> Soon after the war, Northern capitalists invested largely in Western railroads. At the same time they advertised by flameing posters, write ups and in every effective way possible, throughout the South and North, attracting all emigrants and thousands of people from every section, so that for 15 years the whole tide of immigration flowed westward. The result was the upbuilding of immense cities . . . and a phenomenal growth of the whole section and an increase in railroad lines that not only brought immense worth to their owners but placed their bonds at a premium. To-day . . . Northern capitalists are turning their attention Southward and are seeking investments here. If the same ratio in this direction is kept up for 30 years that has marked the last two, Mr. Reynolds argued that the bonds . . . would be worth dollar for dollar and the investment regarded as a paying one.

The bond issue passed, and the new spur was soon completed. Winston — and R. J. Reynolds's company — was poised for expansion.

In Bristol, brother Abram followed the path his father had set up for him: the ex-Confederate soldier had become the God-fearing family man, business leader, and pillar of the community. His growing family was quiet and studious, as well as devout. Daughter Sue Sayers would later write books about religious leaders; several of the sons would enter universities at early ages, and one became a doctor. Abram's charities were his glory. The Methodist Church of Bristol often acknowledged his help; when the YMCA was all but defunct, Abram rekindled the flame and donated a building site for the organization; his wartime reputation combined with philanthropy, and the Bristol armory and militia came to be known as the A. D. Reynolds Rifles.

Wilbur Cash suggests that during Reconstruction one group of

Southerners turned toward the past, to a retroactive ennobling of Confederate heroes, to an intense interest in their forebears, to an evangelical religion more fundamental and puritanical than that of frontier times. The other group focused on the future and followed a business and social ethic introduced from the North; those embracing this second way were rebels who ascribed neither their willpower nor their success to adherence to God's principles.

Cash's formulation describes the different directions taken by Abram and R. J. Reynolds, begun in the 1870s and perfected in the 1880s. While Abram took up the cudgels in the crusade to ban alcohol, R. J. lobbied to obtain for Winston a second railroad that would help his business.

But Abram was still first. When brother Walter finished his advanced studies at Randolph-Macon College, he went to work with Abram. Nancy Jane and sixteen-year-old Nancy Kate settled in Bristol in a new house that Abram had commissioned. Rock Spring was left in the care of brothers-in-law Lybrook and Critz, who experienced difficulty with the farm-based operation. Critz and his family moved to Bristol, where he opened a factory right next to Abram's called Critz and Reynolds. Lybrook's life was immensely complicated by the death of his wife, Mary Reynolds Lybrook, in 1888, which left behind eight children ranging in age from twenty to seven and, as Lybrook wrote, "a miserable heart broken and unworthy husband."

For about ten years, the belief had been growing in Abram that sleepy Bristol could be transformed into the seat of an industrial colossus, the Pittsburgh of the South. Iron ore and coal honeycombed the nearby mountains and spurred development. From the mid-1870s to the mid-1880s, according to a pamphlet that Abram prepared, "the neglected mountain country has become an El Dorado . . . and the whole country has been in an active industrial commotion. Science has sought the way which has been followed by the practical work of men." Abram's pamphlet touted Bristol's three railroads, all booming with freight and plans for new spurs. There were no major towns except Knoxville between Chattanooga and Norfolk, a distance of 650 miles. Abram joined other local luminaries in concluding that the opportunity for Bristol to grow into a "commercial center" would prove irresistible to investors.

With the gleam of development in his eye, Abram did something R. J. never in his life tried: he diverted money from his tobacco business and threw it wholesale into an almost entirely unrelated

venture — the transforming of Bristol into a different city. Abram
founded a new railroad company, the Bristol & Elizabethtown, to
connect Bristol directly to some of the great coal and iron deposits.
Shortly, there were a thousand men laying a roadbed; when this
line eventually met up with a new spur of the Richmond & Danville,
Bristol would have two carriers from the ore fields and three to the
Mississippi and the Atlantic Coast. Competition among its railroads
would lower freight rates and boost the area's profitability. To give
added flesh to his vision, Abram helped build a railroad depot to
service all three major lines into Bristol and erected a new hotel
that would be worthy of a great industrial city.

The Fairmount Hotel, center of dreams, opened to the public in
July of 1889 in an event reported even in the New York City papers.
It was a magnificent structure of a hundred rooms whose amenities
included a private lake and greenhouse, tennis courts, riding stables,
ten-pin bowling alley, billiard room, gas and electric lighting, the
first bathtubs in Bristol, and a resident orchestra for dancing. The
Fairmount's musicians doubled to play for the equally charming
Harmeling Opera House, emblem of Bristol's new cultural maturity; before the opening of the Harmeling, operas had been presented in the big hall of Abram's tobacco factory. These grandiose
buildings anchored Abram's other projects, ventures in which he
was joined by brother R. J. Combining forces in the Bristol Land
and Improvement Company marked the first time in their lives
since early Reconstruction that the brothers had worked together.
R. J., though, was only an investor — he could hardly do less than
put money into something that Abram embraced with such fervor;
Abram's pamphlet seems to indicate that R. J. may have allowed
him to use his name mainly as a drawing card with which to lure
other successful businessmen into the fold.

In any event, Abram and R. J.'s land company owned valuable
tracts between the new train station and the Fairmount, a downtown mule-drawn streetcar line, acres in across-the-road Virginia,
and other plots. The company graded several miles of roads. Abram
and R. J. built large houses. Abram moved into his, and R. J.'s
seems to have been used by the Critzes or by Nancy Jane. They
brought their friends into the business, including members of the
Parlett family, who had been associated with Hardin earlier and
now were important wholesalers for R. J. in Baltimore.

Abram roped in such influential men as General Thomas Ewing,
president of two Bristol-connected railroads (who was given a one-

quarter interest in the Bristol Land and Improvement Company), as well as others from New York, Philadelphia, and Richmond. They, the Reynolds brothers, and the Parletts persuaded their banks to invest several million dollars in the Bristol area in the late 1880s, and Abram put up a substantial amount from his own fortune. By this time, R. J. had far exceeded the $100,000 he'd once told his father he wanted to make before retiring and was considered one of the wealthiest men in the state, his net worth probably in the half-million-dollar range. Abram's precise wealth at this time is unknown, but, judging from later estimates, he wasn't far behind R. J.

Then, suddenly, in 1890, the idea of Bristol as a new Pittsburgh vanished almost as quickly as a dream. Iron and coal were discovered in the Upper Midwest. The Bristol luminaries were unable to persuade the biggest potential investors — Andrew Carnegie, J. P. Morgan, John D. Rockefeller — to direct their influence and money to Bristol rather than to these new areas, and the whole boom collapsed. Many land companies went bust. Railroads headed toward receivership; on the Elizabethtown spur, one employee had "the only bottle of ink on the railroad," while other clerks wrote with pencils. The rooms of the Fairmount Hotel emptied. The mule barn of the streetcar line burned to the ground. Abram's hopes were dashed. He was left with little more than maps, deeds, brochures, and ownership of tracts of land that now seemed to have no value.

Chapter Four

Plug Wars

IN 1890 R. J. was forty years old, hale, hearty, his beard just beginning to show touches of gray. One of the wealthiest men in the state, he didn't act as if he were above the masses. He didn't live in a big house, but in the Merchants Hotel. He didn't flaunt his money, but plowed it back into his business. Blacks in his factories knew that if they could stop and talk to him when he walked through the manufacturing floors, they could air a grievance and possibly even get a raise on the spot. He was fair with them, though he did treat them as members of an inferior race, as did nearly all white men of his class at the time.

Although R. J. worked hard, he relaxed with equal vigor, and in the accepted ways. He didn't take off three months of the year and go to Saratoga or Hot Springs. Weeknights he played cards and took a buggy ride or two. The newspapers dutifully recorded dozens of instances in which he was a member of a wedding party or appeared at the performance of a traveling minstrel troupe or visiting opera company. On the weekends, he had his share of social dinners to attend — but preferred to go hunting and fishing with relatives and friends, out among the fields or in the lakes and forests of the mountainous country to the northwest of Winston.

One frequent hunting companion was his first cousin and lifetime friend, Zachary Taylor Smith. Zach and R. J. were about the same age, and Zach had grown up in Patrick County before moving to Mount Airy, North Carolina, near the border with Virginia. He was not only a member of the Cox family but also counted among his forebears U.S. presidents Zachary Taylor and Andrew Jackson. A farmer and small industrialist, Zach had a passel of children. His eldest daughter was Mary Katharine, always called Katharine.

R. J. used to dandle her on his knee when she was quite young, and in 1890, when she was ten, he gave her a gold bracelet and teased her that he'd marry her someday.

R. J.'s pleasure in such commonplace pastimes and refusal to take up the ways of the wealthy were the seeds from which tales grew of his "humble" past. Notions of his "smattering of education" came from another obvious source: his bad spelling and unwillingness to commit things to paper. Although his origins had been decidedly comfortable and his inability to write was a direct result of his dyslexia, R. J. didn't deny these stories, for they encouraged business rivals to underestimate his abilities.

In December 1891, Winston threw a gala celebration as the last spike of its second rail link was completed. The day of independence they called it. R. J. boasted that the new railroad would "enhance the valuation of real estate in Forsyth County by at least four million dollars inside of ten years." That last spike marked a turning point for Winston — and for R. J. It was generally known in Winston that he'd been buying up real estate, some parcels for his new factories, others just for investment. He had also taken further steps to ready himself for a great leap forward to a higher level of doing business.

After fifteen years of operating as a one-man show, he had finally incorporated. He kept 1,700 of 1,900 shares and allowed younger brother Will and bookkeeper-treasurer Henry Roan to buy 100 each. The three of them constituted the board of directors, and by the end of their first year as RJR, Inc., they'd done incredibly well — a profit of $120,000. R. J. ordered a million bricks and built a six-story-high, block-long, steam- and electric-powered fireproof plant, the largest plug factory in the state. Conveyor belts brought tobacco in at the top floor; it was then slowly processed downward, a floor at a time, so that the product reached street level ready for shipment.

Erecting the factory cost a lot of money, and buying leaf to operate it at near-capacity strained R. J.'s resources. The RJR, Inc., debt began to increase; it wasn't unmanageable, just an added burden, one of the prices an industrialist paid for moving up into the category of larger manufacturer.

R. J.'s state of mind at this time was crystallized in a circular he aimed at wholesalers that used a proverbial saying about bottom and top fence rails to make its point:

How the Bottom Rail
gets on top and all be
Benefitted by the Shuffle

Not by slight of hand but in an open, fair handed way. Requires years of hard work to accomplish it and benefit all who are instrumental in building it up. When they have this ability and are not circumscribed as to territory, there is no limit as to what they can accomplish with the most popular chewing Tobaccos offered . . . R. J. Reynolds' Level Best, Double Thick 8-oz., and R.J.R. Pocket Piece. . . . They have recently equipped the largest and best Tobacco Factory in the South, and are now much better prepared than ever to make the shuffle.

Long ago, he'd boasted of achieving a good market share using only "word-of-chewer's-mouth." Then came the Schnapps kicking machine. Now R. J. more fully embraced advertising — he issued calendars, one featuring "a ravishingly beautiful olive skinned and dark tressed maiden." He wanted the advertising to boost him from medium-sized to large-sized manufacturer but hadn't yet perfected an equivalent style.

In part, he was forced to alter his ways because the whole tobacco industry was changing. No reader of *Tobacco* or *Southern Tobacco Journal* could be unaware of the combining of auction houses or that leaf speculators were being squeezed out of existence and farmers getting progressively lower prices for their raw leaf. Such journals said baldly that these calamities were being forced upon the industry by the sinister and monopolistic tactics of the newly formed American Tobacco Company, under the chairmanship of James Buchanan "Buck" Duke.

By 1890, while R. J. was still a local celebrity, Buck Duke, who was of the same generation and from a background largely similar to that of R. J., was a giant.

Buck's father, Washington Duke, born in 1820, fought in the War Between the States and returned home to his small farm afterward with only a fifty-cent coin in his pocket. He went into the smoking-tobacco business with two of his sons, Ben and Brodie. Their product was called Pro Bono Publico, and most of it was shipped out by rail from nearby Durham, which was dominated by the Bull, the world's largest producer of smoking tobacco. Elder son Brodie moved to Durham in 1869 and set up a plant there.

When youngest son Buck tired of attending New Garden College, the rest of the Dukes moved to Durham and evolved a successful joint manufacturing and sales strategy. While Wash, Buck, and Ben went out "drumming" the products, Brodie stayed home to supervise production. At the same time — the mid-1870s — R. J., Abram, and their father were all in the chewing-tobacco business, but their factories were competing against one another, not cooperating. If they'd worked in tandem instead of pulling in three different directions, the Reynoldses might have had as much success as the Dukes.

In 1880, at age twenty-four, Buck was acknowledged as the genius of the Duke family. Though the youngest, he was clearly the smartest and had great vision. After taking in two new partners and semiretiring his father, Buck decided that it was silly to continue to try to outmanufacture the Bull. He put the company's resources into a new product, cigarettes.

Cigarettes were luxury items, rolled and cut by hand. In a bold move, Buck convinced 125 Polish Jews from New York to move south; the double immigrants rolled 9.8 million cigarettes in their first month in Durham. To sell the product, Buck pioneered new techniques. In Atlanta, a prominent actress posed with the cigarettes — she wasn't depicted smoking, for that would have been evidence of moral degradation, but the advertisements caused a sensation anyway and sold many a boxcar-load. Buck sponsored a roller-skating team that traveled throughout the Midwest, playing "polo" matches against local opponents that were avidly reported by newspapers. As spectators left the rink, each gentleman received a five-cent package of Cross-Cut cigarettes, while each lady had to settle for a small pack of photographs of actress Lillian Russell, various potentates, and historical oddities. Soon rival manufacturers were scrambling to offer better "Russell cards" and other premiums because they were losing market shares to the Dukes.

Now Buck did something that R. J.'s character would not allow him to do: sensing that the way to the very top required the rubbing of shoulders with those who had the greatest leverage, Buck transferred his headquarters to New York. For this move, he asked each partner to put up an additional $20,000. Richard Wright, one of the outside partners, balked and even refused to deliver money he was to have paid earlier for entering the partnership — so Wash Duke foreclosed on Wright's real estate in Durham. This legal

the sale of shares of stock to the public. From its start in 1890, Buck Duke headed the ATC, which made between 90 and 95 percent of the cigarettes sold in America. In the five previous years, thanks to the cigarette-rolling machine, his family's assets had soared from $250,000 to $3.75 million, but most of this money was tied up in plant and equipment. Now, with one magic stroke, he translated the family's assets into ATC stock worth $7.5 million.

The ATC was so large that it was soon dictating the buying patterns in the auction houses and forcing lower prices on tobacco growers for their raw leaf. Josephus Daniels, editor of a North Carolina newspaper owned by Julian Carr, the man who had made the Bull, labeled the ATC in the pages of his paper an incarnation of evil that was condemning farmers to bankruptcy and would soon gobble up smaller manufacturers. He'd previously been a friend of Wash Duke's — they were both stalwarts of the state's Methodist organization — and when the old man came in to the paper's office to cancel his subscription personally, they had a confrontation. After Daniels cited figures to document his contentions about the trust, Wash Duke contritely whispered that hurting tobacco growers was a terrible mistake and that he wished "Buck had never put us into the [A.T.] Company and that we could carry on our business like we used to do it. We were making lots of money and did not have any criticism."

Daniels was seconded in his newspaper campaign by *Webster's Weekly* of Reidville, South Carolina, and both fights were backed, personally and financially, by R. J. Reynolds. Daniels later wrote that R. J. "was even more severe on Buck Duke than my newspaper and endeared himself to the farmers by his plain talk."

It was a time of desperation for the less powerful segments of the tobacco industry, an era of odd alliances. Farmers had never liked any of the manufacturers — or leaf speculators, for that matter — but were forced to fight alongside small manufacturing firms and pinhookers against the trust, which not only controlled leaf prices but was coercing the railroads into giving it special anticompetitive rates. Critics lambasted the railroad trust of J. P. Morgan for joining hands with the tobacco trust of Duke, two fat robber barons settling matters over an oyster dinner at Delmonico's, in New York. The struggle of the farmers, auction houses, small manufacturers, and newspaper editors was joined by religious organizations that hated tobacco altogether.

During this period, doctors traced eighty diseases to cigarettes and smoking and attributed to them twenty thousand deaths annually in the United States. The use of chewing tobacco, though lamented as unsightly, was tolerated as less hazardous than smoking. Preachers invariably characterized "backsliders" from religion as "victims of tobacco." The Methodist Conference of Western North Carolina even tried to condemn cigarettes as "injurious to health and weakening of the intellect," but Wash Duke, a major benefactor of the conference, was aghast at this and leaned on Bishop Kilgo (whose college had recently been moved to Durham and would soon be renamed Duke University in honor of the family's gifts) to pull enough strings to defeat the resolution.

The coalition against the tobacco trust lobbied more successfully in state legislatures for the enactment of laws against sales of "coffin tacks" to minors. Some states even forbade their sale to adults. Virginia's legislature retroactively removed its approval of the ATC's charter. Duke simply reorganized the trust in New Jersey.

R. J. Reynolds watched the trust with a mixture of envy and fear. He admired the way that Duke was making a big splash—but he knew that the waves would eventually come in his direction, even though the trust at first seemed to be interested only in cigarettes. His fears were confirmed in February of 1891, when the ATC bought a controlling interest in a Louisville plug maker. In April Duke traded stock and a small amount of cash for two Baltimore smoking- and chewing-tobacco firms. Soon, despite the fact that they manufactured a different kind of plug from that made in Winston, these ATC firms were cutting into the Winston crowd's markets, selling chewing-tobacco products practically below cost to wholesalers, while at the same time threatening the "jobbers" that if they wouldn't handle ATC plug they wouldn't be allowed to sell the increasingly lucrative ATC cigarettes.

Some of the smaller fry in Winston and other tobacco-manufacturing cities of the South began to go under. RJR managed to stay afloat, but whereas R. J.'s firm had made $120,000 in 1891, in 1892 it was all he could do to break even. If the trust turned up the pressure in 1893, what would he do?

=

It was early 1893. Bristol had changed greatly since the boom and bust of 1890. A newspaperman concluded that the debacle had brought Bristol "from the worst-paved town of its size on earth to the best; cast a blighting shade over a few good men, but profited the community." The newsman had noted, in the same article, that Abram's tobacco factory "had made its usual clear profit of $1,000 a week." With such a money generator, Abram was slowly rebuilding his fortunes. But he was being squeezed by the American Tobacco Company's takeover of several of the Louisville plug makers, which Duke had consolidated into one and renamed the National Tobacco Works.

The ATC challenge was also causing problems for R. J. in Winston. Thomas Farrow, head of RJR's prizing department, and Henry Roan, secretary and treasurer of the firm, had both become uneasy. R. J.'s response to squeezing by the ATC plug makers was to expand rapidly — too rapidly for Roan, who thought him a "reckless plunger." Farrow, who'd worked for R. J. since 1876 yet had only recently been allowed to buy stock, was unhappy because R. J. was keeping most of the profits in the business rather than allowing the new partners to take some extra money home. R. J. pointed out to the dissidents that the advent of the second railroad in Winston afforded great new distribution opportunities, which, if pursued aggressively, could counter pressure from the ATC. They disagreed; push came to shove, and both men resigned. Brother Will Reynolds temporarily assumed the duties of secretary and treasurer — but, at a crucial time, R. J. had gaping holes in his management.

A few months later, the country plunged into its worst depression in twenty years, known thereafter as the Panic of 1893. It made the trough of '73 seem like a picnic. Prices crumbled in many industries, farms went under, and so did many small-to-midsized businesses that didn't have adequate reserves. Throughout the whole of the American economy, there was a shaking out — a realignment that had the effect of aiding the largest firms, especially the trusts, but sinking those that were only marginally viable. Because R. J. had kept so much money in his business, RJR, Inc., managed better than most. Abram's business suffered more severely but didn't go under completely.

However, there were two Reynolds business casualties of the Panic of 1893 — the joint operation of brother Walter and brother-in-law Critz in Bristol, and the enterprise of brother Harbour in Winston. The failure of these companies produced a turning point in the family and a new cast to the old competition between Abram and R. J. Within months, both Walter and Critz had moved to Winston and were working for R. J. The scholarly Walter took over Farrow's duties as head of the prizing department, and Critz shortly became the firm's secretary, elevating Will to the office of vice president. Harbour, whose factory was only a stone's throw from R. J.'s, closed his shop — sold it to R. J.'s competitors, in fact — and went to work for Abram, in Bristol.

Why did Harbour flee to Bristol when he, too, could have gone to work for R. J.? For years, in Winston, Harbour had tried to maintain an independent identity; newspaper stories invariably refrained from mentioning that he was R. J.'s brother, though they were quick to point out the family alliances of the Haneses, the Browns, and other firms. Perhaps Harbour insisted on being R. J.'s rival, not his kid brother. Then, too, Harbour had a drinking problem, one that undoubtedly contributed to his firm's bankruptcy in 1893. Court records show him often involved in minor infractions, some on his own, the rest as bail poster for known moonshiners and men who sold liquor to minors. It seems to have been the sense of the family that he would benefit from a stint working for teetotaler Abram and might even, under Abram's tutelage, get rid of his infatuation with demon rum.

As important as these business moves was the change in venue of mother Nancy Jane Cox Reynolds, who chose this moment to leave Bristol for Winston. It was as if the queen bee had shifted hives and ennobled the new one with her presence. R. J. took the opportunity to move out of the Merchants Hotel, site of his bachelor shenanigans, and for the first time took up residence in elegant, upright surroundings — his first mansion, on Fifth Street — together with his mother, his brother Will, and sister-in-law Kate Bitting Reynolds.

This was a grand home. Outside, the building looked like a wedding cake, with two large turrets rising above the third floor, a wide curved porch and piazza, a driveway leading to a covered entrance, a formal garden, and many other amenities — a home that one later observer called "the ultimate in Victorian fantasy." It was large enough so that Kate and Will, Nancy Jane, and R. J. all had what were in effect separate grand apartments. Soon society writers took notice of the newly elegant R. J. driving around town in his "nobby" vehicle, a spider phaeton, the latest in carriages.

The Reynolds brothers now helped to found the summer colony of Winston. This was Roaring Gap, a resort of spectacular scenic beauty, high in the mountains ninety miles northwest of the city.

The big hotel there was considered a fine one, even if it didn't yet have any bathtubs.

In 1893, Buck Duke's attack on the plug makers was spurred on by some of his own problems — familial and legislative. His ne'er-do-well brother Brodie, recently dried out at an "institute" in Illinois, went on a binge of unbridled speculation during the panic that left him bankrupt and put a drain on family resources. Also, father Wash was continually importuning Buck about the advertising of cigarettes, writing him that because "we owe Christianity all the assistance we can lend it in any form," it was necessary to stop distributing "lascivious photographs" of women in tights, a practice that turned good Christian men against cigarette makers and strengthened the hand of those who were passing ordinances against cigarettes in state legislatures.

Because of such pressures, Duke decided that the time had come to stop pushing cigarettes exclusively and go after the plug industry. There were twice as many chewers as smokers in the country. At that moment, the three biggest plug firms were Liggett & Myers, Lorillard, and Drummond, producing each year 27 million, 20 million, and 14 million pounds respectively, while Duke's own National Tobacco Works made 9 million and had nearly doubled its output in three years under the ATC. By comparison, R. J. Reynolds was making just more than a million pounds a year. R. J. also made a different product than the other four — "bright" plug, as opposed to the "burley" leaf plug.

Duke's expansion into plug was opposed by his major partners in the ATC, but he formed an alliance with Standard Oil millionaire Oliver H. Payne, and they bought out the others, a maneuver that actually made Buck stronger than ever before. Buck wrote to brother Ben of his determination to "make the Plug Mfgrs hustle like we once did Cigarette Mfgrs." Duke cut the price of NTW's Battle Axe from 50 cents per one-pound bar down to 13 cents, of which 6 cents was revenue tax. The three leading plug manufacturers fought back by lowering their own prices and by marketing some cigarettes of their own.

What became known as the plug wars began in earnest. They were costly for Duke. In the next three years, his competitors wrested 15 percent of the cigarette trade from the ATC. The combine's share of the plug market increased, but losses from selling plug too cheaply mounted to more than a million dollars a year. Although Duke's partner grew nervous, the war continued.

One of the beneficiaries of the war among the big four in plug was RJR. With new machinery, a new flavoring — saccharin — and more money spent on advertising, R. J.'s firm grew larger. By 1897 he had quadrupled his output to more than four million pounds.

R. J.'s battle against the tobacco trust took an oblique turn and came to embrace a fight against a lateral trust, J. P. Morgan's railroads, which now included the Richmond & Danville. It was another fight in which R. J. allied himself with crusading editor Josephus Daniels. When Morgan's minions yanked Daniels's pass to the railroad, R. J. sent him a check so he could travel wherever he wanted to, because, R. J. said, Daniels was fighting "in the interest of the people of North Carolina for three generations to come." Daniels framed the check rather than cash it. R. J.'s campaign enabled the state of North Carolina to obtain higher revenues from the railroad, though it didn't do very much for RJR, Inc.

However, in the years of the middle 1890s RJR did very well. R. J. quadrupled his business, eclipsing Hanes, Brown, and others in Winston. The big problem was the firm's debt, which multiplied not four times but nine times, to $270,000 per year. RJR was making a lot of money; however, as the debt ratio grew, R. J.'s business became a high-stakes game in which he could either continue to win big or, in a few tough years, lose everything.

R. J.'s time for head-to-head battle with Duke was coming, but first it was Abram's turn. The crunch for him arrived in 1897, and it coincided with a crisis in his personal, religious life. For years, Abram had been involved in fighting alcohol. Many people saw liquor as the ruination of society, were aghast that Americans spent more on whiskey and tobacco than they did on bread and other staple groceries. Some businessmen went so far as to state that liquor sapped the ability of laborers to work. Only a few voices dared say that the campaign against the bottle diverted energy from fighting the trusts that were taking over tobacco, oil, lumber, railroads, the financial structure, and almost every other aspect of American life.

Abram was in the forefront of the movement in Tennessee. He led anti-alcohol parades down Main Street on horseback, ignoring threats on his life. He sent his brother Harbour to dry out at the clinic that had "saved" Brodie Duke. He was a leader of the Bristol Band of Hope, a youth temperance group that gave out badges to its members. Most of the badges were anti-alcohol, but at least one bore the pledge "I will use no tobacco forever."

Fellow members of the Band of Hope pressed him to get out of the tobacco business. For years, Abram had maintained that if the Lord wanted him to give it up, He would provide a sign. The sign appeared in 1897, after a half-dozen fruitless years of fighting the ATC, when Harbour walked into Abram's office with a tentative offer of a buyout from Abram's local partners, Harbour included. In a few hours, the transaction was consummated. Over the years, Abram estimated, he'd made about a half-million dollars from his tobacco firm, and in 1897 he took $30,000 for his interest, $5,000 of which he immediately lent back to Harbour to shore up his brother's stake in the firm.

Common among the devout was the idea that if the Lord asked you to give something up and you did, He would eventually enable you to gain much more than you had lost. After selling his tobacco business, Abram searched for an investment that would fulfill that promise — and cause him no more moral headaches.

A crucial state election was held in North Carolina in 1898. The Democrats, backed editorially by such firebrands as Josephus Daniels and such major employers of blacks as R. J. Reynolds, saw the election as a referendum on race. The *Winston-Salem Journal* of November 7, 1898, put things baldly: "There are really . . . two parties and but one issue . . . the white man's party and the negro party, white supremacist or Negro rule. Which will you take? Are you a White man or a White Negro?"

The racism of Southern whites in those days was a given, but politics was not so simple as white against black. R. J. Reynolds was essentially a man wholly within the scheme of his culture. His rise to manhood had occurred principally during Reconstruction, and he had a deep belief that the "wrongs" of that era — committed against men like his father — had to be redressed. Reconstruction had been controlled by the Republicans and forced down the throats of old-line white Southerners with the aid of docile Negro voters. That was one of the reasons that R. J. became a lifelong Democrat and an anti-Republican. There was another reason: the Democrats were antimonopoly, and, in the 1890s, that was an important consideration for him. The Republicans were associated with the monopolies (with the Dukes, in particular), and R. J. wished to ally himself with the opposite pole. In the election of 1898, that made him a Democrat and, ipso facto, a supporter of white supremacy, a stance that also fit comfortably with his upbringing.

The Democrats won the election. Their victory reinforced white supremacy through the enactment of poll taxes, grandfather clauses, and other disenfranchising measures. All these set back for several generations the movement for equality of blacks.

Nothing, however, seemed able to retard the impact of Buck Duke on the plug-tobacco industry. That same year, 1898, at the onset of the Spanish-American War, the federal government imposed new, higher taxes on tobacco, which further cut into the profits of the competing plug companies. Duke bought the third-largest firm, Drummond, slashed in half the price of its leading brand, and was closing in on the second-largest company, Lorillard. Duke then offered Pierre Lorillard a deal previously unheard-of in the industry: Lorillard would be allowed to continue marketing products under his own label, while the ATC controlled his company. The Lorillard model deal enticed several other midsized plug companies to quickly join with the existing ones in a new holding company called Continental Tobacco, chartered in New Jersey at the end of 1898. Continental issued $62 million in stock, of which Duke and Oliver Payne took $30 million in exchange for their four plants.

Alarm bells rang for R. J. Reynolds. His competition was now a giant that could produce eighty-four million pounds of plug per year and could easily run him out of all his markets. His debt had mounted almost beyond his control. He had to do something. First, he applied to the North Carolina legislature for permission to increase his capital stock to $12 million. Then, while this application was still pending, he met with Buck Duke in New York — secretly, to keep his intentions from the trust-hating public of Winston.

The historic meeting of the two rough-hewn tobacco men from North Carolina was at Duke's headquarters, 111 Fifth Avenue, an imposing brick building in the commercial district. Duke's office was a true mixture of the strains in his character, housing rich wood paneling, brass ornaments, and, in a place of honor, a photograph of old Wash Duke on the porch of the log cabin in which the Duke boys were born.

Duke was now a man of the world, immensely wealthy, with a fashionable mistress, a country estate in southern New Jersey, friendships with Morgan and Rockefeller. R. J., though well-heeled compared to the rest of the world, was still pretty much the country cousin. Yet they shared similar backgrounds, a love of horseflesh, female company, the game of business. Each respected what the other had accomplished.

The dance of negotiation began. Duke initially feigned a lack of interest, saying that Continental didn't know how to manufacture the flat plug products that Reynolds made and sold so well and therefore wouldn't be interested in buying RJR. R. J. accepted the blandishments and pushed on, saying he needed new capital. Duke countered: he wouldn't agree to buy the RJR company unless Reynolds would stay and run it — in the manner of the Lorillard deal.

R. J. didn't want to give up his hard-won business for ATC stock. He'd rather have Duke come in and do so in the guise of an investor who was putting needed capital into the business. R. J. would have pointed out that if it became widely understood that the ATC or Continental had purchased RJR, the antitrust Winstonians would somehow revolt. Duke agreed.

The deal would be kept quiet. Now for the figures: Duke offered a million for the company. R. J. objected, pointing out that the RJR stock was on the books at around $1 million and, with plant and real estate, was worth more. With a little haggling, R. J. was able to get Duke to raise the offer to $3 million (in real dollars, not ATC stock) for a two-thirds share of RJR, Inc. The company would be kept intact. Buck Duke and his lieutenants at Continental would control RJR, but the current Reynolds management would continue to run the show.

R. J. wired his brothers to "prepare for good living." Now, on paper, at least, R. J. Reynolds was a millionaire. But he was also— on paper — under the thumb of Buck Duke.

Josephus Daniels was shocked when he learned of the sale. He had thought Reynolds was "more than a match for Duke." When Daniels and R. J. met, not long after the transaction, Daniels expressed his regret that R. J. had "sold out to the Tobacco Trust." Reynolds answered,

> Sometimes you have to join hands with a fellow to keep him from ruining you and to get the under hold yourself! . . . Buck Duke will find out that he has met his equal, but I am fighting him now from the inside. . . . You will never see the day when Dick Reynolds will eat out of Buck Duke's hands. . . . If Buck tries to swallow me he will have the bellyache the balance of his life.

Chapter Five

Under the Trust

WEEKENDS IN EARLY 1900, at the start of life under the trust, the Reynolds brothers could be found at one of their old favorite pursuits — cockfights. Held inside barns, cockfights brought people from afar to watch, drink, and gamble on whether a gray cock could kill a red one or vice versa. The spurs, three-inch-long needles wired to the talons and bent into short curves, were lethal, and the cockfights were extremely bloody. It was not so much a sport as occasion for frenzied rounds of betting, the odds changing from moment to moment as the damage inflicted by the spurs each cock wore increased. Bettors would place several wagers on each two- to five-minute fight, winning and losing in quick succession until one combatant died. The heaviest gamblers sat closest to the ring, and the more timid ones toward the back.

The Reynolds men also regularly took part in horse racing, hunting, fishing, and card playing — all lubricated with whiskey — but they continued to be the first ones in the office every day and the last to leave at night. Office hours began at 7:30 A.M. and ended at 6:00 P.M., except on Saturdays, when the office closed at 5:00. (Naturally no business was done on Sunday, the Lord's Day.) The management was still mostly family: boss R. J., his brothers Walter and Will, brother-in-law Robert Critz, a Lybrook nephew, and Ed Lasater, who was shortly to marry a Lybrook girl. (Widower Andrew Lybrook was dying, and R. J. was taking care of his children's futures.) In one of his few concessions to luxury, each morning R. J. rode his horse at a leisurely pace from the Fifth Street mansion to his office, doffing his hat to passersby in a manner unchanged since Robert E. Lee had perfected it in the aftermath of the War Between the States.

In that office, R. J. was playing a dangerous game. On the one hand, he was baldly lying to his salesmen, telling them in a broadside that RJR would not be "taken into either of the trusts nor be identified with them," while on the other he made quarterly trips to New York to get his marching orders from Duke. His lie was a prudent one: in 1900, many products of American manufacturing proudly displayed labels and had advertising slogans that announced them as "not made by a trust." If he didn't flaunt his connection with Duke, his business would do better.

Both he and Buck preferred doing business in person to committing to paper things that might later reveal their more questionable practices. R. J. traveled to New York because, although he had a telephone in his office, he could not yet reach New York through it. Buck was becoming more involved in expanding his business overseas and soon left to his lieutenants the process of tutoring R. J. on the ATC's methods and extracting quarterly, monthly, and sometimes weekly reports. R. J. hated the system: in one memo he cheekily demanded to be told what the current "song and dance" was and as much as said that he sent in the requested reports merely to keep the paper shufflers happy.

In one sense, though, R. J. must have been delighted to deal with lieutenants and not with the big man, for Buck might have seen through what R. J. was planning. At first, after receiving his new money, R. J. did the expected: he wiped out his debts, commissioned a new factory, and did some fancy promotion work. With new capital, he let loose his imagination on the task of making the most out of an already proven winner. He told the maker of the Schnapps bag tags to deliver to Winston a million of them per week and advertised that he'd exchange 75 tags for a fine English steel razor, 2,000 for a dinner set, 14,500 for a Mason and Hamlin organ. He even commissioned a Bristol firm owned by Abram to do nothing but make cast-iron stoves for his exclusive use as giveaways. No rival's offerings could match these, and the market share of Schnapps increased.

R. J.'s problem was that he knew how to manufacture and sell chewing tobacco but was a babe in the woods when it came to mergers, acquisitions, and the stuff of being a grand industrialist. By playing dumb — or, at least, naive — he persuaded the ATC/

Continental men to guide him along without alerting them to the nature of his ultimate goal, which was to take over the flat plug industry of North Carolina and Virginia. He wanted control not only because he was ambitious, but because he sensed that if he didn't grow in size and establish a big power base, RJR eventually would be swallowed up by the ATC/Continental giant.

In April of 1900, a scant three months after he went into the ATC, R. J. bought out a firm down the street in Winston: T. L. Vaughan & Company, to which R. J.'s former partner Henry Roan had unwisely jumped seven years earlier. Vaughan wanted the purchase price to include $10,000 for "goodwill." R. J. was inclined to give it to him, but Continental overruled this, crossed off the $10,000, and substituted $1. Vaughan signed on the dotted line. Lesson One: Be tough.

R. J. was also directed not to publicize the sale and to hold key documents, unregistered, in his own safe — because disclosure of the sale would feed antitrust sentiment. The compliant local newspaper reported that Vaughan had sold out and retired because of poor health. Lesson Two: Keep your cards to yourself.

Next to fall was RJR's largest competitor in Winston, Brown Brothers. R. J.'s own favorite chew was Brown's Mule. Once, while aboard a train, he'd been enjoying some and spat out the window; the juice landed on the face of a trackside bystander. When the fellow charged into the parlor car, R. J. was ready to apologize, but the man only wanted to know the name of the chew, since he intended to switch to it instantly. In the past few years, three of the principals of Brown Brothers had died. The remaining ones saw the handwriting on the wall and decided to get out, selling to RJR for a fire-sale sum. Lesson Three: Aim at weakness.

Lesson Four: Reward friends when necessary and, if possible, in stock and not in dollars. On the same day that RJR agreed to buy out Brown Brothers, the company's board also voted to acquire the next two largest competitors, both operated by R. J.'s chum Pleasant Hanes. B. F. Hanes had died recently, and P. H. was ready to go on to other things. The buyout price was $470,000 in cash and two thousand shares of RJR capital stock. A third Hanes brother, previously in the company management, decided to take his profits, buy a cotton-goods factory making undergarments, and enlarge its capacity. This became the nucleus of the great Hanes hosiery empire.

For R. J., this last big acquisition did the trick. After a year under the trust, RJR was the largest single employer in the state of North Carolina. Rather than run all his new companies as separate entities, R. J. consolidated and condensed; ran steam lines from old factories to newly acquired ones; amalgamated leaf supplies, insurance coverage, and a hundred other details. He did this with a sure hand, as if he'd been waiting for the opportunity all his life. It was another instance of seeing the main chance and reaching to grasp it. Now he was not only bigger, he was more competitive, too. Murmurs of discontent about monopoly swept through Winston, but RJR had grown too powerful to be gainsaid.

An odd irony capped this period of expansion. The old Abram Reynolds business in Bristol, managed by Harbour and associates, tottered, fell, and was absorbed into another branch of the ATC. The trust decided that Abram's flat plug brand should become the property of RJR; so, in effect, R. J. had finally bought out Abram — and Harbour. The kid brother didn't give up easily, though. He took his share of the sale, relocated in South Boston, Virginia, and started up a new chewing-tobacco business, only to have it devastated in a fire. After that, he moved back to Rock Spring and began farming the old place, his dreams of being a manufacturer laid to rest.

At the turn of the twentieth century a social historian wrote that, in contrast to earlier eras, everyone seemed now to be obsessed with obtaining money: "Birth, breeding, rank, accomplishments in literature, eminence in art, eminence in public service . . . when combined they are only as the dust of the balance when weighed against the all-prevalent power of money. The worship of the Golden Calf is the characteristic cult of modern society."

A newspaper named the millionaires in the United States in 1902 — all 8,000 of them. Ten years earlier there had been only 4,700. The gap between the millionaires and the general populace was huge: the lowest third of the nation's families had incomes of only $400 a year, and two thirds of all families made less than $900 yearly. Most of the men on the millionaires list had previously owned small manufacturing concerns that they had sold for fantastic prices during the waves of consolidation that had recently swept through American industry. The 1902 list included four Dukes, Pleasant Hanes of Winston, and A. D. Reynolds of Bristol — but not R. J. Reynolds. Abram made the list not only because of his tobacco profits but because the lands that he had bought up during the Bristol boom and that he had once been told were worthless were now increasingly valuable.

R. J.'s exclusion was ironic. Although he was the largest employer in the state of North Carolina, in terms of disposable dollars he was not yet among the nation's wealthiest. Almost everything he had was in his business.

R. J. was in his early fifties now and on the verge of his biggest successes. He was surrounded by family, and yet he was alone at the top. If it could be said that he lacked anything, he did not have two elements of happiness: a wife, and a son to bring into the business. Now, in middle age, he set out to remedy those lacks.

On one of R. J.'s trips to New York he was accompanied by a chaperon and Katharine Smith, his young cousin once removed, who was acting as his stenographer. Katharine, now twenty-one, had grown from the charming, bright child who had sat on his knee into a tall woman with jet-black hair and deep blue eyes, the very picture of what a contemporary artist was elevating to an icon as the Gibson girl. With her hourglass figure accentuated by yards and yards of cloth shaped into ruffled skirts, mutton-leg sleeves, and a tight waist, Katharine was a striking young woman. Like the heroines of many contemporary novels, she was chaste, overflowing with moral rectitude yet deeply romantic. She was also quite different from most of the young women of class in Winston. In recommending her for college, her grade school principal had described her as "possessing a splendid intellect" and being "farther advanced and more thorough than any student" he'd seen. She attended State Normal School — the first college for women in North Carolina — until a typhoid epidemic shut it down. A roommate remembered her "precise way of speaking and a bit of a tendency to persuade people to do things for their own good." She transferred to Sullins College, down the road from Abram in Bristol, where she studied art and became something of a portrait painter.

She was treasurer of her senior class when she graduated in 1902 with a degree of Mistress of English Literature. Bright, apt at figures, Katharine was unintimidated by R. J., whom she had known since childhood. She was also unusual in that she wasn't out husband hunting but wanted to work.

At that time, only a small fraction of women worked outside the home, and most stenographers in the country were men. To take down R. J.'s stuttering discourse and translate it to the page was no easy task, but he trusted his young cousin to do so. Back in Winston, R. J. held a companywide competition to see who could write the best letter touting the virtues of RJR. Katharine won the prize of one thousand dollars. R. J., teasing, swore he'd have to marry her to get his money back.

R. J. seemed to be surrounding himself with young people at this time. One Christmas, when visiting Abram in Bristol, he had found his nephew Richard S. Reynolds up at six in the morning, reviewing his studies. Always a brilliant student, R. S. had begun junior college at thirteen and law school at seventeen, first at Columbia University and then at the University of Virginia. R. J. told his nephew that if he were so industrious as to get up early during a vacation and study, he ought to quit law school and come to work in Winston. R. S. said that he really wanted to be a lawyer. R. J. snorted; as a lawyer he'd always do someone else's work, but as an industrialist he'd hire lawyers.

R. S. asked for details. R. J. was willing to start him at a hefty $50 a week, perhaps two and a half times the average national wage. Since room and board in Winston would come to only $11.50 a week, R. S. decided to take the job, invest the remainder of his salary, and learn the tobacco business as personal secretary to a titan. Uncle and nephew were soon inseparable. R. S. was R. J.'s aide-de-camp, and R. J. seems to have tutored him closely in the workings of the tobacco business — and the way to the top. Had R. J. married and had children earlier, it seems certain that he would have brought his sons into the firm in just this manner.

In March 1903, Nancy Jane Cox Reynolds died. She was seventy-eight. The family buried her in the old graveyard at Rock Spring, next to Hardin. After the funeral, R. J. moved his parents' marital bed into his own bedroom at Fifth Street.

A month after his mother's death, he wrote to "Dear Cousin Kate" that "your proving a favorite with the older people is a good indication that I judged you correctly, as one of the few that is so constituted or has the capability of enjoying whatever you may do that will make yourself most useful during life." They began to court more seriously. After the requisite mourning period, he rode up to Mount Airy to see his cousin Zachary Taylor Smith and to ask for Katharine's hand in marriage.

"Katharine has other suitors and can take care of herself; perhaps she'll pursue a career as a portrait painter," Zach told him. "Why don't you marry her younger sister Maxie, instead?"

R. J. managed to convince his old friend and cousin that Katharine was the one he wanted for a wife, and Smith finally consented. Then, as was proper, R. J. asked Katharine herself, who accepted in writing. R. J. signed his rejoinder to her note "From your most trusted lover and forever yours."

R. J. seems to have deliberately waited until his mother was dead to propose. This was not necessarily because Nancy Jane disapproved of R. J.'s marrying a blood relation; that point would have been moot, for although Katharine's grandmother and R. J.'s mother had been sisters, Nancy Jane's most famous relative, Joshua Cox, had also married his cousin once removed. Also, in the plantation South, "kin" marriages had always been accepted. A more likely stumbling block would have been the age difference. Katharine was almost thirty years younger than R. J. Possibly Nancy Jane had expressed no opinion, but it is interesting to note that, like R. J., Harbour also waited until his mother was dead to propose to a young lady. His intended was a schoolteacher in the Rock Spring area.

R. J. had not yet informed any of his other relatives about proposing to Katharine when, one evening in 1904, R. S. tiptoed into his uncle's study in the Fifth Street house with the idea of telling R. J. that Julia Parham had just accepted his own marital proposal. When he got inside the door, however, there was silence, and neither man spoke for several minutes. R. J. seemed as embarrassed as the young man. Finally, R. J. cleared his throat and announced, "R. S., I am to be married in January" — and the nephew had to laugh and confess that he'd come to relate the same message.

They had a bit of a tiff. R. J. wanted R. S. to postpone his marriage for six months so the young man would be at the tobacco company's office while R. J. took an extended honeymoon. They compromised. R. S. speeded up his preparations and was married in December of 1904. That way, the stage was set for the early February 1905 marriage of R. J. Reynolds to Katharine Smith.

Just before the wedding, R. J. wrote to Katharine:

I feel that no one on earth is blessed with a more noble, earnest, and sincere, lovely, sweet or better wife than I will have in you. I love you and respect you so much more than I ever did anyone else, that I really feel I never knew what true love was; it must be god's blessing in having me to wait for you and receive more happiness than earlier marriage would have given me.

The wedding took place at Zach Smith's home in Mount Airy, a small, still rural town near the Virginia border, northwest of Winston. R. J. was in a morning coat with cutaway jacket and striped trousers. Katharine wore a modest beaver hat, a deep blue cloth blouse with long shirred sleeves, and a skirt trimmed with chiffon, white silks, and plenty of lace — in those days blue, not white, was the color of choice in weddings. The cut set off her hourglass figure, and the color highlighted her blue eyes. A talented home sewer, she had made part of her outfit herself; she had also created many of the items in her trousseau. All the Reynolds brothers and their children attended, as did other officers from R. J.'s company — except R. S., who was in Tucson taking care of his bride, who had become ill after their wedding. Buck Duke was away but sent an extravagant gift, as did many other important people in businesses up and down the Eastern Seaboard. The local newspaper breathlessly reported that R. J. was the wealthiest man in the state, his personal fortune exceeding three million dollars. Guests grumbled at having to show up in Mount Airy early in the day, but the morning ceremony allowed R. J. and his bride to catch a train reaching New York in time to board an ocean liner. R. J.'s first trip abroad, and the one for which Katharine had yearned since her college days, was a lengthy honeymoon to Paris, Vienna, and Switzerland.

=

The reason that R. J. had been so adamant about having R. S. in the office while the elder Reynoldses took their honeymoon was that this was a crucial moment for the RJR company: Buck Duke was in trouble, on two counts.

The general public had for some time been against the trusts, which were consolidating American enterprise at an alarming rate. Gigantic combines in railroads, banking, lumber, shipping, and tobacco — among other industries — were practicing capitalism in a particularly ruthless way, using their size not only to wipe out or absorb competitors, but also to force consumers to pay whatever price the trusts chose to charge. Now, however, the public outcries were stirring elected representatives to action. Under President

Theodore Roosevelt, federal prosecutors had begun to use laws that had been on the books for years to try to break these trusts. A big blow had been landed in 1904: federal prosecutors won a case brought under the Sherman Anti-Trust Act that forced the dissolution of Northern Securities, a holding company owned by J. P. Morgan, John D. Rockefeller, and other financiers. Previously, the Sherman Act had been used mainly against labor unions. The Northern Securities case was a clear warning to all trusts to mend their ways or be broken up. Duke's response to it had shown R. J. that his boss and rival was in a sensitive position. In actions taken to forestall government prosecution, Buck collapsed all of his paper entities into one operating company, the ATC. He issued orders to the smaller units in the ATC, like RJR, to stop buying companies so that the appearance of competition would be maintained.

To foster the illusion of local autonomy in their subsidiaries, Buck and his brothers also removed themselves from directorships of these units — at RJR, they were replaced by R. J.'s associates, a maneuver that effectively loosened the reins on R. J., though Buck retained financial control of RJR. R. J. understood that, despite all Buck might do, sometime soon the tobacco trust would be dismantled. What he referred to as the day of emancipation might not come this year or the next, but it was inevitable. He must prepare for its arrival.

As if these business worries were not enough, Buck's private life was also in chaos. He had long been in thrall to Lillian McCredy, a divorcée of some notoriety. Associates noted with amazement that he would come out of important business meetings to take her calls and that the normally astute Buck seemed blind to the faults in Lillian, which were glaringly obvious to others. He had installed her in a brownstone near Central Park, squired her to the opera, to his Newport cottage, to his country estate in Somerville, New Jersey — but for years had kept the relationship hidden from his father, Washington Duke. In September 1904, Washington finally got wind of Lillian's existence. Summoned to his dying father's bedside, Buck had pledged to live no more in sin, and he married Lillian in November. The new couple then left on a two-month honeymoon trip to France and Italy.

In apparent reaction to Buck's marriage, elder brother Brodie went on a rampage. For two weeks he staged a massive drunk in a disreputable New York hotel and, to cap it off, married a prostitute and gave her promissory notes on his share of the family fortune. It took quite a bit of fancy footwork to undo the damage, but eventually the knot was severed and Brodie temporarily committed to a mental institution.

By this time, Buck was hurrying home from Europe because his father had taken a turn for the worse. The old man lingered a few more months. By the time Wash passed on, Buck's marriage had gone sour, and he regretted ever having made it. Lillian's distaste for the New Jersey estate was the focus of continual fights. Also, some retainers on the estate told Buck that Lillian was having an affair, so he concocted another trip for himself to Europe and set detectives and ATC executives to follow her while he was away. Evidence of adultery was easy to obtain, since Lillian flagrantly continued her decade-long dalliance with sixty-six-year-old Frank J. Huntoon, mineral water company president, racetrack devotee, and theater first-nighter. Part of what attracted Huntoon to Lillian was that she had been the mistress of another man and was now that man's wife: the excitement seems to have sprung from the illicit nature of the liaison. A week after Buck returned from London, he filed for divorce, naming Huntoon as corespondent.

Lillian countersued, accusing Duke of infidelity with a Somerville housekeeper and such "acts of cruelty" as making her ride across Europe in bad weather in an open carriage and not paying her bills. She also charged that he drank too much, which "inflamed his brutal spirit and increased the infliction of wrongs and indignities" upon her. The New York tabloids had a field day with the trial. Among the revelations: Huntoon had placed cryptic notices in newspapers begging Lillian not to wear low-cut gowns to public galas when they would have no chance for intimacy later in the evening.

R. J. Reynolds must have taken a certain satisfaction in Duke's discomfort, which he, along with many others, saw as the result of trying to keep up with the swells in New York. R. J. had made a conscious decision not to go to New York and joust in the arena of the titans of finance; he had remained true to his roots, while Duke had given up his. Like Duke, R. J. had married when he was middle-aged — but Duke's bride had not been chosen carefully. Katharine was a proper wife for an up-and-coming tycoon; Lillian was a disaster.

It took until mid-1906 for the New Jersey court, observing that Duke had already given Lillian a quarter million in property and jewelry, to award Duke an unconditional divorce with no alimony payments. By that time, R. J. Reynolds had taken many steps to consolidate his control and ready himself for a big push.

In that interim period, for example, R. J. had additional stock in the company issued and helped several employees to buy some, even if they lacked the cash to do so, by accepting promissory notes from them that were to be paid out of future stock dividends. By issuing stock and promoting from within, R. J. built a close and fiercely loyal cadre of managers who helped him expand his business empire.

The business family was together night and day. Fifth Street was becoming an enclave of wealthy RJR executives. R. J. and Katharine, returned from their honeymoon, took up residence in the family mansion alone. Will and Kate had moved to their own house, a few doors away. Brother Walter, nephew R. S. and his bride, and nephew-in-law Ed Lasater and his wife also lived within shouting distance of R. J.

Another Fifth Street neighbor was Bowman Gray, who had begun with RJR in 1885 at a salary of $5.75 a week and was now the firm's top salesman. Gray was known as the most frugal employee, a man who used pencil stubs until they were too short to handle. On Sunday afternoons, R. J. would amble over to Gray's home, where they would sit on the porch, expectorate their chews into conveniently located bushes, and talk about tobacco. One day, when Gray was off on a selling trip to Baltimore, R. J. bought some of the new stock for him. When the cheapskate returned home, he said he didn't want to spend the money for the stock, and the two men had an argument — Gray had the reputation of being the only employee tough enough to stand up to the boss. It took all of R. J.'s persuasive powers to get Gray to grudgingly accept the deal that within ten years (and with *no* out-of-pocket expense) would make him a millionaire.

R. J.'s plan was a flanking attack on the ATC, by way of its smoking-tobacco business. R. J.'s deal with Duke called for RJR to stay out of the smoking-tobacco field; in return, Duke was supposed to steer clear of flat plug. But since the start of life under the trust R. J. had regularly received reports from wholesalers that Duke-controlled firms were trying to muscle in on RJR territory, offering some of their plug brands at below the cost of making them. Why Duke would encourage war between two of his own subsidiaries remains a mystery, but he had often used such tactics to build his fiefdom and continued to employ them when they were clearly counterproductive. In this instance, all they served to do was get R. J. Reynolds angry.

RJR had been in the smoking-tobacco business in a modest way for nearly a dozen years, using scrap tobacco left over from the cutting of plug — as Duke well knew. Buck had allowed this minor sideline to continue because it presented no threat to him.

Now, in 1906, R. J. came out with a smoking tobacco made mostly of bright leaf. Called Refined, it took a gold medal at an exposition but then met disaster as the product rotted in its bags and wholesalers returned it unsold. Shortly thereafter, the death of Refined was discussed around the dinner table by brothers R. J., Walter, and Will; R. J. talked about developing yet another bright-based brand. Walter erupted, angrily accusing R. J. of trying to push water uphill out of a misplaced loyalty to nearby farmers who raised bright tobacco. Burley was the way to go — and Walter had been saying so for several years. R. J. now agreed with Walter, and he sent Will to Louisville to buy, secretly, enough burley to start a new line. There was some thought of calling the new product Kaiser Wilhelm, but R. J. didn't want to name it after a living individual and decided instead on Prince Albert.

With package designs and such still hanging fire, R. J. and Katharine took a vacation in a touring car to Bretton Woods, New Hampshire, a watering place of the wealthy. Katharine had given birth to Richard Joshua Reynolds, Jr., in April of 1906 and was now pregnant with a second child. R. J. was overjoyed at the arrival of his son and looked forward to having more children. His honeymoon to Europe had finally convinced him to take a few real vacations from Winston — not only to Roaring Gap, which was full of Winstonians, but to places far from home where he could enjoy the company of his wife and family without distractions.

Even at Bretton Woods, R. J. fretted over the packaging of Prince Albert: the picture of the prince in his characteristic coat had to be just right. RJR was readying an enormously expensive advertising campaign to launch the new brand and couldn't afford any mistakes. In order to claim in the ads that the flavor of Prince Albert had been developed in a German university, R. J. had even bought a useless patent from a Salem resident who'd briefly studied abroad.

The reason for the intense pressure to meet a deadline soon became clear — loads of Prince Albert were sent to wholesalers in mid-1907, just days after the federal government filed a major antitrust suit against Buck Duke, other officers, and the entire structure of the American Tobacco Company trust.

Between 1904 and 1907 the war on the trusts had lost a little steam. Protrust congressmen espoused the idea that good trusts practiced economies of size and scale and only a few bad ones were monopolistic. Even good trusts, Theodore Roosevelt fumed, often intimidated smaller producers and thus worked against the interests of consumers. Finally TR managed to shepherd through Congress a new interstate commerce law that made the prosecution of trusts easier. He had long wanted to go after Duke, and in this pursuit he was joined by his new attorney general, Charles Joseph Bonaparte (grand-nephew of the French emperor).

Bonaparte in turn entrusted the pursuit of Duke to his chief assistant, James C. McReynolds, who quickly became convinced that Duke and his cohorts were "rich, powerful, conspicuous and guilty." He started the case against Duke right away — but it went forward slowly.

While it progressed, R. J. moved against the ATC with Prince Albert. His first big target was the Bull. The Durham company, once the largest in the tobacco field, had long since been eclipsed by the rise of the ATC; Duke had even had the satisfaction of buying it and making it a subsidiary. It still sold well, until Prince Albert came onto the scene. Within a few years, the *Southern Tobacco Journal* was calling Prince Albert a twentieth-century wonder that was shipping ten million pounds a year and had severely cut into the Bull's market.

The ATC fought back by trying to corner the market on burley tobacco so there would be no raw material for Prince Albert. But RJR men found middlemen who hated the trust enough to accumulate leaf secretly for Reynolds. R. J. also took the initiative by heavily advertising Prince Albert. He had the N. W. Ayer Company of Philadelphia concoct displays in such leading magazines as the *Saturday Evening Post*, *Colliers*, and the *Literary Digest*. The ads, as well as a large, blinking electric sign above New York's Union Square, touted "Prince Albert — The Nation's Joy Smoke." The symbol for the tobacco, aside from the prince on the package, was a well-contented (and rounded) older man, shown blissfully puffing away.

Shortly after the launching of Prince Albert, the *Baltimore American* interviewed R. J. and noted that "success has not given him an undue idea of his own personality, and he has the bearing of the old-fashioned kindly-disposed Southerner." He was shipping thirty million pounds of tobacco products per year, made by four thousand hands and paced by the rapid growth of smoking tobacco. R. J. remarked that now "we are more a nation of smokers than chewers." However, he still liked to chew, and insisted that "tobacco chewing . . . is far better from the standpoint of health than smoking. I know plenty of men in the[ir] seventies and eighties who have been chewers from early boyhood. Another thing is that its use in this way is unquestionably a preservative of the teeth."

Unfortunately for the devoted chewer, spitting had recently been discovered to be decidedly unhealthy. It spread the germs of tuberculosis, one of the most feared diseases of the age; all over the United States, people were being warned not to spit in public places. One bar sign read, "Gentlemen WILL not, others MUST not spit on the floor." In such a climate, R. J. was wise to start pushing another kind of tobacco.

Duke might still have crushed R. J.'s efforts, but he wasn't applying his full attention to business. He had met an extraordinarily beautiful woman, Mrs. Nannaline Holt Inman, the widow of an Atlanta businessman. They were married in July of 1907 (the time of the introduction of Prince Albert) and moved temporarily into Ben Duke's rented mansion on upper Fifth Avenue. The new Mrs. Duke loved New York, so they commissioned an ornate white marble mansion from an architect who had built palaces for major ATC stockholders. Though Buck dwelt with the mighty, he continued to have private railroad cars bring to his New York residence from Durham provisions of cornmeal, chicken, hams, and turnips.

In early 1908 R. J. took heart as the government won an opening-round suit against an ATC subsidiary for monopolizing the sale of licorice paste, an essential element in making plug. James McReynolds then brought to trial in New York City a larger suit against sixty-five corporations and twenty-nine individual partners of the ATC. In his years of consolidation, Buck had bought up all his important suppliers — not only the makers of licorice paste, but also the manufacturers of boxes, foil, and canvas bags to hold loose tobacco. He'd maintained a countrywide system of industrial espionage that kept the ATC abreast of all the marketing ideas of rival companies; agents sent their clandestine reports to private post office boxes and, when they weren't spying, provoked strikes. Competitors' key personnel had been lured into joining ATC-controlled "bushwhackers," supposedly independent companies that made tobacco items at a loss in order to undercut real independents. Then, too, the directors (Duke, Payne, and a few others) had mercilessly milked the paper companies so that a few people had made millions while small stockholders got almost nothing.

All of these shenanigans began to come out in the New York courtroom. Everyone in the country could read Buck's bald declaration on the witness stand that "I never bought any business with the idea of eliminating competition; it was always [with] the idea of an investment." That must have produced a few guffaws at RJR, Inc. Buck had sought to avoid detection by not writing things down, but a mountain of evidence based on his associates' letter books and testimony clearly revealed his monopolistic practices. On December 15, 1908, the federal court found the ATC guilty of violating the antitrust law and prohibited it from engaging in interstate trade "until conditions existing before the illegal contract and combinations were entered into are restored." The ATC appealed to have the decision overturned.

By this time, Teddy Roosevelt was a lame duck, a month away from turning the presidency over to William Howard Taft — a fat, amiable, probusiness man who wanted the appeal delayed. McReynolds wrote a scathing letter saying that delay would, in effect, license the ATC to engage in illegal activities that were netting the trust a million dollars a month in profits. Bonaparte forwarded the letter to Taft and made it plain that if the suit weren't pursued, the consequences would be on the new president's head. Taft reversed his position, and the appeal to the Supreme Court was filed.

Approaching sixty, R. J. was a vigorous, robust man who spent a fair amount of time with his children in the Fifth Street home. R. J. was discovering fatherhood and liking it. However, his relationship with the children seemed to have been more typical of what would be expected of a grandfather than of a father. He played with the children a bit in the evenings, took them out for rides along the few paved roads in the chauffeured horseless carriage (one of the first touring automobiles in the state), and for a month each summer took the entire family by train to Atlantic City and other family-oriented resorts. On stormy nights he'd gather all three children to his room and tell them stories to banish their fears — as his mother had done with him and his siblings more than a half century earlier.

His main model as a parent, though, was his father. Hardin had been fifty years old in 1860, when R. J. had been ten — a middle-aged man who was, in Abram's phrase, a "fine disciplinarian" whose guidance had been most in evidence as his sons approached manhood, not when they were in nappies. R. J. looked forward to raising his son to be a good man. As with most fathers of the era, when his children were young he left day-to-day interaction with them to his wife. The Reynoldses were all rather formal with one another: around little Dick, Mary, and Nancy, Katharine referred to her husband as Mr. Reynolds and he referred to her as Katharine.

Although the family had plenty of money, Katharine continued to sew some of her own clothes and to hand-paint china for wedding gifts to friends. Katharine had given up her own job to become Mrs. R. J. Reynolds. Earlier in life she had been interested in the welfare of the masses and had her notions reinforced at State Normal School; now she translated those into concern for the working and living conditions of RJR workers. R. J. had always been in the forefront of those few white men in Winston who contributed to black causes, and most of his workers were black. Katharine urged him to expand his benevolence, to promote both more sanitary housing for black hands and a day nursery at the factory for the children of black female workers, and to subsidize a hospital serving the black community.

As the family and the business grew, both Katharine and R. J. came to feel that — at last — the maker of millions should enjoy his wealth. Like many other titans of this period, R. J. had put off marriage, and had even put off reaping the benefits of his elevated economic station in life, until well into middle age. Andrew Carnegie had done the same. Unlike Buck Duke, R. J. Reynolds had not rewarded himself with a lavish life-style. Now, the Reynoldses reasoned, North Carolina's principal employer, the effective laird of Winston and Salem, ought to have a grand estate, a beautiful country home that would celebrate and confirm his new stature. The fulfillment of that dream became Katharine's special project, one to which she wholeheartedly devoted her considerable energies, intelligence, and artistic gifts.

Katharine decided to assemble a great tract of land on the outskirts of Winston and to erect there more than a residence — an entire feudal village. Let Duke and his bride reproduce in Manhattan a pretentious Italian-French palace! She would give rein to her imagination in a more appropriate style, and in a more natural and capacious setting. In addition to a large "bungalow," the estate would feature a dairy farm, a school for the area's children, a church, and grounds landscaped for pageantry, hunting, and family games. This self-sustaining unit, this inspiration and model for the lower classes, would be called Reynolda.

Katharine and R. J. began to buy up tracts alongside Yadkinville Road, beyond the last building in town and three miles from its center. The countryside was rugged and desolate but of rare beauty. Price was no object; if a parcel was unreasonably dear, they bought it anyway, until they had assembled one thousand contiguous acres of all sorts of terrain. Katharine read all the magazines of design, architecture, and style, and hired first the noted landscape architect Louis L. Miller. She gave him ideas, and he laid out a rough placement of the major buildings as well as the gardens, which featured cryptomeria, a pine from Japan, together with flowering cherry trees, shrubs, and bulbs from a dozen other countries. When Miller's plans didn't entirely satisfy Katharine, she found in the pages of the magazine *Arts and Decoration* his replacement, the only man in America who actually taught landscape architecture, Thomas W. Sears of Philadelphia. Sears incorporated Miller's designs and added more ideas. He put in an artificial lake edged by two and a half miles of bridle paths. He planted sixty thousand daffodils in the surrounding woods. He sited the formal gardens and hothouse within walking distance of the main house yet separate, so the public might come in and enjoy them without disturbing the serenity of the Reynoldses. He concealed underground the water, electricity, and heating systems, carefully working around the eighteen springs on the property.

To design the several-story bungalow, Sears recommended an architect whose specialty was the Dutch Colonial style, Charles Barton Keen. Katharine wanted a simple yet grand residence, and Keen responded with a burst of inspiration, a sixty-room house that managed not to look overbearing yet had both the magnificence of a castle and the coziness of a family country home. There was no exterior marble but plenty of wood, stucco, and three different shades of green tiles. For detail work they went all over the world to get the best: ironwork by Samuel Yellin, the greatest craftsman of his day; ceramic decorative tiles by Henry Mercer; roofing tiles by Ludowici-Caladon, in Italy. The result was a small cottage writ large, with wonderful details and with outbuildings that echoed the glory of the master's residence.

During the springs and summers, while the main house and grounds were being prepared, the family often camped out at the site in tents. A servant blew reveille, mess, and taps on a bugle to demarcate the sections of the day. In between, the children picked dogwood blossoms and traipsed through the woods. Once they held a costume party; the children copied the grown-ups as they tried the new dances — the bunny hug, the grizzly bear — to the music of a wind-up gramophone. As a surprise, R. J. dressed up as Robert E. Lee and rode a horse into the uncompleted living room.

From 1908 to mid-1911 the ATC case's appeal wound its way slowly through the Supreme Court's review process. In May 1911, the Court handed down a momentous and far-reaching finding: the tobacco trust, "as well as each and all of the elements composing it, whether corporate or individual," was decreed to be "in restraint of trade and . . . a monopolization within the first and second sections of the Anti-trust Act." The Court directed a lower court to plan for the dissolution of the trust and to re-create out of its elements "a new condition which shall be honestly in harmony with and not repugnant to the law." Roosevelt, Bonaparte, and Mc-Reynolds hailed the Supreme Court's decision as the most significant victory over monopoly of their entire public service careers.

It took six months for Buck Duke and his lawyers to work out a plan of dissolution with the new attorney general, whose name was George Wickersham. On November 16, 1911, the trust was divided. There were three big slices — a whittled-down ATC, a rejuvenated Liggett & Myers, and a similarly new Lorillard Company. The much smaller RJR Tobacco Company was spun off from the trust as a separate unit.

In North Carolina, Josephus Daniels fulminated in the pages of his newspaper against the decree, which did no better than to leave former ATC directors in control of the new firms because they owned the majority of the stock. He called the scheme a "Wickersham" and continued to rail against "Buck-aneering." But for R. J. Reynolds, the decree meant freedom. The day of emancipation had arrived.

Chapter Six

King of Tobacco

JUST A FEW DAYS before the final dissolution decree, in November of 1911, Katharine and R. J. Reynolds sent out cards announcing the birth of their fourth (and what would be their last) child, Zachary Smith Reynolds. "Hearty congratulations and best wishes to Mrs. Reynolds and the boy," Buck Duke wrote back. Despite their battles, R. J. and Buck were still cordial. Buck's wife was also pregnant and would shortly give birth to Duke's only child, Doris.

It was a time when many aspects of American daily life were changing. The introduction of the safety razor was starting a trend toward a beardless generation. Some people were wearing wrist-watches, though many thought men should not so do, since such ornaments were associated with the gentler sex. On the roads, automobiles vied with ox carts and mule-drawn trucks. A national magazine characterized the temper of the times: "This is a get-things-done-quick age. It is a ready-to-put-on-and-wear-home age, a just-add-hot-water-and-serve age, a new-speed-record-every-day age, a take-it-or-leave-it-I'm-very-busy age." When a woman from a foreign legation asked President Taft at the White House if she could smoke, there was consternation, but an aide found a safety match and lit her cigarette.

Cigarettes: R. J. Reynolds decided he must switch his major effort to this new area. The RJR Company was still quite a bit smaller than the big three — for example, the reorganized ATC had a capital stock of $92 million, while RJR's was $10 million. And, despite the success of Prince Albert, RJR sold less than 12 percent of the smoking tobacco in the country and only a quarter of the chewing tobacco. To pull level with his rivals, R. J. would have to go after the tobacco product that now outsold all others.

But first, he had to regain control of his company. Two thirds of the RJR stock was still in the hands of Buck Duke and his associates: Oliver Payne, Pierre S. Du Pont, Harry Widener, Nelson Aldrich, Gertrude Whitney, and corporate raider Thomas F. Ryan. How could R. J. get control back from Duke?

A part of the dissolution decree allowed RJR to issue new stock. If enough of the new issue could be gotten into the hands of R. J.'s allies, then control by what the Winstonians referred to as the New York crowd would be diluted. Unfortunately, stock could be issued only by rule of the board, which Duke controlled. R. J. devised an ingenious plan and went up to New York with brother Will to sell the idea to Duke personally. As a quid pro quo for permission to offer the new issue to RJR employees and friends, they'd first set aside hefty profits, more than 22 percent on investment, for previous stockholders. Duke liked the sound of that and gave his consent. In 1912 the company issued $2.5 million in new stock, which R. J. helped his employees and friends finance through loans — and R. J. was closer to full control of his company than he'd been since 1900.

For many years before 1911, R. J. had believed cigarettes were harmful to health; in particular, that the paper wrapper caused problems when it burned. Others in the company thought this was nonsense and cited the public's obvious appetite for cigarettes as reason enough to manufacture them. Then Walter, always the scholar, supervised tests made at laboratories in New York, Chicago, and Pittsburgh, all of which concluded that the paper was harmless. Only after receiving this evidence did R. J. decide to go ahead and manufacture cigarettes.

Since cigarettes were to be packed in a "cup" of tinfoil, R. J. supposedly sent nephew R. S. to Germany to learn the tinfoil business. This may or may not be true — there is no hard evidence — but since it is known that R. S. eventually achieved great success in the tinfoil field, this legend may only be a retroactive seed planting.

What is known definitively is that in 1912 R. S. did become restless at RJR. In ten years, R. J. had taught his surrogate son well and had consistently rewarded him: R. S. was now an officer of the company, on a par with his uncles Will and Walter. Still, when R. S. took a good look at R. J., he saw a man in his sixties, happy with his family, especially with his two blood sons — and realized that R. J. would want Dick and Smith in the family business as soon as they were of age. Furthermore, R. J. would want them to ascend to the leadership of RJR. If R. J.'s sons took the top spots, what would be left for R. S.? Or for R. S.'s own two little sons? He was now about as well trained as any young executive in the entire country. He had also endured the domination of the trust and was on speaking terms with Duke and other captains of industry. Now, before it became too late, R. S. made up his mind to leave the RJR Tobacco Company.

He went not only because he saw no future with RJR, but also because of what was happening to his father at that moment. The greatest single day in Abram's later life had come on Halloween night, 1907. For a quarter century, Abram had battled against liquor, particularly against the twenty-one grog shops in Bristol, which sold shots of Google's Pure Corn or local beer for a nickel. In pursuit of his dream of temperance, he had bankrolled newspapers and revival campaigns, even given up his allied business of tobacco manufacturing. To Abram, it was as clear as God's daylight that drink was the ruination of the country and that when Prohibition became the law of the land, America would be returned to the paths of righteousness. The battle had to be won territory by territory, and at seven on that evening, the last dozen functioning saloons in Bristol shuttered their doors. Finally, his hometown was dry. An elated Abram led a parade through the town streets. Two years later, the Tennessee state legislature passed statewide Prohibition and joined other states in a call to try once more for a constitutional amendment proscribing liquor.

Since then, though, things had turned a bit sour. One of Abram's sons, William, died in 1911 at the premature age of twenty-four. Moreover, Abram was restless — he hadn't really found a business to take the place of chewing tobacco. He had his million dollars (primarily from real estate), myriad charities, and a few investments, but he yearned for the thrill of business again. Just recently he had discovered something in one of the old properties he had acquired during his boomtown days: a mountain of silica, a material that could be processed to make commercial cleansers. Here was a morally unambiguous business for a God-loving man and his now well trained son! And, of course, there was a victory of sorts in taking the young man back from his old rival, R. J.

Although R. J. offered R. S. approximately $100,000 to stay with RJR — "a fabulous sum, for one so young," as R. S. later wrote — in the spring of 1912 he left the man who had been his surrogate father to go into business with his actual father, Abram.

In Bristol, there was a real feeling of the passing of command. Abram was not in charge of the new Reynolds Company, although he was an officer and although the firm employed two of his other sons (who had previously been selling automobiles). As with the Duke family, the star had finally come to the fore: the venture was basically R. S.'s show. Once the protégé came out from under the mantle of the titan, he did spectacularly well. It was a dream business, cheap and easy to operate; the silica was on the surface or just below, so mining was relatively simple. For about fifty cents per ton they could quarry the rock and move it to a crushing plant at the bottom of the mountain. There the "scrubbing crystals" were ground fine, coated in a bath of pure soap, and packed three different ways: Spotless Cleanser in sifter-top cans was for industrial use; Lustre Box was a window cleaner in a metal container; the housewives' preparation was called Bubbles. In no time at all, the business was thriving. The semiretired Abram had to conclude that, indeed, the Lord worked in mysterious ways.

Abram's major interest at this time was a tract of land in nearby Mitchell County, North Carolina, that he had started putting together in boom days and pursued thereafter, piece by piece, until he owned 22,000 acres outright and the mineral rights to an adjoining 38,000 acres. A contemporary observer went over the 60,000-acre tract and marveled:

A better idea of its extent is obtained when a measurement of its transverse diameter shows a distance of 12 miles, requiring a horseman 4 hours to ride across it, while a measurement of its length, from northeast to southwest, shows a distance of 25 miles, requiring 8 or 9 hours to ride through it on horseback . . . frontage on Toe River of 15 miles or more . . . 60 miles of available water power. . . . [It is] one of the greatest, best and most important magnetic iron ore districts in the world . . . schist and hornblende, gneiss and epidote . . . float and seed ore, indicating and marking the underlying large body of ore.

At $25 per acre, the tract had a potential value of $1.5 million. In a characteristic move, Abram vowed to give a quarter of any profit he made from the sale or lease of this acreage to a newly founded

Methodist missionary society that was bringing the word of God to the heathen in foreign lands.

If R. J. felt the loss of his nephew — a man who called him "my greatest friend in all the world" — he hardly had time to think about it. He was frantically busy getting ready to make cigarettes. He had a stroke of luck (or was it foresight?) when Bonsack's patent on one of the original automatons ran out and couldn't be renewed. Now there was nothing to stop R. J. from buying the appropriate machinery.

Six distinct types of cigarettes were then on the market. The fastest seller was Turkish-blended Fatima, made by L&M. R. J. decided to make something similar. He tried four names and packaging techniques: Reynos, Osmans, Red Kamels, and, in early 1913, a blend of Turkish tobacco with the burley leaf that had done so well in Prince Albert and the bright leaf that had long sustained his plug business, which he named Camels. The name showed R. J.'s marketing genius. Short and evocative, Camels smacked of the Near East and could be represented by that ultimate goal of all advertisers, a single image, a lone animal against a backdrop of pyramids, minarets, and other Orientalia.

In September of 1913, when the Barnum and Bailey Circus came to Winston — an annual excuse for closing the factory for a day — R. J. took his wife and four children to the show and had photographs made of Old Joe, the mean-tempered dromedary, as well as of a more docile camel. An employee scurried to a dictionary and reported that while technically a two-humper was a camel and a one-humper was a dromedary, you could also call a one-humper a camel. R. J. was delighted — one hump would be more distinctive and simpler than two, even though in the photograph that came out Old Joe had his eyes closed and his neck outstretched as if he were angry. The dromedary's yellowish color also fit in with the marketing scheme of the package.

"Don't look for Premiums or Coupons, as the cost of the Tobaccos Blended in CAMELS prohibits the use of them," said the package put together carefully by the very man who had used premiums so successfully to sell Schnapps. The slogan had only a smattering of truth in it: the real reason for eschewing coupons (which nearly every other manufacturer then offered) was that R. J. wanted to keep the cost down. Fatima, the Zubelda of Lorillard, and the Omar of the ATC all sold for 15 cents a pack, but R. J. had worked out ways to make a profit selling Camels at 10 cents a pack.

The first N. W. Ayer ad started a whole new trend in advertising: the "teaser." That one merely showed the camel, mentioned the name, but gave no indication of what the product might be. A week later it was "The Camels Are Coming," and a week after that, "Tomorrow there'll be more CAMELS in this town than in all Asia and Africa combined!" Not until the fourth ad was the product actually identified: "CAMEL Cigarettes Are Here!"

The campaign worked beautifully, but it was the blend (perfected by brother Walter) and the five-cent-lower price that made Camels a winner. As an ATC executive later testified, within months after Camels were introduced, "territory after territory swung over into the Camel column. Our brands could not stand up against it." During the first year on the market, there were 400 million Camels sold; the next year, 2 billion. Then, with two winners in Prince Albert and Camels, the RJR Company and its principal owner were racing off into the stratosphere, closing on the big three.

=

The year of the Camel, 1913, was also known in Winston and Salem as the year of the golden hyphen, the moment when the two cities combined to become Winston-Salem. For decades the towns had shared a post office, several newspapers, streetcar lines, and the like but had rejected affiliation; now the citizens embraced it. The new city of nearly twenty thousand people led the world in production of tobacco products per capita and was also the largest manufacturer of fine knit goods in the South as well as a center for making wagons and furniture.

Nineteen thirteen was also the year of the first federal income tax. Some rich people howled because it would take a hefty 2 percent levy from incomes of fifty thousand dollars a year. People with lesser incomes — which weren't to be taxed at all — joked that someday they, too, would be eligible to support the government. Former New Jersey governor Woodrow Wilson was inaugurated as president. R. J. contributed to Wilson's campaign, while Duke backed the sitting president, Taft, who had split the Republican vote with "Bull Moose" Teddy Roosevelt. R. J. liked Wilson because he was a progressive Democrat, a Southerner by birth and inclination, and because his cabinet included R. J.'s old friend

Josephus Daniels as secretary of the navy and James McReynolds as attorney general — the latter selected because he had fought so hard for the dissolution of the trusts.

R. J. was in a new phase now, one of increasing benevolence. The Duke family's millions had brought Trinity College to Durham, where it had become Duke University. R. J. couldn't compete with Buck on the scale of his donations, but everything he touched with his money had a personal connection. R. J. funded schools at the Brown Mountain crossroads where his mother had been born, at Rock Spring, in Winston, and at Reynolda.

He sold off or donated his other holdings so he could concentrate on Reynolda. For example, he closed down a farm and racetrack that he'd owned for many years, took the animals to Reynolda, and gave the land to City Memorial Hospital, which planned to use it to expand its facilities for black patients. The bungalow still wasn't completed, so R. J. used the Reynolda grounds for company picnics and outings to which both white and black employees were invited. It was reinforcement of the idea that the tobacco company was "family."

The Reynoldses continued to live at Fifth Street. The children were getting old enough to send letters and postcards to R. J. when he was away on business. On his return he brought presents, though not extravagant ones.

He told an interviewer, "A rich man's boy has only half a chance to make good, and I do not want my boys hampered by the money I have made. It is not fair to them." This was a fear common to rich men at the time and expressed more fully in the plot of Rudyard Kipling's *Captains Courageous*, published in 1897. For R. J. to let his emotions show in public, as they did in this statement, demonstrates how important the subject was to him. He was keenly aware of being an older father and of the dire consequences of having sons who might grow up rich yet without active paternal guidance.

R. J. had done very well in helping Abram's son R. S. along the path to industry, wealth, a normal and useful life. It is clear that he wanted to do the same for his own sons. Unfortunately, he would not survive to see them reach adulthood — and for them, the consequences of his absence would be central problems in their lives.

As time went on, Katharine became more and more involved in the building of the estate. With her ladies' walking club, she hiked the three miles to Reynolda; then the society ladies tramped over the hills, through streams, sometimes shinnied up a tree, in pursuit of healthful exercise. Her obsession with Reynolda was total; she was in control of the making of the estate. She wrote to architect Keen about the sixty-room bungalow, "I am anxious for it to be a beautiful as well as a comfortable house." She took complete charge of all the contractors, paying the bills — as well as all household accounts — and keeping an eye on the costs. She read blueprints almost as well as an engineer.

At Reynolda, hundreds of workmen toiled on the church, the school, the cottages for employees, the formal gardens and fountain, the stables, the dairy, the smokehouse, blacksmith shop, post office, artificial lake, the nine-hole golf course that wound through the trees, gardens for vegetables, pastures for livestock, enclosures for poultry. Keen and Sears added more refinements: tennis courts, an outdoor swimming pool next to the lake, whose water came from artesian wells. The three barns began to fill with the prize Percherons from the old farm, Tamworth porkers, Jersey cows. There were even two potato houses, one for Irish spuds and the other for sweets. Gardeners lived on the grounds and planted or moved about hundreds of elms, southern pines, Japanese cherries, and many other trees, and enough flower varieties to provide fresh blooms throughout most of the year.

While the Reynoldses were away on vacation one summer, one of the Reynolda contractors misread the plans and poured the foundations so that the back of the bungalow was at the front, and the front at the back. There was consternation for a moment, but then the mistake took on the air of a stroke of good fortune. Turning the building around enhanced its basic modesty. Actually, it was just fine to take what was to have been the imposing front entrance, with columns and decorative urns, and have that be what people saw when they ascended the slope from Lake Katharine. And it was more fitting to have as a front entrance a rather ordinary-looking porte cochere at the end of a long driveway. The whole effect was to accentuate the bungalow's country feeling, produced by its white walls and green gabled roof, partially covered by clinging ivy and smilax.

The first big building to be completed at Reynolda was the church. For R. J. to have on his home grounds a Presbyterian church rather than a branch of the Methodist church of his upbringing suggests that he left the choice to his wife. During most of his life religion was not something he felt deeply; he perhaps associated it with the stifling aspects of being brought up at Rock Spring or, later, with the domain of Abram. As R. J. ascended the scale to "pillar of the community," however, he attended church more regularly, possibly believing that such behavior was expected of him. As far as choosing between Presbyterianism and Methodism, they were similar Protestant churches, but Presbyterianism in that era seemed to be less exacting than the brand of North Carolina Methodism that had tamed the frontiers and that still carried with it traces of hellfire and brimstone.

In contrast to R. J., Katharine was quite devout. She not only went regularly to the Presbyterian church in downtown Winston but also carried on an extensive correspondence with minister Neal L. Anderson and worked hard to convert R. J. to Presbyterianism. The "mission" at Reynolda was, in fact, originally conceived by a Sunday school class of which Katharine was a member and was designed to serve the souls of country folk who were unable to make the long trek every Sunday to the First Presbyterian of Winston. Thus the dedication of the Reynolda church in 1914 was a moment of triumph for Katharine: she watched proudly as R. J., converted at last, walked down the aisle of "her" beautiful little church together with his eight-year-old son Dick, and they all became members of the congregation.

In midsummer of 1914, the Great War began in a conflagration that pitted most of the countries of Europe against one another. Although the United States initially was not one of the belligerents, the war managed to touch the country in several ways. For R. J. Reynolds, it meant that moving into his long-awaited estate would be delayed for some time because of a shortage of building materials. For the RJR Company, it meant difficulties in obtaining many supplies, among them part of the packaging for Prince Albert; on the other hand, the war also brought a large increase in the sale of cigarettes.

For many people, the onset of the Great War was occasion for feelings about the close of an era; sensing the approaching ends of their careers and lives, both R. J. and Abram gave long personal interviews to newspapers. Somewhat disingenuously, R. J. claimed to have ascended to his present prominence in spite of starting out as a lowly manual laborer in his father's business. He even said that he'd been promoted to superintendent of manufacturing there at age eighteen. Usually he told stories like this as homilies, to stress the importance of hard work or rising above circumstances.

This time, Abram took umbrage at his brother's boasting and told a reporter that R. J.'s interview "has done himself and the family an injustice by creating in the minds of the public the idea that he has risen from an ordinary factory hireling to president of the R. J. Reynolds Tobacco Company." Abram pointed out that Hardin was relatively well-to-do, that most of the manual labor in Hardin's factory had been done by slaves, and that he, rather than R. J., had been superintendent of manufacturing. He was quite proud of having set the pattern that R. J. and, later, the other sons all followed.

This imbroglio spurred Abram to pen his *Recollections* in a ledger book. In them, he was the hero through and through. There was no mention of business losses or setbacks, the deaths of young sons, or even the success of R. S.; R. J. was a minor character, and so was Abram's wife, Senah. Abram was writing to set the record straight, but perhaps he was a bit envious of the enormous recent success of R. J., which had far outstripped his own. Abram was a wealthy man, whereas his brother was a multimillionaire.

If all the Camels made in a year were laid end to end, they would circle the globe. The company was adding two and sometimes three new buildings to its Winston facilities yearly. Because of RJR's freight volume, Winston-Salem had surpassed Atlanta as the largest railroad shipper in the South. RJR was in court, fighting collusive railroad rates and lobbying the federal government to have Winston named an official port of entry for the country so that sugar, licorice, and other supplies could be received directly at RJR warehouses, thus saving additional transportation charges.

R. J.'s influence was so great that in a local political campaign it was alleged that R. J. and Will had gone to Washington and successfully lobbied against the locating of a rival firm in Winston. The brothers vigorously denied this rumor, but R. J. allowed that he was backing James Gray, brother of RJR's Bowman Gray, because Gray was on the right side of the central issue in the same campaign, the social conditions in Winston-Salem.

R. J. ran what he thought were modern, safe, sanitary factories that paid realistic wages. Employees on the manufacturing floors made several dollars a day. Henry Ford was at that time astounding the economic powers-that-be of the United States by offering five dollars a day to his workers while most companies, especially in the South — and especially those with black hands — paid less. RJR had successfully resisted trade unionism but no longer had an ample supply of labor. One of the reasons for that was the less than comfortable social conditions in Winston-Salem.

R. J.'s social conscience was being prodded by the necessity of finding and keeping good workers, and by gentler persuasion from Katharine. He and Katharine joined a local reformer, Lenora Sills, in supporting the extension of the city's water supply and sewage system to houses that were still using open wells and privies. They pointed out to the city government that Winston-Salem had the South's highest death rate from communicable diseases; better sewage facilities and unpolluted drinking water should improve matters.

Even within RJR, conditions were far from ideal. Employees were eating quick, paper-bagged lunches while sitting on piles of lumber or on street curbs, and foremen berated hands who spent too much time in the toilets, even though the sanitary conditions in there were hardly conducive to goldbricking. Now the company installed a free ice-water dispenser, and opened a new rest room and lunchroom for white employees. This cafeteria was one of the first in a U.S. factory; for five cents, an employee could enjoy soup, crackers, corn pone, beans, and a pickle. A lunchroom for blacks soon followed. Some management diehards were aghast that the lunchrooms were operated at cost, which they thought capitalistically unsound. The same people fulminated when Katharine persuaded R. J. to cut the six-day workweek back to five and a half days, and they fought against incoming child-labor laws that would change the working conditions of children from twelve to sixteen — who were generally paid less — in the factories.

Katharine encouraged RJR employees to become literate through evening classes. She had the company start and help fund a day nursery for children of black female workers, a project overseen by Mrs. Sills. A similar nursery for white children was planned.

Because the company needed more employees and because Winston's housing was inadequate, R. J. announced that he would pay part of the cost of erecting fifty houses for blacks in East Winston and then bought a tract of land farther out and put up a hundred more houses for whites. Employees who already had their own homes but were paying exorbitant mortgage rates were offered low-interest loans, which they could turn into ready cash or use to refinance the properties. As production in the factories continued to increase, Mrs. Sills, Katharine, and Kate Bitting Reynolds, Will's wife, backed a drive to make a YMCA-style dormitory available to the hundreds of rural young women flocking into town to work for RJR. These young women were part of a national trend toward urbanization that left smaller towns and smaller farms bereft, a trend soon to be memorialized in the popular song that asked, "How're ya gonna keep 'em down on the farm / After they've seen Paree?"

R. J. contributed ten thousand dollars personally to the reelection campaign of Woodrow Wilson, who was returned to office by a narrow margin in late 1916 on a platform that stressed the theme "He kept us out of war."

Despite efforts by Wilson, the United States was gradually slipping toward full involvement in the Great War. Earlier, the British had done the provoking, but by late 1916, German attacks on American ships were on the increase. R. J. was delighted in retrospect that he hadn't named his smoking tobacco for Kaiser Wilhelm. Neutrality was fading.

In early March 1917, R. J. told his family and management colleagues that he wasn't feeling well, and he did something quite unusual for him — ignored some pressing business to attend to himself. He went to a series of doctors in Winston, but they either couldn't or wouldn't adequately diagnose his internal ailment. Most likely they didn't want to tell him what they suspected. Uncomplaining, R. J. took the train up to Baltimore, where doctors with greater expertise — and fewer ties to Winston-Salem — told him the truth. He had cancer of the pancreas. Nonsurgical treatment was begun.

=

After discovering he had cancer, a lesser man might well have stayed at home and left the burden of work to others. R. J. Reynolds did just the opposite. He plunged into the continued aggrandizement of the business: a last great effort could reap a grander harvest for his widow and four small children. Also, after forty-five years in harness, he did not know how *not* to keep pressing on. He seems to have understood implicitly, if he did not know directly, that this was an illness the doctors could only ameliorate, not cure.

A few weeks after R. J.'s cancer was diagnosed, in April of 1917, Germany resumed unrestricted submarine warfare and sunk several U.S. ships. Wilson asked Congress to declare war on Germany and Austria, and the country began to throw its might into a fight to make the world "safe for democracy." In the draft of men to go into the armed services, some RJR people were called up. R. J. solemnly touched his Joshua Coin to their gold coins, tokens, teeth fillings. All those who had been similarly touched by the totem in the Civil War and the Spanish-American War had survived; R. J. hoped the coin's magic would still be potent.

The treatments took him back and forth to Baltimore. On a trip north, R. J. stopped in Washington, D. C. The capital had been a drowsy, slow-moving city for nearly a hundred years; now it was being roused out of lethargy to gear up for an international war. R. J. went directly to the office of Secretary of the Navy Josephus Daniels, just across from the White House.

"Are you an honest man here in Washington as you were in North Carolina?" R. J. boomed at his old friend. He had a little problem he wanted to discuss. The army had purchased great quantities of cigarettes, both Camels and competing brands, at a price that the navy considered too high. The navy was offering 75 percent of the price the army had paid, in cash, the balance to be subject to negotiation between the manufacturers and the government. R. J. didn't like that deal. It wasn't the profits that bothered him but the principle. The navy's stance implied that the manufacturers had overcharged the army, which R. J. held not to be the case. Daniels wouldn't budge from the navy's official position. When the issue was resolved contrary to his liking, R. J. continued to sell Camels to the army at full price and, in essence, sold them to the navy at cost. It was billed as a grand gesture — and anyway, the navy's requirements were much smaller than the army's.

Demand for Prince Albert and for Camels skyrocketed all through the war, and RJR was hard-pressed to keep up with it. The metal used for smoking-tobacco tins was requisitioned by the government to make guns and bullets. Toluene, the most important ingredient of saccharin, was similarly requisitioned because it was needed to make trinitrotoluene, which was just becoming known to the wartime public as the fearsome TNT. Substitutes for these commodities were found, but there was no good replacement for the special cigarette paper, made only in France, to wrap Camels. So, in the summer of 1917, the board of directors sent Walter Reynolds to France, carrying gold and notes in hidden money belts. He was to get cigarette paper at any cost, even if that meant buying the factory outright.

The time had now come, R. J. told his fellow board members,

for RJR to act like a giant. It made no sense to run a company that was generating $10 million in profit each year on $12.5 million capitalization. The directors authorized raising the capital to $20 million, but even that wasn't enough. A company lawyer found another solution: RJR would offer a new class of stock, a B stock; those who bought it would have no voting rights but would get a whale of a dividend, especially if they traded in their A stock for it. The main sales target was the block of A stock still in the hands of the New York crowd, but R. J. also wanted to sell B stock directly to lower-rank employees. This idea was too radical for brother Will, who, during R. J's increasingly frequent periods of illness and absence from the office, had assumed the day-to-day management of the company. The proposal was tabled for a while.

That summer, on the grounds of Reynolda — where the bungalow was finally nearing completion — R. J. took his elder son, Dick, out hunting. It was something that men did together. They golfed a bit, too. Dick was eleven, and the time was coming for R. J. to exert his influence, to bend the sapling so it would grow into a proper tree. Little Smith wasn't even old enough to tie his shoes properly, but Dick was approaching puberty. Yet R. J. must have known that the boy would come of age in an environment wholly different from that which he had faced in the 1860s. From whom would he learn — as R. J. had learned — that life was a competitive game and that the struggle to make something was as much a prize as the money it brought? Dick would be enormously wealthy someday. Not immediately, of course, for R. J. had written a will that would allow for the slow escalation of his children's access to their money from childhood through age twenty-eight and had deliberately put in a provision that would encourage them to go into their own enterprises.

It must have pleased R. J., then, that in the summer of 1917 young Dick started his first business — a weekly newspaper, published with his friend Bill Sharpe. A downtown neighbor, equally young Bosley Crowther, was a junior associate. (Many years later, Crowther became drama critic for the *New York Times*.)

"The Three Cent Pup, a weekly illustrated paper," was a learning tool that displayed the boys' upbringing. It featured local news items — Uncle Will Reynolds had a minor automobile accident; R. J. and family were back from a month at a hotel in Atlantic City; Bill Sharpe was now over the mumps; unknown assailants on Halloween had taken certain Ford cars for joyrides. There was a weekly section, properly belligerent, called "Nipping the Kaisers Heels," which also reminded readers to observe food czar Herbert Hoover's meatless, wheatless, and butterless days. There were gratuitously vulgar jokes in Negro dialect. More lofty philosophy was expressed in essays on "That tyrant — school" and homilies such as "A truly great man always wins and holds the love and esteem of the lowly. Show me a man who's friends are only among the great and I'll show you one wholly unworthy of confidence."

If that had been put in as a paean to R. J. Reynolds, it was certainly apt, for in his last years "the founder" continued to be held in great esteem by his work force, even as he caught up with the very wealthiest people in the country. RJR was about even with the third-largest tobacco company and was continuing to surge upward.

A week before Christmas, 1917, R. J., Katharine, the four children, and a passel of retainers at last moved into the sixty-room bungalow on the thousand-acre estate. Recently returned from a stay in a Baltimore hospital, R. J. told friends and associates that he felt much improved. The family went to Reynolda in order to settle in, but also because during the terrible "Spanish Lady" influenza epidemic they felt the country would be more healthful than the city.

The children and parents picked out bedrooms along the second-floor corridors, which extended like wings from the square body of the house. Katharine and R. J.'s bedroom faced the spectacular rear, with its gardens, fountain, and gentle slope down to the lake. On that same level there was a central balcony running the length and breadth of the living room and overlooking the top of a great crystal chandelier and the enormous space below. The balcony was rimmed with intricate metalwork; on the walls surrounding it, Belgian tapestries hung. Concealed in the walls behind these flowered, medieval hangings were the speakers of the huge aeolian organ whose other working parts took up portions on each of three floors.

Descending one of the twin staircases at the rear of the balcony, one entered the only architecturally exciting space of the mansion, the two-story-high rectangular living room. It was breathtaking, a grand open expanse like the hall of some English baron; almost as wide as the entire building, the room flowed toward the rear, where a curve in the wall matched the gentle arc of the columned portico outside. The living room was dominated by an enormous white marble fireplace in which were set love seats and inglenooks. A single pair of couches or chairs would have been lost in this great room, so there were several sets, giving a variety of small areas for conversations or activities. In a far corner, hardly noticeable, was the console of the built-in organ, which could be played manually, by pushing keys and pedals, or automatically, by rolls. There were also modest-sized oil paintings of R. J. and Katharine, which had been executed by Eugene Pirou in 1905, when they had first been married. Adjoining the living room were dining rooms, libraries, and studies. Kitchens and servants' quarters were hidden on the far edges of the downstairs portions of the wings or on the third floor.

It was in the grand living room that the Reynoldses celebrated Christmas, 1917. The winter was cold, people were somewhat afraid of going out lest they catch the flu, and the holiday was not entirely a happy time. At Reynolda the children had more space and amenities than they had ever enjoyed at Fifth Street, things like perfect miniature dollhouses that contained replicas in sterling silver and china of the family's own possessions, properly rustic log cabins for the boys, horses used to junior riders. But Nancy, just nine, didn't like living on a big estate, isolated behind walls and iron gates, miles from her old home. She missed having playmates for after-dinner hide-and-seek. And now that Dick and Bill Sharpe weren't spending as much time together, the publication of *The Three Cent Pup* languished. The children knew that on Fourth Street, this time of year, there were coasting parties; Reynolda had plenty of hills and sleds, but not the crowd of kids to enjoy them with. Reynolda also had Prince and Albert, two big white Percherons like the ones that drew the fire wagon, but it wasn't the same as going out on Friday night and watching the fire company with its horses practice its rapid drill. On Fifth Street, the harbinger of summer was the old man who trundled his cart of ice around the cobbled lanes and yelled "Five cents a cake." Next summer at Reynolda, what would take the place of that?

There were signs that R. J. knew this might be his last Christmas. Although he wouldn't show that he was hurting, at times he'd tell people quietly that the pain was intense.

Shortly after the first of the year, Walter was sent word to return home from France because R. J.'s health had worsened. That winter and spring, R. J. drove into Winston in a chauffeured Pierce Arrow. He didn't go into the office every day; he was letting go. Nevertheless, he was pleased that, after Will saw the light, B stock was being issued in an amount that would double the company's capitalization, to forty million dollars, enough for an assault that would overtake the big three.

Wartime restrictions on tobacco had been mild, since the armed services were buying large quantities of tobacco products. By now the company's yearly output of Camels, more than reaching around the world, would stretch to the moon and back. In 1917 R. J. personally had made so much money that he'd paid the highest personal income tax in the state, double that of any other man.

When asked by a subordinate how the company would ever get along without him, R. J. said he had "written the book" — set the pattern — that others could easily now follow. When young John Whitaker spent too many hours and too much foolscap trying to figure out how to double the capacity of a licorice-paste can and then went to the boss with his problem, R. J. gave him his own countinghouse edition of *Bryant and Stratton's Commercial Arithmetic*, which had formulas to solve such problems. For years R. J. had told friends that he wanted to write his own text on mathematics; now, the implication was clear, he wouldn't have time to do it and so could afford to give away casually a book he'd guarded for forty-five years.

In the early months of 1918 R. J. shuttled back and forth to a hospital in Philadelphia where doctors attempted to halt the inexorable progress of his cancer. He was increasingly bedridden and in pain. Doctors marveled at his stamina, his refusal to stop being concerned with the world around him. Now, in the midst of a terrible war, there were more charities to think of — the American Fund for the French Wounded, the YMCA, the hospital for blacks, the schools whose names would honor R. J.'s mother and father. In early June, he went back to the Philadelphia hospital, and the doctors performed an operation.

Afterward, believing the end was nigh, R. J. asked the company's lawyer and two RJR associates to come to Philadelphia for some adjustments to his will. Katharine and young Dick hurried there, too.

From his hospital bed R. J. dictated an important codicil to his will. The founder wanted to make certain that his executors would continue to honor the loans he'd made to RJR employees that had enabled them to buy company stock. The price of the shares was down slightly on the open market, but he didn't want his successors to panic and attempt to recoup their own losses by calling in those loans. He predicted that the stock would soon regain its past level and, in the future, would be worth much more than it was at that moment.

Even as he lay dying, R. J. looked toward the future. It was the hallmark of a man who had always seemed to have known where he was going and had gotten there. Many of the robber barons who made fortunes in that era had also been business visionaries, but few had made as much money as R. J. without ruining many smaller businessmen. R. J.'s purchases had always been managed with dignity. Also, in contrast to Edward Harriman, Rockefeller, and Morgan, while R. J. had competed fiercely with every rival company, he'd done so in ways that were legal and ethical. His major fault in business was that he had been as exploitative as the next titan when it came to paying very modest wages to his manufacturing employees; however, unlike most of them, he had been generous to those employees he thought of as equals, principally his management team. Nearly alone among the giants, R. J. consistently took the steps that would make his relatives, friends, and senior employees millionaires. And, wherever possible, he spent his money and made his contributions to charity close to home, thereby enhancing the prosperity of Winston-Salem and North Carolina.

In business, then, he had made few mistakes. By the standards of the day, R. J. was a winner. But business had taken up so much of his energies that he hadn't married until he was middle-aged, and his personal life lacked the sweep, scope, and satisfaction it might have provided had he found a proper wife when he was on the way up. His life with Katharine was, as he had hoped just before their wedding, all the sweeter — but it was achingly brief. Now he was going to die without having been able to guide his sons and bring them along properly in the business that had made him rich.

On July 20, 1918, accompanied by Katharine and Dick, R. J. came back to Winston in a private railroad car and took to his bed at Reynolda. Outside the bungalow, on the grand estate that had been his home for only a few short months, the formal gardens were in their best bloom; the small school was out, and children could be heard wandering through the less manicured portions of the woods, riding horses on the bridle paths, hitting tennis and golf balls, splashing in the pool. The model farm attracted visitors from around the countryside, and the small chapel was a weekly magnet for worshippers. The activity at Reynolda was continuous, and, for nine days, R. J. listened to it.

At one in the morning on July 29, 1918, lying in the parlor at Reynolda, surrounded by family, R. J. Reynolds died at the age of sixty-eight.

Chapter Seven

Katharine and Ed

THE PUBLIC was invited to pay its respects to R. J. at Reynolda. All businesses in Winston-Salem were closed in honor of the leading citizen, and after a religious rite and mourning attended by thousands, he was laid to rest in the old Salem cemetery. "It was his good fortune," the city council said, "to dream of a great future and make that dream a reality."

After estate taxes of $370,000 — the largest ever in North Carolina — and last-minute bequests to two hospitals for another $240,000, the vast bulk of R. J.'s holdings (which, excluding Reynolda, consisted of about $11 million in RJR stock, shares in other ventures, and some real estate) was divided between Katharine and a trust for his four children. Dick, twelve, had watched his father die slowly over the eight months in which the family had lived at Reynolda. Mary and Nancy, ten and nine, grieved, but Smith, just six, deliberately was not immediately informed of the death.

Katharine mourned, and for at least a year after R. J.'s death she wore black. But she was a mature and accomplished woman who had brought a magnificent estate into being and who had helped her husband in the last munificent phase of his career. She had seen R. J.'s death approaching for some months and had evidently determined that her life would not perish with his, that she should not simply become the keeper of the flame; at thirty-eight, she was far too young to retreat forever into distinguished widowhood. Within a few months of his death she began to appear regularly in Winston, wearing a long rope of pearls to set off her widow's weeds.

She threw herself into starting a local chapter of the National Civil Federation to encourage improvements in working and living conditions for industrial employees and then initiated a chapter of the Junior League to give young society women uplifting projects. She donated $300,000 as seed money for an auditorium and high school, both to be named for R. J., challenging the city to raise an equivalent amount. And during the remaining months of the war, she held displays at the Reynolda cannery to demonstrate proper methods of putting up food to send to soldiers. In the fall, the little primary-grades school at Reynolda opened, and she supervised that, too.

Will Reynolds assumed the presidency of RJR just after R. J.'s death; he'd been doing the job in fact, if not in name, for about a year. At first, he did little to alter the style, aims, or methods of the company that R. J. had established. Pleasant, relaxed to the point of being phlegmatic, Will was not an innovator. Never a titan himself, he continued doggedly along the path laid out by his elder brother. The company's growth was paced by two great thoroughbreds, Prince Albert and Camels. They were the best horses going, and all Will had to do was hitch up his buggy and make sure they didn't stray from the track. Within a year of R. J.'s death, RJR was able to declare a spectacular dividend of 200 percent on some new categories of its stock; this greatly increased the value of R. J.'s estate, and continued growth in its holdings was conservatively estimated at 20 percent a year.

Earlier in the war, the real inheritor of R. J.'s sense of vision had had a crisis.

Just at the moment when the factories making Spotless Cleanser, Bubbles, and Lustre Box had reached their highest single day's output, R. S. Reynolds saw out of his office window in Bristol three of his night watchmen chatting with two well-dressed visitors. At 4:30 the next morning he was awakened by a phone call: his factories were on fire. Jumping into his car, he raced to the site and, as he later wrote, "saw my dreams consumed by flames." The arsonists were never found; R. S. was certain that the dirty work had been instigated by his competitors but couldn't prove it.

The Louisville, Kentucky, town fathers had recently set up a low-cost loan fund to lure new business, and R. S. quickly relocated there, while his father, Abram, remained in Bristol, managing the raw materials and staying busy with a new farm he'd bought.

Then, in the spring of 1918, when wartime priorities were set for various industries, R. S.'s soap products were deemed nonessential — not crucial to the national defense — and railroad cars formerly used to bring coal to his factories and carry his cleansers to market were taken away from him and instead allocated for use by defense-related industries. This action effectively gutted R. S.'s cleanser business. By the time of R. J.'s death, R. S. was personally and financially devastated. Every day he'd go to his empty office and sit there "amid the strong silence where once the music of automatic machines" had played. He had no orders for goods. His father seemed to have no new answers for him, and the uncle whom he called his "greatest friend in all the world" was dead. Adding to R. S.'s feeling of being persecuted was his discovery that while his own products were enjoined by the emergency, those of his competitors were traveling by rail to their usual markets.

As his father had done many years before, R. S. turned to God, and a voice "stronger than any human" one urged him to go to Washington. He went. Haunting war-related procurement offices, he tried to find something he could manufacture for the government. On his third trip to the capital he saw a postcard with the motto "Somewhere the sun is shining and someday it will shine on you." He sent it to his wife, who was a constant source of moral and emotional support.

Moments later, or so it seemed, an associate found a military officer who needed to find a way to keep gunpowder dry in something other than a steel drum. Within five days, R. S. built a prototype of a container made from paper, asphalt, and tin. The officer took his sample container and gave out a contract to manufacture it — but to a larger competitor, not to R. S. Determined to fight, R. S. went to see a man to whom he refers in his memoir as "another officer" but who may well have been Josephus Daniels, since he asked R. S. if he was related to "my friend, R. J. Reynolds." When R. S. said that he was R. J.'s nephew and had been his protégé, the unnamed officer reversed the subordinate's decision and awarded the contract for powder canisters to the Reynolds Company of Louisville. Within months, the government had ordered fifty boxcar-loads of canisters, and R. S. shortly recouped everything he had previously lost to fire, skulduggery, and the arbitrary decisions of dollar-a-year men.

At the eleventh hour of the eleventh day of the eleventh month of 1918, an armistice was signed, ending the Great War. That benefited the tobacco industry, but it also meant a considerable slackening of demand for powder canisters. In early 1919, R. S. Reynolds excitedly told Uncle Walter that he'd recently completed the purchase of machinery needed to make tinfoil, had lured away a man from the monopolistic company that virtually controlled the field, and wanted RJR to become his partner in a new tinfoil enterprise.

Walter and Will found this idea tempting. RJR had been having problems with its supply of the tinfoil used to package cigarettes because they'd been forced to buy their entire stock from Conley Foil of New York. In their nephew's plan they saw — as R. S. intended — an opportunity to get away from dependence upon Conley and to make a profit on both ends, cigarettes and foil. So they hatched a joint venture, signing a document saying that once R. S. actually began to manufacture foil, the parties would create a new company, U.S. Foil, in which Reynolds of Louisville would have a 49 percent share and RJR 51 percent, though R. S. would run the company. RJR would guarantee the new entity a standing order of twenty thousand pounds of foil per day for the next ten years. It was a wonderful deal for R. S., and he itched to get started, but RJR dragged its feet because Walter and Will didn't want their rivals in the tobacco industry to know that RJR had stolen a march on them. In this era, the giant tobacco companies were competitive, but only to a point — each was making plenty of profits, and it was no longer considered good business to war upon one another. Essentially, the tobacco trust still lived, though now it was a gentleman's agreement.

Over the summer, because the plan was not implemented, R. S. was terribly squeezed — financially overextended because of his uncles' caution. He told them so, and they said he could borrow some money from them until they worked out the details. He took a loan of $150,000 to pay off the equipment he'd earlier bought. At the same time, Will took the U.S. Foil idea to, of all people, Buck Duke, whose current post was with the British-American Tobacco Company. Duke and his partners came in on the deal, thus sloughing off part of the risk and also blunting the potential anger within the tobacco industry. With BAT aboard, production finally began at U.S. Foil.

Will and Walter's protracted negotiations had certainly cost the new company dearly. However, at the close of business in 1919, when R. S. suggested in a memo that RJR therefore shouldn't participate in the foil company's profits for the year, his two uncles hit the roof. Walter replied with a caustic memo of his own and cut U.S. Foil's ten-year contract back to three years. U.S. Foil prospered, but not without bad blood between the tobacco and metals branches of the Reynolds family.

At Reynolda the three younger children had been attending the little school on the estate ever since its opening. Dick had been chauffeured each day to a downtown public school. In the spring of 1919, to accommodate demand from area parents, Reynolda's school was expanded from five to eight grades. Katharine had intentionally kept the fees low and the standards high, and this, combined with a thorough curriculum including art and foreign languages, attracted many people. To administer the larger school, a professional headmaster was hired.

John Edward Johnston was twenty-six, a South Carolinian by birth. He had graduated from North Carolina's Davidson College in 1914, spent several years as a teacher, and gone overseas in 1917 as a lieutenant with the Fifth Field Artillery battalion. Ed was tall and handsome, and Katharine told the female teachers at the school, with whom she was quite friendly, that one of them ought to set her cap for him.

She then went after him herself. Still a relatively young woman, Katharine saw no reason to remain forever in mourning — or without male companionship. The couple took things slowly, though; it was, after all, only a year since R. J. died, and they didn't want to shock the surviving Reynolds brothers or Katharine's children.

Nevertheless, their liaison upset the children. It wasn't that Ed Johnston was a bad man, but he was obviously no titan; in the children's eyes, no one could replace their father, and certainly not a young, practically penniless teacher whom they suspected of courting their mother for her millions. Dick, now thirteen and rather husky for his age, donned a false beard that made him look uncannily like the dead R. J., surprised his mother and Ed in an embrace, and upbraided them; another time, he took a punch at Ed and decked him.

=

As the romance of Katharine Reynolds and Ed Johnston flowered, everyday supervision of the children was increasingly left to Henrietta van den Berg, whom the children referred to affectionately as Bum or Jette. Katharine was often away from Reynolda and kept in touch with the children's progress by an exchange of letters with the governess. When Katharine and Miss van den Berg went on vacation together, Smith seemed more concerned in his handwritten scrawl to Katharine with having her tell Bum about the exploits of his various canaries and squirrels than with sending regards to his mother. Nancy's letters to Katharine, on the other hand, though generally chatty and reserved, invariably closed with emotionally charged, plaintive lines requesting her to come home soon.

The children were an ordinary, dark-haired foursome, none of them particularly striking; in portraits around 1920 they seem well dressed and subdued. First-born Dick, chubby and tall for fourteen, was outgoing and polite on the surface but sometimes aloof; he had an angry streak that would bubble up and be vented now and then. Mary was the social daughter; she played the leading role of Minnehaha in the *Hiawatha* presented lakeside at Reynolda and had her mother's sense of display. Nancy was more reserved than Mary, nearsighted, not very attractive, an average student (as were all the Reynoldses), athletic and strong-willed.

Smith, the baby of the family, was at times docile and at others petulant. Like Dick, he frequently came down with pneumonia, which weakened his lungs. He, too, was slightly overweight and tall for his age, though not robust.

On June 11, 1921, after a two-year courtship that was the talk of Winston-Salem, Katharine and Ed exchanged marital vows in front of the fireplace of the enormous Reynolda living room. Mary and Nancy were flower girls, all decked out in white and crowned with blossoms, and Smith was a ring bearer in a Little Lord Fauntleroy suit, but Dick refused to attend. He said he was ill, although family physician Dr. Lilly examined him and said there was nothing physically wrong. He was an adolescent boy, distraught over losing his mother to another man. In fact, he would never get over what seemed to be his mother's betrayal: it would affect his view of women — and marriage — and his relationship to his children throughout the remainder of his life.

Dick's actions at the time of the wedding were a trial to his mother. Bum had to expend a lot of energy on Dick — sitting with him in the evenings, going for long rides — so that the Johnstons could leave on their honeymoon to London and Paris without fearing that the family would fall apart in their absence.

To reassure Katharine, Bum sent a long letter that reached the steamer in New York just before it sailed; in it, she told "Dearie" that the children "are so happy in your happiness." She also told her employer that she had Dick well in hand, which was not the case. The split in the family's allegiances came glaring through the letter, for in the next line Bum also reported that, the previous evening, Nancy had whispered to her before going to sleep, " 'Bum I am so happy, it is wonderful to have a Father again.' " Perhaps Nancy's habit of loyalty to her mother was the reason why, when the girl had turned ten, Katharine had presented her in a quiet ceremony with the gold bracelet that R. J. had given her back in 1890. One would have thought it should have gone to Mary, who was Katharine's namesake.

Nancy's attitude seems to have been changed by the fall. At that time, the children's antipathy toward Ed as stepfather was so vigorous that he and Katharine took an extraordinary step. Rather than attempting to overcome the children's understandable emotional resentment, the pair abandoned their responsibility, moving out of the bungalow and into one of the estate's smaller cottages, leaving the children and their retainers alone in the big house. In a single stroke, they removed the last vestiges of direct parental supervision.

Why would Katharine do such a thing? The evidence is skimpy but suggests that she decided — consciously or unconsciously — to choose a new life with a new husband, which had the possibilities of excitement, over the more difficult task of overcoming the hostility of the children in order to give them the sort of guidance they clearly did not like. In her youth she had married an older man, had quickly borne him children, and then became his nurse as he sickened and died. During her childhood and marriage to R. J. she had never had a chance to kick up her heels. Now, married to a younger man, she was going to do just that. For the first time in her adult life, she was going to put her own happiness ahead of anyone else's.

In all likelihood, by this time Katharine had come to hate the shadow of the giant, the dead R. J., whose presence in the form of the children and the money could continually be felt; perhaps she was angry at the children for not allowing her to change and grow after R. J.'s death. The children would be financially well off, so why couldn't loyal retainers see them through the next few years until the emotional storms quieted down?

It was an understandable choice, but in moving out of her children's lives, Katharine made a fundamental mistake: she confused their fiscal health with their emotional well-being. From this point on, Dick, Mary, Nancy, and Smith wanted for nothing — and yet they were in desperate need of the very thing that money couldn't buy and that was now denied them, the moment-to-moment care and supervision of close parenting.

Since the time of R. J.'s death, Will Reynolds had tried to lend Katharine a hand with bringing up the children, but, for a man who had played uncle to dozens of nephews and nieces, he made efforts that were singularly uninspired. He agreed with R. J.'s philosophy that money too easily come by could spoil the chances of a rich man's son, yet had no idea how to apply this to Dick. For example, when the boy was twelve, he decreed make-work: Dick got 25 cents for moving bricks from one spot to another on Will's farm; next day he got another 25 cents for moving them back. It wasn't a stimulating or meaningful task. Now, in 1922 and 1923, when Dick was sixteen and seventeen, Will gave him a job in an RJR factory. It was a man's work, Dick would later tell one of his sons, tending a cigarette-making machine eight to ten hours a day for 10 cents an hour.

That wasn't exactly stimulating or meaningful either. Assembly-line work was dull, and Dick felt that he had no real responsibility. He knew that at his age, his father and uncles had shouldered quite a bit of the management of Hardin's enterprise. If R. J. had lived and Dick truly had been brought into the company and nurtured, as R. J. had done with R. S., the result might have been different. But Uncle Will now held the reins and had no intention of grooming a young hotshot to supplant him, particularly if the young man was the image of the elder brother who had overshadowed Will for so long. Perhaps if Dick had pushed hard, he could have made his way anyhow — but here, as his father had feared, the disrupting influence of inherited money came into play. Dick already knew that his father's will would soon be providing him $50,000 a year, a very princely sum, and that he would be able to increase the amount yearly until, at age twenty-eight, he came into many millions of dollars. Next to that, starting up the ladder at 10 cents for an hour of hard labor didn't seem very appealing, nor worth fighting for.

From the first, the Reynolds family had attempted to downplay the fact that the children would be multimillionaires when they grew up. They searched for ways to handle the situation, but, as with many families that come quickly to riches, they were unsure how to set about the task. Families with a long tradition of wealth often sent their children to schools where their rough edges would be knocked off in the competition with their equally moneyed class-mates. The Reynolds children had gone first to school on their own estate, then to the high school named after their father in the town of which he had been the leading citizen. Now Dick was sent to a Southern boarding school, Woodberry Forest, to which many of the Winston-Salem elite sent their sons. Boys fought for the priv-ilege of being his roommate. Meanwhile, at Reynolds High, the other girls in Miss Flossie Martin's Latin class would wait until Nancy collected her handful of scratch paper before taking theirs. What could Katharine's care in dressing the children unostenta-tiously avail against this kind of deference?

Dick was seventeen, still carrying some baby fat but now six feet tall, with prominent dark and sensuous eyes, when in the summer of 1923 he decided to go to sea. Concealing his real name and answering to the moniker Kid Carolina, he signed on as a cabin boy of the *Finland*, which hauled cattle across the Atlantic. He thought he was running away, but Katharine somehow learned of his plans and sewed $10,000 in cash into his seaman's jacket. (Fiscal responsibility again, but lack of firm supervision.) That summer he made several trips on the North Atlantic run, New York to Hamburg by way of Cherbourg, in France, enjoying the freedom and license of life away from home. He had a grand time, and it seemed somehow connected in his mind with concealing his identity as a Reynolds — when it probably had more to do with the usual pleasure a young man takes in escaping all that he has previously known. In any event, when he returned home in the fall, the jacket with the money inside it was still intact. He hadn't even discovered the $10,000 on his trips.

In 1921, Walter Reynolds died at age fifty-five. A lifelong bach-elor, he had always been scholarly in a family not known to revere learning, a loner in a crowd that flocked together. His genius had been expressed in developing the blends that led to the success of Prince Albert and Camels. When R. J. and his family had moved to Reynolda, Walter had taken over the Fifth Street mansion; he rambled around in it because it was so big. That stately house, and everything else of Walter's, were left in limbo for a while, since he died intestate (without a will). However, in an action that showed there was still tension among the branches of the family, his prop-erty was divided by Will among the surviving brothers and their children — but R. S. got none of it. Further, a lawsuit was filed in Bristol over the sale of some lots Walter had owned there, perhaps since the boom of 1890. The suit pitted Abram against Will and R. J.'s children. The amount in question was so small, $800, that it was overshadowed by the legal fees involved. In response to this sort of suit there arose in the Reynolds family the saying that a dollar won by suing another Reynolds was sweeter than any other currency.

Walter's death stirred Abram to bring his memoirs up to date. He reminisced about his saintly mother: "Under the grace of God men & women are what our mothers make us. . . . we Cant all be great but we Can all try to be good and meet mother and father where we will never say farewell any more." He pronounced himself grateful beyond words to have enough worldly goods to care for elderly clergymen, build up the YMCA, and fund dozens of other religious-based causes.

The sixty-thousand-acre tract Abram had been tending all those years was on the verge of being sold, and he pledged a quarter of the profits to the Methodist Missionary Fund. However, to ensure that this missionary fund would never want, he decided to turn over to it what he now knew to be the best investment possible — stock in the RJR Company. R. J. would have gotten a good belly laugh out of that.

In mid-1922, Katharine and Ed had begun making frequent trips to New York City and took an apartment there. Ed was now a partner in a small brokerage firm, as well as an officer of Winston's Wachovia Trust, and the couple's visits to the home of the stock exchange may have had something to do with this new association. Having an apartment in New York served further to decrease the time they spent in Winston-Salem and with Katharine's children. Then, late into a pregnancy, Katharine had a miscarriage. Caring for her afterward, doctors learned that she had a weak heart and an overtaxed circulatory system. She and Ed were warned by doctors not to try to have another child because such an attempt might prove fatal to Katharine.

By early 1924, however, Katharine was pregnant again. She was forty-four and wished to have this late baby in order to enter fully into a new life with Johnston. Ed wanted the child, too, but perhaps for a darker reason: should the child survive, it would be an heir to the Reynolds fortune, and as its father he could never be cut out of a hefty chunk of money. In the few short years since R. J.'s death, that fortune had already grown to between $30 million and $35 million. Katharine didn't seem fazed by the possibility that Ed was only after her money, or if she was, she chose not to view it as an impediment to their happiness. In fact, cognizant of the likelihood that bearing the baby might prove fatal, she drew up a will that named Ed as one of her principal executors and co-guardian of all her children in the event of her death. Whether or not Dick and the rest of them liked Ed, if she died, they'd be stuck with him.

The pregnancy proved to be so difficult for Katharine that she and Ed moved up to New York, where doctors could more easily manage its final phase. In mid-May of 1924 Katharine entered Harbor Hospital in New York. There, on May 21, she gave birth to J. Edward Johnston, Jr., and, three days later, while still in the postnatal ward, suffered an embolism as a blood clot broke loose and traveled to her brain, killing her.

Will had her body brought back down to North Carolina, where it lay for a semipublic service at Reynolda. In his eulogy Bishop J. Kenneth Pfohl felt it was important to point out not only that Katharine had "accomplished great good" in her time but also that "to be rich is not a sin." The Reynoldses buried Katharine — and Ed allowed them to do so — not as a Johnston but as a Reynolds, next to R. J. in the Salem cemetery.

Ed displayed great grief. He pledged to have a monument to Katharine erected on the Reynolda grounds, to bring up their baby as best he could, to be a good guardian to the four children of R. J. It was impossible to tell whether he was sincere.

We have only hints of what happened next, but it is clear that Dick, now eighteen, and Will Reynolds made their anger known. Quite possibly they threatened lawsuits in which they could charge that Ed had deliberately pushed his late wife into a life-threatening pregnancy. Ed may have pointed out that he could tie up the estate during such a suit and as co-guardian make things difficult for everyone. A compromise was reached. Ed and his son were guaranteed enough money to keep them happy for life — in exchange for agreeing not to lay extravagant claim to the Reynolds fortune. An immediate departure was deemed inadvisable; it might start tongues wagging. And Ed could keep his guardianship, just as long as Uncle Will ran that show. The main thing was to keep the whole affair quiet.

The formal opening of the R. J. Reynolds High School and the accompanying grand auditorium was held less than a month after Katharine's death. The ceremony was bittersweet; Reynolda manager George Orr called it at once the dedication of a place of learning and a memorial to the spirit of Katharine Reynolds, who had contributed more money in one chunk than R. J. had donated in his lifetime and by doing so had pushed the city to build these institutions. The ceremony was well attended — but none of Katharine and R. J.'s four children was there. Mary, Nancy, and Smith were off on a first-class tour of Europe under the wing of a chaperon, while Dick and his cousin May Lybrook, with another chaperon, were on a similar tour of South America.

Reynolda, except for the employees, was empty — a caretaker's paradise.

PART TWO

PLAYBOYS

Chapter Eight

Fly-boys

IN THE SUMMER of 1924, Uncle Will Reynolds and J. Edward Johnston, executors of Katharine's estate and co-guardians of teenagers Dick, Mary, Nancy, and Smith, sat down to decide how to rear the orphaned millionaires, who ranged in age from eighteen to thirteen. It was a tricky task. How could the trustees keep the teenagers in line and yet adequately ready them for assumption of great riches?

The middle years of the Roaring Twenties were characterized by a pronounced catering to the whims of the wealthy: there was an emphasis on elegance, style, and youth. Yet all around, society reverberated with warnings about inherited wealth. Henry Ford grumbled, "Fortunes tend to self-destruction by destroying those who inherit them." William K. Vanderbilt dryly said that "inherited wealth is as certain death to ambition as cocaine is to morality." And the famous émigré sociologist Pitirim Sorokin dourly observed of American millionaires that whereas the generation of the fathers had worked hard, spending money only late in life and not in a particularly profligate manner, the heirs often manifested a "weakness and longing" for material goods and conspicuous consumption, mixing a "pecuniary standard of living" with "pecuniary canons of taste."

It wouldn't do to have the Reynolds heirs live like paupers and suddenly, when they were twenty-one, put large amounts of money into their pockets — not when America was booming and each child's quarter of the estate was producing dividends in excess of $300,000 a year in an era when the average annual family income was about $3,000.

In horse-racing terms — Will was very fond of horses — the

solution was to loosen the reins yet maintain control. So Will and Ed decided that the children would be introduced to their money slowly, in ever-increasing amounts. They would learn the value of money by paying for some things so that when they reached the age of twenty-eight and took complete possession of their fortune, they would destroy neither R. J.'s legacy nor themselves.

The guardians allotted each child $10,000 to $15,000 a year. This was enough for spectacular life-styles; but they were charged many thousands for the maintenance of Reynolda, first-class trips to Europe and South America, and generous salaries for chaperons. The children's funds underwrote an oil painting of Katharine that hung in the high school, the Winston revival missions of Billy Sunday (the model for Sinclair Lewis's forthcoming novel, *Elmer Gantry*), some of Will's own pet charities, the upkeep of their horses and of the family cemetery. When all of these had been debited, the children were left with relatively modest amounts of pocket money — but were permitted to charge back to the guardians almost everything they needed, even down to such petty items as a $1 rubber stamp and a $1.75 magazine subscription.

However, an allowance doesn't control a child's spending habits: a parent does. The difficulty lay not with the plan to restrain the children's spending but with its day-to-day administration. By now Ed Johnston commanded no respect from the children, and Uncle Will was too busy running RJR and building up his new Tanglewood estate to supervise R. J.'s brood.

Wearing mourning for their dead mother, the children spent the summer of 1924 touring Europe and South America before they returned to school in the fall. Soon both girls, Mary and Nancy, had left Reynolds High and were in boarding or finishing schools, Mary in New York and Nancy in Bryn Mawr, Pennsylvania. In their guardians' eyes, they were being readied for marriage. The boys were harder to set on the right path. Despite evidence that Woodberry Forest hadn't done much for Dick, Smith was soon a boarder at the school. Dick moved briefly to Culver Military Academy, in Indiana. The fact that all three younger children now had been sent to boarding school testifies to the guardians' belief that the Reynolds children could not be handled well enough at home and to their hope that discipline, standards, and values would be forced into the teenagers by institutions paid for that purpose.

In the fall of 1924 Dick was eighteen, an inch over six feet, slightly overweight at about two hundred pounds, a good-looking, strapping

ing, track, the yearbook. None of these greatly interested him. In the Smoker's Club he was known, of course, as "Camel" Reynolds, pledged to the club's motto, "Smoke now for tomorrow you may burn." He had a crush on one of his cousins and took her to a midwinter dance. When she brushed him off, he was devastated. He wrote a suicide note:

Will.
I leave my car to Ab [Walker, his best friend]. . . . My money to Dick. . . . My good looks to Mary (she needs it). P.S. You think I am tite [drunk], but I'm not. P.S. Hope you don't feel hurt about this will.

Soon Smith couldn't take Woodberry Forest any longer and followed Dick's footsteps to Culver Military Academy. The change was not a success, so the sixteen-year-old went to New York, where he hung around his twenty-year-old brother and took up with show girls and airplanes. As did Dick, Smith could feel the combined approach of his manhood and possession of a grand fortune. The combination was exhilarating.

The death of the Reynolds children's father in 1918, followed by their mother's desertion, remarriage, and subsequent death in 1924, had left Dick, Mary, Nancy, and Smith parentless but in expectation of an enormous fortune. Deprived of what every child needs, the warmth and love of its parents, they also lacked the sort of parental authority that sets boundaries and teaches children strategies for dealing with the world around them. The guardians provided little in the way of affection and assistance. Thus, even though they were ill prepared for that larger world, by the late 1920s the four children, still under the age of twenty-one, had all effectively slipped out of the control of the guardians and were on their own.

=

On April 4, 1927, Dick Reynolds turned twenty-one. It was known legally as the day of emancipation, and Dick took it literally. He formally discharged Will Reynolds and Ed Johnston as guardians. Now he had a greater, though still limited, right to draw his dividends directly from the RJR legacy. His income from the trust rose to $100,000 a year. He wouldn't actually take control of the full inheritance for another seven years.

F. Scott Fitzgerald wrote of New York at this time:

Young people wore out early — they were hard and languid at twenty-one. Most of my friends drank too much — the more they were in tune to the times the more they drank. The city was bloated, glutted, stupid with cake and circuses, and a new expression "Oh yeah?" summed up all the enthusiasm evoked by the announcement of the latest super-skyscrapers.

The description perfectly fitted Dick Reynolds's rebellion against his upbringing.

In New York, he rented an apartment in town and a house on Long Island, the latter with two servants in addition to the chauffeur he hired for his yellow Rolls-Royce. He backed Broadway plays and had affairs with show girls. Liquor was illegal, but speakeasies dominated nightlife, and their illicit charm was part of what made them attractive to customers. Dick was at nightclubs almost every evening. He was known to eat expensive meals, smoke incessantly — Camels, of course — and drink heavily. He rubbed shoulders with fellow millionaires and with racketeers at Texas Guinan's, Jimmy Fay's, and Jimmy Kelley's. He wore tuxedos and took flappers in ermine and pearls to Harlem. He was a regular visitor at such uptown places as Barron's Cabaret and Connie's, where (the *Daily News* said) waiters "whispered that bottles should be carried in the pocket, and not be placed on the floor," else they would be in danger of being kicked over during wild dancing.

In his more sober hours, Dick embraced aviation with the same intensity he brought to partying. Though he already knew how to fly, and no license was required, he took an examination from the only duly constituted body that could issue a license, the Fédération Aéronautique Internationale, just at the time when Orville Wright had been elected its secretary. He passed easily and obtained one of the first licenses issued to a U.S. citizen, and one of the very few signed by the father of aviation.

Many pilots at Curtiss and Roosevelt fields were getting ready to try to cross the Atlantic solo, a feat that had never been accomplished and one that held the promise of a $25,000 prize. Just weeks after Dick turned twenty-one, Charles Lindbergh landed at Roosevelt with his *Spirit of St. Louis,* and one of Dick's pals, a pilot named Harry Bruno, peremptorily took charge of fending off newsmen interested in interviewing the shy man. Bruno told the press that Lindbergh was the only fly-boy around who didn't drink. On a misty morning, Lindbergh taxied his small plane out of its Curtiss

Field hangar and rolled it onto Roosevelt Field, whence he took off for Paris.

Lindbergh's triumph and the atttendant wave of publicity produced ripples of interest in aviation across the country and throughout the world. Just after this historic flight, Dick Reynolds decided to put his money where his heart was: in aviation.

If Dick was trying to emulate his father in picking a fledgling industry to conquer, he was at the right place at the right time. Curtiss and Roosevelt fields were awash with a thousand visitors a week, come to ogle Lindbergh's takeoff site and to feel a part of his adventure. Dick bought Curtiss Field and hired employees to escort the curious through the hangars for a small fee. He also purchased planes to take sightseers up in the air and to teach prospective pilots how to fly. One pupil was brother Smith Reynolds, now sixteen and eligible for Orville Wright's stamp of approval.

At this time, most airports in the United States were located hours away by road from major cities. Amphibians were seen as a way to move passengers efficiently from riverfront cities to the airports. George Ireland's amphibians were considered the best on the market, and his factory wasn't far from Curtiss Field; Dick bought Ireland Amphibian, too.

Dick also made a third purchase. One day, astonished passersby at New York City's Columbus Circle heard the godlike voice of a Metropolitan Opera baritone coming to them from the clouds. It was the inauguration of the Plane Speaker Company, which used loudspeaker equipment mounted on a plane to inform, entertain, and amaze from a thousand feet in the air. Dick thought that the army would want "plane speakers" to broadcast above battlefields; airplanes and airports would use them to communicate with one another, and advertisers ought to snap up the idea as a new way to provoke the public with their messages.

In the company's flagship, a trimotor, Dick circled high above his hometown of Winston-Salem, intoning, "Warning . . . a swarm of killer bees is on the way. Take cover! Warning. . . ." Winstonians did panic, but only until they realized that R. J.'s elder son was up to his usual practical jokes. In this era of collegiate flagpole sitting, crowding into phone booths, or playing marathon mahjongg matches, such stunts were almost expected of young men, especially rich ones, and were seldom punished.

In the summer of 1927 a seemingly casual visitor to Reynolds Airways suggested a little extracurricular activity for Dick Reynolds's planes: occasional trips out over Long Island Sound or the nearby Atlantic Ocean to drop what looked like golf balls on the decks of certain ships. It was all done through intermediaries, but Dick learned that the ultimate customer was Frank Costello, a New York mob boss of some notoriety.

That identification made obvious the intent of the mysterious flights. This was the era of Prohibition, and the ships were rum-runners, cutters that came up from the Bahamas, or other places that still manufactured and sold liquor, and waited outside U.S. territorial waters, where authorities couldn't touch them. The golf balls actually were iron pellets stuffed with information about where the target ships should rendezvous with smaller boats, which, in turn, would take aboard the illegal liquor and make fast runs into port. Should the pellets miss the decks of the boats or roll off, they'd sink quickly, so there'd be no evidence left bobbing in the ocean waters. Dick took the job. He loved the excitement of it. (R. J., in his youth, had imported moonshine into Winston.) But after one of Dick's pilots on a golf-ball mission crashed in the drink — he survived, although the plane didn't — the twenty-one-year-old aviation entrepreneur decided to stop flying for Costello.

Dick undoubtedly wanted to keep his operation clean because he had become interested in trying to land a big potential money-maker, a mail route. For years, the army had carried the mail. Now the business-oriented Coolidge administration was trying to turn that task over to private industry. To compete for the contract on the Chicago–New York route, Dick took offices in the new Art Deco Graybar skyscraper in Manhattan and expanded Reynolds Airways to thirteen planes, which were flown by such Great War veterans as Ed Music. They operated regular flights along the Eastern Seaboard. In pilots, planes, and financial resources, then, RA resembled every other fledgling airline in the United States. To this mix, Dick added one original idea: he planned to locate the eastern terminus of the route in New Jersey, which was as close to New York as Long Island but less crowded. He based his planes at a small airfield in northern New Jersey.

To take over the paperwork of the government application, Dick interviewed Randolph Stratton Coyner, twenty-seven, son of a poor but dignified old Southern family. Strat was a recent graduate of law school and a CPA. In a chauffeured Rolls-Royce, Dick met him at the Winston train station and brought him back to breakfast in the elegant dining room at Reynolda. Then the young heir lit a cigar, moved into the equally grand library overlooking the manicured grounds, and got down to negotiations.

"Those things that tend to facilitate transportation are the things that advance civilization," Dick told Strat, and Reynolds Airways was designed to advance the heck out of civilization. He wanted Strat to move to New York and take over the day-to-day operations of Reynolds Airways and Dick's other personal business dealings. For this he would pay Strat five hundred dollars a month — considerably more than Strat was making in Asheville, where he'd been having a hard time getting his private practice started. Strat took the job, and soon he and Dick were fast friends.

But they didn't get the contract. That went to a new company, set up through the Rockefeller-controlled Chase Manhattan Bank, called United Air Lines. United, of course, went on to become a giant in the field. For a while, Reynolds Aviation continued to operate and even to expand operations slightly. Winston newspapers publicly called on Dick to enlarge Winston's tiny airfield to make it worthy of an expected fall visit by Lindbergh; Dick declined to upgrade Winston's strip but did open a branch of his line at the small field. He boasted to the hometown press that such cities as Rochester were willing to rebuild their airports at their own expense in order to have his planes make scheduled stops there.

Back in New York, after the defeat of the mail-contract bid, Dick let Strat run things and spent even more of his time in nightclubs. Pursuing a chorine, Dick was persuaded to invest in a musical comedy she was rehearsing, a show of dubious worth entitled *Half a Widow*. Beset by poor reviews and having exhausted all its angels' funds, the show limped to Broadway for previews. Dick began to get daily imploring messages from the producers, asking him to give them $4,000 to pay the rent on the New York theater so they could properly open the show.

On September 15, 1927, Dick withdrew $5,000 from a bank account, sold a Packard roadster to his fellow RA officer John Graham, and arranged to send his servants at the Long Island house back home to Winston. That evening, Dick and Graham began drinking at a well-known roadhouse in Oyster Bay. Traveling in Dick's yellow Rolls, they stopped at several more watering holes on Long Island before ending the evening at a favorite spot in Manhattan, the Charm Club, on West Fifty-first Street, a Broadway hangout. In the wee hours of the morning, Dick left the club with dancer Marie Houston.

When the sun was fully up that day, Dick's yellow Rolls was found upturned in the surf off Port Washington, on Long Island. This precipitated a search for its owner. John Graham blithely told police he didn't know where Dick was. Then things got out of hand. One newspaper story suggested that there had been foul play, that Dick might have been murdered. A reporter went to the morgue: one dozen bodies had been found overnight in New York, but none was a white male, six foot one and 210 pounds.

Where was the young heir? According to the newspapers, all America wanted to know. Days passed, Dick didn't turn up, and newspaper interest ran higher and higher. Ed Johnston and Reynolda manager George Orr hustled up to New York to speak with the authorities, while Uncle Will engaged the Hargreaves Detective Agency and offered $3,000 for information on the young heir — who was worth, newspapers estimated, between $10 million and $15 million. RA vice president Carter Tiffany recalled that his pal had been impressed by the film *Beau Geste* and suggested that Dick might have gone to join the French Foreign Legion. This new wrinkle set off a passport hunt; the State Department cabled its legations around the world to check if anybody resembling Dick had come in to obtain a passport. A show girl swore that Dick had taken Marie to the Grand Central railroad station at six on the morning in question but didn't know whether either of them had gotten on a train. Marie was missing, too.

While Dick was gone, but before word of his disappearance had reached the national newspapers (where he might have read about it), there was a tragic accident. On the afternoon of September 17, in heavy rain, RA's eighteen-passenger Fokker crashed soon after takeoff in an orchard in Dunellen, New Jersey. Killed on impact were the experienced pilot, his mechanic, and five passengers who had taken advantage of "Bargain Day" rates. Five more escaped with injuries. That night, employees of RA came from the nearby Hadley Airfield base and burned the wrecked plane. Although the RA people said that the cause of the crash was engine failure, and no local or federal agency pressed any charges, lawsuits were expected. The following day, *Half a Widow* closed.

These events added up to a mess with the missing Dick Reynolds at its center. The truth of his whereabouts slowly came out. The chauffeur for the Rolls admitted that Mr. Reynolds had sent him to Long Island with money for the two servants to go to Winston-Salem and instructions to leave the Rolls at the train station; the chauffeur implied that the Rolls in the surf was a practical joke, a diversion to enable Dick to get away from New York. Next, a tearful show girl in the cast of *Bonita* confirmed that before his disappearance, Dick had come down to Washington but had unfortunately found her in the arms of a rival and become distraught. Then Marie Houston returned to New York and, pressed, admitted she and Dick had gone to St. Louis on a binge. The hunt leapt to St. Louis, but by that time Dick was in Chicago watching one of the most famous of sporting events, the rematch title bout between Gene Tunney and Jack Dempsey for the world heavyweight crown. At ringside with former champ Jim Jeffries, New York Yankees owner Jacob Ruppert, and author Damon Runyon, Dick saw the "long count" that gave Tunney time to recover from Dempsey's blows and win. The contest was so exciting to the millions around the country listening on the radio that during the thirteen-second climax of the fight several listeners died of heart attacks.

On the train back to St. Louis, Dick made friends with a racetrack tout, to whom he showed his dog-track winnings and boasted that he'd been living on them. Once back in the city, the tout pointed the Hargreaves Agency detectives to a chop suey joint, where they found the missing heir in the company of a twenty-three-year-old lovely with long blond hair. Dick tried to pass himself off as John Graham and even produced Graham's driver's license as evidence. After a while, though, he admitted his identity.

Alighting from the train in New York, Dick explained his disappearance to a horde of reporters. "I just got fed up" with the nightlife of New York, "where money talks," he said, and so he'd taken a little vacation. He had, of course, told Graham and others that he'd be at the big fight; they'd just decided to let him have his privacy.

The caper made Dick Reynolds front-page news throughout the country for two weeks and established, as perhaps nothing else could have done, his role as professional playboy. His disappearing act was symptomatic of something deeper. It was a reaction not only to the pressures of being rich and footloose in New York, but also to being pressed in business. Over the next few months, the unsuccessful bid for the airmail contract, the accident suffered by the RA plane, and the residual attention he received after coming back to New York combined to make Dick lose interest in aviation. He did so at a particularly crucial moment: in the following year, 1928, airlines in the United States carried four times as many passengers as they had in 1927, and thereafter the trend was steadily upward. But by then Dick had chosen to put more energy into his life-style than into his business.

=

Abram Reynolds's last year of life was informed by the bitter knowledge that his brother was squeezing his son out of business. Seventy-eight and in frail health, Abram was a director of U.S. Foil, the company jointly owned by R. S. and the upper management of RJR, represented by Will Reynolds. RJR was disappointed with U.S. Foil's performance. There were delivery and quality problems; the big sticking point, though, was a personality clash — R. S. and Will didn't see eye to eye. Finally, the tobacco company gave R. S. an ultimatum: buy out RJR's shares in U.S. Foil for $750,000 (twice what RJR had put up in assets back in 1919) or else the shares would be dumped on the market. R. S. refused to pay what he considered an exorbitant price. Six months later RJR offered the shares for sale and outsiders bought them, which diluted R. S.'s ownership position. RJR also made clear that once the present contract to buy foil from USF was ended, it would not be renewed.

If Will and RJR hoped by these stratagems to sink R. S.'s enterprise, they didn't know their adversary, for R. S. was as tough and resilient in his own way as his mentor, R. J., and his father, Abram. In a poem that R. S. wrote a few years later, he expressed the philosophy of finding opportunities in crises that got him through difficult times:

> Upon the past I turn my back,
> Foursquare I face the sun,
> Tomorrow is my own,
> Trampled under
> By no hoofs of days gone down.
> Through storm and wrack
> Mid multitudes or alone,
> I spell out hope and wonder.

Possibly with money from Abram, R. S. bought one of his company's major customers, the ice cream firm that made foil-wrapped Eskimo Pies. The amalgamation was a success: both entities became more profitable. Within months, R. S. was able to pay a 20 percent dividend to U.S. Foil's shareholders — which, of course, no longer included the RJR concern.

It was just after these maneuvers that Abram died. In its obituary, the *Herald-Courier* called him "the leading citizen of Bristol for the last half-century," as well as the major benefactor of its churches and schools. Most of Abram's fortune was bequeathed to his many charities. As for the rest, his will stated, characteristically, "It has been my policy to treat my Creator as my partner in all my business affairs, and it is my desire that my children will not dissolve the partnership which I entered into with Him in 1875. . . . All that I have is His and I simply commit a part of it to my dear children to use for their comfort and His glory. . . ."

Because of the loss of tobacco-industry revenues, U.S. Foil's overall business fell off markedly in the following two years, 1927 and 1928. Rather than letting the whole enterprise go down, R. S. used what resources he had to buy rival companies and dramatically change the focus of his enterprise. In short order he purchased the Robertshaw Thermostat Company, the Fulton Sylphon Company, and part of Beechnut Foil. He combined these, plus U.S. Foil, into a new entity, which he named Reynolds Metals. His new company used metals — aluminum now, as well as tin — to make foil and in dozens of other ways, too. By the end of 1928 he had tripled the size of his previous operations, quintupled his profits, and brought his brothers into the new concern.

Like R. S., the country's stock market was on a meteoric rise. It seemed that everyone who had money to spare was buying shares: to R. S., this was another opportunity. He started a brokerage firm to cater to people in midsized towns, such as his home base of Louisville, who wanted to make investments. Chartered in Delaware, Reynolds & Company had a license to trade on the New York exchanges. By July 1, 1928, the firm was in the black and mailed dividends of $81,000 to its own shareholders.

In the same 1927–28 period when cousin R. S. was forging Reynolds Metals and creating the Reynolds brokerage firm, Dick Reynolds was dealing with the crisis in his aviation holdings — from a completely different point of view on life. Rather than struggle against fate, Dick simply chose to pocket his profit and get out of the troublesome matters in which his businesses were enmeshed. He sold part of Curtiss Field to the owners of Roosevelt

Field for $800,000, much more than he'd paid for it. Then, leaving Reynolds Aviation (Winston) in the hands of Reynolda manager George Orr, and Reynolds Airways (New York) to Coyner and Tiffany, Dick went on a more or less permanent vacation, back and forth to Europe. He took an apartment in London, sailed on some yachts, frequented expatriate hangouts in Paris, and generally had a good time — sometimes so good a time that he wouldn't be able to come out of a binge for several days. In June of 1928, when his old flying buddy Wilmer Stulz piloted Amelia Earhart across the Atlantic, Dick met them in London, where Amelia gave him for safekeeping the pontoons of the *Friendship*, the plane in which she had become the first woman ever to complete a flight over that ocean. He lost them.

In the fall of 1927, royalty descended from the heavens on Winston: on the outskirts of the city, on the grounds of what had been the Forsyth County farm for black delinquents, Charles Lindbergh landed his plane. The Lone Eagle's stay occasioned red-carpet treatment the likes of which had not been seen in Winston-Salem since the funeral of R. J.: motorcades, speeches of welcome, crowds that included everyone in town. Lindbergh was the greatest hero in the world; Smith Reynolds was eager to shake hands with him.

At sixteen, Smith was one of the youngest pilots in the country. To him, airplane fuel was an exotic, addictive perfume: he lived to hang around the Winston airfield, fiddle with the machines, and talk shop with the men of Reynolds Aviation. In Winston, those who frequented the field were an odd mixture of grease monkeys and the sons of rich men — C. G. Hill and "Fat Charlie" Norfleet, in addition to Smith.

Often, Smith took up a plane to practice touch-and-go landings and takeoffs on the Reynolda golf course. By studying and flying all the time, Smith had not only obtained his pilot's license but was in the process of passing the tests for the mechanic's and transport pilot's licenses, which were considered much more difficult to obtain; in time he'd get these, too. Toward the end of 1927 Smith started talking to Uncle Will about getting money from the estate to buy a plane. Smith had his eye on a particular Waco Whirlwind for sale by a reputable dealer. It was only $8,000.

Now, in the eyes of "Mr. Will," nephew Dick was already out of control. Will argued with Smith about the plane. Yes, he'd allowed Dick to buy one, but Dick was older. Smith continued to press for the Whirlwind. Will sought guidance from his lawyer and friend, Clement Manly, an RJR board member. Manly understood immediately that the problem was far larger than whether or not Smith could get his toy — he saw that Smith's request put the entire trusteeship setup in jeopardy. Manly knew that the dividends declared by RJR and the price of RJR stock were soaring; the children's dividends alone were running at a million a year each. Upon reaching age twenty-eight, each of R. J.'s children would be assured not of $10 million to $12 million but of double that amount. Manly told Will, "Those boys can get four or five times as much money as you allow them if they went into court and asked for it." He advised Will to give Smith the plane, double quick, and while he was at it, to loosen the purse strings on the four trusts.

Will considered it. After all, Smith was less trouble than Dick, and perhaps if he were satisfied with the plane, he wouldn't be as worrisome as the elder playboy. As Will later said, "The only thing [Smith] ever took any interest in at all was aviation. I could never get him interested in anything else and I tried as fully as I could. I saw there was no use trying to break him off from it and that was why I let him have the money. . . . I wanted him to have a good plane."

Smith bought the Whirlwind and took it to air shows, where he competed in various races: five times around a triangular course, speed sprints, touch-and-go competitions. He won prizes. One day, Smith and a cohort flew the plane together over a farmer's field near Madison, North Carolina, and Smith jumped from the Whirlwind — just to try the parachute. It worked. Uncle Will didn't learn of the exploit for several months.

Ed Johnston remarried, moved to Baltimore, and in 1928 gave up his position as guardian. He was replaced in that post by Ed Lasater, who had married Will's niece, was close to Will in age, and had been in the management of RJR for many years. Even though Lasater was sympathetic to aviation and liked Smith personally, the new guardians would allow him only $3,600 that year, with a promise of $18,000 next year — but by the spring of 1929, Smith needed more money.

Reluctant to approach Will directly, Smith asked Lasater for the extra money from the estate. Lasater didn't encourage him, so Smith went to sister Mary. She was turning twenty-one and thus had greater access to her quarter of the fortune. Smith probably also felt that Mary had reason to act in a benevolent manner just at that moment because she'd recently become engaged to twenty-nine-year-old Great War veteran and financial specialist Charles Babcock, one of the most eligible bachelors in Winston. Smith importuned Mary for a loan of $4,000 so he could buy the Monocoupe agency for Winston. He planned on becoming the local dealer for the nifty-looking small planes, which, he was sure, buyers would instantly line up to purchase. Mary wrote out a check for $4,000 and didn't even bother to ask him for a note promising to repay.

On May 14, 1929, in London, Dick Reynolds and twenty-two-year-old English accountant Ronald Bargate rented a green Buick and set out for Hurley, about twenty-five miles west, to play golf. Rain made golf an impossibility, so they repaired to a bar in a nearby hotel, where they spent the afternoon and early evening hours knocking back glasses of Pimms Cup #1 — gin and lemonade — and playing "cricket darts." Around 9:30 P.M. Dick loaded Bargate, who had passed out hours earlier, into the backseat and got on the road to return to London.

A half hour later, going through a small village, Dick felt a bump as he went off the road, up a curb, and onto a footpath next to a hedge. He reversed the car and continued on, weaving from side to side until at Chiswick a police constable pursued and stopped him. The constable asked him to get out.

"I don't know that I shall. Why should I?" Dick said. When the constable insisted, he emerged rather unsteadily.

"You are drunk, sir."

"I certainly am not," Dick replied. Later, at the station house, a local doctor also pronounced him inebriated. Police noted that the car's mudguard was bent and a front headlight was missing. Dick made up an explanation: he'd done the damage at the hotel in Hurley. Later, the constabulary compared reports with police in the hamlet of Burnham and concluded that Dick's car had hit a motorcycle ridden by one Arthur Reginald Graham, who was currently in critical condition at Windsor Hospital with broken ribs and ruptured liver, pancreas, and kidney. The missing headlight was found at the accident site.

When told of Graham's injuries, Dick said to the constable, "I must have been drunk." After spending the night at the Chiswick station, a rather subdued Dick offered to give the Chiswick police inspector money for a specialist to attend to Graham. "I wouldn't advise you to do that, sir," the inspector said, pointing out that there could be legal repercussions — such a gift could be construed as accepting responsibility for having caused the accident.

"I'd do the same for any man," Dick insisted. When the police refused to take the money, Dick arranged through another channel for a specialist. It was too late: after three days of great pain, Graham died. Dick was hauled before a judge in London and charged with manslaughter. "American in Green Car Mystery" screamed a British billboard advertisement for a London tabloid.

For some time, the American press almost missed the story entirely because a wire service reported the hit-and-run driver's name incorrectly and so there was no identification of him as R. J.'s son. George Orr sailed to London to represent the family's interest. Winston businessman Frank Fries arranged to be on hand as a character witness for Dick. In London, Dick hired a team of five English lawyers and many experts to testify for him. During the weeks before the trial, to friends in London Dick appeared concerned about the death but not overly remorseful.

When the trial opened on July 22 at the Old Bailey, England's most famous courthouse, there was great interest in the galleries in the spectacle of a wealthy American playboy in the dock. The bewigged prosecutors presented witnesses who described the drinking at the hotel bar, the weaving of the car on the road, the drunkenness of the occupants, the hitting of Graham from behind. The motorcyclist's rear light had been working, but Dick hadn't seen it, and on impact Graham was thrown forty-two feet down the path. The constable reported Dick's words at the time of his being apprehended and on his hearing of Graham's injuries. Prosecutor Sir Henry Maddocks, K.C., concluded his case by saying that Dick's "drunkenness was the cause of that young man's death."

For the defense, Sir Norman Birkett, K.C., contended that Dick had not been drunk and that Graham's carelessness had caused the accident. The barman was called to the stand to say that Dick's steadiness at cricket darts attested to his sobriety even after having six Pimms Cups. Medical experts testified that the amount of gin in those drinks was not enough to impair ability. Yes, there had been an accident, Birkett charged, but Dick had been blinded by oncoming headlights. On cross-examination, the constable admitted that after initial stumbling Dick had indeed been able to walk to the station; a medical expert stated that Dick's natural walk contained a bit of a lurch. Birkett stressed Dick's attempt to get medical assistance for Graham even after being told that this would impugn his legal position.

"Were you drunk on May fourteenth at all?" Birkett queried his client in the dock.

"No, sir."

"Was there anything you could have done to avoid the tragedy?"

"No, sir."

On July 25 it was revealed that the jury foreman had spoken casually with one of the witnesses — they were friends — and the judge declared a mistrial, taking pains to state that "I am satisfied that Mr. Reynolds had nothing at all to do with the improper conduct." He ordered a new trial.

By now the case was sensational on both sides of the Atlantic. At the retrial, the *New York Times* reported, Dick "appeared more nervous." Most of the testimony was repeated for the new jury of eleven men and one woman. Among Dick's paid experts was a knighted pathologist for the Home Office, who was lambasted by the judge for offering comments far outside his specialty and being too obviously willing to say whatever would help Dick's cause. In his charge to the jury, the judge said that even if Dick's money would later be used to comfort the widow — she was to receive more money than Graham would have made in a lifetime — Dick would have been obliged by law to do something similar anyway; therefore, "you will try him just as you would a London costermonger charged with knocking somebody down through driving his cart furiously." He noted that Dick had admitted having a large number of drinks in a few hours, with nothing to eat. The jury took only half an hour to return a verdict of guilty.

The prisoner in the dock took the verdict calmly, as if he'd expected it. Birkett outlined the settlement to the widow and had Orr and Fries testify to Dick's good character. The judge's sentence was the most lenient allowable under the statute, "five months imprisonment in the second division." This meant no hard labor and included the possibility of time off for good behavior. Dick was whisked off in the Black Maria to Wormwood Scrubs prison, in South London, where he was outfitted in a khaki-colored suit adorned by broad black arrows. Editorials in U.S. papers praised the British system of justice. The Greensboro, North Carolina,

daily said unctuously that imprisonment would give the unspeak-
ably wealthy young playboy "time to think things over."

=

On October 24, 1929, stocks traded on the New York Stock
Exchange experienced a phenomenal crash. More than twenty billion dollars in valuation disappeared in a single day. The debacle
turned into a horrendous downward spiral, and the apparent prosperity of the Roaring Twenties was replaced by the economic
depression that had already engulfed most of Europe. RJR's sales
remained strong, however, and the tobacco giant was considered
more stable than General Motors or U.S. Steel, so the crash didn't
even cause a momentary pause in the Reynolds heirs' style of life.

In North Carolina, seventeen-year-old Smith Reynolds was
courting a young lady he'd met that summer, eighteen-year-old
Anne Cannon of Concord, North Carolina, also an heir to a fortune,
as granddaughter of James W. Cannon.

J. W. Cannon had created an empire in textiles similar to R. J.'s
fiefdom in tobacco: Cannon Mills was the world's largest towel and
cotton-goods manufacturer, with ten thousand looms in four Southern states. During the Great War the American doughboys were
issued Cannon towels inscribed with "In God We Trust" on one
side and "To Hell With The Kaiser" on the other. Cannon steadfastly refused to advertise — even to sew labels on his towels. Once,
a delegation of Buck Duke and R. J. Reynolds begged him to
advertise, but he would not be moved. J. W. retired in 1916 and
died in 1921. His disinherited son, Joe Cannon, clawed his way
back into the upper management of Cannon Mills and by 1929 was
a principal.

Anne Cannon was Joe's daughter, a cousin of Ella Cannon Hill,
Dick's old flame, and of Charley Hill, one of Smith's flying friends.
Still a schoolgirl, Anne drank, smoked, partied, and cursed with
the toughest of the boys. Smith flew to Concord to take her on
joyrides. He was fond of doing outside loops in the Whirlwind.
Anne decided that Smith Reynolds and the danger and excitement
of flying were better tonic for life than simple involvement with
her long-term boyfriend, F. Brandon Smith, Jr.

As Smith pursued Anne, Dick continued his incarceration at
Wormwood Scrubs, on the outskirts of London. Except for the
bars, he didn't have a bad time. His only chore was light house-

cleaning. He was able to write and receive letters and see his solicitors, who were mounting an appeal. He told a friend that the service in prison was better than he'd received in some of Europe's most distinguished hotels. When this remark was made public, the warden retorted, "It don't make much difference who this chappie is. 'E gets no more raisins in 'is duff than a Whitechapel leather snatcher." The warden's belittling notwithstanding, rumors persisted that Dick was being furloughed on weekends and enjoying conjugal visits with girlfriends.

While still in prison, Dick learned of a suit for $3.2 million filed against him and Reynolds Aviation on behalf of the victims of the 1927 plane crash.

One of Dick's solicitors talked the Chiswick police into taking a stance that reduced Dick's charge to dangerous driving. The judge then overturned the manslaughter conviction. On November 13, 1929, Dick emerged from prison, once again a free man. Upon getting out of jail, he bought an old Italian freighter of three hundred tons known as the S. S. *Harpoon*. Converting the officers' quarters into luxurious guest suites took only a modest investment. He saw the ship as a perfect way to combine business with pleasure. He could haul cargo across the ocean and take advantage of a provision in R. J.'s will that would award him two dollars for every dollar he earned on his own — and he could run the freighter as if it were a yacht. For cargo, he arranged with one of RJR's competitors, the Glass Staples Tobacco Company, to haul tobacco from Norfolk to Amsterdam. On board the *Harpoon*, Dick was a good and playful host for what became almost continuous parties, entertainments held far away from a too prudish society. Sometimes he charged friends a modest fee for passage, primarily as a tax dodge so he could deduct what he'd paid for renovating the accommodations. The guests would drink more in champagne than they paid for tickets.

The world was plunged into economic depression, but Dick sailed through it in a never-ending party. He wasn't blind to the ironies: in fact, it was during this era that his philosophy of spending money first began to crystallize. "Being too stingy or thrifty with my money won't benefit society," he'd say. "If there's anything I hate, it's a rich miser."

Two nights after Dick got out of jail in London, Joe Cannon returned to his mansion in Concord and surprised Smith and Anne in an intimate embrace on the living room couch. All three were drunk. The elder Cannon demanded that the teenagers immediately be married. At the point of a shotgun, he and a chauffeur hustled them into a Cadillac and drove them to the nearest town that could perform a ceremony without waiting. They reached York, South Carolina, shortly after midnight. A policeman was prevailed upon to roust a probate judge out of bed. York was known as a town to which out-of-staters came to get married — though usually not at this hour — and the wedding was soon performed with the policeman, license clerk, and judge's daughter as witnesses. When news of the nuptials was discovered, wags could not resist referring to it as a "cannon" rather than shotgun wedding.

Next day, in Concord, the newlyweds transferred to Smith's green Lincoln convertible with chromium-spoked wheels for the drive to Winston-Salem. Reynolda's bungalow was occupied by Mary, Charlie Babcock, and Nancy, so Smith and Anne rented the ninth floor of the downtown Carolina Hotel Apartments.

For a month or so, Smith and Anne seemed happy in their forced marriage, flying to air shows, outfitting their apartment, entertaining. Smith's friend Dwight Deere Wiman, heir to the John Deere tractor fortune, came down from New York to celebrate with Smith; Wiman was a Broadway producer with a current hit, *The Little Show*, starring Libby Holman. Anne had relatives in Winston-Salem. She was a friend of Mary's and Nancy's, and she also knew many people in Smith's set. Apart from the youth and spoiled-brat nature of the participants, the Smith and Anne pairing didn't seem a bad match.

During Winston's most illustrious annual affair, the Christmas dance at the Robert E. Lee Hotel, Smith and Anne had a quarrel that did not abate even after they returned to the apartment and had dinner with some of Smith's pals. Ab Walker and Jim Baggs weren't as wealthy as the Reynoldses and Cannons, but Smith was more comfortable with them than he was with the swells. From them he got both respect for his aviation heroics and a bit of awe for his money. This night, however, both young men were embarrassed as Smith and Anne shouted profanities at each other. Smith hit Anne a few times — enough to quiet her — and put her to bed. Then he sat next to an open window and silently sailed the dinner plates out: they fell nine stories, hit the streetcar tracks, and broke into pieces.

In early 1930, the marriage between Smith and Anne shattered, too, even though Anne was pregnant. Anne began again to see her childhood sweetheart, Brandon Smith. She also went on the town in New York with Mary Babcock. They were both pregnant and, after a night spent downing many drinks, sat up on adjoining beds and watched their bellies move as the babies kicked. Mary wrote Nancy of one wild night in the company of Anne's father, Joe. It took place at Texas Guinan's nightclub, where Anne and Mary talked the owner into letting a drunken Joe go backstage; soon, decked out in a girl's costume and makeup, he came onstage in the middle of the chorus line during a production number. His daughter and her sister-in-law hid under the table and laughed themselves silly. Next night, Joe went back to Texas Guinan's, and the girls had to find another place where they could drink; in the Prohibition era, that wasn't hard to do.

In a sense, what old Abram Reynolds and his generation of anti-alcohol reformers had done in managing to attach to the U.S. Constitution an amendment forbidding the sale of liquor was to increase the allure of alcohol and to push those who drank toward greater excesses than had been the norm when liquor was legal. In the 1920s, getting drunk was the way young people showed that they knew how to enjoy themselves; if one didn't drink, one was considered so straitlaced as to be insufferable. To be outside the law and having fun was the essence of youth. As journalist Warner Fabian was writing just then, "They're all desperadoes, these kids, all of them with any life in their veins; the girls as well as the boys; maybe more than the boys."

A few weeks later the group on the town included Smith, in company of a chorine; Dick, fresh from his freighter; and Nancy, out for a last fling before her impending marriage. They hit Barney Gallant's on Washington Square and many of the same clubs where Mary, Anne, and Joe Cannon had gone, places where the smoking, drinking, and nightlong parties seemed never to stop.

Occasionally, on the nightclub circuit, Smith and Anne would run into one another. Almost out of funds, Anne hesitated to ask Smith for money; Mary acted as a go-between. No reconciliation was in sight, but they could all be sophisticated and civil, couldn't they?

The whole clan returned to Reynolda in April to get ready for Nancy's marriage to a young man from the advertising department of Condé Nast, Henry Walker Bagley. Spring was the most beautiful time at Reynolda, and the mansion was a perfect setting for a wedding. Aunt Maxie, Katharine's sister, had taken charge of everything and was going to be the hostess of the reception. All that remained to be done by the bride-to-be and her siblings was relax.

At Reynolda, the night before the wedding, Smith, Dick, Mary, Charlie Babcock, and Nancy stayed up late, talking and drinking. They were a small fraternity of a family, a core group that shared a unique heritage and legacy; often, in Winston especially, they had to behave with decorum to uphold their social position — so, at home alone this night, they let loose. Everyone had a lot to drink, many laughs, a good time. Perhaps Dick even said to Smith, as he had avowed privately to the others, that if he'd been home at the time of the "cannon" wedding, Smith would never have gotten married, because Dick would have done his utmost to prevent or annul Smith's folly.

Getting on toward dawn, the kid brother and the brother-in-law and the bride-to-be gave up and went to bed. Mary and Dick walked through the great house with baskets of fresh eggs, tossing them at wall hangings, pieces of furniture, the crystal chandelier. They entered the second-floor bedroom where Nancy lay, comatose, her hair done up especially for the wedding; Mary cracked her last egg and emptied it into her sleeping sister's coiffure.

It was hell to clean up, but what was a staff for? By the time the guests arrived for the wedding ceremony in front of the great fireplace, where both Katharine and Mary had had their weddings in earlier years, the house had been restored to magnificence. No one even noticed the extra sheen in Nancy's hair.

Chapter Nine

Smith and Libby

O N THE EVENING of April 12, 1930, after a drunken party in Concord, North Carolina, the pregnant Anne Cannon Reynolds returned to her father's home, escorted by Tom Gay Coltrane. In the morning Coltrane was found dead in the next yard, and the coroner announced the cause of death as alcohol poisoning. There were many such fatalities among young revelers in the age of illegal liquor; it was one of the risks people took when drinking booze that could have been distilled with the wrong kind of alcohol. Reporters following the story learned of Coltrane's date with Anne, asked a few questions, and made headlines by making public for the first time the separation of Smith and Anne.

A few days later Smith went to see his friend Dwight Deere Wiman's touring company of *The Little Show*, in Baltimore. Dressed in riding boots and jodhpurs, Smith came in after the show had begun, sat in the first row, and was dazzled by the performance of Libby Holman, who sang "Moanin' Low."

He was not alone — the critics recently had been struck by her as well. She was twenty-five and had sung professionally for a half-dozen years without particular notice until *The Little Show* opened in the fall of 1929. It featured just three performers, Fred Allen, Clifton Webb, and Libby. Reviews elevated her to instant stardom. With her bee-stung lips, languorous posture, husky voice, and intense eyes, she seemed a new version of the 1920s sensation Clara Bow, the "It" girl. But while silent-screen star Clara Bow had faded from the scene when talking pictures revealed her nasal, rasping tones, Libby's quality — her sexiness — was heightened by a low, growling, emotion-packed voice. In an age of black blues singers, she was a white one; in an age of crooners, she was a belter of what had been essentially black music, torch songs. Libby was unique and unforgettable. Elinor Glyn, the author who invented "It," described the quality as having allure to men and women alike; Libby, a confirmed hedonist, was conducting affairs with men as well as with Louisa Carpenter, a Du Pont heiress.

After the show Smith begged Wiman for an introduction to the songstress, which was soon made. Smith followed up with flowers and notes. If he had hoped Libby was just another chorine who would dream of his money and sleep with him, he was rudely surprised. Libby was earning $2,500 a week. She'd had moneyed admirers before, run through them, and tossed them away. At first, she was polite to Smith — he was, after all, a friend of her show's producer. But Smith was not even nineteen, six years her junior, and he was married, as well as hopelessly naive when compared with the bright and sassy company she kept.

Smith was driven wild by the combination of Libby's obvious appeal and her refusal to accept him as a lover. He saw her a few times in Baltimore, at least once in the company of his brother. Dick had met Libby years earlier and, although impressed by her talent and charm, was not attracted to her, probably because of her reputation as a bisexual.

Smith followed Libby to Florida. She was surrounded by admirers, and he was just one of the pack. She treated Smith, one biographer writes, "like an amiable buffoon." After she returned to the tour of her show, Smith went off to do something daring.

A man named Frank Goldsborough had just set a record by flying from New York to Los Angeles in 34 hours and 3 minutes, not counting time on the ground during stops. Smith believed he could do better. With an outwardly casual air, Smith climbed in an RA Monosport in Winston and told a man at the airport that he was going to New York for a few days. He went to New York but then lit out for Los Angeles in an attempt to break the cross-country speed record. He actually did so, with a time in the air of 28 hours and 5 minutes. However, because Smith hadn't bothered to have certified checkers present at takeoff and landing, the time was, alas, unofficial. Smith's feat didn't enter the record books. Some said that Smith's not having the checkers present was not simply an oversight; rather, it was a reflection of his obliviousness to all but what he wanted to do. He'd felt like breaking the record, so he attempted it, bettered the time, and that was that. He didn't really care who else knew about it. Flying buddies at the Winston airport must have tipped off the local paper, because its article on Smith's journey authoritatively said that his manner in this affair "was very symbolic of all his flying. Aviation is his hobby, but he never 'opens up,' conversationally, so far as his own experiences are concerned. When he is ready for a hop, he hops, but very seldom makes any previous announcement of where he is going or when he will be back."

Libby passed the early summer at Louisa Carpenter's house on Long Island, visiting with Bea Lillie, Irving Berlin, Ed Wynn, and the Bankhead girls, Tallulah and Eugenia. Eugenia, known as Sister, was also having an affair with Louisa. Smith flew up and took a cottage nearby, met Libby's friends, buzzed Louisa's home and boat with his plane. Libby and Louisa sailed for Europe. Smith followed them. Through private detectives he traced the women to where they were staying in Paris, then arrived on their doorstep. They took him along to clubs and parties of American expatriates.

All four Reynoldses, accompanied by various spouses and girl-friends, were in Europe that summer. Mary also had along, in her suitcase, millions of dollars' worth of stock and bond coupon books, entrusted to her care by the Baltimore bank. She had to clip and send in the coupons on time or the estate and the trusts wouldn't receive their quarterly dividend incomes. She tried to set up a family reunion in Berlin — "Couldn't we have a free-for-all in full force?" she wrote to Nancy. "I'm all excited about a good old drinking boute." It didn't work out.

Smith returned to the United States with a plan to unite the two passions of his life. For the first time, the shy young man would attempt to set an aviation record publicly. He would do what had never been done before: fly around the world. By circumnavigating the globe he hoped to catapult himself into that pantheon of adventuresome heroes currently occupied by Lindbergh and Admiral Richard Byrd. He searched for the right plane — an ordinary one wouldn't do — and to handle the publicity, he chose childhood chum "Slick" Shepherd, a fledgling reporter. Slick would write up the voyage and feed it to the papers. Smith would become a front-page hero, and that, at last, would make Libby take him seriously.

Precisely nine months and one week after her marriage Anne Cannon gave birth to a daughter, Anne Cannon II. From New York, Smith sent Anne a telegram of congratulations. Their divorce was not being pursued actively.

Smith begged Libby to forget Louisa and spend time with him

as he waited for the right plane and otherwise planned his journey. She told him to go away. Obedient as always to her whims, he did. For the remainder of the summer he occupied himself flying across the country, drinking and gambling in California and Colorado, calling Libby on the telephone.

In the fall, Smith was back in New York to see Libby open in *Three's a Crowd*. The producers had included the memorable "Body and Soul" expressly for her voice and sultry personality; singing it increased her stardom. Smith attended nearly every performance of the show, sitting on the aisle in the front row so he could slip in late or leave early. When the curtain fell Smith and Libby would take a gang of Broadway luminaries to Tony Soma's speakeasy in midtown or to The Yeah Man in Harlem. The conversation would sparkle with the wit of songwriters Howard Dietz and Arthur Schwartz, and *New Yorker* humorists Peter Arno and Robert Benchley. Smith would buy the drinks. He didn't say much — this wasn't his milieu — but he dreamed of making his mark and had told Libby of the great coup he was planning. For the moment, it was a secret they shared.

Libby continued her affair with Louisa. She told friends that men were beasts and that if she ever married it would be to someone sensitive, well mannered, and rich — but not to Smith Reynolds, although she also told friends that he had a secret treasure inside. Her pals thought Smith's only treasure was blatantly apparent; they judged him dull, sullen, and shy, a lapdog that Libby allowed to follow her around.

The comparison was partly true. Libby liked conquest — she often bragged of the men and women she'd bedded — and Smith was a very visible one. Further, once turned by Libby into a devoted admirer, he was neither threatening nor competitive, as were some of the more assertive men she encountered. The pair were seldom alone, but when they were, or during the endless telephone calls that Smith made to Libby, he importuned her to leave show business. His allowance from his guardians was unreasonably tight, a mere eighteen thousand dollars a year now — but he'd have money to burn when he turned twenty-one. She tried to make him understand that her career was going too well, that she had worked hard to get to this point and there was no sense stepping away from it when the rewards were finally coming her way. Smith had to admit the logic of her argument. That didn't make him like it, though.

Libby also saw Smith as a kind of insurance policy. One year after the crash, the country was solidly in the grip of the Depression. Entire industries were shutting down. Each Friday, another hundred thousand people got pink slips and joined the unemployed. When nightclubbers emerged into the dawn after hours of spending money as if the well would never run dry, they were greeted on the streets by apple sellers. For lack of an audience able to afford the luxury of entertainment, many Broadway shows closed. In such a climate, Libby felt it was a good idea to keep Smith around, if only on a back burner.

In late 1930 Dick Reynolds's continuing debate over his allowance escalated into a formal suit against nearly every living relative he had: Nancy, Mary, and their husbands; Smith; Anne Cannon; Abram's children; and various Lasaters, Critzes, and Lybrooks, as well as Uncle Will, Ed Johnston, and the Safe Deposit and Trust Company of Baltimore. At issue was the "two for one" provision of his father's will, which Dick believed to have been improperly administered. Dick's lawyers contended that the will said the offspring would be entitled to "two dollars for every one dollar earned or SAVED" and wanted to apply the clause to Dick's entire income. For example, they argued that from his birthday in 1928 to his birthday in 1929, he'd received from the trusts and his businesses a total of $215,000, against which he claimed $85,000 in expenses and taxes — and wanted the estate to pay him $2 for each of the $130,000 that he'd "saved" above his outgo! Dick actually won the case in the lower court, and judgments were entered against the trust for the years since 1928 for amounts averaging about $125,000 per year. On appeal, however, the award was reversed. Dick got nothing for his effort but legal bills. Within the family, there was no lasting bitterness about this suit; the elders considered it a nice try.

While Dick tried to get into the trust of the Reynolds millions by the back door, Mary went in through the front. Later in 1931 Mary made an arrangement with the guardians to obtain $320,000 from the trust, which she then lent to her husband, Charles Babcock, so he could buy into the brokerage firm established in 1928 and operated by cousin R. S. Reynolds. As with most brokerage houses in the aftermath of the 1929 crash, Reynolds & Company was teetering a bit. The new infusion of capital put it back on a sound financial footing; shortly, as the Depression deepened, the company flourished and began to buy up older firms. Babcock was soon more involved in the day-to-day management of the firm than R. S., whose interests lay primarily in metals.

In 1931 a national magazine profiled Winston-Salem and its hard-working rich people as "The Town of A Hundred Millionaires." The fortunes in textiles, furniture making, real estate, and insurance were said to have come from providing services to RJR or from ownership of its precious stock. The article described how RJR executives worth millions went to their offices in the new twenty-two-story Reynolds skyscraper at the crack of dawn, managed their domains with sleeves rolled up, led quiet lives, and were never ostentatious in the display of their wealth. At a party, an apocryphal story went, a visitor's Lucky Strikes were thrown away and Camels substituted; the guest then started taking off his shirt to change his offending underwear to Hanes — which got a hearty laugh from a millionaire's wife.

The article didn't mention that RJR stock was doing reasonably well even though cigarette consumption was down slightly in the midst of the Depression. Nor did it mention the playboy sons of R. J. Reynolds, who held, together, about fifty million dollars in RJR and other securities. However, since the magazine's readership would have been aware of Dick and Smith through the daily papers, the playboys were an unwritten presence in the article and in the readers' minds, the profligates against whom the more sober Winstonians were measured.

Winston-Salem didn't like the article. There weren't a hundred millionaires in town, people said, there were only fifty or sixty. Well, maybe seventy.

=

In the spring of 1931 Smith got the plane he wanted for his trip around the world. The Savoia-Marchetti amphibian was capable of a speed of 85 miles per hour and had a range of a thousand miles on a full tank of fuel. Its cost was rumored to be ninety thousand dollars but was probably half that; some of the money was possibly lent to Smith by Dick, since the guardians' records do not mention it. He may also have lowered the cost by convincing the Port Washington company that made the amphibian that there was publicity to be gained from his voyage. Gulf Oil was "contributing" fuel, and Dick's *Harpoon* would meet him along the way with spare parts.

The round-the-world journey was not quite that. For one thing, as with Smith's flight across the United States, it would be made in short hops, and the only time counted would be that actually spent in the air. For another, Smith would be traversing only the more or less contiguous land areas from the British Isles to the tip of Asia at Hong Kong. His route would follow the edge of the continents along southern Europe and northern Africa through the Middle East, India, the Indochinese peninsula, and the southern rim of Asia, a total distance of seventeen thousand miles. The across-the-seas aspect of the circumnavigation would be completed by boat. He and the plane would first travel to England aboard a ship and then become airborne. He'd dropped the idea of publicizing the venture daily in newspaper articles, but Smith planned to keep a carefully worded journal for later publication.

In June, just after *Three's a Crowd* closed, Libby told an interviewer the goals she hoped to attain in her life: acting in many dramatic roles, owning a villa in France, continually enriching her mind, writing poetry, being the hostess of a salon, and bearing a child. "I want at least one great love," she explained. "Maybe more, but no millionaires. I want a man who has achieved something in the arts. He must be more than my match in physical vitality and artistic achievements. You can say that I have not met a soul who qualifies."

Was Smith really out of the running? More likely, in this public way Libby was enforcing her domination of him through humiliation. In effect, she was telling Smith that in order to win her he'd have to make good on his promise to accomplish something.

While Libby stayed at Sands Point, Long Island, Smith rented a home nearby. Though there is no conclusive evidence, it seems likely that this was the moment when they began their sexual relationship, Libby possibly going to bed with him to make up for what she'd said in the interview.

That summer on Long Island, Smith had a roommate, Ab Walker, a friend since childhood, the son of a middle-class Winston family. Ab was not particularly brainy or cultured, but he was attractive in his own way, both to men and women. He was a drinking buddy, a "good old boy" who hung around Smith for lack of anything better to do and perhaps because Smith paid for everything.

People who knew both Smith and Ab suggest the possibility of a homosexual relationship between them, which may have been initiated during boarding school and been masked by liquor and the idea that what happened while drunk was excusable. Modern psychologists have written that the lack of a father's affection and an overbearing mother are often conditions that contribute to homosexual tendencies in men. R. J. had died when Smith was six, and after R. J.'s death Katharine alternated in her behavior toward her children between the extremes of strictness and absence. People acquainted with Ab in later life were convinced he had eventually become bisexual; whether he had been so when younger no one was ever willing to say. There is no conclusive evidence of homosexuality on the part of either Ab or Smith. However, during that summer on Long Island, there was no doubt that Smith's closeness to Ab was fueled by Libby's continuing liaison with Louisa Carpenter. Louisa's father's yacht, a 137-footer, was anchored off Sands Point. Louisa, Libby, the Bankhead girls, and Libby's sister cruised up and down Long Island Sound for a week, without Smith — or Ab, whom they had also met and professed to tolerate.

Libby did spend some time with Smith. They had a few trysts as well as several quarrels. As their intimacy increased, so did Smith's jealousy. Finding Louisa at Libby's house one afternoon, Smith raised a ruckus, then left and drove his car into the ocean.

On another occasion, when Libby had been invited to a party at Bea Lillie's and he hadn't, Smith drove hurriedly to the airfield. Tears in his eyes, he told instructor Peter Bonetti that Bea Lillie was trying to break up his romance with Libby and that he was going to end it all by flying into the ocean. Before Bonetti could object, Smith took off over the Atlantic. The instructor waited seven hours until, long after dark, Smith returned. Bonetti had known Smith in Winston-Salem and thought that in this instance Smith had been lucky — he had almost run out of fuel, and, flying over the ocean, any minor engine problem that cropped up would have caused him to ditch far away from land and probably would have killed him.

Was he really trying to kill himself, or was he just letting off steam? Yes, Smith did put himself in a situation that could have been life-threatening, but actually he did no more than worry his parent of the moment. Most people who are truly intent on committing suicide don't do it halfheartedly. Smith was an excellent pilot; as his long-distance hops showed, he knew his machines and their tolerances very well. Had he wanted to die in the air, he wouldn't have turned back with enough fuel to make it home. The same understanding must be applied to Smith's prep school suicide notes: they were no more serious than those of hundreds of other young men in the grip of raging hormonal changes, teenagers who felt despondent at one point but never carried through on a suicide threat. In the case of Smith, these notes were construed as significant only later, after his tragic death.

Libby later reported that other incidents had taken place that summer. She told of Smith's sometimes sleeping underneath a bed and leaving a dummy on top. Hearing footsteps, he would lurk about with a pistol, which Libby begged him to put away. Once he fired off the gun accidentally in her house. Another time, when he was with Libby in the back room and heard people talking in the front, Smith jumped out the rear window and ran two miles to get the police; of course, the authorities found nothing. He did these odd things, Libby said afterward, because he was petrified of being kidnapped for his money.

It is important to recognize that many of these stories about Smith, for which Libby Holman's later testimony is the only source, must be taken with a grain of salt. For example, Smith had been around firearms since childhood and habitually carried guns or kept them handy. Then, too, police reports of the gunshot incident and the suspected prowlers have never been found. Further, Libby's recollections of Smith's fear of kidnapping were first heard in the period just after the spectacular kidnapping of Charles Lindbergh's baby; at the time that Smith was supposed to have feared kidnappers, this phobia was not yet part of the public's consciousness.

Smith was about to leave on his voyage when he filed a will in New York. It divided his share of R. J.'s estate into three parts — for Mary, Nancy, and Dick — and left five specific bequests, of which the largest by far was fifty thousand dollars for Ab. Curiously, the will made no provision for Libby. The document seemed to have more in common with the division of his property in his adolescent suicide notes than it did with a will of a mature individual.

Five days later Smith bade farewell to Libby (who was enmeshed in rehearsals for a road tour of *Three's a Crowd*), taxied the Savoia-Marchetti alongside the Cunard liner *Berengaria*, and had a derrick haul the plane aboard as part of his baggage. If this was unusual, these were hard times, and the *Berengaria*, which had acquired the nickname of the Bargain-Area because of a lack of passengers, was only too glad to comply with a rich man's wish and bill him accordingly.

In London, while obtaining the permits necessary for an international flight, Smith came down with the flu. He wrote despondent letters to Libby:

> I would gladly come home if you were not going on with the show.
>
> I'll gladly give up this trip or anything I have to devote all my time to you, if you would do the same for me. If I get to the point where I simply cannot stand it without you for another minute, well, there's the old Mauser with a few cartridges in it.
>
> I guess I've had my inning. . . . It's time another team went to bat.

With this letter, Smith's repeated attempts at suicide become clearer: they were a form of emotional blackmail, a sort of "I'll give up my life for you if you won't give up your work for me." Libby was so tough a nut for Smith to crack that he had to resort to the ultimate threat of killing himself in order to obtain whatever affection he could from her.

The transitory nature of his threats was apparent as he pursued other women. In Paris, with Sister Bankhead, Smith wasn't so desperate. They bent elbows at Chez Florence; she called him Myth because he was sloppily romantic and intrigued by legend. He proposed marriage but she laughed — both of them were already married, not to mention her known homosexuality. They hatched a plan: he'd fly over from London and pick up her mother's silver, take it to Hong Kong on the plane and thence back to the States as a surprise for the family. He started out but never showed up, cabling her, "Plane sank. Love, Myth."

Actually, the plane was okay, but the flu had aggravated an old weakness, which developed into a mastoid infection. Smith decided he must return to New York for surgery. The world could wait; he would fly around it when he felt better. Aboard the *Leviathan* Smith met Nancy Hoyt, a much-married older woman who wrote romantic novels; her brother was then the husband of Sister Bankhead. Smith and Nancy Hoyt had a shipboard affair during which, she later averred, Smith never mentioned Libby, although he did report that he was already married. So was she. They plotted to get divorces and then hitch up.

When the boat landed in New York, however, the affair ended, at least in Smith's mind. He was again in Libby's orbit, and she was, at last, responding to him. After his surgery, she agreed to fly down to Reynolda with him for a long weekend. She'd never made that much of a time commitment to him before. In the air, of course, he was in complete command, and she a helpless passenger. Just before landing at the Winston airport, Smith circled the thousand-acre Reynolda estate, hoping it would impress Libby. It did. She showed her gratitude — and her own power — by singing "Moanin' Low" for a dinner party at the edge of Lake Katharine and wowing Smith's friends. At the end of the weekend Libby went back to her show tour, for which she was receiving reduced wages because the Depression had sapped much of the potential audience. As she sang for her supper in the boondocks, Smith flew Anne Cannon to Reno to complete the divorce proceedings.

Anne, ill, stayed at Cornelius Vanderbilt, Jr.'s, dude ranch, where she could avoid publicity. All had agreed to a settlement in which she and her daughter would receive $100,000 now and trust funds of $500,000 each when Smith reached the age of twenty-eight. In the depositions, Anne said Smith used foul language that made her "terribly nervous and upset," and he avowed that the cause of the marital split was that "she likes big parties [and] I like small parties." If society needed reasons to dissolve an early, ill-considered marriage, these would do.

While Smith was in Reno, Libby was reported as having a brief fling with another young heir, in Chicago. This occasioned the now usual calls, missives, and suicide threats from Smith, this time reminding Libby that he was getting divorced from Anne to marry her.

Smith's divorce seems to have removed the last rationale Libby could muster for refusing to marry him. He had shown that he didn't want to cramp her style, that he would tolerate a certain level of infidelity and allow her to remain on the stage if she wished to do so. Besides that, his riches would always be there if she flopped or decided to retire. And in the early 1930s there were no surefire hit shows on the horizon.

Also, she was beginning to paint him in her mind as her very own romantic hero, about to dare something never done before — for her. She told a friend that Smith was "like an arid surface in which a geyser suddenly springs up." Nobody quite knew what that meant. Libby whispered to Smith about her accompanying him on the plane, but — darn it, darling — she couldn't get released from her road-tour contract. He'd have to go it alone.

As for Smith, he considered marriage to her the equivalent of winning a prize no other man had been able to carry off. By marrying the sexiest woman in America he would prove himself as a man.

On November 23, 1931, the divorce decree came through; Anne left Vanderbilt's ranch on a stretcher to obtain treatment in the Midwest for what they told the press was rheumatoid arthritis. It may well have been exhaustion or alcoholism. Two days later Smith met Libby in Toledo, Ohio, and they drove to a small town in Michigan, the only state where a minor could be married without his guardians' consent. Smith and Libby were married by a justice of the peace in his parlor. Their marriage license was marked "Do not publish," and they took delight in the secrecy of their union.

They stayed together one night. By December 1, Libby was back on her road tour, and Smith watched the Savoia-Marchetti plane being hauled aboard a ship for the third time. She was the S. S. *Paris*, bound for England. The fly-boy and his songstress vowed to meet at the Repulse Bay Hotel, in Hong Kong, on April 1, 1932, to celebrate the successful completion of his daring deed and to enjoy a proper honeymoon.

This, then, was the beginning for Smith of a private, unwitnessed, and, for a long time, unreported adventure. It was a great and wonderful exploit, though it did not always smack of the derring-do that he construed as necessary to such feats and for which he had yearned. Flying by compass, landmarks, and the seat of his pants, Smith piloted his plane across and around dozens of countries. There were forced landings, near-misses. His foot nearly froze in cold air. The plane almost went under in a high Swiss lake. He came close to being jailed a couple of times, contracted yellow fever in Egypt, and was all but stranded in Afghanistan and Thailand.

At nearly every stop the plane had to be repaired before it could get into the air again; Smith, who held a mechanic's license, learned to coax the most from his machinery.

Every day was a challenge. He flew fifty to one hundred feet above deserts, which threw sand in the propeller and engine, or at treetop level over trackless jungles where a sudden downdraft could have meant the end. He followed railroad spurs and rivers where there were no roads, skittered low through narrow valley passes because he didn't have the oxygen or cabin heating to go over the adjoining mountains. Through caution and pluck in the air and charm on the ground when he needed a spare part or a square meal, Smith worked his way east toward China. It was a tremendous journey. He was a boy of just twenty when he began, but at the end of the hop he was surely a man.

Unfortunately for him, Smith's handwritten, sixty-page diary doesn't truly reflect the hair-raising nature of his trip nor how often he cheated death. So intent was he on his task that nearly every line he wrote contains a comment on a technical matter — the myriad problems, how he went about convincing people to help him fashion spare parts, the devilry of the weather. All the hindrances were treated in a matter-of-fact way. Smith held on tightly to his emotions, as if keeping out of his notes and his consciousness his joy, sorrow, excitement, hate, and longing, lest such things overwhelm the pages and him. Nonetheless, some sentiments came through: the Taj Mahal by moonlight was so beautiful that he had to stop "raving on and on" about it. He wondered how the RAF lads at Basra got by without wives during their two-year tours of duty; surely it was "unhealthy" without women. Upon reaching a milestone stop, "I proceeded to get a little tight. . . . It has been a long time since I have seen much of anybody." He was amazed by the great statues of Buddha in Burma, by a fortune-teller in India, by the streetful of ugly prostitutes in Tunis, by camel rides and elephants, by the enthusiasm of the maharajah of Jodhpur for flying, by the occasional friendliness of people whom he met at points along the way and who knew him as a daring flyer and not as heir to a fortune.

After a ride in a hollowed-out log across a river in Indochina, Smith passed a sleepless night: "I was so near to my destination. All at once thoughts came to me that had been squelched for months. Though so near, I still had to be careful."

Libby sailed from the United States in late February and arrived in Hong Kong on April 1. There, everything was wrong. War had begun between China and Japan, so the town was full of Chinese soldiers. An outbreak of influenza had hit the colony. The Repulse Bay Hotel hadn't heard from Smith Reynolds. She wandered around town, located an old acquaintance, and befriended a waif who fleeced tourists.

Smith knew he was late and sent a telegram from Hanoi, but it got lost. On April 4, he made the hop from Haiphong to Fort-Bayard (present-day Chanchiang, China) but almost ditched and had to lighten the plane by throwing things overboard. On landing at Fort-Bayard he discovered that the engine was shot and that he wouldn't be able to take off again without extensive repairs — an overhaul that could not be done on the spot. He'd been stopped cold on the very last leg. After sending a cable addressed to Libby in Hong Kong, he hitched a ride on a Gulf Oil steamer 270 miles to the Crown Colony.

Libby's waif told her that an American fly-boy had come into the bay on a boat and that she should go see him. Afraid it wouldn't be Smith, she disguised herself in a coolie hat and traveled by junk out into the bay. Smith was indeed there, in a white suit, standing on board the Gulf Oil ship — but neither recognized the other. Later, at the dock, Smith and Libby were reunited.

Smith was completely manic. He embraced Libby passionately in public and told her that while civilians weren't permitted to carry cameras or pistols in Hong Kong, he had both with him. He pulled them out of his pockets and waved them around. Having flown around the world and married the sexiest woman in it, he could do anything, break any law; nothing could stop him! She had never seen him so happy, so self-assured, so attractive.

For two weeks in Hong Kong, Smith and Libby took a hedonistic joyride: gambling in Macao, dancing in hotel ballrooms, smoking opium on Pok Fulam. At times Smith was self-assured and Libby found him — for once — very sexy. But when Libby made herself alluring to other men or when Smith himself got too drunk, he lashed out at her and she answered back in kind. It was the first two weeks they'd ever spent alone together, and it was a roller coaster of a honeymoon.

=

While Smith and Libby were still in Hong Kong, he began to believe that because he hadn't completed those last 270 miles by air, his adventurous voyage had failed and he was not a hero. This notion was a disservice to the risks he'd taken and the things he'd accomplished. Properly packaged for public consumption, an account of his journey might well have made Smith a hero in the public's mind — but he wasn't one in his own. He put his journal away, didn't allow Slick Shepherd to write any articles, and otherwise maintained silence about his long trip. Whether Smith's belief in his failure was exacerbated by Libby's attitude is impossible to say; however, it is clear that the honeymoon phase of their relationship faded during the latter part of their weeks in Hong Kong.

They retrieved the plane from Fort-Bayard and had it hauled onto the *Empress of Russia*. Aboard the ship in Hong Kong harbor, two days before departure, Smith locked Libby in their stateroom and went ashore alone. When he came back, they fought. She made vicious remarks about his occasional impotence. His weapon was the Mauser, with which he once again threatened suicide. They came to a compromise: for one year, she would give up the theater and devote herself to him; in return, he would do everything in his power to make her happy.

They landed in British Columbia. Libby went on ahead to New York, and Smith followed. Because of a mix-up in registering at a hotel, the newspapers learned that Smith and Libby were married and besieged them for interviews. In response, the pair drove through the night from New York to North Carolina and on the afternoon of June 6, 1932, arrived at Reynolda for what both hoped would be an extended stay.

The Smith Reynoldses had the magnificent estate to themselves. Mary and Nancy were off having babies and furnishing apartments; Dick was cruising toward Dakar, Senegal, the best place to have the *Harpoon*'s deck retarred; Uncle Will was harness racing on the circuit and was out of town. At Reynolda, Smith could relax, surrounded by servants like Pluma Walker, who'd known him since his infancy and understood his needs.

The question in everyone's mind was how long the new Mrs. Reynolds would be diverted by the charms of the estate. Smith and Libby swam together in the spring-fed pool, had picnics by Lake Katharine, picked out bouquets from the formal gardens, rode horses along the miles of trails. Smith offered to teach her to fly, but that was his talent and she didn't want to learn. When the servants were asleep, Smith curled himself inside the dumbwaiter and went down to the kitchen to fix them a snack.

For their sleeping quarters the couple spread out over several bedrooms along the entire east end of the second floor; when it was hot they spent the night in a double bed on the breeze-cooled porch at the end of the wing. Libby had closets so large she couldn't fill them. To change outfits she simply stepped out of one and put on another; a maid would come along and pick up after her.

They quarreled. They had passionate patchings up. They made an adjustment to their shipboard compact: both would take lessons, Libby from Blanche Yurka, who would stay for a while at Reynolda to prepare Libby for dramatic roles, and Smith from recent New York University graduate Ray Kramer, who would also live in and tutor Smith to enter NYU's aeronautical engineering program in the fall.

As weeks passed, there was more tinkering with the arrangement. He entertained his friends, she brought hers down from New York for weekends and had her parents visit from Cincinnati. Alfred and Rachel Holman came in the Cord roadster Smith and Libby had given them for Christmas. Smith had never met the Holmans, and some people later thought him dismayed to discover that they were Jewish.

Smith's friends — Ab Walker, Charley Hill, Fat Charlie Norfleet, and the other fly-boys — found Libby exotic and glamorous. She didn't mind them hanging around; she liked to fascinate men. She also didn't mind singing for Aunt Maxie or for other associates of Smith's long-dead mother who would drop by Reynolda to hear her. Smith didn't like her singing "his" songs for other people. However, since he'd promised to make her happy and knew she loved performing, he endured it.

His fortitude was taxed by Libby's friends from New York, a bunch of whom seemed to arrive almost every weekend. The most frequent visitors were the suave Clifton Webb, actresses Bea Lillie and Spring Byington, and his old nemesis, Louisa Carpenter. In his own home Smith was a reasonably gracious host, and when he couldn't take their banter he'd wander outside.

Most of the time, Smith and Libby kept their sets of friends apart. However, on one occasion a flagrantly homosexual companion of Clifton Webb's tried to embrace Smith's pal Jim Baggs; later, as Smith and Jim stood apart from the Broadway crowd, Smith confessed to Baggs that he'd gotten in over his head with these "fairyish folk." During this period, Smith's North Carolina buddies found him moody and sullen, increasingly retreating into shy silence and drink. When Webb, Lillie, and actress Peggy Fears arrived for a repeat stay at Reynolda, upon entering the bungalow from the porte cochere they came upon Smith, obviously drunk, hanging over the balcony above the fireplace and the enormous living room. To the applause of Smith's drinking companions, strewn about on the couches and sofas, he was shooting out the crystals of the grand chandelier. The Broadway sophisticates turned on their collective heel and entrained back to the more civilized streets of Manhattan.

In quieter moments, when Smith and Libby were alone, he'd convey the fear that, unable to keep up intellectually with her friends, or unable to make her happy emotionally or sexually, he'd never manage to hold her here at Reynolda. Libby tried to allay his doubts with assurances and embraces, but her restlessness with rustic life was as apparent to him as it was to their many visitors. He was no dummy; he could see that Libby's actions didn't square with her promises. For example, she'd agreed not to go back on the stage, but then her agent and manager, Walter Batchelor, came down to discuss a Czech play that Blanche wanted Libby to star in. Smith wandered in and out of their initial reading. Libby's part was that of a prostitute who seduces a young married man and gets him to divorce his first wife and marry her. She then continues to sleep with lovers; when one of the lovers discovers her in bed with the new husband, he murders the husband. Then the ex-prostitute becomes embroiled in making the murder look like an accident.

Aside from the odd foreshadowing that the murder and cover-up in this play represented, there were many aspects of the drama that must have struck Smith like a slap in the face. When he'd first met Libby he had been a married man, and she had continued to see lovers long after the time when he had emotionally committed himself to her. The play implied that she would continue to sleep with lovers. Smith's reaction was quick in coming. That evening, over coffee in the great living room, the guests examined the Reynolds family Bible; in it there was a notation next to Smith's name saying that he'd been born on Sunday morning, November 5, 1911, at ten minutes after five o'clock. Smith picked up a pen and wrote in the Bible, alongside the mention of his birth, "And died of old age shortly thereafter." This was another mock suicide threat — the only communication, Smith knew, that made Libby sit up and take notice. It worked again. In front of the company, Libby screamed about tempting fate. "You take everything so seriously, darling," Smith said, laughing and putting his arm around her. For once he'd won a round.

During the second reading of the Czech play, held in the wood-paneled library next afternoon, Smith plopped down alongside the bathing-suited Libby. She lay down with her head on his knee; Smith put his hand on her bare thigh; she removed it. "You shrank from me," he accused. They quarreled.

Telling Libby that he was going to talk tomorrow to a doctor about "seeing things that aren't true," such as her recoiling from his touch, Smith then headed downtown, accompanied by Ab Walker and a full bottle of bootleg Scotch. At the Robert E. Lee Hotel, Ab registered them under his name. They spent the night drinking, talking, and having sex with two prostitutes. Before morning Smith convinced Ab to leave his 18-cent-an-hour job and work as Smith's personal secretary for $125 a week plus board and residence in Smith's old room down the hall from the newlyweds at Reynolda.

In the morning Smith and Ab went to the airport to see Smith's plane, which was being outfitted with landing lights and radio gear; then Smith returned to Reynolda and apologized to Libby for the previous evening's uproar. The couple agreed to throw a party the next night, July 5, to celebrate Charley Hill's twenty-first birthday. Ab was sent to buy moonshine. Invitations went out to twenty people. Some were away; others were unable to persuade parents to let them attend what was expected to be a wild evening at Reynolda.

Eleven people gathered on the concrete patio of the boathouse on the bank of Lake Katharine on the evening of July 5, 1932. It was a warm night; basic drinks were corn liquor, home-brewed beer, and White Rock soda water. Besides Smith, Libby, Ab, and Blanche, the guests were fly-boys Hill (who'd competed with Smith and was Anne Cannon's cousin), Lew McGinnes (Dick's pilot), and Fat Charlie Norfleet (also head of the trust department of the local bank). Charley Hill brought Virginia Dunklee (a classmate and good friend of both Mary and Nancy Reynolds); Jim Shepherd (Slick's cousin), who owned an art gallery, brought tall twenty-eight-year-old widow Babe Collier Vaught, who worked at a downtown department store. Tagging along was Billy Shaw Howell, a radio salesman who'd flown in the Great War.

The young men mixed their own drinks from a bar while Pluma Walker served the canapés and other servants walked back and forth with extra supplies along the hundred yards or so that separated the patio and the colonnaded rear portico of the bungalow. The guests could see that Smith and Libby weren't really talking. After having spent a weekend with her agent and drama coach, Libby now had to be the hostess of a party for boys and girls, some of whom had had to ask their parents' permission to come to the house where the wicked lady of Broadway reigned. Libby chatted with the only other mature woman, Babe Vaught. Babe not only worked — which set her apart from most of the others — but she also had a tangled past, which included a husband who'd died. Babe and Libby had a drinking contest. Shot glasses of 100-proof corn liquor were poured into the home brew to make "divebombers," and the trick was to drink down the concoction before the liquor settled to the bottom of the beer glass. The other men may have applauded and urged on the two women, but Smith didn't like this display, Pluma Walker noted; she could tell because he said nothing and just nursed one beer. Having attended Smith since childhood, Pluma recognized the outward signs of his anger: the retreat into his shell, the refusal to speak about his discomfort, the inability to eat.

By 7:30, Babe and Libby were extremely drunk, trying to sing together, laughing, knocking things over. Smith whispered angrily to Libby, but she brushed him off.

Though Ab changed into his bathing trunks, he didn't go into the water. Libby, in a white flannel lounging suit, flirted openly with Ab. Smith propelled her up the slope toward the bungalow, where they had a quarrel. After it, Libby disappeared for several hours. During her absence, Smith told Ab that he wasn't accusing his friend of untoward behavior; Ab said, surprised, that he hadn't done anything.

Ab searched the grounds for Libby and reported that he couldn't find her. As they waited, Smith became quieter. After several more hours of desultory drinking by the guests, at about 11:30 most of them left; Smith told McGinnes to be sure to have the new landing lights on the plane checked so he could take it up next evening. Blanche Yurka went to bed. Jim Shepherd carried Babe Vaught up the Reynolda staircase to a second-floor room where she could sleep off the booze.

A half hour after midnight, as watchman W. E. Fulcher ate a

sandwich while he sat on his car, which was parked at the back of the bungalow, he saw Libby walking unsteadily up the slope. To Fulcher, she seemed drunk. She had grass stains on the knees of her white pajama outfit. Fulcher's dog made some noise, and Ab came out and joined Libby as she walked the last part of the way to the columned back entrance. As Smith went to the door to meet them, he saw his friend and his wife stumbling forward. Libby grinned at him, and he grimly took her inside.

In the living room, probably in front of Shepherd and Ab, as well as Smith, Libby disrobed, dropping her pajamas on the floor in a deliberate, provocative gesture. Smith hurried her upstairs to Ab's bedroom, which was down the hall from their own.

Why Ab's room? Later testimony by reliable witnesses begins to get fuzzy at just this point, but the likely explanation is that Smith wished to confront Libby with the fact that some of her clothes were under Ab's bed. Below, in the living room, Ab and Shepherd heard a loud argument between Smith and Libby. Discretion being the better part of valor, Shepherd decided to leave Reynolda, borrowing Ab's car to do so. The plan was for him to return in the morning and fetch Babe Vaught home at that time.

About what happened next there remains to this day great confusion. There were six people left in the bungalow after Shepherd left and watchman Fulcher had resumed his rounds. Babe Vaught and tutor Ray Kramer, who were in close proximity to the event, later said that they were asleep through it all, and Blanche Yurka would always claim that she slept through most of it. That leaves Smith, Libby, and Ab. In considering the following tale, we must continually take into account that what was later said by Libby and Ab — and by many of the other people who were at the party that night — may have been biased by their own possible culpability.

According to Ab Walker, after the altercation Smith came downstairs and told Ab that their proposed round-the-world trip as well as Ab's secretarial job were canceled because he was going outside to "end it all." Ab understood him to be in despair over the marriage. Smith tossed Ab his wallet and implied Ab could keep its contents in lieu of a week's wages. Because he wore only a pocketless bathing suit, Ab took the wallet upstairs and wedged it into a sofa. He did not go outside and try to prevent his friend's suicide; moments later, Smith came back in and walked up to the sleeping porch.

There was an argument from the east wing. Blanche said she heard voices, awoke, and asked Ab over the railing what was going on. Ab told her he was closing up the house. She went back to bed. After even more loud but unintelligible voices from upstairs, Ab heard what he thought but couldn't be sure was a single, muffled gunshot. Blanche came out of her room and said, over the balcony to Ab, that she'd heard someone scream. Libby emerged from the east wing, wearing a peach-colored negligee, yelling Ab's name. He rushed up the stairs; she collapsed on the hall settee, saying, "Smith, Smith shot himself." Ab ran into the sleeping porch and discovered the unconscious Smith facedown on the bed, blood seeping from a head wound. Ab raced down the back stairs, phoned for an ambulance, and then, before it could arrive, decided to drive Smith to the hospital himself. With minimal assistance from the women, Ab dragged Smith down the stairs, out the entrance, and into Libby's green Cadillac. Ab drove, Libby was next to him, and Smith's body lay in the backseat next to Blanche as they sped four miles to the Baptist Hospital. When Smith was wheeled into the operating theater, Libby was shown to a private room. Ab attended her there.

From this point on, we have some less involved witnesses. The stories they told — some in the wake of the event, others not until decades later — cast doubt on the idea of a simple suicide. Nurse Ruby Jenkins came into Libby's private room and overheard Ab instruct Libby not to talk to anyone about anything. They asked Jenkins to leave and she did, but a bit later, hearing a thud, Jenkins came back in and saw Ab and Libby on the floor together, having just fallen out of bed. Both were practically nude, Ab in his bathing suit and Libby in a skimpy negligee. "Oh, my baby," Libby said. "What do you mean by that?" Ab asked. "Don't you know that I'm going to have a baby?" Jenkins heard Libby say before the door was closed on her. The fall could have been two inebriated people taking a tumble, but reports persist that the couple had been sexually entwined before ending up on the floor.

In the hospital, Ab neglected to call the police but did get two of Smith's relatives on the phone, guardian Ed Lasater and cousin by marriage J. T. Barnes. When they came to the hospital Ab told them he wanted to go to Reynolda to clear the place of illegal liquor before the police searched it. In the meantime, at the estate, Fulcher and manager Stewart Warnken met the ambulance driver, who was annoyed at having to come out to Reynolda and then finding no one to take back to the hospital.

At this point Warnken and Fulcher didn't know anyone had been shot; Fulcher thought Smith might have gone to town, as he often did at late hours. In the downstairs living room the men found a half-empty gallon jug of corn liquor, bottles of gin and whiskey, glasses with booze in them — and Libby's lounging pajamas. On the sleeping porch they saw blood; Fulcher then remembered having heard a single shot, which he had supposed was just Smith shooting out the crystals in the chandelier again. Now he looked for a gun and couldn't find one on the porch.

At three in the morning, Barnes and Warnken made a second search of the sleeping porch. No gun. Ab, who had come back to Reynolda from the hospital, bringing the news that Smith had been shot, now told the men that he wanted to change out of his bathing suit. While Ab showered and put on a shirt and pants, they searched the sleeping porch for a third time. Still no gun. The men went downstairs. Fifteen minutes later Ab rejoined them, fully dressed, and handed them Smith's empty wallet. As they all rode back to the hospital, Barnes wondered aloud where the gun was, and Ab said it was on the sleeping porch. If this sounded suspicious, they didn't immediately act on it. After all, Ab was Smith's best friend, it looked like a suicide — and, most important, should Smith recover, it would be best if the Reynolds family's basic privacy were not violated by any shocking stories. Thus, the main elements of a cover-up of what had actually happened to Smith were already in place while he lay dying.

Bob Critz, another Reynolds cousin, also a flyer, was at the hospital when Ab returned with Barnes and Warnken. At 5:25 in the morning, the doctors came out with bad news. From the moment Smith had been brought into the hospital with a bullet in his brain, all that the doctors could do was make him comfortable. Now, at age twenty, Zachary Smith Reynolds was dead. Critz reported his death to the police; the doctors signed a certificate listing the cause of death as suicide.

Chapter Ten

The Mystery

AN HOUR after Smith's death, still near dawn on July 6, the Mauser was found lying on the carpet of the sleeping porch, three feet from the bed. When Ab Walker returned to the estate, Bob Critz accused him, saying, "Ab, I don't believe you're telling everything you know." Ab replied that "there is something I'm going to take to my grave." He didn't say what it was, and Critz got nothing more out of him.

Sheriff Transou Scott talked to him, and Ab contended that Smith had committed suicide after talking about it for weeks because, "well, the truth of the matter is, Smith just thought too much of that woman." Scott tried to interview "that woman" right then and there, but family members said she was too distraught. Scott felt powerless at Reynolda to override their concern; after all, these were the Reynoldses! The sheriff fumed as Ab went upstairs and had a one-hour unobserved conversation with Libby.

At a respectable time of the morning, guardian Ed Lasater, senior member of the Reynolds clan present in Winston-Salem, told the gathered press that Smith's death was a suicide. Mary and Nancy, who arrived later by plane, and Uncle Will, who came in by train from Cleveland, concurred in this verdict, though all said they knew no reason Smith would have wanted to kill himself. A spokesman released a statement suggesting that since R. J.'s will had made no mention of the spouses of his children, Libby would probably not inherit anything from the estate. Security guards were hired to keep outsiders from entering Reynolda; the family did not want its private grief on display for the curious.

Later in the day, Blanche Yurka and Charley Hill took a sequestered horseback ride on the Reynolda grounds. During the ride, Hill later said, Yurka informed him that no one would ever tell exactly what had happened on the night Smith was shot.

The coroner convened an inquest. In North Carolina, such inquests were to be held as soon as possible after the death, as near to the point of death as practical, and the oath was to be administered to jurors in the presence of the dead man. Accordingly, the day after Smith died, six male jurors were sworn in next to Smith's casket at Reynolda. The jurors had a brief wait while the family held a funeral service at the house, and then Smith's body was taken by hearse to the old Salem cemetery, where it was buried next to R. J and Katharine. During these ceremonies, Libby cried uncontrollably and Ab fainted.

The inquest began the following morning (that is, two days after Smith's death) in Smith and Libby's bedroom in the east wing. From their folding chairs the jurors could see the sleeping porch where the fatal event had taken place. Maids and police investigators had moved objects from their previous spots on the porch, pinned up draperies, and outlined stains on the carpet. On this first day of the inquest, a legal ruse kept reporters away from the proceedings — which only added to the confusion and mystery.

Dr. Fred Hanes, who examined Smith at the hospital, described the path of the bullet (from upper right temple to an exit point below the left ear) and a contusion the size of a "small orange." He concluded the shot had been fired at point-blank range.

Dr. Alexander Cox, a young intern who had ministered to Smith before Hanes, felt later, on reviewing the inquest, that Hanes either lied or just hadn't understood the situation medically. As Cox told Jon Bradshaw, author of a recent book about Libby Holman, he was certain that the bullet had traveled from left to right and that the gun had been fired from a distance of more than eighteen inches from Smith's head. The differences in the accounts were significant, yet either interpretation made simple suicide unlikely. Smith was a left-handed shot, so a self-inflicted wound would almost certainly not have followed a right-to-left path. And if Dr. Cox was correct, a man attempting suicide wouldn't hold the gun eighteen inches from his head. Both of these things argued for a verdict of something other than suicide and might have occasioned quite a stir had they been made public at the time — but they weren't. Cox was not summoned to the inquest, and he didn't volunteer information. Dr. Hanes was, after all, from one of the town's leading families, and it wouldn't do for a lowly intern to contradict him.

The questions asked of Ab Walker in the first session of the inquest indicated that the coroner had been apprised by Sheriff Scott of his serious misgivings about Ab's version of events. Referring to Ab's conversations with Scott and Critz, the inquiry gave Ab occasion to deny having said he'd take a secret to his grave, or having wanted to put the house back in order before police arrived, or having told anyone that the gun was on the sleeping porch when three previous searches hadn't located it. Ab said he didn't know why Libby's slippers were under his bed or why her sweater was in his bathroom. After eliciting these responses, the questioners didn't try to shake Ab's testimony, perhaps because they planned to recall Ab after others had made their statements.

Blanche Yurka gave the panel a series of lies. No one had been drunk. Libby and Smith were deeply in love. The apparent suicide stemmed from "some utterly unexplainable impulse." Discrepancies between Blanche's recounting of events and Ab's also went unremarked. It soon became obvious that no one who had been at the party that evening would give a clear and detailed picture of what occurred.

The negligee-clad Libby was questioned as she lay in her bed, while her lawyer father held her hand. Libby's story was the most blatantly blank of all. She claimed not to be able to recall the entire day and night before Smith's death:

> The last thing I remember is Monday night. . . . The next thing I remember, and it is just a flash, is hearing my name called and looking up and seeing Smith with the revolver at his head, and then a shot, and after that I don't remember anything. . . . I have this feeling that Smitty was in my arms and I felt this blood, but it is a haze, it is blurred.

After hearing this amazing non-story, the questioners neither scoffed nor demanded details that would substantiate Libby's claim of amnesia. She was presumed to be in a state of shock; fortunately for her, this was still the era when women were allowed to faint in the presence of terrible things so that later they would not have to speak of them. Libby also threw sand in her questioners' eyes by mentioning that she'd missed her period on June 25 and was, she felt, very probably pregnant.

The mention of her pregnancy, though not made public at this time, made an impact on the Reynoldses. Just as the surviving child of Katharine Reynolds Johnston and Ed Johnston had been a legal heir to the family fortune, so this unborn child could be a legitimate claimant to Smith's portion of the Reynolds millions. Instantly, Stratton Coyner and other lawyers began to riffle through Smith's legal papers, looking for a will, and through law books, seeking precedents on which to defend the family's millions.

Forsyth County solicitor Carlisle Higgins adjourned the inquest until the morning. Blanche, Libby, and Ab were to be held as material witnesses, the ladies at Reynolda and Ab in the county jail. Upon hearing of Ab's potential incarceration, Mary Babcock and Nancy Bagley interceded with Higgins, and Ab was allowed to spend the night under guard at the Robert E. Lee, where the accommodations were more comfortable and the food was tastier. Their indulgence toward Ab was consistent with what they told the press representatives outside the Reynolda gates early the next day: the family "felt like it was suicide."

By this time, around twenty-five reporters, including those from the wire services and the New York, Cincinnati, and North Carolina papers, were petitioning state courts to let them into the inquest. Many top crime reporters had just left the Lindbergh baby kidnapping story. Slick Shepherd, not deemed experienced enough to write of the death of his friend, was doing spadework for the United Press. The angry reporters harassed cars entering the estate, demanding to know who the occupants were. Family members found this especially upsetting. In Winston, Reynoldses were used to deference from the press.

On Saturday, July 9, the family, the jurors, and authorities — but no reporters — heard Ab change his story and omit having been in the sleeping porch at any time before carrying Smith from it. Again, no one pointed out the discrepancy between this and his earlier avowal. Warnken said unequivocally that Ab had been alone on the porch just before the search that had finally turned up the gun.

Another Reynolda employee said it was obvious that "someone" had attempted to wash bloodstains from the bathroom door but had been only partially successful. Sheriff Scott reported finding pieces of the bullet on the floor of the sleeping porch and a hole in the porch screen that was six feet high — too far up to have been made by a shot fired, as Libby had implied, downward by Smith as he leaned over her on the bed. The inquest was adjourned until Monday. Ab and Libby were again ordered held in custody as material witnesses.

By this time it was so obvious to the Reynolds family that the major participants were lying that the family withdrew its protection from Ab Walker. He was jailed in the basement of the courthouse. Family members let the press know that they felt Libby also should have been locked up rather than allowed to remain at Reynolda. Newshounds were delighted; they had felt in their bones that there was more to the story than the spectacle of a rich boy shooting himself. On Sunday the news organizations located a judge who gave them permission to attend the last session of the inquest.

That session was held on Monday afternoon at 1 P.M., five and a half days after Smith had died. This time, to accommodate the circus of reporters, the proceedings were held in the library adjoining the living room. Telegraph and messenger facilities were made available to the newsmen, and the staff tried hard to be polite.

Jim Shepherd told the jurors of having taken a two-hour ride with Babe Vaught in the middle of the party but said he couldn't remember having seen Libby just before she went upstairs with Smith. Later, Jim asked his cousin Slick if his testimony had been believeable; after Slick replied that Jim's lies were obvious to all, the cousins didn't speak for thirty years.

Then came the more damaging testimony. Various nurses and other witnesses who had nothing to gain from keeping quiet gave alarming details about Libby and Ab's conversations and the lack of blood on the sheets in which Smith had been taken to the hospital. Since head wounds bleed profusely upon first being opened, this lack of blood indicated that Smith had been left without medical attention for some time, during which the blood flow had subsided, before being brought to the hospital. Such a gap in time raised the question of whether Libby or Ab had delayed calling an ambulance because of guilty involvement in the shooting.

It was late afternoon. Although almost a week had elapsed since the tragedy, Libby appeared in a diaphanous nightgown and made a spectacular entrance to the proceedings. As she walked into the library, she went out of her way to pause in front of a stream of sunlight from a window. Various reporters commented on the wonder of her well-exposed figure. Then she sat down in a chair, flanked by her father and her mother. If the coroner's jury of six men was upset by this entrance, no one said so.

By this point, District Attorney Higgins had taken over the questioning. However, when confronted by the apparition of one of America's sex goddesses in a revealing outfit, he asked questions gently, almost as if he were a defense attorney trying to let his client paint her own picture rather than a prosecutor leading the investigation of a death. Soon, Libby was offering long disquisitions on how she had given up the theater willingly because of her love for Smith, providing inordinate detail about conversations that had taken place — if ever — months before. How she could remember these yet nothing of what happened on the night of Smith's death bothered some reporters, but Higgins didn't suggest any discrepancy. Forty-five minutes into the questioning, Libby began a soliloquy:

> He was very sensitive and I had to be conscious all the time to be close to him and tell him that I loved him. . . . He had an inferiority complex. . . . We used to have arguments lots of times, and Smith would imagine things that weren't true. . . . I didn't want to annoy him and aggravate him, but wanted to leave him alone when he got in one of those moods, because before Smith had threatened to kill himself, and would come in with a gun at his head. I didn't know when he would get in one of those moods and magnify something.

Her self-portrait was without warts; during Smith's previous suicide threats,

> I would have to throw myself on him . . . push the gun back with my hand . . . so that the bullet wouldn't touch him. That was my only thought, to save him. . . . If he had shot then he would have shot me, too, and then I wouldn't care so much; the bullet would go through me, too. Once when we were in Winston-Salem he got that same feeling that he wasn't making me happy . . . and that I was being too nice and thoughtful and unselfish, that it wasn't human, and he came in and sort of pointed that gun at me, and I said, "Smith, I want you to understand, if you want to kill yourself I want you to kill me too; I don't want to live without your love."

Higgins finally intruded with an intelligent question: "If it was a disease of the mind . . . how do you explain the fact that it manifested itself only in your presence and not in the presence of anyone else?"

"Because I knew Smith."

"You mean he could restrain himself in the presence of other people?"

"Absolutely. . . . I wouldn't discuss Smith's condition with any-body else; I didn't have the right to tell anybody. It was something that was sacred to me."

Higgins failed to follow up, and Libby recaptured the initiative. She broke into sobs and, with her head in her mother's lap, launched into the heavy stuff: Smith had been impotent with her, she said, and had even suggested that she have an affair — which, of course, she had refused to do. After this shocker, and a reiteration that Smith had a wish to take himself out of her life because he wasn't making her happy enough, she capped her testimony with docu-mentary evidence: two suicide notes of Smith's, from prep school days, that she had managed to save from his personal papers though he had ordered her to destroy them in the event of his death.

Two jurors were in tears. Libby was blubbering. Alfred Holman told her to "buck up. I can't bear it for you. I wish I could." For Higgins to continue to press this frail, pathetic creature after two and a half hours of testimony would be cruel. He ended the inquiry.

Today, nearly fifty years after the event, Libby's testimony reads like a script written and delivered by an expert playwright and actress. Its various parts build on progressive, emotionally intense revelations to the point where the audience is intended to believe that Libby was the innocent, loving victim of a deranged, incom-petent young man bent on self-destruction.

Near midnight, at the Forsyth County courthouse, Higgins an-nounced the verdict of the coroner's jury: Smith had died "from a bullet wound inflicted by a party or parties unknown." In other words, rejecting Libby's explanation, the jury specifically excluded the idea of suicide.

=

Sheriff Scott took the judgment of the inquest as a spur to further investigation and put the matter before a grand jury. Behind closed doors, he told the panel that disparities in the testimonies of Walker and Holman led him to conclude that both were lying and that they had had ample opportunity to conspire and make up a story absolving both of them of responsibility. As to the physical evi-dence: the gun was so clean that fingerprints had to have been removed from it. There was also the matter of the bloodstains in the house, which had been mopped up — why would anyone have bothered about the blood if it had been an accident or a suicide?

Also, why did Ab and Libby wait so long before calling for help that the flow of blood from Smith's wound had a chance to stop?

The panel returned an indictment of Ab and Libby for first-degree murder — but, as sometimes happened in those days when there hadn't been enough time to nail down all of the evidence, the "presentment," or finding, was sealed. This grand jury was aware that another one would shortly be empaneled and hoped that the second would consider all the evidence and hand down an indictment that could not be controverted.

After the inquest verdict, Ab and Libby had been released as material witnesses. Libby left Reynolda and went into hiding. Blanche Yurka and tutor Ray Kramer returned to New York, and when the mansion was empty, Mary, Nancy, and their husbands moved into Reynolda to escape the clamoring press. After the foreman of the first grand jury claimed to reporters that they hadn't even considered the case and that it would be July 25 before another panel began, many big-city reporters left Winston-Salem, much to the relief of the Reynolds family.

Everyone in town awaited the arrival of Dick Reynolds, who in later years would say that the news of his brother's death reached him in Dakar while he was chained to a tree trying to get rid of the D.T.'s, delirium tremens, the shakes brought on by imbibing too much alcohol. He never said who'd chained him to the tree. Upon being released from his confinement, he'd gotten a speedboat from Dakar to a point farther south on the coast, where he boarded a ship crossing to Brazil. His passage was delayed, and then an insurrection in Brazil cost him further time. While the inquest and first grand jury proceedings were in progress, he was still struggling to get home.

Will Reynolds offered to help the public officials buttress any possible murder case. Prosecutor Higgins resented the intrusion but, since this was the Reynoldses' town, said he wouldn't object to having more evidence. Will hired a former FBI man to investigate and also talked personally to Ab Walker. The boy was only nineteen and beholden to the Reynolds family. With Will, Ab was reserved, but he provided Will with a depressing picture of Smith's deteriorating marital situation in those last few days of his life.

Sheriff Scott was receptive to help, and, over the next several weeks, the Reynolds family exchanged several dozen letters with him, based, most likely, on information they'd turned up and theories they thought he might not have considered. It was clear that Will no longer ruled out the possibility that Smith might have been murdered.

Higgins later told the story that one night a limousine pulled up at his office and Mary Babcock emerged from it to tell him that she was sure, now, that her brother had committed suicide. On what she based her contention he never said. The possibility exists that he invented or distorted this incident in later years to counteract what seems to have been serious foot-dragging and a willingness not to try to break the cover stories of the most likely suspects. Further reasons for his actions became apparent a few weeks later.

Libby announced that she had asked that Will Reynolds be appointed executor of Smith's estate in her stead. Actually, she had little choice in this matter since she was residing out of state and wouldn't have been able to make proper claim to executorship anyway. It was one of her first salvos in a public relations war that shortly consumed the entire affair. Next, Libby's father sent a telegram to Higgins — also released to the newspapers — saying that any murder indictment would be "an injustice equaled only by that of ancient times and the barbarous middle ages," i.e., that to indict his Jewish daughter would be anti-Semitic.

The new grand jury panel heard Sheriff Scott, W. E. Fulcher, Stewart Warnken, J. T. Barnes, and Dr. Hanes — and, on August 4, issued an indictment of Elizabeth Holman and Albert Walker for premeditated murder. The foreman later said that the panel didn't believe Ab and Libby were guilty of first-degree murder but indicted them to force the suspects to stop lying and reveal what had happened to Smith.

The defendants were ordered jailed without bail until criminal court convened on October 3. Ab Walker surrendered after hiring as his lawyer Bailey Liipfert, the chairman of the Forsyth County Democratic party executive committee. Liipfert, then, was the man in charge of choosing who ran for district attorney. Alfred Holman argued that Libby need not be incarcerated and said she would appear whenever the trial was held. He engaged two local lawyers, Benet Polikoff, a young Jewish man who had done some work for Higgins, and William Graves, who had been Higgins's campaign manager in the last election. Thus, opposing District Attorney Higgins were two men, Graves and Liipfert, from whom he needed political support. Liipfert convinced the judge that evidence to support a charge of first-degree murder was meager and that Walker should be considered only an accessory after the fact and should be released on $25,000 bail. Higgins agreed. A bail bondsman was found, Ab's family pledged some property as collateral, and he was let go.

To the disappointment of a caravan of reporters, a heavily veiled Libby showed up briefly in a small upstate North Carolina town and was released on $25,000 bail — money provided by Louisa Carpenter, who dressed for the occasion in such mannish clothing that she was written up as Libby's new male suitor.

Although the same arguments hadn't been advanced for Libby as for Ab, because Libby paid the same in bail as he did the charge against both of them had now been effectively reduced from first-degree murder to manslaughter. Higgins hadn't agreed to a lesser charge, but after these bail proceedings it would have been difficult, though not technically impossible, for Higgins to prosecute them on the more serious charge.

On August 10 Dick had gotten as far as Trinidad. Strat Coyner flew south to meet him, a copy of the inquest in hand. From reading the transcript it would have been obvious to Dick that most of the witnesses had lied, including Ab and Libby. Ab's story in particular was full of holes. That Libby and Ab had to have been involved in Smith's death was an inescapable conclusion.

Reaching Winston-Salem without fanfare, Dick hid out at Coyner's house downtown. Perhaps at Dick's instigation, at midnight on August 23 several doctors exhumed Smith's body from the Salem cemetery and peered at it in detail. Even to conduct an exhumation implied that the examination of Smith on the night he died hadn't been properly done. However, most of these autopsy physicians were the same people who had looked at Smith in the hospital and who had a vested interest in confirming what they'd written up seven weeks earlier. This time Dr. Hanes's group said Smith had been shot "at close range," which suggested that the barrel of the gun had not been up against Smith's head, as previously suggested. This new interpretation of the physical evidence left open the possibility that hands other than Smith's had been involved in holding or firing the gun.

Virginia Dunklee, who was friendly with the Reynoldses as well as with the Shepherds, told Slick Shepherd that shirts with the R.J.R. monogram had shown up recently at her family's laundry, to be cleaned and returned to Coyner's home. In response, Slick went to Coyner's and insisted on an interview with Dick, whom he had known since childhood. Dick was closemouthed but, the next morning, was forced out of hiding to make a statement.

Dick told reporters that he'd known Smith better than any other person — a refutation of Libby's boast during the inquest — and that Smith was not the type to take his own life. Dick didn't reveal the autopsy findings, which were still secret, but they may have been the basis of his forthright statement that "in view of all the facts available at this time, I believe my brother's death was murder." He announced that he was going to aid the investigation and intended to stay in Winston for the trial.

His cover blown, Dick moved into Reynolda. Mary and Nancy had returned to New York. He lived in the west wing, amid some of the furniture from the old downtown mansion — his father's things. During the next few months Dick threw parties for friends and attempted to return the estate to gaiety. (Ab was not invited; Dick wouldn't speak to him.) The gatherings delighted the younger social set of Winston-Salem even as they shocked the parents, who thought them improper so soon after a tragic death.

As time went on and Dick learned more about Smith's, Libby's, and Ab's tangled lives before the event on the sleeping porch, Dick pulled back a little from his hard-nosed stance at the news conference. There were a number of possibly sordid notions associated with the case that no Reynolds would want permanently linked to the family name. Quite naturally, these all had to do with sex. They included the persistent rumor around town that Ab and Libby had been sexually involved; the suspicion that the baby Libby was carrying might not be her late husband's; Smith's obvious sexual confusion; Libby's homosexuality and inferences of similar behavior on the part of Blanche, Ab, and even Smith.

Just when the twenty-six-year-old Dick was considering what would be good for the Reynoldses — as contrasted though not yet opposed to how the mystery of his brother's death could be solved — he fell in love with one of the frequent guests at the Reynolda barbecues. She was twenty-three-year-old Elizabeth McCaw Dillard. She'd been invited to the Reynolda party on the night Smith died but had been whisked off to the resort of Roaring Gap by her mother.

Elizabeth Dillard had been a childhood playmate of the family's. Just Nancy's age, she was the daughter of a wealthy building contractor and granddaughter of Bill Taylor, a tobacco manufacturer whom R. J. had never succeeded in putting out of business. In the nineteenth century, "Old Man Bill" Taylor had been called a socialist for trying to imbue his workers with religious fervor. Stories still circulated that R. J. had been helped by Taylor in the early 1880s and that when told by Duke to swallow up the Taylor firm, he'd let it survive.

Like Mary and Nancy, who were in her social set, Elizabeth had gone to an acceptable college (Sweet Briar), "done" Europe, taken lessons in riding and golf. Unlike Mary or Nancy, she was striking, with an oval face and a slender, appealing figure. But it was her personality more than her appearance that attracted Dick. As was Anne Cannon, she was a bit of a rebel, given to smoking, drinking, and talking tough with the boys. Dick nicknamed her Blitz, and the appellation stuck. Soon Winston was abuzz with rumors. Dick wasn't sure yet whether their romance was serious. His interest in his old flame Ella Cannon Hill, who'd resurfaced in Winston, might have been rekindled, but she was being courted by Emory Flinn, from Atlanta. The Flinns and Reynoldses had known each other for ages, and Dick wouldn't poach on a friend's territory. Then, too, Aunt Maxie was pushing hard for him to pay more serious attention to Blitz; Maxie thought that two such good bloodlines ought to marry, principally because they'd produce terrific children.

Several years earlier, Dick had left Winston-Salem and had not really intended to return. He preferred cosmopolitan New York and round-the-world parties. Smith's death, as well as the marriages and pregnancies of Mary and Nancy, put a lot of pressure on him to change his life and settle down. The era of close guardianship was nearly over. Dick's income was about $1 million per year; soon he'd turn twenty-eight and come into personal control of more than $25 million. If Reynolda held too many memories for him, he could build a new estate. He ought not do as his father had done (indeed, as Joshua Cox and all previous holders of the Joshua Coin had also done): wait until he had reached middle age before marrying and having children. The name and the line of R. J. Reynolds had to be continued.

In the country at large, wealthy patrician Franklin Delano Roosevelt had recently been nominated for president and was expected to be easily elected. That fall, Dick became a fervent admirer of FDR's and a contributor to his campaign. In FDR, Dick saw a hero to whom he could relate directly: a rich family's son who followed (as Dick's father had) the principles of Woodrow Wilson, had an aristocratic manner, yet pledged to do something for all less fortunate people in the world. FDR was also a sailor, like Dick, and vowed to end Prohibition.

Labor Day came and went, there were more parties at Reynolda, and the date for the trial drew nearer. In late September, Libby broke her silence in an interview with Broadway columnist Ward Moorhouse: "It's the knowing that I'm going to give birth to the child of the man I love that affords me my only gleam of happiness, that gives me any desire to live at all. The fact that within four months I will have a child — HIS child — makes me strong enough to fight for a complete and absolute vindication. God in Heaven knows that I did not kill Smith Reynolds." While knitting small pink garments, she depicted Smith as a misguided, tormented, inadequate youth who gave up his puerile pursuit of aviation to dote on her. She'd pleaded with him to get himself disinherited; they'd have lived on her Broadway income, which was more than his own. Now, "I don't only want acquittal. I want a complete apology." The Moorhouse column was a clear indication that during any future trial Libby would defend herself with vigor and in doing so would splash as much mud as possible on Smith's reputation.

In reaction, Dick and the family decided on an aggressive public relations campaign of their own. Dick and Charles Babcock, acting for the family, met in New York with Harry Bruno and Dick Blythe — publicists for Charles Lindbergh and flying buddies of Dick's — and mapped out a strategy to inculcate in the public's mind the idea that Smith "was a youth of courage, determination and breeding . . . [To show] the first true facts regarding the achievements, ambitions and personal qualifications of Z. Smith Reynolds." In addition to a press release, the firm would assist in the publication of Smith's flight diary, circulate retouched photos to replace those "unflattering to the boy," and encourage his posthumous induction into the Ligue Internationale des Aviateurs.

Newspapers of October 7 and 8 were mainly interested in the other document they had released, the will that Smith had made before his marriage to Libby. Front pages of newspapers told how Smith had left Ab Walker $50,000, made similar bequests to Anne Cannon and their daughter — and, omitting Libby, left everything else to his brother and sisters. The New York Evening Post reported that "unusual precautions" made the will difficult to contest; no one named as a beneficiary could assert that the will was invalid on pain of losing benefits from it.

Larger newspapers sought opinions from lawyers, who pointed out that a will made before Smith was twenty-one was not valid and that the operative will was old R. J.'s, which said that a dead heir's portion should go to the heir's children: in this case, little Anne Cannon and Libby's unborn baby. Also, Smith's divorce agreement with Anne Cannon superseded his will by settling $500,000, rather than $50,000, on their daughter.

Dick received the several-pound sheaf of clippings from Bruno and Blythe and commented that the job they'd done was "not so hot."

By this time, the family was in despair. There could be no doubt that a trial would damage Smith's reputation and the family's with it. Libby would take the stand and expound on Smith's impotence, drinking, suicide threats, and bad habits. Moreover, for the prosecution to make any sort of a case Higgins would have to allude to infidelity and a wide marital rift between Smith and Libby. The mention of such moral breaches would not help the Reynolds family; the publicity could, perhaps, be endured if a strong possibility of a conviction existed, but in the absence of a confession by Ab or Libby, the evidence was circumstantial and weak. Dick believed that both Ab and Libby had been in the room with Smith and that at least two of them — possibly all three — had had their hands on the gun. Beyond that, it was anybody's guess.

Today, after many years, we can more reasonably reconstruct what happened, based on the character of the participants and their history. There was a screaming fight, exacerbated by liquor and an actress's love of dramatic confrontation, a fight most likely instigated by Smith's having found Libby's clothes in Ab's bedroom. (Ab was known to sleep with any woman he could get his hands on.) Libby might have admitted an affair, or denied it, or accused Smith right back of a homosexual involvement with Ab.

Ab would have been drawn into the fight, and then or shortly thereafter the gun would have been taken out. If Smith threatened to shoot himself, Libby, drunk, could have dared him to do the deed at last and stop manipulating her with threats. Perhaps Ab tried to interfere and grabbed the gun; he could have moved it from Smith's head but not succeeded in wresting it completely away, so that when the pressure of at least two hands jogged the trigger, the shot went through Smith's head at an odd angle. It was even a possibility that Smith wasn't pointing the gun at himself but at Ab or Libby and that Ab — or Libby — lunged to prevent him from shooting them.

Arguments against a pure suicide are buttressed by evidence from Smith's past and Libby's later actions. Smith had threatened suicide before but had never fired a shot at his head — and, in fact, had refused several times in his life to go through with killing himself, the prime example being the episode of semisexual humiliation on Long Island, after which he took his plane out over the ocean but managed to return without harming himself. Also, more than a decade later, in the 1940s, Libby's second husband (like Smith, he was young, sexually confused, and drunk) committed suicide after being clearly driven to do so by Libby's actions.

The totality of the evidence suggests that there were more hands on the gun than Smith's alone. After the shot, feeling that they had participated in it, Ab and Libby guiltily conspired to wipe away the evidence, hide the gun, and concoct stories to absolve themselves. Quite possibly Libby sealed her pact with Ab by giving herself sexually to him. They may even have sworn Blanche Yurka to silence. Fifty years later, Yurka asked an author for fifteen thousand dollars to tell what happened that night and, when the money was not forthcoming, kept her silence. What had she to tell if she had been, as she testified, asleep?

Our conclusion is that the death of Smith Reynolds was unpremeditated manslaughter — what we'll call assisted suicide, done with the complicity of Ab and Libby. At the time, there was no way to know definitively what went on in that sleeping porch, and, at last, there was no willpower within the family to try to press the contention of murder.

On October 18, with the trial still not begun, Will Reynolds sent a remarkable letter to Carlisle Higgins, simultaneously released to the press. It said, in part,

> I am convinced that [Smith's] attitude toward life was such that he would never have intentionally killed himself. Nothing that I have been able to learn about the case has been sufficient to change my mind in that respect. On the other hand, it is equally true, in my opinion and in that of Smith's brother and sisters, that the evidence fails to prove conclusively that Smith was murdered. . . .

Will's letter then went into specific recommendations:

If in the discharge of your further official duties . . . you come to the conclusion that it is right and fair and in the public interest that the cases be dropped then that action on your part will certainly have no criticism from me or from the other members of Smith's family. In fact, I think that under the circumstances, all of us would be quite happy if it should be your decision to drop the cases.

Dick told reporters that the death "might have been accidental" and that a lengthy trial would not clear up the mystery but would cause "undue hardships for the accused and heartaches for all concerned." He concluded that the "whole truth of what happened that night at Reynolda House will probably never be known."

Libby proclaimed herself furious; she wanted a trial to clear her name. Higgins reserved decision on whether he would proceed. Dick privately offered Libby quite a bit of money if she would stop insisting on a trial, not contest Smith's will, and just go away. Libby supposedly accepted the money; in mid-November, when Higgins finally said he'd drop the case, Libby didn't object.

And so the trial never took place. Outside the Forsyth County courthouse, across the street from the Reynolds company skyscraper that was a smaller version of the Empire State Building, souvenir vendors had to throw away thousands of photos of Libby and Smith, and crude postcards with plans of Reynolda overlaid by the words "bloodstains" and "path of bullet."

On Christmas Day, 1932, Blitz and Dick announced their engagement, and they were married on January 1, 1933. The ceremony at St. Paul's Episcopal Church was elaborate. The couple entered the building to the strains of one hundred choristers singing "O Perfect Love" and between lines formed by one hundred of North Carolina's most elite couples. It was deeply regretted that Smith could not be his brother's best man, but to the newspapers and the family the wedding was a symbol that, despite tragedy, life went on.

Chapter Eleven

Dick and Blitz

DICK AND BLITZ Reynolds were on their honeymoon when newspapers reported the premature birth of a boy to Libby Holman. Two Reynolds family lawyers stationed outside Libby's delivery room declared they could not be certain whether the boy was Smith's, although Libby soon named him Christopher Smith Reynolds.

There were no blood tests for paternity then, so the fatherhood of "Topper," as Christopher was called, was never truly challenged. Thousands of Americans counted the months on their fingers and figured that he had been conceived at Reynolda in early June. At the Shell gas station near Reynolda where Ab was working as a pump attendant — the only job he could get — friends burned Ab's fedora when the news came, traditional horseplay for friends of a new father.

Next Dick read that Libby's lawyers believed Smith's 1931 will to be invalid and were preparing to argue in court that Smith had died intestate, therefore making Libby and Topper entitled to Smith's entire fortune. Dick was incensed. He'd given Libby money to go away — and here she was, coming back for more; her actions seemed proof that she'd never loved his brother and had always been after his money. A day later, Alfred Holman was quoted in the papers as suggesting that Libby would be satisfied with a "modest sum" and that the remainder of Smith's estate might stay in the Reynolds family if the Reynoldses were prepared to take "certain altruistic actions."

Then another claimant to Smith's fortune came forward, by means of a suit filed on behalf of little Anne Cannon II, ostensibly against one guardian by another. This stratagem allowed the Cannons to contest the Smith-Anne divorce settlement of $1.1 million and lay claim to half Smith's estate. They contended that while in Reno, Anne had been under the influence of morphine and so had not been competent, thus rendering her divorce from Smith and Libby's marriage to Smith invalid and making Anne, rather than Libby, the true widow of Smith Reynolds. The Cannons avoided mentioning the fact that after she divorced Smith Reynolds, Anne had married F. Brandon Smith and by this time had divorced him, too, and married for the third time.

Soon Aubrey Brooks, Anne's attorney, was bargaining directly with Uncle Will and Alfred Holman. Every once in a while, bulletins on the progress of these negotiations would reach the newspapers. The fight for Smith's estate was a royal mess, a diverting scandal in the spring of 1933 that took people's minds off the political revolutions being made by newly installed heads of state: Franklin Roosevelt in Washington and Adolf Hitler in Germany.

In May, a North Carolina judge ratified a deal awarding $1.5 million to Anne Cannon II (in addition to the half million previously promised), $2 million to Topper, and a half million for Libby. It also allowed Anne Cannon to keep the $600,000 agreed to in her divorce. The remainder of the estate, currently estimated at $7 million, would be deeded by Dick, Mary, and Nancy to a new foundation, named for Smith.

After this deal was struck, however, the Holmans and Cannons claimed the Reynoldses were hiding assets, and they went back to court to assess properly the value of Smith's estate. The process dragged on and on.

It is hard to overestimate the effect on the Reynolds siblings of the death of Smith Reynolds, the publicity surrounding the investigation, and the subsequent wrangling over Smith's estate. After these events Dick, Mary, Nancy, and their spouses all took nosedives into conformity and eschewed former patterns of high and licentious living. They tried very hard to stay out of the public eye and to lead "normal" lives. In the next half-dozen years, they would produce twelve children, four to each family.

When Dick and Blitz came back from their honeymoon and started life together in Winston-Salem, a fundamental problem faced the twenty-seven-year-old heir. Should he go into business or simply pursue investments and a life of leisure? He decided that, as a major stockholder, he wanted to become involved in RJR —

in particular, he wanted a seat on the board. Neither his temperament nor his position as a person of wealth suited him to an ordinary sales or marketing job from which he could climb the corporate ladder. Had his father still been alive, he might have taken such a starting slot, but R. J. was long gone. Dick didn't want to be an underling; he felt he belonged on the board.

As far as Uncle Will was concerned, Dick's interest in RJR came at an awkward time. For one thing, Will had retired as chairman, so that day-to-day management of the company was now in the hands of Bowman Gray and other nonfamily members. Also, over the past fifteen years Will had been actively engaged in downplaying the notion that R. J. had single-handedly been responsible for the success of the RJR Company and was substituting the idea that all of the Reynolds brothers, especially himself, had combined to make the company great. To have a young man named R. J. Reynolds, Jr., on the board would give the lie to this subtle leaching of historical reality. Will, Gray, and others voted to deny Dick a seat. Besides, to them Dick was still a profligate of dubious business achievements. Although Dick had made money in aviation and with the *Harpoon*, he had little else to show the RJR elders as evidence that he had left behind his past wildness.

It was perhaps unfortunate that the board didn't give Dick a chance, because just then, in the middle 1930s, he was trying very assiduously to change his life — or, at least, other people's view of it. But he didn't fight the board; rather, he plunged into buying up real estate around Winston and backing several local businesses. These were sidelines, though, to entering the Winston social scene. He and Blitz were the darling new couple of Winston. In short order, they began a skeet-shooting club and gave the first of what would become annual parties. They also started racing trotting horses.

Dick could hardly avoid trotters, for Uncle Will was emerging as one of the most important men in America in the sport. Will believed that the turn of the century (when he had been in his thirties) was harness racing's golden age. The advent of automobiles and the urbanization of the country's population had sent it into decline. To return the sport to its former prestige, Will helped set up the Grand Circuit, stakes races that now awarded the sport's richest purses — some of which he was currently winning himself, with horses from his own stables. Will was treasurer of the Hambletonian organization. Perhaps as a sop to his nephew, he had Dick elected to that board.

Will liked to name horses after family members. It wasn't quite the same as brother R. J.'s naming chewing-tobacco brands after girlfriends; it was more like a pleasant though noninnovative echo, for Will was a likable though noninventive version of rough-and-ready R. J. One of Will's fastest colts was Dick Reynolds, who made it around the harness track in what was considered excellent time, under two minutes. When Will retired that horse and took advertisements out in sporting papers to announce "Dick Reynolds at Stud," Blitz framed the ad and gave it to her husband. It was a tongue-in-cheek gift — and, after all, she was pregnant.

On October 28, 1933, a note came to Reynolda threatening to kidnap the pregnant Blitz if Dick did not immediately pay ten thousand dollars in cash. Instructions for delivery of the money followed. Dick didn't tell his wife but had Strat Coyner get in touch with J. Edgar Hoover, who advised him to pay the money and have authorities watch the drop site. At 1 A.M. a few days later, Dick left the cash in the designated garbage can on a street corner in Winston-Salem. Five hours later the police apprehended the man trying to retrieve the money, John Lanier, a young out-of-work textile hand and part-time Reynolda security guard.

Some of the newspapers were surprised when Dick asked the court to treat Lanier gently. Dick suggested that the man had conceived the plot because he was unemployed and desperate for money. Lanier was convicted and sent to jail; when he came up for parole, Dick again interceded on his behalf. This episode marked the first demonstration of Dick's developing understanding that great wealth could harm those who, like moths, were attracted to its flame.

Partly because of this scare, and partly because sister Mary wanted to live at Reynolda, Dick and Blitz decided in late 1933 to get ready to move out. Richard Joshua Reynolds III was born that December. In four months, Dick would turn twenty-eight and take possession of $28 million in stocks, bonds, real estate, and cash. Then there would be no more guardians, no more finagling to get two for one from the trust. He would be one of the wealthiest men in the country — far wealthier, for example, than Uncle Will.

Reynolda was beautiful, but it was the creation of Dick's parents. Moreover, it had seen too much unhappiness: the death of R. J., the pain of Katharine's remarriage and early demise, the trauma of Smith's brief life, as well as the kidnap scare. Dick and Blitz decided to maintain a smaller residence in Winston and to put their considerable resources into creating an estate of their own. Following the example of Katharine and R. J. twenty-five years earlier, they started assembling properties. This time the land was not the suburbs of Winston but the foothills of the Blue Ridge Mountains, fifty miles northwest of Winston. They planned an estate ten times the size of Reynolda; they would call it Devotion, a name — an action — that reflected the young couple's feelings for each other.

A striking woman, with a rounded face and a figure trim enough to make her a model in the fashion shows Winston women often staged to raise money for charitable causes, Blitz moved easily among the upper reaches of Winston society yet liked at times to be independent of that crowd. That aspect of her character reflected Dick's. Blitz was an excellent match for Dick in background and temperament. At this stage of their lives, they were deeply committed to each other, to their marriage and family. Blitz was rather easily able to persuade Dick to give up one of the former loves of his life, the *Harpoon*, by arguing that life at sea (which she hadn't sampled) was no venue in which to bring up the children they both wanted to have.

Symbolically, Dick used the proceeds from the sale of the *Harpoon* to purchase the first piece of Surry County property that would make up Devotion. That first parcel, situated along the tributaries of the Mitchell River, was only a few hundred acres, but Dick and Blitz kept buying until they had eleven thousand acres, miles and miles of rugged hill country, with wide glades, pastures, forested knobs, lakes, streams, and waterfalls. If the thousand-acre Reynolda was a village, Devotion was the equivalent of an entire valley.

At this time, early into Roosevelt's first administration, even some wealthy Southern Democrats went along with FDR because Hoover's attempts to halt the Depression hadn't worked and they believed new measures had to be tried. But few FDR admirers went as far as Dick Reynolds when he made the building of Devotion his own private WPA project. Rather than contract the work out, Dick chose to hire three hundred men, mostly from Surry and surrounding counties, to pay them double and triple the prevailing hourly wage, and to have them work wherever possible by hand rather than by machine in order to keep them at work longer. This employment enabled many to get off the relief rolls. The workers formed an army that gradually reshaped the thousands of wilderness acres into the new design of Devotion. As he had with the labor, Dick insisted that the materials be indigenous: gray slate and stones; black pine, chestnut, and oak cut down locally and made into carved, cabinetlike interior walls and shelves; structural beams; and custom furniture.

Reynolda had been built as self-sufficient; Devotion would be more so, with the ability not only to grow its own food but also to provide its own power, and with its own gas station and storage tanks. Reynolda's inspiration and guiding hand was Katharine; Devotion's beauty was the result of Blitz's vision in the interiors and Dick's in the grand design. Devotion was more ambitious in its scope than the fantasy of the previous generation. Two lakes, for example, were carved out of the hills, one of twenty and the other of forty-two acres. They gave a feeling of placid serenity to the otherwise rugged land. The circumferences of both lakes, several miles of shoreline, were lined with slate. Each lake led to a waterfall. One, near the main house, was eighty-five feet high and was used to turn the flywheels of huge, concealed generators that made electric power. The other waterfall was even higher, and its only purpose was scenic. Terraced walls and walkways leading to these waterfalls were faced with local granite, hand-hewn and hand-carried to the spot, then cemented into place. At the foot of the higher waterfall, the stream gave onto experimental fish ponds, then flowed on as an irrigation system for crop fields and cattle pastures.

The largest residence, Long Creek, was a hunting lodge in the mode of English and Scottish backwoods retreats, built along the side of the five-hundred-foot-wide dam and into the gorge through which the western waterfall spilled. The lodge had nearly two dozen intricately paneled rooms, on almost as many levels, that hugged the lake shoreline or extended into the hillside adjacent to the gorge. Below, cut into the hillside, were capacious kitchen quarters that could produce a hundred meals at a time and dining rooms that could seat the same number of people comfortably.

Trailing behind the lodge, like so many goslings behind a mother goose, were workshops for wood and metal, a large movie theater, a cheese-making facility dear to the heart of chef Karl Weiss (recently of the *Harpoon*), and other buildings. In another cluster of buildings down by the separate farm, there were a slaughterhouse and poultry and feed barns. Elsewhere within the property were guest and staff cottages, some of them large enough to accommodate whole families. The woods overflowed with quail, deer, bear, pheasant, and rabbit. There were miles of trails for hikers, horse-back riders, and skiers. The main lake was stocked with trout, and a boathouse held a small flotilla of rafts and canoes. Within walking distance of Long Creek Lodge were a tennis court, a skeet-shooting range, a steel jungle gym, and other paraphernalia of a full-sized playground. There were even caged bears for guests to feed.

Devotion, in short, had everything that could be fancied for a four-season family vacation home. As befitted a labor of love, its construction proceeded slowly, through the 1930s, as the four sons of Dick and Blitz were birthed about two years apart. Visitors felt the special nature of the place when they came through its gates and wound their way up to the lodge. The rightness of Devotion was symbolized for Dick by a tree he had discovered on a high forested plateau overlooking the smaller of the two lakes: it had been molded by the wind into the outline of Blitz's aristocratic face.

=

In 1934 Dick and Nancy sold their shares in Reynolda to the Babcocks; thereafter Mary and Charles lived most of the year in Connecticut and spent summers and vacations at Reynolda. When Mary came into her quarter of the fortune, she began to remodel the bungalow, making a new main entrance at the east wing, for example, something that would afford the family some privacy since the public was now allowed onto the grounds to drive to the gardens. In the basement the Babcocks installed a bowling alley, pool table, and shooting gallery, as well as a mirrored bar, and beyond the east wing they added an eight-bedroom guesthouse and an indoor swimming pool. By the late 1930s, Reynolda finally became what Katharine had hoped it would be twenty years earlier — a complete family estate.

Toward the end of Reynolda's reconstruction, cousin R. S. Reynolds sold most of his portion of the brokerage firm to Babcock; this left Charles as senior partner and major stockholder in Reynolds & Company.

A contemporary article listed Mary among the country's richest women, one of two dozen who each controlled more than $25 million. The editors seemed upset by what they noted as a sharp difference between Mary Reynolds Babcock and such female millionaires as Doris Duke and various Paysons, Whitneys, and Dodges: despite her money, Mary, they said, lived in comparative

Rock Spring *(below)*, in southern Virginia, seemed a very modest starting place for two separate fortunes. The founders of those fortunes: *above left*, eldest brother Abram Reynolds, about 1872; *above right*, second son Richard Joshua Reynolds, early 1880s.

Following their father's model, all five Reynolds brothers went into the tobacco business. Some worked for R. J., others for Abram, and later switched. *Seated, from left:* R. J., Abram, and Harbour; *standing, from left:* Walter and Will; about 1915.

R. J. and Katharine's family life was full in the days just before the Great War; while they built Reynolda, they lived in a Victorian wedding-cake house on Winston's Fifth Street. *Above, from left:* Mary, R. J., Katharine, Nancy, Dick, and Smith. *Right:* Smith at age four. The baby of the family was at times docile and at others petulant. *(UPI/Bettmann Newsphotos)*

Libby Holman, singer of torch songs *(left)*, before her marriage to Smith, and at a court hearing *(facing page)* after being indicted for his murder. (Both, *UPI/ Bettmann Newsphotos*)

Smith's plane *(facing page)*, in which the twenty-year-old *(left)* made it almost around the world. *(UPI/Bettmann Newsphotos)*

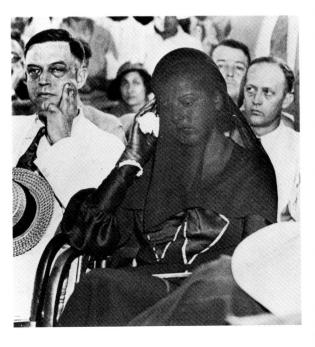

Above: The thousand-acre Reynolda estate, photographed in 1932, just after the tragic death of Z. Smith Reynolds. *(UPI/Bettmann Newsphotos) Below:* The interior of the great living room at Reynolda as it appears today. *(Tony Lalor)*

Above: "I know it's a lot of money, but I can't get excited," Dick Reynolds told reporters. Dick and Blitz, 1934, as they took possession of his inheritance of more than $25 million. *(UPI/Bettmann Newsphotos) Below:* Dick and Blitz planned an estate ten times the size of Reynolda. They would call it Devotion, a name — an action — that reflected the young couple's feelings for each other.

Above: Part of the estate at Sapelo, an island off the coast of Georgia, twelve miles by four, which became Dick Reynolds's fiefdom. About half of it was kept as a private game preserve, used for fashionable shooting parties. *Below:* Dick and Blitz, near the center, with a day's results, mid-1930s.

Above: Dick's sloop *Blitzen*, with himself as skipper, was the overall winner of 1939's most grueling yacht race, the 2,085-mile trans-Pacific route from San Francisco to Honolulu. *Below:* The winners, who took fourteen days to cover the distance, pose for the press. Dick is center, bottom row. (Both, *UPI/Bettmann Newsphotos*)

Marianne O'Brien, late 1944. When Marianne opened her first letter from
Dick Reynolds, out fell several hundred-dollar bills. Dick told her to have
pictures taken of herself, to mail him copies, and not to object, because
"the money is better spent helping your career than moldering in some
bank." (*Bruno of Hollywood*)

Lieutenant Commander Richard J. Reynolds, Jr., former mayor of Winston-Salem and former treasurer of the Democratic National Committee, at the time of his wedding to Marianne O'Brien, 1946.

Above: Michael, Dick, Marianne, and baby Patrick, 1949, before the fantasy crumbled. *Below:* Marianne accompanied by attorney Louis Nizer and her mother at the time of her divorce from Dick, 1952. She didn't get nearly as much as Blitz had gotten. *(UPI/Bettmann Newsphotos)*

Above: Dick with Muriel Greenough Reynolds at a nightclub in the mid-1950s. In marrying wife number three Dick left behind a second set of sons, having earlier abandoned the four boys from his first marriage. *Below:* The six sons of R. J. Reynolds, Jr., at the time of Zach's wedding in 1959. *Front row, from left:* Patrick and Michael; *back row, from left:* Josh, Will, Zach, and John. *(Coppedge Photography Inc.)*

Above: Dick's shipboard wedding to Annemarie Schmitt, 1961. The Lindemanns flank the new couple, and Gunther Lehmann is to the right of Mrs. Lindemann. This initial attempt at marriage was later ruled invalid when Dick's divorce from Muriel was overturned on appeal. *Below:* Dick had, he believed, only a short time to live — and would now spend some of it in a courtroom, doing battle with a woman he hated; 1962.
(Both, *UPI/Bettmann Newsphotos*)

Above: "Dr. Zach," with the largest collection of motorcycles in the world, 1975. *Below:* Muriel and Marianne in later years. The two former Mrs. R. J. Reynoldses continued to commiserate and to believe that Annemarie was somehow involved in Dick's seemingly premature death . . . though they thought they'd never prove it.

Above: Patrick Reynolds interviewing one of Dick's former employees at Hog Hammock, on Sapelo Island, 1987. *Below:* Patrick speaks out against the tobacco that was the foundation of his family's fortune. *(Boston Globe — Mark Wilson)*

moderation. The magazine suggested that she'd learned to live modestly from years of having been "forced" to exist on only $50,000 per annum.

That was nonsense; however, the article did sum up her real motivation in choosing an anonymous, unostentatious life-style:

> Because both her parents died when she was young and she and her sister spent years travelling through Europe as orphans with a chaperone, she has the deepest feeling for simple home life. Because the Reynolds family has been dislocated by headline tragedies, she wants more than anything else a sane, normal, unobtrusive existence.

It was an accurate reading for both Mary and Nancy.

About Dick Reynolds, not quite the same could be said. In his new life centered on Winston-Salem and Devotion, Dick missed one thing — the sea. That was soon remedied.

In 1935 Dick was invited by an Atlanta real estate man for a shooting vacation. The location was one of the Golden Isles off the coast of lower Georgia. These barrier islands stretch from the northern edge of Florida to the coastal metropolis of Savannah. During colonial days they had been plantations and had remained private farms until the early-twentieth-century crop of millionaires began to establish vacation homes on them. Dick's destination was Sapelo, owned by Howard Earle Coffin, who'd made his fortune building Hudson Motors and who was then engaged in developing Sapelo as well as neighboring St. Simons Island. A lavish spender, Coffin had entertained Presidents Coolidge and Hoover on Sapelo and in 1927 had commissioned what one newspaper called "the nation's most palatial yacht," the 124-foot *Zapala*, the Spanish name for Sapelo.

Coffin lived in a mansion, South End House, that he had rebuilt according to the plans of a previous owner of Sapelo, Thomas Spalding. In the early 1800s, after having been owned by waves of Spanish and French owners, most of the island passed into the hands of Spalding, an inventor, agriculturalist, and writer of Renaissance virtuosity. He cultivated a sugar plantation — indeed, founded the sugar industry in Georgia — pioneered techniques for growing sea island cotton, and perfected the use of tabby as a building material. After the Civil War, the island lay fallow until the early 1900s, when Coffin bought it.

By means of his own prodigious energy and a commitment of

more than a quarter-million dollars annually, Coffin had reinvig-orated Sapelo. He cultivated crops and livestock, even harvested oysters from nearby marshes. Part of the island he made into a hunting preserve, stocked not only with native deer, turkey, pos-sum, and black bear but also with *chachalacas*, pheasantlike birds he imported from Guatemala.

Sapelo's beauty had been featured in the pages of *Country Life* and *National Geographic*. What those spreads did not say, however, was that in developing Sea Island (an island off St. Simons con-nected by landfill), Coffin had overextended his financial resources. The Depression had taken its toll. He and his partner, Bill Jones, had invited Dick to Sapelo to get him to invest in the Sea Island Company. But Dick had been told the invitation was for a turkey shoot.

To assure Dick's good humor, one morning before dawn he was led to a place where turkeys had been salted ahead of time. A guide made a call, and a flock of turkeys answered, but two other guests raised quick shots and killed four turkeys. The rest flew off. Dick didn't get a single bird.

After the millionaire had been plied with drink and a good meal at the magnificent wood-paneled South End House, Coffin broached the subject of investment. Dick was incensed — or at least said he was. (He knew very well why they'd brought him to Sapelo; his anger may have been a negotiating ploy.) He railed against having been lured to Sapelo under false pretenses and said he didn't like being played for a fool. He refused to put up money for Sea Island, but he offered to buy Sapelo. Knowing the Coffin and Jones company was in desperate straits, Dick made a low offer: $700,000 for the entire island, and, if they'd throw in the *Zapala*, he'd up that to an even $750,000.

Sapelo was Coffin's passion and his home. The $50,000 offered for the yacht was a fraction of its commissioning cost. But in 1936 very few people had as much money as Dick Reynolds, and the Morgans, Vanderbilts, Goulds, and Rockefellers already had homes on nearby Jekyll Island. Eventually, Jones helped Coffin realize that he had little choice; for the resort of Sea Island to survive, Sapelo must be sold. Coffin begged Dick to keep the deal secret for a year so that publicity surrounding the transfer wouldn't ad-versely affect Sea Island's development. Dick agreed. Soon, Dick had his seafront residence and one of the world's great yachts, obtained at a fire-sale price, perhaps 10 percent of their real value. Coffin moved to St. Simons; within a year, the sixty-four-year-old carmaker was dead, a suicide.

Dick's new estate was a rectangular paradise twelve miles in length and from two to four miles wide. Seen from the air, as Dick often viewed it from his private plane, most of the outlying portions of the island were revealed as low salt marsh and white sand beaches. On the Atlantic edge, there was an untouched beach stretching several miles in a virtual straight line. The interior was more elevated than these low portions — only a few feet above sea level, actually, but high enough to be densely packed with vegetation, with perhaps ten thousand acres of ground solid enough for cultivation. The forested stands of live oak, laurel oak, bay, holly, magnolia, cabbage palm, and slash palm were all hung with Spanish moss, which filtered and cooled the hot sun's rays. The underbrush consisted of wax myrtle, broom sedge, and panic grass.

Aside from the South End House and some tabby ruins, there were a few scattered communities owned by blacks, families descended from slaves who had been on the island for generations.

South End was a jewel. Although on the mainland it might have seemed modest, placed in Sapelo's junglelike vegetation it exuded a certain stately grandeur. Dominating the approach to the mansion was a cross-shaped outdoor pool graced with Florentine statuary. The house itself was laid out in a manner similar to Reynolda's design, though not so roomy, with a two-story-high central living room flanked by kitchen and bedroom wings.

The first floor had libraries, studies, and drawing rooms alongside the living room. Dick and Blitz took bedroom suites in back of the living room, divided one from the other by a small patio that faced an indoor pool. They had the bottom of that pool flecked with gold and commissioned a well-known muralist to paint the walls of the patio with fantastical banana trees, winking owls, and playful monkeys. On the walls of a third-floor space that the Reynoldses converted into a ballroom, the muralist did circus scenes, and the motif was carried out in a circus tent hung from the ceiling, chandeliers that boasted terra-cotta monkeys on trapezes, and floor statuettes of performing seals. A finished basement was decorated to honor pirate Blackbeard, whose island was actually at Sapelo's northern end. Dick liked to set up empty champagne bottles as the pins in a basement bowling alley and knock them down. He also put in belowstairs wine cellars, walk-in freezers, and generators to make the island independent of outside food and power.

While Mary acquired and remodeled Reynolda and Dick built Devotion and upgraded Sapelo, Nancy began her own estate in Greenwich, Connecticut, located in an ocean-edge granite quarry from which had come the foundations of the Brooklyn Bridge and the base of the Statue of Liberty. In her youth Nancy had told her diary, "If I go through life and accomplish comparatively nothing, yet leave to the world one spot more beautiful because I have lived, I think I will not have lived in vain." Quarry Farm was to be her beauty spot, and she, too, spent lavishly when she came into her share of the fortune, to make it a great residence.

Mary's Connecticut home was not far away, and the two sisters continued to be close, competing seriously in garden and flower shows, going on clothes-buying trips to New York and Europe. A few years later, Nancy bought Musgrove Plantation on St. Simons Island, which was only a few miles south of Sapelo. Often she would bring her family down there for vacations and visit back and forth with Dick and his brood. And, of course, there were millionaires on other neighboring islands to see as well.

In the mid-1930s, because of all the activity at Sapelo and Devotion, Dick employed hundreds of people and dozens of contractors. His business interests included complicated real estate transactions and the buying and selling of stocks and bonds; in the mid-thirties, while stock prices were down, he invested in such blue chips as Chrysler, Cannon Mills, Autolite, General Motors, and Atlas Powder. He spent about a million a year and habitually kept at least a million in foreign banks, while buying gold and silver in foreign countries against the fluctuating values of currencies.

He prided himself on buying the best of everything, and in quantity. When a liquor dealer found twenty cases of pre–Great War bourbon, Dick snapped them up, put them in the Sapelo cellars, had the bill sent to his office, and never knew what price he'd paid for a drink he stocked only for guests; he himself preferred Scotch.

Dick's business transactions were so complicated that lawyer Strat Coyner devoted his entire practice to them. Similarly, Dick's accounts occupied accountant Grey S. Staples full-time. In the middle 1930s, quite unexpectedly, Coyner and Dick came across evidence that someone had skimmed $150,000 from the Reynolds accounts that should have gone to pay contractors. The trail wasn't hard to follow, and it led directly to Staples. Evidently Staples had become convinced by Dick's hands-off style that the millionaire would never really examine his own account books. Dick confronted him with the evidence; shortly thereafter, the accountant committed suicide.

Dick was upset over the death. If he had confronted Staples in a different way, would the man not have killed himself? It was impossible to know. He concluded, however, that Staples's embezzlement — like Lanier's kidnapping threat — had been provoked by the proximity of so much money. Perhaps Staples had been a good man momentarily corrupted by having too much money at his fingertips. Dick expressed his regard for Staples in the only way he knew how, by hiring Ledyard Staples, Grey's brother, as his new accountant. Thereafter, as if to demonstrate his trust, Dick continued to remain aloof from the day-to-day details of paying for his multimillionaire's life-style.

=

It was 1936, and the dust surrounding the estate of Smith Reynolds had finally settled. Dick, Mary, Nancy, Uncle Will, various spouses, and Coyner met to formally set up a foundation and find proper projects for its millions. Until this time, the family's donations had been sporadic and haphazard; pushed into starting a foundation, they were not in complete agreement as to its character. Dick was the driving force behind the Z. Smith Reynolds Foundation, Coyner later said, but other family members also had strong opinions. Mary didn't want to erect buildings; she thought they ought to do more socially constructive things such as send dentists to the back hills of North Carolina. The Reynoldses decided that the charter should mandate the foundation to concentrate on helping the region, giving seed money for projects that might not otherwise come into being. The first large ZSRF grant set up an innovative program to combat syphilis, a disease then rampant in the Southern states. Within a year, this pilot program was taken as a model for a federally supported national campaign against venereal diseases.

The other major push was to upgrade Winston's rather small airport by adding a new terminal. The expectation was that after the WPA had cooperated by grading the runways, Forsyth County would rename the airport for Z. Smith Reynolds — a fitting monument to the memory of the aviator brother.

As Dick soon found out, charitable giving was as full of backbiting and power plays as any business. For years he'd been quietly sending ten thousand dollars annually to North Carolina State to help fund its athletic program. Then a small fracas erupted: the other major donor, textile magnate and publisher David Clark, had been trying to exercise control over football with his contributions. Dick had given his money with no strings attached. Now he had to sit for interviews, testify before a panel, take some criticism. It was a lesson in learning to choose carefully among the many organizations asking for his money. One he had gladly funded was the university's agricultural research program; as an experimental farmer on Sapelo and at Devotion, he understood the value of such research in spurring the development of the region.

By the late 1930s Dick was becoming more skilled in using the power of his money for socially conscious ends: one example was a contribution of land for what became Winston's Reynolds Park. Here, the contribution was tied to a pledge by the WPA to build the structures; when the park was completed, it had a golf course, tennis courts, a swimming pool, a gym, and amenities usually reserved for members of private clubs. Dick was present at the opening ceremonies and made a speech. This, too, was part of what he was learning: to be comfortable as a public figure. He discovered that he didn't mind the glare of publicity as much as he had in former years; obtaining applause for being a pillar of the community was gratifying.

Dick's position as leader of the second generation was increasingly challenged by the social aspirations of Mary's husband, Charles Babcock. In the late 1930s a group of younger families led by Babcock, and including Dick, dropped out of the venerable Forsyth Country Club, which was in financial difficulties, to form a new club, the Old Town. Babcock donated one hundred acres of Reynolda for Old Town's eighteen-hole golf course. It seemed a certainty that Forsyth Country would shortly close its doors. But Babcock and the other Young Turks made a mistake: they elected Dick Reynolds, in absentia, to the Old Town board. Insulted by having his cooperation taken for granted, Dick reacted by resigning from that board, going back to the almost bankrupt Forsyth Country Club, and subsidizing its renovation and refinancing.

Dick's charities and business investments didn't take up a great deal of his time. Coyner and others on his staff acted as filters on all matters so that Dick had to make only the final decisions. Accordingly, Dick and Blitz's life-style was unfettered by the press of everyday business. It featured a good deal of moving from residence to residence, lots of entertaining, and a continual search for creative ways to enjoy their leisure and their money.

In the late 1930s most of Dick's energy went into Sapelo and Devotion. On Sapelo, he sought to swap tracts with the blacks, who had been scattered around the island, so that their community would center on Hog Hammock and Dick would have clear title to all other areas. As an inducement, he brought electricity to the island and had all the blacks' homes hooked up. He also paid a schoolteacher to come over and instruct the black children, many of whom had previously been kept home because of the long journey required to attend school on the mainland. Since nearly all the residents now worked for him, he sometimes held court like a feudal lord, adjusting disputes, meting out small punishments.

The *Zapala* was another mansion, containing five mahogany staterooms; Oriental rugs; a walnut-paneled dining room with china, crystal, and silver services; brass railings within and chrome without; teak and cedar decks — all serviced by a crew of eight. It cost Dick and Blitz about twenty thousand dollars to make their annual crossing to the French Riviera. The *Zapala*'s more usual cruise was up and down the Atlantic coast.

The Reynoldses became famous for their parties — several couples aboard the *Zapala* for a champagne cruise to Bermuda, fifty guests and a small orchestra flown to Sapelo for a weekend, dinner for a hundred after a mass pheasant hunt at Devotion. Every birthday, anniversary, local or national holiday was excuse for celebration. In public, Dick was a gracious, charming host who made his guests feel comfortable.

The luxurious journey through life was not always smooth; indeed, the couple's wealth and freedom from want may have contributed to their difficulties. Their houses were beautiful and perfect, their servants were ubiquitous and took care of their every need — as a consequence, the couple had few of the usual worries of American families in the Depression years. Moreover, small dissatisfactions that a couple in more ordinary circumstances might have tolerated were blown up to the status of nagging problems. Then, too, Dick and Blitz, both strong-willed, had short emotional fuses. Dick drank heavily at times and when in his cups could turn in an instant from courteous to scathing. When Blitz desired a trip to New York, or a new maid, or a pair of earrings, she would allow nothing to stand in her way; she'd argue until she won. No matter how Blitz and Dick tried, they could not keep their stewpot from bubbling over, and Winstonians eager for gossip soon learned of their fights, which became well known. Perhaps in reaction to this, at parties Dick would discourse on the impossibility of having a marriage without fights and say that it was good for partners during a dispute to slam doors or drive away from a house. He'd sometimes stalk out of Long Creek Lodge, start up one of the automobiles, and go out past the gates for a ride. He'd always come back, though it might not be for a day or two; then there would be apologies and protestations of love on both sides. He liked the drama of such stormy episodes. If he'd gone astray while not at the hearth, he seemed ready on his return to atone for his lapses with gifts. Tongues in Winston wagged long and hard to figure out what Dick had done to enable Blitz to extract from him the donation of an entire new building for the Junior League.

While Dick traveled to oversee construction at Devotion and on Sapelo, Blitz was at home in Winston more often than not. Sons arrived at approximately two-year intervals (R. J. III, or Josh, late 1933; John, 1936; Zach, 1938). There was also the Winston social scene: she was a stalwart of the YMCA and the Junior League and even designed costumes for children's plays. She conceived a passion for her wardrobe and modeled the latest styles from New York for her Winston charities, often buying the clothes in which she strode down the ramp. She liked being Mrs. R. J. Reynolds, buying whatever she wanted, having the prestige and social position that came with the name.

In late 1937 Dick acted on a passion of his own: to have a racing yacht and compete in international regattas. He'd been a master sailor for years. Now he told Sparkman & Stephens, premier sailing yacht builders of the era, to spare no expense in putting together the *Blitzen*, named after Blitz. She was a fifty-five-foot sloop with one mast and sails fore and aft. As soon as she was launched, in the spring of 1938, she was a serious competitor. Like only a handful of other yacht owners, Dick captained his own boat; in the *Blitzen*'s first, short race, he finished a respectable second.

Dick joined the New York Yacht Club and another club based on St. Simons and became part of the yachting set. Blitz seemed to like this world of moneyed people, dockside cocktail parties, and wind-driven boats as much as Dick did. In June of 1938 the *Blitzen* entered her first world-class race, from Newport, Rhode Island, all the way down to Bermuda. Sloops, ketches, and yawls had come from England, Germany, Canada, and several other countries, as well as from the United States; five were Sparkman & Stephens designs.

Each day en route to Bermuda produced headlines on sports pages around the globe. Although Dick did not come across the finish line first, his handicap allowance — based on weight, draft, and other factors — caused his sloop to be declared the winner of the Class B division and established the *Blitzen* as one of the world's fastest sloops. The *Blitzen* also made a good showing in the British Fastnet: a third place, even after a breakdown. Germany, then annexing Czechoslovakia and making a pact with the British and French at Munich, was still trying to appear civilized by putting into the water excellent competitive yachting teams. On the international circuit Dick met several high-ranking German naval officers and also Christian Nissen, an ordinary German seaman who years later became his employee.

In racing yachts, Dick found something that combined his competitiveness, love of the sea, and zest for the good life in the company of people who accepted his inherited wealth without rancor. He took the *Blitzen* everywhere in 1939 — second prize in the Miami-to-Nassau run, first prize in a Nassau course, two more firsts going from St. Petersburg, Florida, to Havana and from Havana to Key West.

In June 1939 he freighted the *Blitzen* to San Francisco for the ultimate long-distance yacht race, 2,085 miles to Honolulu. In the shadow of the Golden Gate there were problems with off-loading and qualifying time trials, but there also were diversions, nearly continuous parties thrown by the yachtsmen in the bay, which was the site of an international exposition. As tens of thousands watched from the Golden Gate Bridge, the shorelines, countless boats, and even a blimp, on July 4 hundreds of yachts set out to sea.

Dick struck a southerly course across the Pacific. This turned out to be a good choice, because boats that opted to ride the northern trade winds were soon becalmed. After ten days, he was third, behind the 106-foot *Contender* and the favored *Fandango*.

Early on the evening of July 18, 1939, the *Contender* finished first, but the *Blitzen* and *Fandango* were sail and sail, just at the horizon.

Rounding Diamond Head, Dick's sloop lost her spinnaker, and he and the crew frantically gathered wind in the mainsail. Near midnight, they crossed the finish line, beating the *Fandango* by fifty-two seconds. Once more, because of the handicaps, Dick's *Blitzen* was declared the overall winner of a yacht race — this one, the most grueling of the year. With this feat, Dick proved himself to be at the top of the list of the world's racing captains; in today's terms, the equivalent to the man who wins the America's Cup.

Six weeks later, Hitler's armies invaded Poland, the British and French came to Poland's aid, and World War II began. Among its early casualties was the international yacht-racing circuit. Thus the cross-Pacific was the *Blitzen*'s last important victory. After it, Dick had to find something else to occupy his energies.

Chapter Twelve

Politics

IN EARLY 1940, the world was at war — except that it didn't feel much like war because the major belligerents, Germany, France, and Great Britain, weren't actively engaged in killing one another. The "phony war" was a doldrums, a time of waiting. Even the president had not made up his mind whether to run for an unprecedented third term. Many people were aghast at the notion of a third term, which they likened to crowning a king. If the war heated up, Roosevelt was expected to run; if not, people thought, he'd better retire. FDR's former aide Ray Moley contended in a 1940 book that *After Seven Years* the Roosevelt revolution had completed its course and it was time for a political change.

Dick Reynolds was restless, too, and also looking for a change. He decided to put his money to work for him — something he hadn't done since he'd bought the old *Harpoon*. Over a few months in the spring of 1940, he made purchases in three different business arenas. First, he transferred his love of yachting to an interest in shipping by making a successful bid in February for the bankrupt American Mail Line of Pacific steamers. The freight carrier, based in Seattle, was awash in red ink: its half-dozen boats were old, the U.S. government had withdrawn mail subsidies, and Pacific routes were being challenged by the expansion of Japan. He purchased the assets for a fraction of what they were once worth. If he made money, he'd be a hero; if not, he could write off the loss against his other income. It was the sort of purchase easily available to wealthy people even at the tail end of the Depression. The *Seattle Post-Intelligencer* hoped he was a savior for the line and assessed him favorably: "There is nothing in Reynolds' air or appearance to indicate his great wealth. . . . He is a tall, well-built young man, with an engaging grin and a complexion that shows he's spent a lot of time in the open."

To turn the company around, Dick initiated a flurry of activity, arranging to sell the freighters for scrap, rent others, and have new ones built. Dick and Strat Coyner started shuttling monthly to Seattle. There also were trips to Washington to intercede with various government agencies involved in shipping. These activities took Dick out of town on business at least one week of the month.

During this period Dick also bought more RJR stock, for two reasons. When as a teenager Dick had tended cigarette machines in the factory, his boss had been John Whitaker, who was now ranking vice president, slated for the chairmanship. Dick had faith in Whitaker; moreover, Whitaker had always been partial to Dick and was willing to listen to the man who was now the largest stockholder. The purchase also put him in line for a seat on the executive board — Uncle Will was expected to retire soon, and there would be a vacancy that "solid citizen" Dick could fill.

The third major purchase was actually several, in aviation. Dick became the largest stockholder in the underfinanced Eastern Airlines, not merely because he believed in the future of aviation, but also, as with the RJR stock buy, so that he could use his resulting leverage with the company. There was a plan for Eastern to bring regular scheduled service to Winston-Salem. The Z. Smith Reynolds Foundation had pledged money to upgrade the airport but made the grant conditional on regular scheduled passenger service being brought to Winston by a large airline such as Eastern. Winston's negotiations with Eastern took the better part of the next two years.

Later in 1940 fledgling Delta Airlines got in trouble and turned to Dick; his purchase of a large block of stock enabled Delta to stay in business. Then a third air carrier came to him for rescue. Years earlier, with a loan from Dick to his personal pilot Lew McGinnes, the North Carolina remnants of Reynolds Aviation had become Camel City Flying Service. In addition to ferrying people on short hops, McGinnes was also distributing Piper Cubs and other aircraft. By 1940, however, the enterprise wasn't making money. The network of wealthy Winstonians got to work. Charlie Norfleet, trust officer at the Wachovia Bank and secretary of the Forsyth County Airport Commission, put Dick and McGinnes together with Thomas H. Davis, a young man of some means. Davis agreed to repay some of the loans, and Dick agreed to forgive the rest so that

Camel City Flying Service could become Piedmont Aviation. In later years, few people realized that at a crucial juncture for the aviation industry, Dick Reynolds played a part in ensuring the survival of three of the country's major airlines.

Dick also made a small investment for another old friend and fellow liberal, Bill Sharpe, with whom he'd once published *The Three Cent Pup*. Sharpe had become a columnist for the Winston papers. When Dick's contemporary Gordon Gray (son of Bowman Gray, board chairman of RJR in the 1930s) formed a consortium that bought the Winston papers in 1937, he asked Dick to join. Dick was ready to do so until he discerned that Gray was going to run those papers with a heavy hand, and he declined. Bill Sharpe then proposed to Dick a new paper that would express their anti-establishment views and work to make the city more progressive. Dick backed Sharpe's weekly, *Thursday*, which developed into a widely read social critique that spared few and was a constant gadfly to the Winston power structure. Dick's dalliance with Gray but ultimate refusal to join him, and his backing of Sharpe, demonstrated his unique position: at that moment he was both in the Winston establishment and rebelling against it.

His rebelliousness, combined with his continuing admiration for Roosevelt, led him inevitably into politics. Dick's open third-term advocacy put him at a distance from many of the old-line Democrats in Winston, especially Uncle Will Reynolds and the management of RJR. They had actively supported FDR in 1932 and 1936 but had become disenchanted. Exacerbating their disapproval of Roosevelt was a major antitrust suit against the tobacco companies (for price fixing), which shortly would name Will Reynolds and the upper RJR management as individual defendants, along with RJR and the other giant tobacco companies.

In May 1940, Hitler invaded France and the Low Countries. When the war spread, Roosevelt said he would run for a third term. This was too much for old-line stalwarts; in North Carolina they withdrew support from the Democratic party, and it almost fell apart. People who had been Democrats since the era of Woodrow Wilson now pledged to vote for the Republican nominee, Wendell Willkie.

Charles Babcock challenged Will Reynolds to publicly wear a Willkie button — for $500. Uncle Will pinned one on his coat and contributed Babcock's $500, plus $3,500 of his own, to the Willkie campaign. Dick told a reporter that old R. J. had always been a

Democrat and that his son saw no reason to change now. Will responded in a letter to the editor that R. J. had once voted for William McKinley. Soon, uncle and nephew weren't speaking. However, Winston would not be allowed the spectacle of a public feud between them: no old biddies could even wonder about such a thing when the announcement was made that Dick's fourth son, born in 1940, was to be named William Neal Reynolds II.

Like the FDR presidency, after seven years the marriage of Dick and Blitz was a bit tired — to friends, Dick seemed restless. There were four boys now. Sometimes Dick called them his pride and joy; at other times he disliked their constant clamor for attention. He alternately spoiled them and ignored them, and overall supervision was left to Blitz.

For this now large family, Dick and Blitz were building a new home in Winston, Merry Acres. It would border the Forsyth Country Club, just as the new Old Town golf club (Charlie Babcock, founder) would border Reynolda. Dick had sketched what a newspaper called a "fantasy of decks and turrets, towers and cantilever porches" and turned the project over to an architect to complete. Blitz and he disagreed on many facets of the design; for example, Dick wanted the house air-conditioned and Blitz didn't. Things between them weren't the same as when they were fashioning Devotion.

Bill Sharpe wrote in *Thursday* that Blitz, "whose nickname is indicative of her strong personality, frankly told her friends that she didn't know what would happen to [her marriage] if Roosevelt were re-elected." She disliked FDR now and was planning to vote for Willkie. That, of course, was anathema to Dick.

In September, Dick was offered the post of financial director of the North Carolina committee in charge of raising money for FDR's campaign. Dick agreed, on condition that the task encompass more than anteing up and soliciting his fat cat friends. In this post, he could express both his political leanings and his anti-Winston-establishment posture; it also kept him away from home just when he and Blitz were disagreeing over politics, air-conditioning, and alcohol consumption. He moved into an office in Raleigh and began work.

He took to the job like a yacht to water. Years of being affable to countless party guests, of moving effortlessly among the wealthy and their servants, seem to have prepared him well for politics. Sensing support from cab drivers, shopkeepers, and other ordinary people, he deliberately sought small contributions. In 1936 Dick had given $20,000 to the Roosevelt campaign (and loaned tens of thousands more), and other wealthy men had pledged similar amounts. This time, the recently passed Hatch Act restricted individual donations to $5,000 or less. Dick buttonholed wealthy friends and resisted the temptation (embraced by other campaigners) of taking potshots at the rich in the name of upholding FDR, choice of the common man. However, he was not very successful at squeezing donations from his peers. To his chagrin, he was among the very few well-to-do people in the country who continued to support FDR. The New Deal was requiring the rich to pay somewhat higher taxes, and it seemed that the allegiance of those with money had now, after a temporary fling with Roosevelt, returned to its old home, the Republican party.

Only once did Dick give rein to his temper in public: he had a fistfight with a utilities executive who was backing Willkie and beat him silly. Though more than one newspaper called this "unusual behavior" from someone they saw as a charming, publicly reserved man, news of the fight leaked out — and didn't hurt Dick's popularity with small contributors.

Dick stumped the state, was tireless on the telephone, and came up with innovative ideas to involve younger people in the campaign. The *Raleigh News and Observer* commented, "The job as finance director . . . is throwing the ambitious and democratic scion of the tobacco family into contact with people who count politically, in the nation as well as the State." That was so. Dick met with Democratic National Committee chief Ed Flynn and treasurer Oliver Quayle and was praised for his good work.

Later, these men called his attention to a crisis. Roosevelt had won by landslides in 1932 and 1936, but now the president was not considered a cinch to be reelected; in September, some polls showed FDR even with Willkie, some had him slipping behind. If the president made a series of radio addresses in the closing days of the campaign, the politicians felt, he would win; if they were not made, Willkie might win. Unfortunately, the national committee had run out of money. Would Dick "lend" the state committees of Michigan, New York, and New Jersey about $300,000 so that these committees could then pick up the tabs for the radio broadcasts? Dick assented instantly.

There was some opposition from radio companies that had broadcast Willkie more often than FDR; with cash on the line, NBC and

CBS agreed to sell time for the president's speeches. Between October 23 and November 4 the president spoke six times on the radio. These speeches asked listeners not to change horses in midstream and stressed Roosevelt's experience in foreign affairs, so necessary at a crucial time. They swung enough votes into the Democratic column to give FDR the election.

When the donations were tallied, it was found that, primarily through Dick Reynolds's efforts, North Carolina had been second among the states in money raised, and its $80,000 had been amassed from many more individual contributors than in former years. Unhappy with Oliver Quayle's performance, Roosevelt and Flynn decided to offer Dick Reynolds Quayle's former job, treasurer of the Democratic National Committee. Dick accepted, requesting only that lawyer Strat Coyner and his old friend John Graham (who had worked hard on the campaign in Winston) be hired to assist him.

At a news conference at Washington's Mayflower Hotel on January 4, 1941, Flynn announced the reorganization of the DNC and Dick's appointment as treasurer. Flynn described him as part of the Reynolds tobacco family but not connected with RJR.

A few days later, the questioning of a Democratic state congressman from New Jersey by a Senate subcommittee investigating campaign financing revealed that Dick had lent the New Jersey Democratic Committee $100,000; the note was dated October 31, for ninety days. No attempt had yet been made by New Jersey to repay, and Reynolds had not tried to collect. Immediately, the subcommittee subpoenaed Dick.

Dick took the witness chair on January 10 — the day he was to formally assume his duties as DNC treasurer — wearing a gray business suit and a green shirt, and with a demeanor described by the *Washington Post* as "suave." Under questioning by Republican senator Charles Tobey of New Hampshire, Dick denied that his appointment was the result of his loans but did admit advancing the New Jersey, New York, and Michigan committees $300,000. "I expect the loans to be repaid," he said, explaining that they had been made "because . . . I was told this money would carry those states for President Roosevelt, whose reelection I thought was vital."

He showed the senators the notes and made the mistake of saying he thought Michigan's was for three months when it was for six. Tobey moved in for the kill: "I wish I was in a position that I did

not know the length of notes." Tobey then suggested that Dick
expected repayment for the loans in the form of favorable Maritime
Commission rulings on the American Mail Line. Dick countered
by pointing out that most of the line's dealings with the commission
had been concluded before he'd bought the company. (Actually,
at year's end Dick had received word that his efforts had already
succeeded in putting American Mail in the black; profits for 1940
were about $340,000.) The hearing soon dissolved in partisan bick-
ering. To deflect Republican pressure from Dick and department-
store magnate Marshall Field, the Democratic members insisted
that Republican contributors be compelled to testify. The Du
Ponts, Pews, and Rockefellers, in giving more than $100,000 each
to various Willkie committees, could also be accused of circum-
venting the Hatch Act.

The following Monday a Washington grand jury called Dick to
testify on the loans. The night before his appearance, Dick got
drunk. It had happened often enough in private, but this time it
threatened to spill over into his public life. Lew McGinnes found
him in a Washington bar and first brought him back to the Mayflower in a wheelbarrow, sobering him up with a shower. Only
then did he go to the witness stand, where he answered questions
blithely and escaped without a scratch. Bill Sharpe commented, in
Thursday, that if Dick was going to be in politics, he should recognize
such public scrutiny and infighting as the norm, and added that he
hoped Dick would develop a "thick skin and a . . . sunny dispo-
sition," as well as employ a good lawyer.

=

The whirl of activity surrounding the third inauguration of Roosevelt, in early 1941, swept up both Dick and Blitz; they became
part of the Washington political-social set. Their differences were
shunted aside. The new DNC treasurer needed a wife who could
be a trouper, and Blitz relished her new roles as member of the
women's affiliate of the DNC and, later, chairwoman of some small
gatherings. She proved a whiz at political dinners and on reviewing
stands; opening the Reynoldses' new home, Merry Acres, she
played hostess for visiting dignitaries with great success. Sometimes
she and Dick would attend the same events, but often there were
so many obligations that they split the work and appeared at different functions.

In the early months of 1941, Dick bounced from Washington to

Winston-Salem to Raleigh, with occasional trips to Seattle. If in ideology he followed FDR, in the mechanics of politics he emulated Ed Flynn, the son of poor Irish immigrants who was a ward boss in the Bronx before appearing on the national scene. Dick and Flynn became close friends, the crafty, self-made Flynn serving as mentor to the young millionaire. Dick devoted one or two days a week to raising money to eliminate the $400,000 deficit from the election campaign. The usual vehicles to obtain that kind of money were countrywide Andrew Jackson Day dinners, scheduled for various dates around the end of March.

Although planning for these went smoothly at first, there was a hitch when prospective attendees at the Washington, D. C., dinner balked at paying $100 each after learning that the president would speak to them by radio and not appear in person, since he was vacationing on a boat off Florida. Dick tried to rescue the Washington dinner by having a telegram sent from the president. He didn't get an answer from FDR's boat far enough in advance and so canceled the dinner. A flap ensued — in a memo to FDR, presidential counselor Jim Rowe said Dick had acted like Pontius Pilate. But Flynn and others took the view that it was simply the mistake of a man who was still an amateur. No real harm was done to Dick's political career.

A man more accustomed to the struggles of business or politics might have learned a fundamental lesson here — watch your back — but Dick's previous experience and basic optimism seemed to prevent that particular lesson from taking hold.

Charles and Mary Babcock came to a party at Merry Acres honoring the Flynns, even though the country club feud was still simmering. In Winston, even if you were fighting you observed the niceties. Mary's letters show that she and Blitz didn't like each other very much, but the two women flew to New York to cheer Nancy's entry in a prestigious flower show; it took third prize. Later, Mary wrote Nancy that at a Winston party she'd been asked to do her "famous" burlesque bump and grind, had been drunk enough to comply — and hoped no one would remind her of it at the next gathering. Tallulah Bankhead was appearing in *The Little Foxes* at the Reynolds auditorium; Blitz went to see her and perfected a wicked caricature of Tallulah, which she displayed as the queen in the Junior League's *Snow White*.

For many years the mayoralty of Winston-Salem had been a fiefdom of James Gray of RJR. In 1941, Mayor Jim Fain, a Gray man, was considered the front-runner in that year's race. Other candidates included previous mayor Bill Coan and Marshall Kurfees, a perennial gadfly and also-ran whom Dick had supported in his unsuccessful bid for the mayoralty in 1939. Kurfees and Dick were in the library of Merry Acres one afternoon, sipping cocktails and discussing the local situation, when Jim Gray called on the telephone to ask whether Dick was going to run for mayor.

"What of it?" Dick said. Gray asked if he and Fain could come over. The prospect of a Reynolds running for office in a town that revered Reynoldses obviously had alarmed them. Kurfees hid in an adjoining room. Gray told Dick he'd make a fine mayor someday, but that it was customary for mayors to serve two terms and he wanted Fain now. Dick said he didn't care much for custom and believed that the last time around Kurfees had been bilked at the ballot box. Gray caved in, saying that if Dick wanted to run, Fain would pull out. Dick shouted, "Let him run. I don't give a damn. . . . I'm going to run and I want him to run." Dick announced a few days later. Within the week the major candidates had withdrawn in his favor.

One needs to have a large ego to stand for elected office, and Dick must have been flattered by the other candidates' precipitate scurry to get out of his way. However, he may well have counted on having an easy path in his hometown. The idea of running for office had been growing in his mind since he first took the North Carolina finance post in 1940, and in his first try he had decided to enter a race that he had a good chance of winning.

His platform was solidly New Deal. For six years Winston-Salem had officially sanctioned the notion that no slums existed in the city. But it was a quarter century since R. J., Katharine, and Lenora Sills had tried to upgrade conditions in the town; certain black neighborhoods had whole square blocks without working toilets or drinking water, many homes needed to be replaced, and some city streets were little more than dirt roads. Dick called attention to these defects, pledged slum clearance, and said he'd apply for WPA help and federal housing funds to rebuild poverty-stricken districts. Coming from an intimate of powerful political figures, this promise made sense to Winstonians.

Dick won election easily on April 21, but before he could actually take office, a political fight blew up. The unexpected death of Congressman Lon Folger left vacant his post of male DNC representative from North Carolina. There was an immediate flurry of interest in the job, not because it was a prestigious position but, rather, because it was seen as a stepping-stone to the 1944 senatorial nomination. The most substantial candidate was former governor Clyde Hoey, who, with his brother-in-law O. Max Gardner, also a former governor, had run Democratic politics in the state for twenty years. But Hoey was viewed by younger Democrats as a conservative who had also been lukewarm to FDR.

Dick Reynolds decided he'd try for the national committeeman post. Though it was a minor position, it would bring him greater statewide recognition, accentuate the shift of leadership to the younger, more liberal faction of the party, and put him in position to challenge Robert "Our Bob" Reynolds — no relation — in the 1944 senatorial race. The other Reynolds was considered vulnerable because he'd deserted FDR in 1940 and was also a dim-witted windbag.

In this battle, however, Dick underestimated his opposition. As a neophyte in politics he didn't recognize (or perhaps didn't care) that his candidacy would upset the machine politicians of the state. Governor J. Melville Broughton could not allow his power to be undermined, and former governors Hoey and Gardner couldn't permit an upstart to steal their thunder.

In May, the conflict broke out publicly, with both Hoey and Dick opening offices in Raleigh to lobby actively for votes. At stake were the ballots of the limited number of voters, all of whom were from the ranks of Democratic party officeholders and other state functionaries. Dick wanted a closed ballot so that people could maintain their support for him without the old guard's knowledge. Hoey wanted an open vote. Dick sent his plane to Washington to bring back one congressman who said he'd vote for him, but Hoey's men twisted the fellow's arm. A female state executive thought Dick was the best candidate but was forced by the governor to give a proxy vote for Hoey. Another delegate was threatened with the loss of a state job held by a close relative. Nine of twelve delegates in a third district held jobs subject to the governor's pleasure. An old hand in Raleigh called the tactics of Broughton, Gardner, and Hoey "the most ruthless exhibition of political pressure I have ever seen."

Dick had won the Winston mayoralty with a plurality of more than 90 percent. However, the committeeman vote overshadowed both his victory and his first weeks in office. While Mayor Reynolds presided at a meeting with the city aldermen, attended a high school graduation, and spoke over Gordon Gray's radio station, Hoey kept chipping away at his support. In late May, the vote was finally held — by open ballot and with fistfuls of proxies. Hoey won easily.

In this affair Dick not only suffered his first political defeat but also, at the outset of what promised to be a long career, had his nose rubbed in the mud. And that he never forgot. Had he learned earlier to watch his back, or that success in politics was assured more by cultivating the power structure than by unnecessarily challenging it, he might have avoided being slapped down by the governors. As things went, the defeat took the bloom off the rose just as the flower was emerging into the sunlight.

=

The weeks following the election for national committeeman were so hectic that Dick hardly had time to reflect on his defeat. Business, politics, family, and charity all mixed at once. In Chester, Pennsylvania, he and Blitz, accompanied by two of the boys, cracked champagne over the bow of the ninety-six-ton *China Mail*, the first of several ships being built for the American Mail Line. In Washington, D. C., Dick did some DNC work, which included a speech to North Carolina Democrats touring the city, and made an attempt to see the president about a judgeship he wished to obtain for a friend. In Winston, he spoke as mayor and a major benefactor on a national radio hookup marking his gift to the local historical society of the Old Salem Tavern, where George Washington had once slept. The Reynoldses flew to Hollywood for a Democratic fund-raiser, and Dick went by himself or with Strat Coyner to Southern state conventions of the Young Democrats.

Back home again, he began aldermanic meetings. He spurred the elected officials to pass a slum-clearance ordinance, but a backlash was growing. There were other clashes in council over the city's budget, blue laws, and a taxi drivers' strike. Dick brought the drivers in to see the officials and said that in the 1920s he'd once driven a cab himself. In championing the drivers, pushing to loosen the blue laws, and taking on the problem of slum clearance Dick reversed the quiescent posture of previous city administrations; although his actions didn't endear him to local politicians, they made headlines and won popular approval.

One weekend in June, Mary and Charles Babcock entertained 150 descendants of Joshua and Agnes Cox at Reynolda. Smiths,

Reynoldses, Bagleys, Babcocks, Critzes, Staleys, and Lybrooks came in profusion. Abram's children mixed with R. J.'s brood; the old rift was smoothed over at five parties in two days, which also spilled over to Merry Acres. Extra lifeguards were hired for Lake Katharine and the pool. R. S.'s son David had a false eye, having lost an eye in an accident; when a party heated up, he sometimes replaced the glass eye with a bloodshot one. When an affair became really wild, he put in an eye that sported a miniature American flag.

Dick and his cousin R. S. were friends, though separated in age by more than a quarter century. At this moment, both were taking business risks. R. S., now sixty years old, was in the midst of the biggest move of his life — a move that paralleled what R. J. had done at about the same age upon being released from the tobacco trust. R. S. was trying to transform Reynolds Metals from a user of aluminum foil into a primary producer of the metal itself. Until the start of World War II, the aluminum industry had been dominated by Alcoa, and R. S.'s $15-million-a-year company had had to buy most of its aluminum "pig" from Alcoa. R. S. had pleaded in public for the government to get into the pig-producing business in 1940 so America could produce the fifty thousand airplanes that FDR wanted in order to be prepared for war.

When the government did nothing, R. S. tried to put his own company into production of pig and faced considerable problems, the most serious of which was lack of capital. No private banks would gamble with him. He'd finally persuaded the Reconstruction Finance Corporation to lend him $15 million and was now pushing hard to build smelting and reduction plants and a sheet mill. R. S. was overextended financially, but if the United States went to war — as both he and Dick believed it would — Reynolds Metals would leap into the category of giant.

Dick was also taking a $15-million gamble, building six ships for AML, and his money had been borrowed easily from regular banks. The real difference between them was that Dick wasn't paying as strict attention to AML as R. S. could give to Reynolds Metals because Dick was also involved in politics and finishing his estates. At AML, as with many of his ventures, in the first few months Dick had put in a lot of time and energy to establish the pattern of management, then had turned day-to-day operations over to others. R. S. delegated power, too, but remained involved personally and daily with his enterprise.

The oldest people at the Reynolds-Cox family reunion were Uncle Will and Aunt Kate, now in their seventies, and Will's venerable older sister Lucy Burroughs Critz. This party marked the last public appearance of Aunt Kate. Later in 1941, the woman who had once been the belle of Winston was declared mentally incompetent. There were worries about Uncle Will, too; that summer, when he took the witness stand at the price-fixing trial, he was accompanied by a nurse.

As the weather warmed, Blitz and the boys moved to Devotion. Dick couldn't go with them because he had to be in Washington for DNC business during the early part of each week and in Winston during the second half of the week for aldermen's meetings. So, in effect, the Reynoldses were separated during the summer of 1941.

Toward the end of June, Dick took on his biggest challenge as mayor of Winston-Salem, an all-out fight in the council chambers over slum clearance. The question before the aldermen was whether to apply for a U.S. Housing Authority grant to build public housing units. Dick cared more about this issue than anything else on the council's agenda. His support for slum clearance and public housing was an expression of his liberal beliefs and of a piece with a lifelong attempt to help the underdogs of Southern society, the blacks. For example, he was an anonymous donor to several black causes and consistently hired blacks for his enterprises. On Sapelo, not only had he instituted an on-island school for the blacks, but he also let the members of the Hog Hammock community know that he would pay for any of them to go north to look for a job — and for their return passage — at any time.

In Winston, Dick had seen the fight over slum clearance coming and had hired out of his own pocket several attorneys to help him present his case. Opposing him was a coalition of slumlords, whose counsel was a local judge. On the evening of the council's vote, while reporters and many interested citizens watched and listened, there were several hours of shouting. The opposition slung a lot of racial insults and even had property owners testify that caring for run-down housing was their version of bearing the white man's burden. They also suggested that public housing, already long embraced by the rest of the country, was un-American. When all the arguments had been aired at least once — and were still going on — Dick gaveled the council to silence and called for a vote. It was unanimous in favor of his plan.

Dick immediately rushed to Washington and arrived on the last day for filing USHA requests. There hadn't been time to get Winston-Salem's proposal written, but through his political connections Dick obtained a personal hearing on the request with Housing Authority chief Nathan Straus. A month later, Straus called Dick to say that USHA had approved $1.4 million out of the $2 million requested by Winston-Salem, enough to build four hundred new apartments. Dick appointed RJR's John Whitaker to head the new Winston-Salem housing commission and also put Strat Coyner and former mayor Jim Fain on the board. These appointments, and the way he went about getting the USHA grant, showed that he'd learned to use political muscle and pay political debts.

He was also learning to keep his mouth shut when opening it couldn't help him. The RJR Company was in trouble on three fronts: the price-fixing trial, a concurrent suit by disgruntled stockholders, and the attempted unionization of its workers. Mayor Dick Reynolds, a major stockholder, steadfastly avoided comment on these issues, though he was known to have liberal ideas that championed organized labor. His silence was interpreted as support by both the company and the union organizers.

Despite that new political sophistication, during the rest of 1941 the Hoey-Gardner-Broughton combination continued to oppose Dick on political posts. As DNC treasurer, Dick picked all the chairmen of the forthcoming 1942 Jackson Day dinners; his choices went unchallenged in all the other states, but in his home state the governor's minions managed to insist on their candidate for the job. The combination did the same in picking who would be the North Carolina head of the Young Democrats. Such pettiness, and the continual squabbles in the Winston city council over minor ordinances, sapped Dick's willingness to continue the infighting that seemed necessary to political advancement. In politics, as in his forays into aviation and yacht racing, a defeat Dick suffered — one that might have been construed as only a temporary setback — loomed larger than that in his mind and set him to thinking about other directions. By late summer, Bill Sharpe's paper was hinting that Dick might soon follow a few other local luminaries and join the U.S. Navy.

On December 8, 1941, when FDR denounced the Japanese attack on Pearl Harbor and asked Congress for a declaration of war, Mayor Reynolds took to the radio to put Winston-Salem on alert: he deputized the airport staff to watch for incoming enemy planes, announced test blackouts, and called on the citizenry to aid the war effort and look out for saboteurs. The unexpectedness of the attack had made even inland cities like Winston-Salem wary, and willing to meet the alarm. In the country as a whole, the declaration of war ended a long period of waiting for the inevitable; now the nation had a clear direction and a task, to beat the Axis. For Dick, the coming of war afforded a perfect excuse to get away from a society, a job, and even a life-style that no longer met his expectations. Perhaps being in the war would enable him, at age thirty-five, to prove himself as a man and not merely as a wealthy son of R. J. Reynolds.

The draft board refused to take him, not only because he was the head of a family and the mayor of a large town — both perfectly acceptable exemptions — but also because he was the principal owner of an "essential" industrial unit, the American Mail Line. His only recourse was to volunteer. Blitz was bitter about this decision. Even though she and Dick weren't getting along that well, she didn't want him to go to war.

He decided to enlist voluntarily. He hadn't flown by himself for a while, and despite the fact that some of his contemporaries — and fellow members of the "Ancient Order of Quiet Birdmen," like General Jimmy Doolittle — were now America's top pilots, he thought that the air corps would want younger men, so he made plans to join the navy. Doubtless he could find a berth appropriate to his experience; there couldn't be too many men who understood the operation of both ships and aircraft to the extent that he did. He kept his intentions private for some time, so private, in fact, that even sisters Mary and Nancy were not aware of them until the last moment.

Over the first six months of 1942, as the United States geared up for war, Charles Babcock, Henry Bagley, and sons of the Gray, Hanes, Graham, and other prominent families all enlisted in the armed forces, though most of them, like Dick, were fathers and could have remained civilians. Mary, Nancy, and Blitz all began work in hospitals.

With the coming of war, some of the New Deal's social measures were sidelined. One small casualty was the public housing grant of $1.4 million for Winston-Salem, deferred for the duration of the national emergency. With that grant gone, Dick's major accomplishment as mayor seemed to evaporate, and this reinforced his disenchantment with politics. During the spring he took examinations, passed a physical, and was scheduled for training by the navy.

In mid-April the RJR board met, accepted the resignation of Will Reynolds, and appointed Dick to Will's former seat on the company's ruling body. It was a goal Dick had long sought. Now he would be unable to enjoy sitting on the board of the company his father had founded because he was going to war.

Dick met with President Roosevelt, who was a bit annoyed by Dick's decision and asked him not to resign as DNC treasurer until he found a successor who was good enough to do as well as he had — come close to wiping out the party's debts and put the Democrats in the black for the first time since anyone could remember. For two weeks Dick called around the country to locate someone with the necessary characteristics; he was finally able to persuade Ed Pauley, a yachtsman and finance chairman of the western states during the 1940 campaign, to take the job.

In a handwritten letter to FDR on June 4, Dick formally resigned, noting that "the Party's finances are in the best shape they've been in for some time." In fact, he'd wiped out the entire deficit, except for what the party owed him personally. Since the DNC's principal outstanding obligations were his own loans, Dick suggested he donate the notes to the charity begun by FDR's friends to fight polio, the Warm Springs Foundation; this action, he wrote, would enable party supporters to "have the added satisfaction of knowing that they were also helping a most worthy charitable cause."

In a "Dear Dick" response, the president congratulated him on a "grand job," during which "I have liked your idealism," but rejected the donation of the unpaid loans because of the problem involved in having a foundation take a political committee's notes. Those notes continued on the books of the state committees, unpaid. Dick was proud of his DNC service and felt a sense of accomplishment in what'd he'd done, but he didn't toot his own horn about it. Months later, Pauley would make headlines by claiming for his own Dick's accomplishment of having put the Democrats in the black, except for Reynolds's loans. By that time, Dick would not be around to correct Pauley's announcement — he would be on a ship heading for battle.

On a Saturday in mid-June 1942, several thousand people gathered on the runways and at the terminal for the renaming and dedication of the Z. Smith Reynolds Airport. It was the last public ceremony to be presided over by Mayor Dick Reynolds; he'd already resigned as mayor, the resignation to take effect after this event. It was a day of splendid sunshine, groaning buffet tables, fireworks, and stunt flying.

It was a Reynolds show through and through. This ground had been the cornfields of the Forsyth County home for black delinquents until in-law Ed Lasater had given the money to make it more presentable to welcome Lindbergh in 1927. Now it had been upgraded again and had an impressive new terminal, thanks to a grant from the Z. Smith Reynolds Foundation. As Mary, Nancy, Blitz, and various members of the family watched, three of R. J.'s grandchildren — Charles Babcock, Jr., Smith Bagley, and Josh Reynolds — pulled the cover off a bust of their late uncle. The head-and-shoulders sculpture of Smith showed him more handsome than he'd ever been in his short life. It was set against a background of stained glass that made it almost seem like the shrine of a saint in some modern church.

Charlie Norfleet, chairman of the airport commission, who'd been at Smith's fateful party at Reynolda, told of a forthcoming WPA grant that would further expand the airport to make it ready for Eastern Airlines' expected use of Winston-Salem as a North Carolina hub of operations. Among the guests was E. Smythe Gambrell of Eastern, representing principal owner Eddie Rickenbacker, who couldn't be there but who sent regards. Gambrell called the structure "the finest terminal building in the United States."

North Carolina and local officials also graced the runway and terminal. Mayor Reynolds, a polished public speaker now, compared this day with earlier Winston firsts, such as the completion of the plank road in the early 1800s and the arrival of the first train, which had lured R. J. to the town. This newly upgraded airport would be the focus of Winston's future growth. It struck some in the audience that day as ironic that Mayor Reynolds would talk so assuredly about the future when it was now well known that he'd shortly be heading off to war, a war whose course was uncertain and one that would undoubtedly place him in danger of losing his life.

Within the week Dick put on a uniform and began his navy training.

Chapter Thirteen

Going to War

ALTHOUGH the battlefronts were thousands of miles distant, rationing of gasoline, foods, and long-distance telephone calls affected families on the American home front. At Reynolda, Mary Babcock felt pushed to provide comforts and entertainment — the swimming pool, boats on the lake — that others could no longer offer. "Every day, I wish we didn't have so much," she wrote Nancy. While Nancy trained nurse's aides, Mary sketched for war-related charities and designed scenery for plays staged for servicemen. Mary proposed that the government use Reynolda as a hospital, but no one was interested; the Babcocks shuttered the bungalow and moved to a Reynolda cottage.

Charlie Babcock spent a weekend at Devotion, where Blitz's four sons seemed delighted to have a father figure around for horseplay. When Mary went "up the mountain" for a similar weekend, Blitz told her there had been very few letters from Dick but volunteered no details. It seemed to Mary that Blitz's moods, up or down, swung on whether she'd heard recently from Dick; she complained that he didn't like writing letters, that Strat Coyner heard from him more often than she did. Occasionally, when Dick was stationed in Florida, he and Blitz would meet on Sapelo.

The process of getting into action, Dick Reynolds discovered, was slow. He spent some time at a training program, then in an advanced school where his expertise as a yachtsman and ship owner was at odds with the more formal schooling in navigation of Annapolis graduates. Mary thought that Dick must be as depressed as Blitz, but when she saw him she reported to Nancy that he looked unusually calm, well rested, and happier than he used to be in civilian life.

That was true. The war gave Dick an opportunity to exercise skills in which he excelled — navigation and working with aircraft. It also provided him with a wonderful excuse to get away from life in Winston, where, he often complained, he was continually called upon to maintain the social posture befitting the son and namesake of R. J. Then, too, the war allowed an escape from a wife with whom he was bickering and a family that seemed to demand more time than he was willing to give.

Late in 1942, after the Allies had taken back some of the territory in North Africa that Germany and Italy had previously conquered and the Pacific had emerged as the navy's main theater of war, Dick was transferred to San Diego as an intelligence officer aboard the *Sangamon*, a baby flattop. Such small "jeep" carriers had thirty planes each and were more maneuverable than larger aircraft carriers. They were useful in a wide variety of battlefield and supply missions. Though the assignment as intelligence officer wasn't what Dick wanted, he reveled in the camaraderie of the navy and in the satisfactions of doing a job well. Using his private income, he took a suite in a hotel in San Diego and invited several other officers to be his roommates. Needless to say, they lived unusually well for servicemen. He developed a close friendship with a navy priest, to whom he confided that the only religion he'd ever respected was Catholicism.

All through 1943 Dick chafed as the *Sangamon* was stuck doing exercises, launching and retrieving its planes, shooting at dummy targets. He asked an old acquaintance, Admiral O. B. Hardison, to get him into the war zone. Hardison respected Dick's abilities enough to offer him a position on his own staff, planning defenses of the West Coast, but Dick declined the offer and continued to press for duty aboard a ship heading for combat.

When Blitz's boys got truly lonely she rented movies and showed them in the big theater at Devotion, or on a Sunday at Merry Acres, and invited the neighborhood children. Blitz and Mary, both of whose men were away at war, had a spat, then made up and were close again — together they coped and hoped and listened to one another's fears about polio epidemics, fatherless children with an excess of material possessions, the danger (which they both courted) of drinking too much and thinking too much.

In early 1944 Dick finally got just what he wanted: the position of navigator aboard CVE-93, a newly commissioned baby flattop, the *Makin Island*. This was an escort carrier, named for a coral atoll in the Pacific taken at great cost by the Allies only months earlier. Stationed at San Diego during the spring and summer of 1944, she ferried aircraft and men to Pearl Harbor, then to ports recently freed from Japanese control, Majuro and Kwajalein. These journeys took Dick closer to the battle zone but not yet in it.

The crisis point of the Pacific war came in early October 1944, in the operations at Leyte Gulf, in the Philippines. When orders came for the *Makin Island* to sail for Ulithi, at the edge of the battle zone, everybody aboard rejoiced.

Before the ship left the United States, senior officers assigned Dick the duty of providing a last-minute entertainment for the crew. Dick called the Warner Brothers studio — he knew some of its executives and was a pal of singer Al Jolson, who'd taken him around the lot — and asked for three starlets to entertain and dance with the crew: one blond, one brunet and one redhead.

Three stunning studio contract players, Becky Brown, Lynn Baggett, and redhead Marianne O'Brien, reported for duty aboard the *Makin Island*, where they danced and sang for crew members, who were noisily appreciative. Later the starlets partied with the officers in their suite at the Del Coronado Hotel. Dick got very drunk. At dawn, Dick gave the ladies his car to drive back to Hollywood — and said they could keep it as long as they wanted, since he would have no immediate use for it. As the *Makin Island* steamed across the Pacific, Dick wrote polite thank-you notes, which he mailed in Hawaii, and had his stateside employees send each of the women a box of candy, orchids, and a U.S. Navy pin embellished with ruby chips, diamonds, and sapphires. He got polite thank-yous from two of them but not from the redhead. He wondered why; she was the only one he wanted to see again.

The *Makin Island* arrived at Leyte Gulf after the battle began, with the second wave of ships. In what is often regarded as the greatest naval engagement ever fought, Admiral William F. "Bull" Halsey's forces defeated the Japanese and opened up the Philippines. The *Makin Island* protected troop carriers as they disgorged battalions of marines on the beaches, but to the disappointment of her crew, the ship encountered little resistance in this first battle.

Back home, Blitz sent out 1944 Christmas cards with two separate photos, one of herself and the four boys, the other of Dick in his battle helmet aboard ship, with a caption: "Although we are separated by the distances of war, we are united in our thoughts of friends far and near. . . ."

When Rear Admiral T. C. Durgin transferred his flag to the *Makin Island*, Dick became navigator for an entire task force. This was no easy assignment. Many of the maps carried by the American ships were a half century out of date and incomplete. It was considered dangerous to maneuver in the coral-filled bays and passageways of the Philippines and other island groups. Dick did it well enough to bring the task force through with no marine mishaps.

Now the fighting escalated until there was all the action anyone could have hoped for. In early January of 1945, in support of General Douglas MacArthur's long-awaited return to the Philippines, the *Makin Island* went up Surigao Strait and encountered what the official navy history labeled as "fierce, almost continuous enemy air attack during the passage to the assault beaches." To avoid Japanese planes, Dick had to put the *Makin Island* through the hazardous maneuver of an emergency turn sixteen times in fifty-eight minutes — that was fancy navigating. The greatest danger to the ships was from kamikazes. At first the Americans had no idea how to defend themselves against these enemy pilots who were willing to commit suicide by flying their planes into American ships. Dick's old ship, the *Sangamon*, took a direct kamikaze hit. To port and starboard of the *Makin Island*, sister carriers were sunk by kamikazes, but Dick's ship remained unscathed.

In a time when four-leaf clovers or other good-luck totems decorated each bunk, Dick's shipmates wondered if the Joshua Coin had anything to do with the *Makin Island*'s invulnerability. Dick had told his roommate Price Gilbert, a Coca-Cola advertising executive, about the coin, and the story of how it had protected people in the Civil War and in World War I made the rounds of the ship. Rather astonishingly — since he believed in the coin's powers — Dick didn't have it with him. Before leaving home, he'd rubbed his own gold-filled teeth with it but then had put it in a safe-deposit box, fearing that the coin might disappear from the family if he were killed and his body lost at sea.

Following the invasion of the Philippines the *Makin Island* led the task force, combining with other ship groups that made up an invasion fleet of eight hundred ships bound for Iwo Jima, halfway between the Marianas Islands and Tokyo. Iwo Jima was heavily fortified and protected by many planes based on the island rather than on Japanese ships nearby. The American marines' commander thought Iwo Jima "the toughest place we have yet to take" and estimated there would be 20,000 American casualties. There were

25,000. During the long siege of Iwo Jima the *Makin Island* again came under heavy fire. One night, three big carriers were ablaze from kamikaze hits in the bay around her, a terrifying sight. She landed some of those other ships' planes, not without crashes. It was the worst fighting of the war. For his actions in Surigao Strait and at Iwo Jima, Dick Reynolds later received the Bronze Star, a medal awarded only to a relatively few men for unusual valor under direct enemy fire.

After the hell of Iwo Jima, there was a lull at Ulithi, a port now out of the battle zone. Dick had gone through a terrible experience, one that affected his view of the future. He promised himself that if he survived, he would live the rest of his life doing what he wanted to do — not what others mandated for him.

It was at this moment that a sack of mail arrived from the United States and yielded a handwritten note to him from Marianne O'Brien. His letter and gifts had been sent astray and then mislaid; that was why she had not thanked him earlier. Her missive was appreciative of his gifts, warm, and friendly: "Some day when I'm a very old lady, I'm going to learn the secret of saying — 'Thank you' — and 'I like you' — gracefully." Dick concluded that she'd already mastered that art, read the letter until he'd memorized its contents, put it in a cigar box above his bunk, and started the first of many answering letters.

=

Marianne O'Brien was living in Hollywood with a friend and preparing for an audition for the role of Joan of Arc. When she opened the letter from Dick Reynolds, she was stunned: out fell several hundred-dollar bills. He'd sent them so that she could have pictures made by Bruno of Hollywood; she was to mail Dick copies and was not to object, because "the money is better spent helping your career than moldering in some bank." She had glossies made that showed her crowned with romantic veils.

On board the *Makin Island*, over bunks near Dick's, shipmates had pinned up photos of Rita Hayworth in a nightgown or Betty Grable in a bathing suit; "That's what we're fighting for," the men would say. Soon, Dick had the picture of an equally beautiful starlet over his bed — a starlet who was writing personally to say that she liked him.

Marianne was twenty-seven, with brilliant red hair, a heart-shaped face and emerald eyes, a buxom figure. She had arrived in

Hollywood by the classic route. In the 1920s her father had abandoned her mother, and in New York City Mae Byrne had raised three children on what she could earn by playing piano to accompany silent movies or by being a hostess at Jimmy Kelley's nightclub. Marianne and Dorothy boarded at Catholic convent schools, while Walter went to a school for boys; the girls were impressed when Mae's admirers gave them rides in limousines and demonstrated in other ways that they were wealthy. In the thirties, Mae, a striking redhead herself, married Abe Attell, a Jewish gambler who'd been the featherweight boxing champion of the world from 1901 to 1912 and had also helped fix the 1919 "Black Sox" World Series. Abe and Mae ran their own restaurant on Broadway.

While still a teenager, Marianne modeled for Sears Roebuck catalogues, then landed small parts in Broadway musicals. Once she was in the chorus of *You Never Know*, which starred Libby Holman. There were always suitors around — one was a gangster who sent five mink coats to her mother's apartment so she could choose one. She returned them all. Dean Murphy, an actor famous for his imitation of FDR, was cast with her in the *Schubert Follies*, which starred Milton Berle; as Murphy watched Marianne enter a room, heads turned, and if they didn't do so immediately she made them turn. At rehearsals for the *Follies*, dancer Janey Neu found Marianne a bit stuck up until Marianne pleaded with the experienced hoofer to teach her how to do the steps; they became fast friends. During a big production number onstage, the mischievous Marianne would goose Murphy.

A road show of a hit, *The Doughgirls*, was looking for someone to play the choice part of a dumb redhead. Marianne wanted that part badly and auditioned for three of the theater's big guns, director George S. Kaufman, producer Max Gordon, and playwright Joe Fields. They thought her wonderful, but the producer of the *Follies* didn't want to release her. Stage manager and boyfriend Freddie De Cordova interceded on her behalf, and she joined the six-month tour. Audiences and critics liked her, too.

Another boyfriend, Charles Martin, writer-producer-director of radio's *The Philip Morris Show*, insisted she choose a Warner's contract at five hundred dollars per week rather than one with Twentieth Century Fox for more money because Warner's had the rights to *Doughgirls* and Marianne could repeat her part on the screen. She signed and went to Hollywood.

However, Warner's gave the *Doughgirls* part to Ann Sheridan, cast Marianne in a supporting role in *The Very Thought of You*, then gave her bit parts in *Cinderella Jones* and *Hollywood Canteen*, possibly to chastise her for not going to voice classes and posture briefings — schooling she thought ludicrous for someone who'd spent years on Broadway. At the same time, her love life turned sour. Charles Martin began chasing Paulette Goddard. Janey Neu was engaged to trombonist and bandleader Tommy Dorsey, Lynn Baggett was shepherding producer Sam Spiegel to the altar, the Warner's contract had just run out, and Marianne was nearing the age of thirty when Dick Reynolds's letter found its way to her.

They were both at vulnerable points in their lives. In their first few letters, they opened up to one another as, they noted in amazement, neither had ever done to anyone else before. After Marianne had confided her doubts about becoming a star, and Dick had confessed his loneliness, there was no stopping the process of writing themselves into each other's heart.

Dick wrote to her daily. He was "leaning over the chart table," he was "between navigational sightings, up here under the stars," it was "very late at night" when he put pencil to the back of a letter from one of his employees at home or to a yellow-lined pad to tell her "what crossed my mind." Topics included the history of the Joshua Coin, the inadequate shipboard food, the joy of receiving liquor in the guise of a can of food sent by Mary, the way the ship resembled a small city of which the captain was the mayor. His letters were "interrupted by almost-continual attacks," but he couldn't tell her where they took place because of censorship. Actually, the *Makin Island* was standing for two months off Okinawa, supporting the invasion.

He was thrilled when she observed that he "would never die for lack of interest in life," delighted to have her discern that he hated being a "solid citizen" and a "stuffed shirt" and for understanding that he wanted to be "a soldier of fortune and an adventurer at heart." He was worried, though, lest "the flood of letters will bore you to death." Marianne's own missives became for Dick his lifeline to a world beyond war, to a playboy style that he had once embraced, then put aside for a decade, and now yearned to take up again. Soon he'd be forty; he didn't want to face a life of numerous responsibilities and no fun.

While the *Makin Island* was stationed off China — he couldn't tell her exactly where, of course — Dick reported to Marianne a reverie that he and other officers were conjuring for their postwar future: a China-U.S. shipping line that would make so much money that they could build, on a high bluff above the Yangtze River, an estate-community for all of them "with a small airport, beautiful gardens, flowers and trees, green grass kept like a putting lawn, dozens of servants, wonderful food, drink, beautiful girls to sing and dance for us," as well as rare paintings and a private theater. The fact that fellow officers could concoct such an idyll must have buoyed him, for it was evidence that he could live the life of which others could only dream — after all, he'd already built two such paradises and owned a U.S.-to-the–Far East shipping line.

He reported that his secretary, Nettie Allen, had been keeping his political options open by signing his name to a newsletter she sent to Winston men who'd gone overseas and that Nettie believed he could win the mayoralty again. But, he told Marianne, he had decided not to return to politics at all. He bragged that he could have run for U.S. senator in 1944 from aboard the ship and won — a shipmate whom he detested had done the same and won a congressional seat, then used the excuse of his post to leave the battle zone. To Dick that was "unpatriotic" and "cowardly."

Given the open hostility between Dick and the Hoey-Gardner-Broughton forces, Dick's boast about having an easy time of it in politics was a little on the optimistic side. He probably could have gone home and fought his way up in the political arena, but, as in many of his endeavors, once having been knocked back, he didn't struggle very hard to continue the battle; rather, he sought other avenues into which to channel his energies. In telling Marianne what he could have done, Dick was simply bolstering his own sense of what he'd be giving up by not returning home and, in the process, making it a virtual certainty that when the war ended he would not go home.

Marianne's letters enclosed good-luck charms, jokes clipped from the newspapers, family stories. She wrote that her mother, Mae, had been telling her about him for years and that Mae said she'd even discussed her beautiful daughter with Dick years ago, at Jimmy Kelley's. Did he remember? And wouldn't he prefer an heiress, say, a Du Pont, to a penniless Irish show girl?

He replied that fifty sailors on his ship had gotten "Dear John" letters in the last mailbag. He suggested that Marianne might be a good match for his bunkmate, the dapper Coca-Cola executive Price Gilbert. She answered, "Darling Dick: You son of a bitch! I can take care of my own love life." He apologized, said he "didn't want

to lose" her, and wrote that his marriage had been essentially mor-
ibund for some time, so that he felt no compunction in "writing
love letters to you." He informed Marianne that he wrote dutifully
to Blitz, but only short notes saying he was too tired to write more.
On the other hand, "I've tried to figure out how you have changed
me, to make me want to sit down and write to you, God knows
that letter writing to me before has always been a thing to avoid
at all costs." By July of 1945, Dick was "sure" that he loved Marianne. It was "just a fact" that he couldn't argue himself out of
knowing.

On July 17, 1945, in Winston-Salem, Blitz filed papers to make
her the sole legal guardian of the four boys, now aged from eleven
to five. This step is often associated with predivorce proceedings.
Its timing — after Dick had been in the navy more than three
years — and the fact that Dick's attorney, Strat Coyner, helped
Blitz file suggest that Blitz as well as Dick considered their marriage
to be over. Blitz took the step reluctantly, as a defensive measure,
because she didn't want a divorce. As for Dick, he hadn't seen his
boys in nearly two years and now considered his freedom to be
more important than his old home life. Even so, Dick didn't mention
the filing to Marianne in his letters.

Rather, he reported that American Mail Lines had been upgraded
from an "essential" to a "critical" industry and that Al Lindner,
president of the line, was pleading with him to come back. "We
have an opportunity to become one of the big Pacific companies,"
he wrote Marianne, but he wondered how she would feel about
"someone thats in the service and gets out before his time was up?"
He was "very sensitive to criticism" that he might be using his
connections to avoid navigating the *Makin Island* back to a mainland
U.S. port.

Marianne replied that she'd be waiting whenever he landed but
wouldn't yet promise to love him forever because they'd spent so
little time face-to-face. He had a remedy for that: precisely one
year after they'd first met, they'd have a date at a theater in New
York and see how they got on in person.

In early August 1945, atomic bombs were dropped on Hiroshima
and Nagasaki, and, suddenly, the shooting war was over. The
Makin Island remained at battle stations. Dick decided that the time
had come to use his pull to go back to "Uncle Sugar" (the United
States) before his tour of duty was finished.

He waxed emotional about leaving his shipmates, who were some of his "closest friends in the world," and was "ecstatic" when the captain called him the best navigator in the navy and promoted him to lieutenant commander. Roommate Price Gilbert wrote a pictorial history of the works of the CVE (baby flattop) class of ships; Dick helped in culling photos and writing captions and then put up fifty thousand dollars so that the book could be printed and mailed to each of the thirty thousand men who'd served aboard CVEs.

Dick wrote to Blitz and the boys that it would be Thanksgiving before he was home. He didn't inform them that he was making plans to stay at a New York hotel, one where he wasn't known. He wired money to Marianne so she could outfit herself properly to paint the town with him. On August 29, 1945, he received the "first what I'd call sweet letter from [Blitz] since I've been in the Navy." It was too late. His mind was already set on traveling as quickly as he could to New York City, where one day he, the secret Catholic, hoped to "join hands in St. Patrick's Cathedral" with Marianne.

PART THREE

INTO
THE DARKNESS

Chapter Fourteen

Starting Over: Marianne

PRECEDED by telegrams to Marianne announcing the stages of his arrival, in mid-September Dick left the *Makin Island* and flew to New York. Although it wasn't precisely a year to the day they had first met, in every other way their reunion was all they hoped it might be. At first sight they embraced, then were embarrassed, then set out to have a good time; he'd yearned for fresh fruit, real meat, vintage liquor. They attended the theater, ordered the best of everything at The Stork Club and El Morocco, painted the town.

Dick seemed to relax in the company of such characters as Marianne's stepfather, former boxing champ Abe Attell, and sister Dorothy's husband, Axford (Al) Buck, sportswriter for the *New York Post*. They were like the ordinary Joes who'd been his comrades in the war. He was made the subject of Attell's favorite practical joke — Abe surreptitiously attached a wine cork to Dick's pants front so it appeared as if Dick hadn't buttoned his fly. He didn't mind. These people laughed hard, cried easily, were outgoing and often melodramatic; they made a striking contrast to the tightly controlled country clubbers of North Carolina who Dick had so often felt sat in judgment on his own behavior.

Quite early one morning Dick telephoned Blitz to say he was in New York and didn't know when he'd get to Winston-Salem. A few days later he called and said he wanted a divorce. She begged him to reconsider. He disclosed that in a nightclub the previous evening he'd told columnist Walter Winchell that he'd be obtaining a divorce and marrying starlet Marianne O'Brien — so the idea would shortly be public knowledge, and there was nothing anybody could do about it. Indeed, Winchell's column reported that Dick had already given Marianne extremely expensive gifts.

John L. Dillard, Blitz's father, flew to New York to see if he could dissuade Dick from a divorce. Dick told his father-in-law that he was appalled by the visit. More likely he was embarrassed because he knew he was behaving badly. He wanted Marianne and didn't want to go back to Blitz but could see no way to sever himself from his first marriage without hurting people.

After reading in gossip columns that Dick was ill, Blitz went to New York to beard the lion. Dick was incensed to see her in his hotel. Blitz thought his behavior "hostile, unfriendly, humiliating" and was convinced that he was hung over. A whole crowd of Irish and Jewish sycophants, she believed, was conspiring to keep him permanently drunk and away from home.

It may have seemed to Blitz that Marianne and her family were hopping aboard the gravy train, but this wasn't precisely the case. For one thing, Dick was intent on having a high time of it in New York and was spending for his own enjoyment; for another, Marianne and he were deeply in love. To her, he was the embodiment of all she had dreamed about in a potential husband; to him, a middle-aged man, she was the perfect emblem of renewal.

A week after Blitz's visit to New York, when Dick called Blitz and asked her to meet him at the Greensboro airport, she was overjoyed, thinking he meant to come home and ask forgiveness. This was an era when many instances of infidelity and bad behavior on the part of errant husbands were forgiven so that marriages could endure; divorce was uncommon, especially in the South. But when Blitz picked Dick up at the airport and they were driving toward Winston, it was clear that he hadn't come on an errand of contrition. Dick told her he wouldn't be able to stay at Merry Acres because that would delay the divorce.

Dick seemed to be acting as if Blitz ought to understand that the marriage was over and that they ought to bury it jointly and behave courteously toward one another during the funeral. It was one more instance of his naiveté. As he well knew, divorces, especially among the wealthy, were seldom characterized by anything other than all-out warfare.

So Dick slept in a Winston hotel on that trip, and Blitz wouldn't even let him in the front door of Merry Acres to see the boys. In retaliation, he closed some of her store charge accounts, leaving open only those from which she could purchase food, clothing, and other necessary things for herself and the children. She continued with her attempt to obtain sole guardianship of the boys.

Dick stopped at Sapelo to commission repairs and upgrading, then returned to New York, where he and Marianne bought a twenty-two-room duplex apartment on Beekman Place and started redecorating it. Then they flew to Miami and found a beautiful, near-palatial house in Miami Beach previously owned by the Fisher family of automobile chassis makers. It took up five lots on prestigious Sunset Island. If Dick established residence for ninety days in Florida, he could seek a divorce there and not have to contest one in Winston-Salem. In November, from Seattle, Dick called to advise Blitz that he was going to do just that.

Now Blitz had to find a lawyer of her own. Dick's most prominent apparent enemy in the state was former governor O. Max Gardner; the bitterness over the national committeeman fight had not subsided. Gardner was currently in Washington, in a high subcabinet post. He was a wealthy man now, having been helped by the Gray family to buy RJR stock in earlier years. He told Blitz he was happy to advise her, because he saw that she was in a bad way — her whole world seemed to be collapsing. During this period Gardner, a former Sunday school teacher, assisted Blitz not only legally but spiritually as she turned to religion for insight on how to live the rest of her life and how best to bring up her children. Gardner recommended a local lawyer to handle the actual divorce, L. P. Mclendon of Winston, who knew Dick and who was a partner of the lawyer who'd done so well in obtaining money from Smith's estate for Anne Cannon and her daughter. That was fitting, for this was not merely a divorce but a fight over division of Dick's large share of the Reynolds family fortune.

"Mac" Mclendon claimed Dick was worth between $25 million and $30 million, and he demanded half for Blitz, including Devotion, Sapelo, and part of the American Mail Line. Dick was willing to give up Merry Acres and even Devotion — in his mind, Devotion was irretrievably linked to the Blitz he had loved in earlier days — but not Sapelo or any AML stock.

The wrangling between Dick and Blitz inevitably drew in the rest of the family. Mary and Nancy tried to stay neutral, but Mary confessed to Nancy in a letter that Blitz was "hipped on the subject that you and I aren't working on her side." Both sisters were furious with Dick for running off with a "gold-digger," but then, Strat Coyner thought, no family ever likes a second wife. In addition, the publicity attendant on the divorce was being increased by two events that had brought Smith's death back into the public eye. Libby Holman's second husband had just taken a fatal overdose of sleeping pills, evoking comparisons with the end of her first marriage; moreover, a novel by Robert Wilder, *Written on the Wind*, had been published recently and was being reviewed as a thinly disguised version of the Smith-Libby-Ab tragedy. The Reynolds women had their own problems. Nancy was recovering from a serious internal operation, and Mary's doctor had told her that her own abdominal problems were being exacerbated by stress. Both women, always heavy drinkers and smokers, promised each other in letters to go "on the wagon" and dutifully reported when they'd fallen off.

Through the winter and spring, negotiations went on between Mclendon and Dick's attorneys. To keep Sapelo, Dick agreed to a big settlement for Blitz: she'd get $3 million in cash and stocks, Merry Acres, Devotion, and some other parcels of Winston real estate. Blitz wanted trust funds for the boys; that was a sticking point.

In a tender moment with Marianne, Dick wrote out on a napkin his engagement present — a note deeding her the island of Sapelo. She valued the gift more than the ermine jacket, the jewelry, the mansions he was buying for her, because Sapelo was close to his heart.

As a first hearing in the divorce trial approached, the attorneys completed a settlement. Dick agreed to trust funds of a half million for each of the four boys. The total package was worth $9 million, the largest divorce settlement ever. The case went to court anyway. The intent of the lawyers had been to do so merely to ratify the settlement, but Blitz wanted some revenge. In tears, she testified that Dick had treated her badly but had always intended to return to her, and she cited some wartime letters of his: "On my heart I promise not to take a drink after the war is over. I will give you a check for $5,000 for each drink I take. . . . I think I'll just stay home and help you raise the boys. If anyone can point out the pitfalls of life to them, I can. I've got the finest wife in all the world." In response, Dick shook his head. He wouldn't rise to the bait and take the stand, even to refute Blitz's version of what had torn apart their marriage. Custody of the boys was awarded to Blitz. When Dick asked Blitz to return to him the Joshua Coin and his second-most-prized possession, the pilot's license signed by Orville Wright, she refused. He was angry but could do nothing about it.

Mary Babcock was trying to explain to her children that people got divorced mainly for reasons of incompatibility — in the way that her daughter changed roommates when she wasn't happy — when Dick phoned. About to go to New York from Winston, he wanted to bring Marianne to meet Mary. Mary said "I'd rather not" and hung up.

In explaining her actions, Mary wrote Nancy that "I've got 3 daughters who will say that this [Marianne] is what men want, for Uncle Dick turned down Aunt Blitz so [Blitz is] not the type for me to copy. . . . Just pray for your brother during his freedom."

Mary's real prayer was that Dick would tire of Marianne and not marry her, but this was not in the cards — nor in his character. He had decided to divorce Blitz in order to wed Marianne, not to be free. In choosing the beautiful starlet, and especially in abandoning his four sons, Dick seemed to be doing something more than fulfilling a wish to escape from a mid-life crisis. As psychologists would have recognized, he was repeating the emotionally successful behavior pattern of one of his parents: he was emulating his mother, Katharine, who in 1921 had chosen a new life and the possibility of future happiness over the responsibility of raising four young children.

In June of 1946 Dick's divorce from Blitz became final, and on August 7 he married Marianne in a civil ceremony in Mae and Abe Attell's apartment in New York City. His best man was *Makin Island* shipmate Sherlock Hibbs. The bride's sister, Dorothy, was maid of honor, and her brother, Walter, gave her away. Among the guests were various Broadway types and newspaper columnists. The headlines read, "HEIR TO TOBACCO FORTUNE WEDS STARLET." No one from Dick's family attended.

=

In 1945 a new crisis loomed before R. S. Reynolds. Elected officials shared a worry that, after the war, the United States wouldn't be able to absorb all its wartime production capacity for aluminum; consequently, the government was considering the sale of some surplus plants to the giant in the field, Alcoa. If Alcoa succeeded in buying the plants, Reynolds Metals might as well go out of business. Then, at last, the Supreme Court ruled that Alcoa was a monopoly — and an opportunity appeared.

R. S. pushed on his government (and Democratic-party) connections as hard as he could to follow up on the Supreme Court's ruling. The results were soon evident. In January of 1946 Government Surplus Property Administrator Stuart Symington announced that in order to bust up Alcoa's monopoly, he'd sell the surplus aluminum plants to anyone other than Alcoa. Symington had the backing of President Harry S Truman. As a senator during the war, Truman had chaired an investigation that had been appalled by the Alcoa stranglehold on an important strategic metal. Now Truman could strike back legally at Alcoa and its Republican-contributor executives. Within four days of Symington's announcement, Alcoa, in exchange for being allowed to stay in existence, agreed to hand over to the government, license-free, its patents for extracting aluminum from bauxite, the process that had been built into the key government surplus plant — a plant that Reynolds Aluminum was then allowed to buy. This government strategy served to encourage Reynolds Aluminum to become a serious competitor of Alcoa's.

Shortly thereafter, R. S. made St. George killing a dragon the new emblem of his company; he told reporters that the dragon was really Alcoa. He also let it be known that he slept in a bed that was a replica of Napoleon's. A few months later, he introduced in the marketplace a home-use foil that would make aluminum part of everyone's daily life: Reynolds Wrap.

In this same era, Dick Reynolds's American Mail Line had an equivalent chance to become a postwar giant. There were government surplus ships to be snapped up and, with them, the lure of reestablishing and dominating the West Coast–to–Asia routes in the boom that followed the war. AML didn't rise to its opportunities. The reasons are complex, but Dick's personality was at the heart of the failure. He had never thrilled to the challenge of building a company and keeping it on course; the initial impetus was what engaged him — the courting and conquest — not the long haul, which he preferred to leave to subordinates. In the case of American Mail Line in 1946, the diversion of his interest to personal matters coincided with the line's missing its moment in the sun.

Dick missed another chance as well — in government. John Graham, Dick's friend for many years as well as his associate in Reynolds Airways and his assistant at the Democratic National Committee, used his Washington connections to begin a distinguished career in public service. Other old buddies of Dick's did the same; but Dick was in a phase of overthrowing everything that was old and embracing the new, and to him that also meant by-passing opportunities that he might have successfully pursued.

In aviation, he made a move out of spite. During the war years, Eastern Airlines had reneged on its promise to make Winston-Salem the hub of its Carolina operations — a decision that dealt a tremendous blow to the town's further economic expansion. Dick was annoyed at the line's double-cross. So when Delta called in 1946, desperate for money to meet payroll, he sold some Eastern stock and invested the proceeds in Delta. Dick's money enabled Delta to pay its bills, and he emerged as the major stockholder in what became Eastern's chief competitor.

In fact, in this period Dick made a wave of sell-offs to sustain his new life of carefree spending with Marianne, centered on New York, Miami, Sapelo, and several yachts. The Reynoldses and Marianne's dancer friend Janey and her husband, Tommy Dorsey, dressed in formal clothes, were a frequent foursome at El Morocco and The Stork Club. Under the eyes of maître d' Perino, Morocco came alive about eleven each night and boasted in its flashy rooms and on its dance floor a crowd of Broadway and film stars and wealthy South Americans. Sherman Billingsley's Stork, known to intimates as "the Bird," was so exclusive that only guests known to the management were let through the red velvet rope outside, and even fewer were escorted into the inner sanctum, the Cub Room.

Often, in the clubs or elsewhere on the town, waiters would bring the check to Tommy Dorsey, who would laugh and take it, telling Dick, "You may have more money than me, but my face is better known." Dick was used to having to pick up the check all the time, and sometimes he resented it; Dorsey's willingness to pay for his friend was a prime bond between the two men.

In the clubs they frequently sat with people from show business. Marianne was at her best in these situations, where her good looks and ability to banter served her well. She was brassy, outgoing, often overdramatic, traits that helped her exude an air of confidence.

Once, playwright Sidney Kingsley asked Marianne if she planned to return to the stage. It wasn't just a polite question — Marianne had projected well on stage and was a good actress. "What would I do every night from eight to eleven?" Dick responded. However, Dick did offer film producer Walter Wanger a million dollars to star Marianne in a film; Wanger was willing, but Marianne was not.

For Marianne, to consider her marriage more important than reaching for stardom was the grandest gesture she could imagine, the only way she could equal Dick's own sacrifice in giving up his family for her. Completing the circle, Dick not only threw his past life to the winds but also let others handle his business affairs and devoted nearly all his time and energy to the pursuit of pleasure in the company of Marianne.

Marianne loved Beekman Place. As a young girl, she had lived three blocks away and had often gazed at the river through the bars at the end of a Beekman Place cul-de-sac. Now she was the wife of a millionaire who was spending a fortune to have a big picture window built in their new apartment so she could have an even better view of the river — from a few stories higher.

To finance the renovations, Dick sold off odd lots of property in North Carolina and Georgia, for good profits. During the inflation after the war's end, he came to believe that paper money would eventually become worthless and began exchanging some of his dollars for gold (then selling at twenty-five dollars per ounce). He held gold on Sapelo but sent part of his hoard to his banks in Europe. From time to time Dick would offer a piece of property in the United States for a bargain price — if the buyer would pay him in gold and agree to deliver that gold to Dick somewhere out of the country.

In this high-rolling life-style the difficulties at first didn't seem too serious. Under the terms of the fantasy compact, the couple was supposed to enjoy life; to Dick, that meant license to imbibe and let loose, especially on Sapelo, where he was undisputed king of the island. Marianne drank to keep up with him.

The joys and strains of the couple's new life seemed especially evident at a Sapelo New Year's Eve party, for which several plane-loads of guests and musicians were flown down, only to be marooned by the fog for four days. Some guests were friends, others were of the sort that made it their business to hang around the wealthy. Airline presidents mixed with mechanics, major office-holders with ward heelers. Press agent Curly Harris, who'd met Dick in the 1920s and who had also known Marianne and Dorothy before Dick and Marianne were married, was amazed at the party's length and liquidity. Dick got so drunk he performed a routine that terrified Marianne but that she went through because he seemed to enjoy it: as Dick stood in front of the eighteen-inch cannon on the front lawn, it was filled with powder and Marianne fired it off.

Then Dick pretended to have been shot and wobbled around doing a death scene.

Days later, as the master and mistress journeyed still further into the alcoholic haze, the island's blacks came to serenade them as they sipped drinks on the colonnaded front terrace. The guests crowded around to see. Lawyer Strat Coyner climbed up on a glass table for a better view. The table collapsed. Coyner got glass splinters in his rear end and had to be rushed by boat to a mainland hospital. And still the fog continued. Eating, drinking, and partying wore thin. Finally, to get away from the guests, Dick and Marianne fled to a tree house near Cabretta Beach, a two-mile stretch of long-dead trees that had become a bleached grove of driftwood. Blackbeard was rumored to have buried his treasure here, Dick told Marianne as they cuddled in the tree house and cooked chili, away from the intruders they'd invited to their paradise.

Shortly after that party, Marianne discovered she was pregnant. Dick insisted that the baby be born on Sapelo. It would be the first white child birthed there since the Civil War, a conceit congruent with Dick's fantasy of being lord of a well-run kingdom. Medical facilities on the island were rudimentary, but Marianne was a healthy young woman, and the doctor who occasionally came over to see her expected no problems.

The reality of the isolated situation intruded harshly when Michael Randolph Reynolds chose to arrive on a Sunday in mid-1947. Labor was very difficult, and during it Marianne lost a great deal of blood. The doctor said she was in grave danger. Blood banks were closed, but Dick sent pilot Lew McGinnes off in a plane with instructions to "damn well get blood" — pry one of the banks open, if he had to. Mac returned with enough blood to save Marianne's life.

For more than a year, both Nancy and Mary had been estranged from Dick because of his divorce and remarriage. In their letters, the two Reynolds sisters, now in their forties, discussed Marianne in the nastiest of terms. Mary wrote Nancy a short poem on the subject:

> There was an ex-starlet named O'Brien,
> Who corresponded to net her lion.
> Tho he's jungle and sea, quite a mixture,
> He's now her apartment fixture.

Michael's birth afforded occasion for a reconciliation. Nancy wrote Dick to say that she hadn't heard from him in a year; she castigated him for not writing a proper thank-you for her Christmas gift of a battery-powered megaphone, then offered congratulations. "I wish [Michael] the intelligence of his father, the beauty of his Mother, the consideration of one Aunt, and the moderation of the other." Dick answered, and relations were restored. He and Marianne stopped in Winston-Salem to see Mary on the way to New York. At the Reynolda bungalow, Mary told him the Babcocks were planning to move permanently from Greenwich to Reynolda; a doctor believed that her abdominal problems were caused partly by the stress of being a transplanted Southerner. Charles had some medical problems, too, and being head of the Reynolds brokerage in Winston would be less strenuous than commuting to Wall Street.

After Dick and Marianne were gone, Mary reported to Nancy that Marianne was flippant and not too bright. The starlet had charmed the servants easily, but she wore the wrong clothes — too flamboyant — and had committed the extreme gaffe of having a package of clothes addressed to "Mrs. Reynolds" delivered to herself at Reynolda, which had annoyed Mary. Mary was sure that Marianne looked Jewish and was really Abe Attell's daughter, not step-daughter. (Offhand anti-Semitism was common in their letters; Mary thought Marianne's Jewishness was conclusive evidence of bad breeding and manners.)

Mary also told Nancy that, as usual when Dick showed up in town, Blitz made sure to be away. Every time Dick came close to Winston-Salem, Blitz or her father would take the older sons to Cuba or Florida. Mary reported that Dick bore up under the strain of not seeing the boys and didn't drink too much.

In subsequent letters there was more information about Blitz, who had gone and done something unusual but entirely in character: moved to Devotion and set up year-round residence there. The boys now went to school in rural Surry County. On the estate they were made to perform chores in the dairy and chicken farms and were generally kept without money in their pockets. Very few guests were now invited to Devotion, and once there they were subject to the same strictures Blitz placed on the boys — giving them fines for arriving late to a meal, making them do their own laundry and other menial tasks. Most of the longtime servants had fled in horror; Mary considered hiring some for herself but didn't want people to think she was poaching.

She believed that Blitz was doing all of this to counteract problems associated with possession of too much money, the evil that, in Blitz's view, had corrupted Dick. With qualifications, Mary admired Blitz's idea: "I think the boys will come out of it O.K. They'll certainly face life with no inhibitions. She may be drawing the line too rapidly between rich and poor to suit the rest of us but if she perfects this she may have something we 'ain't' (Blitz's favorite word) got for the future generation."

When they were in her sight, Blitz kept a tight rein on her sons. But the estate was vast, and often, Mary reported, the four boys roamed the hills and streams virtually unfettered. They were like other rural children except for the size of their farm and the expense and complexity of their toys. In the next few years, as the boys grew up at Devotion, Mary often told Nancy about them. She worried about Josh, who at fourteen in 1948 was "old enough to remember and appreciate the have-alls." John seemed to hover between being citified and countrified, but the two youngest, Zach and Will, were full-fledged country boys. They were also "characters." Will had made a miniature BB gun and was overeager to demonstrate its prowess in Mary's presence. The man after whom he'd been named — Uncle Will, now in his eighties — would do essentially the same things with the boy that he'd tried with Dick Reynolds nearly forty years earlier: offer little Will some change to do small tasks, such as putting together a plastic boat model. Young Will, however, was a conniver and quickly figured out that his old uncle would pay more money for more complicated projects (up to five dollars for a completed painting), so he worked hard on a series of paintings in order to earn enough to buy his heart's desire, a motorcycle. Zach was interested in shooting everything — guns (he was a crack shot), Polaroid cameras (he captured every moment at a Roaring Gap dance, while simultaneously turning it into a shambles), and vehicles (he drove cycles at high speeds). Mary observed admiringly that they all had spunk and admitted that when they arrived at a party it then took on the proper Reynolds gaiety. Her main worry about them was what she perceived as the lack of male influence in their lives and the presence of backwoods rather than upper-class exemplars for them.

=

During the summer of 1948 Marianne called the Babcocks and asked to come and see them, incognito. Wearing a three-foot-round navy straw hat with streamers, a long taffeta skirt, and a blouse with a plunging neckline, she stepped off the plane in Greensboro: if nobody had recognized her, it would have been for lack of trying. In the airport lounge she poured out a tale of woe: Dick had been going on binges, often leaving her and the baby at home while he sat ringside at a fight or some other sporting event and didn't return for a week. When he did arrive he'd be rumpled, filthy, and often accompanied by strangers he'd picked up en route, to whom she was expected to play hostess. She'd timed her visit so that she could get back to Sapelo before Dick emerged from sleeping off the latest escapade.

"What was there to say?" Mary wrote to Nancy about the flying visit: "Her story was identical to the one she succeeded. . . . Male and female do mighty strange things for love or material things." As Mary well knew, in the 1930s Blitz had endured the pattern of Dick's binges, the shouting matches after them, the gifts Dick would offer along with his smiles to make up for having been a bad boy. Mary suggested that Dick had a problem with alcohol.

The deeper problem was that the fantasy concocted by Dick and Marianne had crumbled in less than two years. Cinderella was waking up in the "happily ever after" and discovering the flaws in Prince Charming; for his part, Dick seemed shocked to realize that his Hollywood starlet had become a mother trailed around by one squalling baby and about to give birth to another. Neither Dick nor Marianne wanted to admit change to the relationship, so things got worse. His drinking continued; to stay companionable, Marianne drank more than she ever had before. They had fights, most of them having to do in one way or another with money. Now, despite having set up mother Mae and stepfather Abe in a new saloon in Manhattan, Dick started grousing that he didn't like Marianne's relatives hanging around. He'd tell Marianne to do whatever she wanted, but when she sent a plane to New York to bring back her sister or mother to Sapelo or took her relatives on a yacht when Dick was out of town, he'd get annoyed. In turn, Marianne would be arrogant and damning in her fury at the band of sycophants who drank with Dick in order to partake of the good life.

She began to smoke. He took the cigarettes away from her, calling smoking a vile and disgusting habit. He couldn't stop smoking, he said, but he didn't want her to start. This was his way of asking her to remain pure, to be the beautiful starlet he'd placed on a pedestal, not some ordinary earthling. She could no more maintain

that image forever than he could continue to imbibe alcohol reck-
lessly and never be stinking drunk.

One morning at Beekman Place, while they were sleeping off
the effects of a night out, the butler woke Dick to say that President
Truman was calling from the White House. Hung over, Dick didn't
want to take the call. The butler was incredulous. "But Mr. Reynolds," he fussed, "it's the president!" "Tell him I'm out," Dick
said and went back to sleep.

Dick knew what Truman wanted — money. In 1940 Dick had
jumped at the chance to help FDR. Now he was more cynical about
political contributions. He wanted to be properly courted for a big
donation. Shortly, an invitation came for him and Marianne to
attend a White House tea. Marianne, pregnant, wore a low-cut
dress and was seated next to Ambassador Averell Harriman, who
couldn't take his eyes off her décolletage. At such an event, protocol
dictated that no one leave until the president had been introduced
and had himself left. Truman was delayed, and Harriman's roving
eyes outraged Dick, so when Marianne said she felt a bit faint, they
went back to their hotel without meeting Truman. Eventually the
president got Dick on the phone and told him that many regular
contributors had given up on the campaign because the polls showed
Governor Tom Dewey with a sizeable lead in the race. These
desertions had put the Truman campaign in desperate need of an
angel.

Dick promised to help but expressed disappointment that he'd
never been reimbursed for his 1940 loans, or for the $96,000 he'd
given in 1944 and the $175,000 in 1947. He wasn't asking for the
money back, but, he said, he could use a tax deduction; unfortunately, at the time, the IRS held that political contributions were
not deductible. Truman said he'd see what he could do — after
the election. Dick put up more money for the campaign, in which
Truman narrowly defeated Dewey. On the last business day of
1948, an IRS deputy commissioner wrote Dick a letter allowing
him to deduct from his 1948 tax return most of his outstanding
loans from 1940 as a "non-business bad debt." A later ruling wid-
ened the edict to include the 1944 and 1947 loans; these rulings
were kept secret for several years.

At Sapelo one night, in their poolside bedroom with the marble
fireplace, Marianne and Dick had an enormous drunken altercation
in which he accused her of becoming pregnant this second time in
order to have a hold over him — as Blitz had. Marianne replied

that it was natural, and her right, to have children and that money had nothing to do with it; then she slammed the door on Dick and settled into bed to read. Dick burst back in, ripped her book in half, and started to choke her and wrestle her to the floor. She began to black out, and for some moments, depressed, she didn't resist; she was going to let him kill her. During her entire pregnancy, the baby had not kicked; now, suddenly, it did. The baby must survive! An influx of energy and willpower enabled her to struggle free and push Dick away. He staggered back, hit his head against the mantel, and fell down, unconscious. Marianne didn't know if he was dead or alive; visions of Libby Holman's ordeal after Smith's death filled her mind. She screamed. Dick showed signs of life, and she helped him into bed, where they both slept off the booze. Weeks later, on December 2, 1948, Patrick Cleveland Reynolds was born; although he didn't know it for some time, he had almost died before he came into this world.

Dick and Marianne left the two babies in care of nurses to attend the Truman inauguration. The Reynoldses and Curly Harris and his wife ran around the capital to the black-tie parties. At one gathering, Dick recognized mobster Frank Costello and asked Curly if he knew him. Dick wanted an introduction, explaining, "I used to work for him, but never met him." Costello and Dick sat and talked over the rum-running days. Meanwhile, Marianne discovered her old chum Lynn Baggett at another table; four years ago, they'd both danced on the deck of the *Makin Island*. Marianne thought Lynn's husband, Hollywood producer Sam Spiegel, old and ugly compared with her own catch, who was handsome, in his early forties, and had much more money.

During a break in the inaugural festivities Dick was received by Truman in the Oval Office. The president said, "I owe my election to you." It was true that Dick's generous contributions had helped him when no one else would contribute on that scale. In return, Dick presented Truman with a statue; it had originally been a matador with a bull charging into his cape, and Dick had had it altered so that the man appeared to be throwing the bull over his shoulder. Dick told Truman it was "an Oscar for politicians," and the president, tickled, kept it in his office for the rest of his term.

For the new year, 1949, the Reynoldses decided to dry out and start their lives going in a new direction; maybe the fantasy could be saved or, like the statue, altered for the better.

At a clinic in the mountains, Dick and Marianne underwent drastic therapy — a cure consisting of insulin shots given at frequent enough intervals to give patients the shakes, after which they were kept in isolation under the eyes of round-the-clock nursing patrols. Dick was annoyed when one of his nurses, on learning that he was a Reynolds, prattled endlessly about her own First Family of Virginia pedigree. Marianne told her sister, Dorothy, that after the insulin shots she felt as if she'd been a mental patient and had gone through electroshock treatments.

For weeks afterward, neither of them drank any alcohol; to that extent, the cure worked. But in the medical profession in 1949 there was little recognition that alcoholism was a disease, nor that sufferers from it ought never to touch liquor again; it was thought possible for reformed drinkers to resume social imbibing so long as they did not drink to excess.

The cure went hand in glove with other plans by Dick and Marianne to change their lives. Since they spent only a few months of the year on Sapelo, they decided to turn South End House into the Sapelo Plantation Inn. A gushing article in the *Atlanta Journal* showcased its beauties. To house forty guests at a time, Dick had apartments constructed overlooking a courtyard that had formerly been the headquarters of the farm. These flats also served to accommodate a group of University of Georgia scientists from a new foundation that Dick was setting up to study coastal marshlands, which were rapidly disappearing. In an era when only experts knew about ecology, Dick was caught up with the idea of studying the environment of Sapelo. At the request of the Reverend Orme Flinn, father of Dick's friend Emory, Dick also established on the island a camp to give poor mainland boys an idyllic summer. To transport the guests, scientists, and campers, Dick bought jeeps — not just a few but an entire jeep agency, lock, stock, and service contracts. Keys were left in the vehicles and numbers painted on their tops so that they were easy to use and could be spotted from the air if they got lost.

The Reynoldses didn't run the inn because they needed the income. At this point, Milton Berle, then the highest-paid entertainer in the world — "Mr. Television" — was earning about $6,500 a week. Dick's income was roughly $25,000 per week. By taking in guests, however, Dick could write off some of the enormous expense of maintaining the island for the times when he was in residence.

While the paying guests were about, a bathing-suited Marianne would emerge to dip in the outdoor pool or just to take the sun. Her movie-star figure made the male guests gawk; they'd talk with her and she with them. That summer the lord of Sapelo seemed to those who knew him alternately proud of Marianne's allure and annoyed when she displayed it for others; but then, Smith Reynolds hadn't liked Libby Holman singing "his" songs for others, either.

Benevolence and anger: alcoholics often veer back and forth between these, embracing extremes of each as the tides of inebriation and sobriety come and go. In 1949 Dick didn't stay on the wagon very long. How could he have guests staying in his South End mansion without having a polite drink with them? He loved being a good host.

Dick told sister Mary he had four rooms reserved for the Babcocks in August, but Mary worried to Nancy about exposing her children to "Uncle Dick" when he wasn't entirely sober. The Babcocks didn't manage to make it to Sapelo that year.

Things started going awry in Dick's business dealings. Despite a pact with a rival line on shipboard passengers, and another with an airline on forwarding freight from West Coast to East Coast ports by air, American Mail Lines was only intermittently profitable. There were labor problems and difficulty in replacing revenues lost when government subsidies were withdrawn. In another investment, Caribou Consolidated Mines, a uranium venture in Canada, Dick relied more on faith than on fact and lost money quickly.

By the fall of 1949, there was no more talk from Dick Reynolds about cures. For the next year he, Marianne, the two infants, a governess, a butler, and other attendants continued to bounce from Miami Beach to Sapelo to New York and by yacht to the Riviera and the Caribbean. No matter where home was at any particular moment, the Reynoldses' consumption of alcohol rose and the tolerance for each other's faults fell. Neither seemed able to give up the fantasy nor to substitute a new reality for it.

One night, Dick and Marianne were out in their finery at 21, a New York nightclub-turned-restaurant that boasted that its bar was the most expensive piece of real estate in the world. Before this evening, the couple's arguments had occurred mostly in private. Now, over steak tartare and champagne, Dick suggested that Marianne was wearing her emerald and diamond necklace and bracelet just to impress people in the restaurant. She retorted by asking why he had given her the jewelry if he hadn't wanted her to wear it. He was, she opined, just jealous because other men were appreciating her good looks. People turned to stare, but by this point the Reynoldses seemed to want their performance viewed by strangers. Dick accused Marianne of having gone after him for his money; she became so angry that she left the table, thrust her jewels into the hands of the owner and said he could keep them, and then returned to Beekman Place alone. Dick stayed out for two days, finally wandering into Abe Attell's bar, where his wife's stepfather convinced him to go home. By that time, Marianne had already retrieved the baubles from the club, and she and Dick were reconciled — for the moment.

=

In the fall of 1950, Dick went alone to the Knickerbocker Ball in New York City, one of the biggest social events of the year. There he met Mrs. Muriel Greenough. Although she coyly waited until Dick had been formally introduced before agreeing to dance, the meeting — at least on her part — was hardly accidental. Earlier in the evening, her escort, an interior designer, had seen her list of eligible millionaires who were going to be at the ball and was told that she aimed to capture one of them for her third marriage.

In other women this idea might have been presumptuous, but Muriel was adept at the business of catching wealthy men. As a teenager in her native Canada in the 1930s, Muriel was intelligent, witty, and voluptuous, though not beautiful. Pushed by her British mother, Muriel married Harold Laurence, a wealthy Californian, and mixed with the literate set of Hollywood — Dorothy Parker, Robert Benchley — at the Garden of Allah complex in Los Angeles. She and Laurence took frequent trips to India, where she fell under the influence of a maharajah. By the age of twenty, she'd divorced Laurence and joined her mother in London. In the British capital, when the war started, she cadged a job from the *New York Times*, reporting on conditions during the blitz. A Nazi buzz bomb trapped Muriel and British journalist Richard Greenough in a cellar for two days; by the time they were rescued, they were lovers. Her second marriage followed. Greenough, too, had quite a bit of money. After the war this marriage soured, and Muriel went husband hunting in Europe and America. One of her favorite ploys was to ask a real estate broker in a fashionable area like Miami Beach to show her some expensive homes; she and her mother would visit these homes and pretend to be able to afford them, though their actual purpose was to meet the wealthy owners, who, often as not, were in the process of being divorced.

As Dick danced with Muriel at the Knickerbocker Ball, he was charmed by her. He knew Laurence and had also met Greenough. After the ball, as was his custom, Dick invited a dozen or more of the guests back to the Beekman Place duplex. Marianne greeted the revelers and looked over the crowd to see if any of the women could compete with her in terms of beauty. She hardly even noticed Muriel and soon retired to her own bedroom, leaving Dick, Muriel, and the other guests to their own devices.

That was a mistake. Muriel wasn't classically beautiful, but she was sexy, sophisticated, literate, and considerably more tolerant of the decadent ways of the wealthy than Marianne. Dick Reynolds, weary of the woman Marianne had become — a new Blitz with babies — was intrigued by a woman who seemed to be her opposite.

Dick and Muriel had a few clandestine dates, but Dick made no commitments. Even though his marriage was in trouble, he did not want to appear to be leaving one woman for another.

During the early months of 1951, Dick and Marianne sailed to the French Riviera. At Monte Carlo, the rich were in their element: one could not wear too many jewels, have too much champagne, arrive in too fine a car, bet too flamboyantly at the casino. The parties moved easily from ship to shore and back. Sometimes Dick would get so drunk that by evening he wouldn't be physically able to leave the yacht, and Marianne would have to stay aboard and watch him deteriorate, then pass out. In the mornings she'd remove the debris, the vomit, the other evidence of the night before — because, after a while, she was too embarrassed to continue ordering the staff to clean it up.

After several such nights and mornings-after, one evening she announced to Dick that even if he couldn't walk steadily down the gangplank, she was going ashore. In the casino, dressed to impress, she had a good time. Thereafter, when Dick started on the booze too early in the day, she'd again fly solo. In the rarefied atmosphere of Cannes and Monte Carlo, no one frowned at a beautiful, bejewelled woman alone. There was always a man to light her cigarette or bring another drink, and the bills could be sent to Mr. Reynolds's office. On such nights, many men paid court to her. Among them were Prince Aly Khan and his close friend, the infamous Latin playboy Porfirio Rubirosa.

Rubi was then at what a newspaper labeled the "zenith" of his charm as a "romantic adventurer." Born in the Dominican Republic in 1909, he became the country's star polo player and at age twenty married the dictator's daughter. His marriage to Flor de Oro Trujillo lasted only five years, but when it broke up Rubirosa was posted as a diplomatic envoy to South America and then to European countries. Intrigue surrounded him; in the 1930s he was implicated but not prosecuted in the murders of several expatriate critics of the Trujillo regime. He was a racing-car driver, a pilot, a tennis player of rank, a diver who sought sunken treasure. In 1942 he married French actress Danielle Darrieux, then described as the world's most beautiful woman. After divorcing her, in 1947 he married Doris Duke, only child of Buck Duke. That marriage also ended quickly, but Rubi got a nice settlement. "The ambition of most men is to save money," Rubirosa was quoted as saying. "Mine is to spend it." He homed in carefully on either beautiful or wealthy women. Trying to understand his appeal, one magazine described his "swarthy good looks, smooth rhythm on the dance floor, faultless tailoring, an intriguing accent, sex appeal," and lauded him as "an easy conversationalist, a graceful athlete, an adaptable companion."

In Marianne Reynolds he saw a beautiful woman on the verge of divorce who would be wealthy in her own right after she split up with Dick. And if there was no divorce — well, Rubirosa never seemed to mind; he was as much a Don Juan as a fortune hunter. Rubirosa continued paying court to Marianne in Cannes, then pursued her from city to city throughout Europe. No matter where the Reynolds yacht docked or in what grand hotel they stayed, Rubirosa would show up, always smiling and attentive. Flattered and interested, Marianne was reluctant to have an affair that would be bound to get into the gossip columns and wreck her marriage. However, when Rubirosa reacted by paying attention to Zsa Zsa Gabor — then ending her marriage to George Sanders — Marianne was jealous.

As Dick sank deeper into alcohol, conducted casual affairs of his own, and appeared oblivious to what she did, Marianne grew bolder. The attention lavished on her by Rubirosa became impossible to resist; they consummated their passion in his Paris apartment. The affair lasted for a week. By then, the news that they were "constant companions" was all over the gossip columns of Europe and America.

Dick was hurt. The Reynoldses' life-style might have withstood reciprocal infidelities — certainly he himself was not constant, and he could perhaps have forgiven Marianne a fling in reaction to his binges — but to cuckold him publicly with the notorious Rubirosa was an affront to a Southern gentleman who in the best of times loved his wife passionately.

Testament to their residual affection for one another was the fact that the marriage did not immediately split apart. After recriminations and apolgies, Dick and Marianne left the Riviera together and returned to New York. They showed their faces in the usual circles, and gossip columnists, allies of Marianne's since her New York stage days, reported breathlessly to readers that the couple's difficulties had been relegated to the past.

One night the Reynoldses and Tommy and Janey Dorsey, all in formal garb, visited El Morocco. After drinks and dancing, they were about to leave when they saw Rubirosa at the bar. Dick and Marianne started to bicker over whether to acknowledge Rubi's presence. Marianne angrily went over and publicly embraced her former lover. Dick was furious; heated words were exchanged, and Dick pulled a knife. Tommy Dorsey grabbed Dick, Janey took Marianne, a cordon of waiters formed around the grinning Rubirosa, and somehow the Reynoldses were gotten into separate cabs and back to Beekman Place.

"Dick's been a bad boy," Marianne told Dorothy a few days after the incident, "so he said to take everybody down to the islands, and he'll meet us there." Marianne, Dorothy, mother Mae, another woman friend, the two boys, a governess, and a maid all cruised to Jamaica and island-hopped around the Caribbean, staying at night in suites at the best hotels.

Once again, Dick was trying to appease a wife with an expensive treat. And by accepting the trip, Marianne was agreeing to this way of atoning. Similar deals had propped up Dick's first marriage; now he was resorting to them to try to save his second. But when he arrived in Jamaica he immediately undermined the scheme by asserting his right to do what he damn well pleased, which was to stay out all night on shore, drinking. Next day, when Marianne, Dorothy, and a Jamaican taxi driver found him in a dive and Marianne was ready to give him hell, he was so charming — insisting that the ladies come in and have a drink — that Marianne just threw up her hands and went along.

Several days later, while at anchor in Puerto Rico, they had what

Marianne later called a "big, knock-down, drag-out drunken fight" about everything and nothing. Dick sent the women and children ashore to a hotel and issued instructions to the management that he would pay their bills for no more than two days. Then he got back aboard the yacht and sailed for Europe by way of Sapelo. On his Georgia island, he destroyed all of Marianne's wartime letters to him, a fitting final gesture for a marriage that had now collapsed.

Dick also closed the Sapelo Plantation Inn and made plans to sell the American Mail Line. Competition from the Japanese, as well as economies being realized in air transport, had lessened the value of AML's nine wholly owned ships and ten leased ones. He found a buyer in a syndicate headed by Texas oilman Clint Murchison.

Then he asked Blitz if he could take all four of his boys on safari to Africa. He'd hardly seen them in the past ten years because he hadn't insisted on parental visits, but he needed them now. As the boys neared adulthood, Dick wanted to reassert his influence; R. J. had hoped to nurture his sons as they came of age but had died before completing that task. Also, in a time of emotional upheaval, having left behind a second set of sons, Dick didn't want to completely lose touch with all of his children. Blitz agreed that he could take Josh and John, seventeen and fifteen. They left shortly for a cruise to England, then to Africa. As usual, Dick had several agendas going at once. Seemingly by accident, he and the boys met Muriel and her mother in London. Of course, Dick had set this up earlier by telephone. Dick and Muriel made plans to spend time together later in the year. From Africa, Dick wrote Tommy Dorsey long, brooding letters full of anger at Marianne's "betrayal." He and Marianne loved one another but could no longer live together, he said.

That reasoning failed to assess the real causes of the schism between them. Dick had little understanding that the fantasy he and Marianne had constructed, unable to withstand changing circumstances, had fallen apart. Marianne had betrayed him, yes, but no more than he had betrayed her by his drunkenness and emotional infidelity, faults that no gift, no matter how lavish, could cancel out.

=

In September of 1951 the first wedding of the generation of R. J.'s grandchildren was held, at Reynolda: Mary Katharine Babcock married Kenneth Mountcastle, Jr. The bride's mother had invited the entire family, including half brother J. Edward Johnston, Jr. Dick came, without Marianne. Uncle Will, however, did not attend because he had recently been taken ill and was in a coma.

Will Reynolds died several days later, at the age of eighty-eight. He was mourned as a great figure, a benefactor of the community's schools and libraries. His money was left principally to the Z. Smith Reynolds Foundation, and his estate, Tanglewood, was to be made into a public park — for whites only. In the year before Will's death his stables had done better than ever before, with four star horses. Also, another dream of his was reaching fruition: the emplacement of Wake Forest University in Winston-Salem. A few weeks after Will's death, President Truman flew in to turn over the first spadeful of the college's new campus; in his speech, the president emphasized that the price of peace in Korea would demand sacrifice on the part of the entire populace of the United States. After lunch at Reynolda, the president took a nap in one of the upstairs bedrooms.

In November of 1951 Dick was taken ill in New York and spent more than a week in a hospital. His illness perplexed him; he wondered to Mary when she came to visit, "How could I, a forty-five-year-old man with a large capacity for liquor, pass out after only two drinks?" Doctors found multiple answers: liver damage, weak lungs, and an overworked heart. They advised him to stop drinking and quit smoking.

He did neither. He tried to be a little more moderate in his habits, but drinking and smoking had been part of his life for thirty years; furthermore, Scotch and Camels were two of his great pleasures, and his life was predicated on the right of a wealthy man to enjoy himself. Nancy and Mary fretted in their letters over his continued indulgence but didn't take him under their wings. Both had problems of their own: Mary's abdominal difficulties were increasing and Nancy's marriage to Henry Bagley was on the rocks.

However, Dick's illness may have pushed him toward the decision, in early 1952, that there would be no reconciliation with Marianne. He instituted divorce proceedings. He had Marianne's phone tapped and sent detectives to follow her and members of her family. His lawyers took a tough negotiating stance, arguing that Marianne had committed adultery with Rubirosa (who would be named as a corespondent) and therefore would be entitled to very little from Dick Reynolds.

While negotiations went on, Dick took Muriel to the Caribbean and then to England. At work for him in England was an old navy buddy, Warren Ritchie, whose marriage had also recently split apart; Dick had hired him to oversee the building of a new yacht, the *Aries*, a sixty-five-foot-long beauty made of teak. Ritchie marveled at how at ease Dick was with both the elegant shipyard owner and the lowly craftsmen. Dick would chat up the "blokes" about every mechanical detail of the construction. He'd also drink with them and after one binge was incarcerated overnight, to the delight of the British press, which replayed the 1929 manslaughter case for a new generation of readers.

While Dick was in Europe, in April of 1952, Senate Republicans unearthed the 1948 IRS ruling on Dick's loans and took potshots at Dick, Truman, and Adlai Stevenson, who would shortly become the Democratic nominee for president. These led to hearings that, in subsequent congressional sessions, formulated laws to better regulate the financing of election campaigns.

That same month, three-year-old Patrick Reynolds was hospitalized in Miami with polio, a realization of the fears of every mother in the years before the development of the Salk and Sabin vaccines. Patrick was in a respirator and a brace; doctors told Marianne he might never walk again. Grandmother Mae and her sisters said round-the-clock novenas for the boy, and Marianne tried frantically to reach Dick. He cabled her, "I see no reason for Patrick's illness to delay our divorce proceedings."

This was heartless — but in keeping with the pattern he'd established during his first divorce, a pattern that echoed his mother's actions in abandoning her children for a new partner and a new life. Dick believed that Marianne had conceived Michael and Patrick in order to gain a financial stranglehold on him; therefore, he wouldn't pay attention to Patrick when the boy was in danger. Such rationalizations prevented Dick from becoming emotionally attached to his children.

Marianne was asked not to visit Patrick in the hospital; doctors feared that if the child saw her, he would lift his arms up to greet her and compromise the work they had done to save his paralyzed back. Unable to stay away, she dressed as Santa Claus to come and see him but got only a brief glimpse; behind her mask and beard, she cried.

As she was returning from seeing Patrick in the hospital, Marianne was unable to remember her address or even her own name and had to be helped by a policeman. After this incident she was briefly hospitalized. Dick didn't believe she'd actually been ill and pressed on with the divorce.

Marianne's energies were focused on Patrick. In six weeks, the boy got so much better that doctors considered his recovery miraculous. Walking again, he showed few traces of the disease; Marianne took him to New York, where he could undergo more therapy.

It was in New York, at the end of June, that she received a letter from one "Danger Jones":

> You are making a complete idiot of yourself, and you are seemingly doing it deliberately, what no one else can understand is why, when given the opportunity of a fair settlement (knowing that you had treated your husband like a dog, and slept with several other men as well, Sinatra included, none I might add, who seemed to want you for long), why you didn't take it and go quietly when you had the chance.

A week later, a second letter arrived, similarly typed and signed, warning her to "go quietly" or the writer would make public such details as her having been a gangster's moll, having had abortions, and conceiving children in order to have a hold over her husband. Marianne believed Muriel had written the letters with information from Dick because they contained a mixture of truth, conjecture, and charges Dick had long made against her. Yes, before she met Dick she'd been the girlfriend of a man associated with the underworld; she'd had a date with Sinatra but not, as implied, an affair; further, Dick was fond of the "treated like a dog" phrase. Of course the letters couldn't be traced — or used in the divorce trial. Marianne's legal position was weak, and shortly after this she agreed to a settlement: $750,000 in cash, a $750,000 trust fund for herself but none for the boys, the New York and Miami Beach residences, three automobiles, lawyers' fees, and an allowance of $5,000 per year for each boy. The total worth was estimated at $2 million, far less than the $9 million Blitz had won six years earlier.

While waiting for Dick's divorce to go through, Muriel had obtained a divorce from Greenough, although under what later proved to be shady circumstances. In an Arkansas town famous for twenty-four-hour divorces, her papers were drawn up by a debarred lawyer, and her chief witness was her mother, who may have committed perjury in answer to a judge's questions.

On August 7, the divorce of Dick and Marianne became final. That same day, at Muriel's home in Oyster Bay, Long Island, Dick asked Muriel to sign a prenuptial agreement on which they'd worked for several months. It was to be executed by a bank and trust company in Canada, and it deeded to Muriel ten thousand shares of Dick's RJR stock (then valued at $100,000). She would get half the yearly income from it and her mother would get the other half. Also included was a gift of $10,000 in cash to go along with approximately $100,000 in jewelry that Dick already had given her. By signing the agreement, Muriel would waive "any and all right, title, etc." to Dick's other property and would have to avow that in case of a future divorce, she would receive nothing more from Dick than alimony of $15,000 a year.

Under the gun, Muriel objected to signing the agreement. That was nonsense, Dick retorted, because they'd begun work on the agreement in Switzerland months ago. If she didn't sign it now, he said, he wouldn't marry her. Muriel asked to insert a clause requiring Dick to pay her an additional $15,000 in cash if he broke a pledge not to drink liquor. He put that clause in as well.

The $15,000 was a trifle to him, the equivalent of half a week's income from his stock dividends. He inserted the clause because he wanted the main part of the document signed. By this time, Dick had understood that his money was at least part of what attracted women to him, especially such a sophisticated woman as Muriel — and it was that acceptance of money as partial reason for the marriage that he was codifying in the prenuptial agreement. This new marriage was to be a realistic one, not a fantasy, or he wouldn't make it. It was the principle that counted. If Muriel wouldn't sign, then he would know where he stood with her.

She signed. Next afternoon at Sapelo, fifty local blacks and a few of Dick's business associates attended the marriage, held under a live oak on the lawn of South End House. After the ceremony, Dick carved into the tree the legend "Muriel and Dick — Forever Married Here August 8, 1952."

Chapter Fifteen

In Danger: Muriel

AT THE EXPLORERS CLUB in New York, one of Dick's older sons was approached by a private detective who'd been following Muriel's tracks for years and who maintained that she was among the "most dangerous women in America," a fortune hunter by trade. The detective offered to sell his information for $10,000; when the young man declined to bite, the detective suggested that his mother might be interested. Blitz refused, saying, "Muriel is not my problem; Marianne WAS my problem."

Indeed, after his new marriage, Dick and his third wife had a cordial visit with Blitz and the boys. Muriel encouraged Dick to rekindle his relationship with his older sons. The Reynoldses also paid calls on the Babcocks and Bagleys before leaving on an extended honeymoon that included a trip to London to launch the *Aries*, flying to Tahiti, and yachting through the South Sea Islands, where they bought thirty acres of paradise for a vacation home. Dick fell far enough off the wagon that he had to pay Muriel the agreed-upon $15,000. For the most part, though, he remained sober and seemed to be greatly in love.

In 1952, as he had done in 1946, Dick sold property to finance his divorce, remarriage, and new purchases. He realized capital gains on 25,000 shares of Eastern Airlines stock and 35,000 shares of RJR but balanced these by writing off as worthless $200,000 in stock and $250,000 in loans to Caribou Consolidated Mines. Even after such transactions, his net dividend income for 1952 was more than $2 million. In fact, his fortune was so large and so stable — $20 million to $30 million, the same as in 1946 — that divorce settlements, bad debts, and spending $1 million a year made no appreciable dent in it.

At the beginnings of his marriages to Blitz and Marianne, Dick lavished jewelry and new homes on them and financial aid on their relatives. Now he did the same with Muriel. In addition to purchasing two adjoining Fifth Avenue apartments in New York and a home in Palm Beach, Florida, Dick lent her brother, Tony Marston, a quarter million to recapitalize his Canadian shoe company; soon Tony was sending more pairs of shoes than Dick could ever wear.

For the next several years, the couple spent about five months of each year at Sapelo, a month or two in Palm Beach, a similar amount of time in New York, and the rest of the time traveling in Europe, where they often moored their yacht off Monte Carlo. Muriel liked to play chemin de fer; she lost thousands of dollars, but Dick wasn't upset by the cost of the entertainment. The marriage was going well, and he wasn't going to quarrel over small matters.

Mary Reynolds Babcock died of abdominal cancer in early July of 1953, one month before her forty-fifth birthday. She had been a heavy smoker throughout her life. At the Reynolda funeral service, the president of Wake Forest University said that the extent of Mary's generosity would probably never be fully known because she had given to the college through so many different channels. About half Mary's estate, $12 million, went into a new foundation named for her. As her friend Emily Rose wrote in a memoir-introduction to Mary's posthumously published book on gardening, "Her eager mind penetrated into all facets of life, particularly those which would bring well-being and beauty into her home."

After a somewhat riotous youth, Mary had lived a successful, near-anonymous life devoted to her children, flower arranging, and many good works. Her solid marriage, and an ability to throw herself into the minutiae of daily living, revealed in her letters to Nancy, counterpointed the high pleasures and low torments that characterized the lives of her brothers. Although she sprang from the same background as Smith and Dick, she had been better able than they to cope with wealth.

Nancy was somewhere in between. A few months after Mary's death, she instituted a divorce from Henry Bagley following a marriage that had lasted twenty-three years and had produced four children. During the divorce, Nancy and Dick grew closer. Reaching middle age, they found that their outlooks on life were similar; like Dick, Nancy seemed to have come to the belief that while money couldn't necessarily buy happiness, it could be used to thrust aside those things that made one unhappy.

That summer, with a governess and a maid, Marianne took the two small boys to Europe, first-class. They hit all the millionaires' spots; Marianne wore her jewelry and trademark low-cut gowns and was courted by Aristotle Onassis and Wooly Donahue, an heir to the Woolworth fortune. To maintain her wealthy image, Marianne was dipping into her capital. The ten thousand dollars per year she was receiving for the boys' education didn't cover the cost of private schooling, the governess, and summer-long trips. To keep the Miami Beach residence going required seven in help, and Beekman Place needed several more. Then, too, Marianne was becoming a magnet for the same sort of hangers-on who had always trailed Dick; before she had despised them, but in the aftermath of the divorce she began to like their flattery.

Josh and John were at prep school, but when Blitz's two younger sons reached high school age she decided that she couldn't bear to have them also go away to school. Zach and Will didn't want to continue their education in rural Surry County, so Blitz brought them back to Winston, where they attended Reynolds High.

With this move, Blitz took the boys out of the country but was unable to take the country out of the boys. By this time, the role models of their rural environment — the "good old boys" who rode cycles, shot guns, and caroused endlessly — seemed to have compromised Blitz's attempts at strict upbringing. The contradictions in the boys' backgrounds were evident; at Reynolds High, for example, Zach played trombone in the marching band and had a girlfriend who was a cheerleader, but his real interest was motorcycles. He raced them, tinkered with them, and was the leader of a cycle pack called the Buena Vista Butt Busters. On weekends and during vacations Zach and Will would ride their bikes through the hills of Devotion and fire guns at road signs. One of their pleasures was to use their swivel-based machine gun on such targets. Zach and Will drove their cycles and cars so fast that they often got into trouble, and Blitz had to put a bail bondsman on retainer. When Zach temporarily lost his license for speeding, he switched to driving a souped-up tractor; there were, he pointed out, no speed limits for such vehicles in North Carolina.

In May of 1954, Dick, Muriel, and the *Aries* were in Bermuda, waiting for a man to come from the States to repair a damaged radio. During this enforced lull, Dick drank heavily and Muriel was inordinately rude to the crew. A fight started between the couple, and Dick jumped in the water and pulled in Muriel, who was wearing an evening gown. Later during the same binge Dick took a bad fall on the gangplank and injured himself. A doctor, summoned to give first aid, told Dick that he was too drunk to know what he was doing and would continue to have "accidents" unless he sobered up; Dick maintained to *Aries* crew member Warren Ritchie that Muriel had rigged the plank to collapse.

The marriage of Dick and Muriel was less than two years old, and cracks were beginning to appear, just as the troubles in Dick's marriage to Marianne had surfaced in about the same span of time. Despite their marital differences, Dick and Muriel crossed to England to examine a new yacht being built for them. At the shipyard Dick again met Christian Nissen, who had been on the crew of German yachts that Dick had raced against before the war. Dick hired him on the spot, together with Nissen's friend, twenty-year-old Gunther Lehmann.

Both new employees accompanied Dick and Muriel on board the new yacht to Bremen, Germany, where further calibrations on the ship were to be made. They sailed around the German coast and the Scandinavian countries, carousing all the way. Often Dick invited crowds of people he'd just met to come aboard the yacht for after-hours parties. As Marianne had done before her, Muriel grew to dislike this practice, and after one such party in Copenhagen, on August 15, 1954, she left the yacht and didn't return that night. Dick assumed she'd gone to see her mother in London and would show up sooner or later.

Next day, from Copenhagen, Muriel forged a cable in Dick's name that instructed Barclay's Bank in Monte Carlo to wire $550,000 to their joint bank account in New York; such telegrams, she knew, were the usual way Dick transferred money. Then she wired the New York bank to send her $25,000 in Paris. Both banks obliged.

Blitz had fought Dick with insults, Marianne with fists — but Muriel went to the real source of pleasure and pain in the marriage: money.

Learning of the cables, Dick moved to stop the transfers and began preliminary inquiries for a divorce. Christian Nissen easily found Muriel in Paris and brought her back to Dick. She admitted the errors of her ways but tried to excuse her erratic behavior by claiming that she'd just found out she was pregnant.

Pregnant? Well, he was forty-eight and did want to have a little girl. He softened. Perhaps, he thought, he'd now been through enough to raise a child successfully. Dick dispatched Muriel to New York to tend the pregnancy while he stayed in Paris, preparatory to taking the new yacht and its crew for a shakedown cruise to Tangier.

Marianne was also in Paris at that moment. She knew that Rubirosa was around and that he was newly divorced, having been married to heiress Barbara Hutton for just fifty-three days. She found and talked to Rubi, but he was no longer interested in her. She drifted to one of Dick's old Paris haunts, Fred Payne's bar, haven of expatriate Americans since the 1920s. Dick was there, on a bar stool.

He introduced Marianne pleasantly to a companion, and for a moment she imagined that the love she still held for him was reciprocated. Then, when her back was turned, Dick commented to his crony that she was looking fat. Marianne erupted in hysterical rage, hitting Dick over the head with her high-heeled shoe and screaming at him, over and over, "Where were you when Patrick had polio?"

Dick could have overpowered her physically, but her pain and the justice of her accusation seemed to keep him from doing so. When Payne tried to come between them, she threatened to break his eyeglasses with her shoe heel, and he backed off. Then she started smashing liquor glasses — fitting emblem of her long battle against Dick's constant drinking. After a while, drained, Marianne left the bar; damage to it was considerable, and her own self-image was no less scarred.

In African waters, aboard his new ship, Dick expressed his own feelings by drinking to excess with Warren Ritchie and the Germans; it was clear to Ritchie that part of the reason they had been hired was to be genial drinking companions. Dick sent Muriel several letters, postmarked Tangier, most of them reiterating the theme "Dearest Doe: Think of you all the time and hope everything goes well with you. All my love forever & ever — Buck."

In a suite at the Ritz Hotel in New York, Dr. Henry Rowan treated Muriel. He observed that she looked exhausted and nervous.

He accepted her statement that she was pregnant but did not do a vaginal examination to check the diagnosis. When Dick joined Muriel in New York, Rowan examined him, too, and told Dick that he was an alcoholic and that he'd better do something about it, quickly.

On the night of December 5–6, 1954, while alone in her bathtub, Muriel had a miscarriage. She told her doctor about it but did not bring him the fetus, which she estimated at about four months. She disposed of it herself. Although by law such stillbirths had to be reported to city authorities, no such report was made, nor did the doctor make an examination of her, which could have verified Muriel's story of the miscarriage. Within a few days of this event, Dick and Muriel left for Palm Beach; Muriel was in such good health that Dick wondered if she had actually ever been pregnant or if that had been a lie concocted to cover up her attempt to take money from him.

=

To show that Miami was her town rather than Dick's, Marianne threw one of the most extravagant parties ever held in Miami Beach, a gala that she dubbed the "Swan Song." On the grounds of the Sunset Island house, in a circus tent lined in pink satin and hung with crystal chandeliers, actor Dean Murphy was master of ceremonies, the Tommy Dorsey Orchestra played, and other performers sang and danced. Show business and socialite guests came in by plane or moored their yachts behind the house. Marianne dieted for a month to fit into a spectacular gown.

After the party she sold the house and moved with her two boys to a much smaller one in the walled-in neighborhood of Baypoint. If there were no yachts anchored out back, there also were no longer seven in help to pay. Determined not to lose her standing in Miami society, Marianne took over the chairmanship of the annual Miami Heart Ball; one year, in response to a surfeit of charity dinners, she conceived the "No Ball," for which donations were taken but benefactors were relieved of the necessity of attending a dinner dance. It was a great success and widely imitated. In the mid-1950s Marianne sold the twenty-two-room duplex at Beekman Place because she couldn't afford to maintain that either. The apartment came into the hands of her onetime suitor Aly Khan. A follower of Islam, which does not allow the drinking of liquor, he ripped out the forty-thousand-dollar bar. He also installed rectangular Persian carpets in the rooms that Dick and Marianne had had built to curve at such great expense.

Marianne didn't get a good price for either property. Soon afterward she moved back into the building on East Fifty-second Street where she had grown up, taking an apartment on the sixth floor that was identical in size and shape to her mother's on the third. The princess had come full circle. Yet she continued to take luxurious trips to Europe, to move between New York and Florida — in short, to act as Mrs. R. J. Reynolds, even though two other woman now bore that appellation. Her capital diminished steadily but not her consumption of food, alcohol, and cigarettes. Sister Dorothy thought Marianne was developing the imperial manner perfected in earlier years by mother Mae.

Michael and Patrick first went to school at private academies in Miami, but by the time they were nine and eight, respectively, Marianne packed them off to boarding schools, at first in the Miami area, where they could return home on weekends, and later to separate schools that were farther away. A product of boarding schools herself, Marianne thought them appropriate surroundings for the sons of a rich man. However, the boys felt isolated; having been cut off from their father by the divorce, they were now out of touch with their mother. At school Patrick learned to keep his identity as a tobacco Reynolds secret, for when news of it leaked out, as invariably happened, he was often ostracized or asked for money. Nonplussed when pressed for details about his father, whom he hadn't seen since he was three, he was also awed and embarrassed by his flamboyant mother, who would come and take him for rides in limousines, as her mother and gentleman friends had done with her when she was a child at boarding school in the 1920s.

Though at times Marianne acted callously toward her sons, just as often she overwhelmed them with love. Sympathetic toward her friends, especially those who experienced hard times, she had bursts of kindness and understanding. When Tommy Dorsey passed away in his sleep, Janey, bereft, couldn't bear to stay in the marital bed anymore and moved into one of her children's rooms. Learning of this situation in a phone call from Florida, Marianne immediately flew to New York and hired a limousine to drive her to the Dorsey home in Connecticut. She kept the limousine outside while she went in and hustled her friend upstairs; they both got into the double bed and spent the night talking about the need for life to go on and for survivors to cope. In the morning Janey felt better and said she'd sleep in the bed henceforth. Marianne got back in the limousine, which had been waiting outside all that time, and returned to Florida.

Blitz's sons were coming of age. As they left Devotion, they found their way into Dick's orbit. When Josh, in his early twenties, wasn't traveling, he lived across the hall from Dick and Muriel in New York, in the extra apartment Dick had bought for guests. Josh was then a beatnik, trying to figure out life; he and his stepmother would have long talks and lunches together. John, two years younger, became a crew member on the *Aries*. Dick chided him severely for trying to impress girls with the wealth he might inherit from his old man. John decided to join the marines.

Zach and Will were still in school, under Blitz's eye, but were becoming wilder. Both were skeet-shooting champions, and Zach was a good skier and motorcycle racer. Zach's daredevil antics reminded older Winstonians of his dead uncle, Smith — an apt comparison since, like Smith, Zach had a shy, repressed side. He also stuttered. When a new baseball field was dedicated at Reynolds High and Dick was guest of honor at the ceremonies, Zach appeared to be hiding on the field behind his marching-band trombone. His girlfriend, cheerleader Linda Lee Tise, asked him why he wouldn't greet his father. Zach said he didn't expect her to understand, because she was from a normal family; he was unable to tell her then that he hadn't spent any time with Dick in the past fifteen years.

Blitz had known Linda Lee's family for ages and hoped that she would marry one of her boys — any one of them. When Zach and Will went up to Devotion for the weekend, Blitz offered Linda Lee and her girlfriends the use of Merry Acres for a pajama party; teenage girls dressing up in outsized men's pajamas was a fad just then. During the night at Merry Acres, Linda Lee discovered that Zach had hidden a microphone to record what the girls might say about him.

When Zach would be arrested for speeding, Blitz would let him spend the night in jail in hopes that he'd learn the error of his ways. He didn't. The battle deepened. Blitz wanted things done her way, but Zach had his own vision for his life. Upon graduating high school he wanted to study engineering, a logical course since he was a born tinkerer and mechanically inclined. Somewhat perversely, Blitz sent him to Wake Forest, which had no program in engineering but which was next-door. Blitz won that skirmish but lost the war: after a year, Zach dropped out of Wake Forest to join the navy.

The sons were rebelling, and not just against Blitz's heavy hand. All were restless and unsettled. They knew they were going to have substantial money from the Katharine Smith Reynolds Johnston trust, a half million each from the divorce, and perhaps even more as they got older, and there was no family tradition to teach them what to do about this money or with it.

Throughout the mid-1950s Dick and Muriel continued their pattern of life: from Sapelo to the Caribbean to Palm Beach to New York to Europe and back, all in the course of a year. As did many wealthy people, Dick considered it a point of distinction not to know the details of his expenditures. He encouraged Muriel to do the household accounts and put $100,000 into her hands annually for that purpose.

His own money came and went — mostly came. He bought the farm next to Tanglewood from his Lybrook cousins, held it a year (during which he took a tax loss for operating it), and then sold it at a 20 percent profit. When he had a big gain in income, he also usually had a loss against which it could be offset for tax purposes. Dick's RJR stock was soaring: in 1953 his shares brought in $200,000 in dividends, and by 1956 the same number of shares returned $300,000. The price of the stock itself had also risen, by a third.

In a typical series of transactions, Dick first lent a man he met in Germany a quarter million for a quick-freezing facility. Initially, this seemed to Muriel like a dumb investment — the sort of thing Dick often did to gratify a friend, sometimes one he barely knew — but it was actually a good idea and sparked others. With the freezing facility and a freighter, Dick started a business that brought frozen food to the Virgin Islands. From this notion, he leapt to the formation of an offshore holding company, an entity that saved money in taxes if it didn't directly generate cash. The Netherlands Meade holding company became the repository for notes on Abe Attell's bar in New York, Tony Marston's shoe company, Emory Flinn's brokerage in Miami, the Andrew Johnson Hotel in Nashville, some

Atlanta property, and the homes Dick bought for a half-dozen present and former employees.

As the years went by, both Dick and Muriel became steadily more eccentric. On Sapelo, Dick kept a pet goose, Gretel, who followed him about; he also had a pond shaped there to resemble the world's oceans and the seven continents. He secreted more and more gold on Sapelo and also made an extraordinary purchase of a million dollars in bearer bonds. Any bearer could turn in these bonds at a bank and collect cash. Dick intended them for emergency supplies when the world collapsed. He kept some in a safe in New York and the bulk on Sapelo, not in a safe but in a locked closet in which Muriel also stored her jewelry. Every month, it was Muriel's task to cut the coupons off these bonds and hand them to Dick so they could be cashed.

Muriel took to wearing turbans, stuck a six-inch dagger in her waist sash, consulted occult books, surrounded herself with statues of Buddha, and burned incense on the South End lawn. Warren Ritchie, Dick's drinking buddy, thought that some of the changes in Muriel were encouraged by her mother, Mrs. Marston, who was a frequent visitor at Sapelo. Ritchie detested the old woman because she was such an obvious leech; in fact, he believed Mrs. Marston wanted Dick dead. When Ritchie told Dick his suspicions, the millionaire just laughed, saying he'd charm his mother-in-law and give her enough money to keep her happy.

It began to take more than monetary payoffs to make Mrs. Marston — or Muriel — happy. One summer, the boys at the camp on Sapelo put on a play-pageant of the island's history, and Dick and Muriel were honored guests at the big performance. The boys did well enough with Blackbeard and former Sapelo owners Thomas Spalding and Howard Coffin but offended Muriel by their portrayal of her. She had a temper tantrum and insisted that Dick close down the camp. Knowing that she'd badger him endlessly, he gave in. It was a turning point in their relationship. Thereafter, especially on Sapelo, Muriel grew bolder, believing that Dick would accede to her wishes in order to avoid marital strife. She became imperious with black employees, who feared her voodoo toys, and when longtime chef Karl Weiss displeased her, she took him off kitchen duty and, while Dick was away, had him lay bricks, which almost killed him.

Concurrently, she tried to gratify what she believed to be Dick's darker wishes. In Germany, in 1957, after Dick had paid a song-stress to continue to warble for hours after her club was closed, Muriel had Gunther Lehmann pay the woman to come into bed with her and Dick. Dick was too drunk to raise any objections.

Later on during this trip Dick became sick in Lisbon, and the illness was traced by doctors to his alcoholism. Both Dick and Muriel went on the wagon in London, fortified by shots of vitamin B_{12}. They also had checkups there to find out why Muriel couldn't conceive. On May 17, Dr. T. M. Creighton examined Dick, who was, he later wrote, "most anxious to have a child," and had a specimen of Dick's sperm inspected in the laboratory, where it was labeled inactive. That was to be expected of a fifty-one-year-old who'd been drinking for decades. Some hope was held out that if the drinking stopped, the sperm would again become viable. Dick consoled Muriel with a promise of sobriety and some new jewelry.

In early 1958, as the *Aries* was dockside in Montego Bay, Jamaica, Warren Ritchie watched as Dick started to drink to be sociable with his guests, the governor of Jamaica and other local dignitaries. Muriel matched Dick glass for glass and soon had drunk so much herself that she insulted the guests. That, of course, made Dick angry — and gave him an excuse to drink himself into a stupor. The dignitaries beat a hasty retreat, leaving the besotted millionaire and his wife on their yacht. Yes, Ritchie concluded, Dick's drinking was a major problem in the marriage, but he now understood that Muriel often goaded her husband to drink.

This binge lasted ten days. Unfortunately, this time Dick didn't come out of it as he had in Lisbon. In fact, he almost died. He collapsed and was hospitalized, first in Palm Beach and then in Winston-Salem. For years his health had been deteriorating; now it was as if his body had fallen over a cliff. He was alive but severely damaged.

≡

Muriel moved into the hospital with Dick and hardly left his side for the several weeks he spent in a private wing of the Winston institution built with his donations. Doctors found his liver damaged, his heart weakened, his lungs almost gone. They diagnosed an "aggravated asthma" because no one seemed to want to label it emphysema. Dick was ordered to stop drinking, to stop smoking, and to eat no salty foods, which would draw fluid into his lungs.

He left the hospital in midsummer with his own portable oxygen equipment — he could breathe regular air only for short periods. The Sapelo patio was being separated from the pool by floor-to-ceiling glass so his rooms could be air-conditioned; while this was being done, Dick, Muriel, chef Karl Weiss, and Sapelo native Fred Johnson went to stay in a rustic, isolated cabin at Fancy Gap, North Carolina, that Dick had recently bought for nineteen-year-old Zach. It wasn't air-conditioned, but the temperature and humidity in the mountains were moderate.

Earlier, before Dick had been taken ill, nine-year-old Patrick wrote a first letter from boarding school to his father: "Dear Dad, I am your son Patrick. Where are you? I miss you and I want to meet you. Love, Me." Dick had been on a cruise with Muriel in the South Pacific; the letter had been forwarded six or seven times but had missed him. When he received it, touched by its pathos, he sent a telegram to Marianne asking her to send the boys to visit him in the summer. The boys were elated. But then a second telegram arrived, saying Dick had been taken ill and could not see them until mid-August; meanwhile, they were to go to camp at his expense.

That August, Michael, eleven, and Patrick, nine, were flown from camp on a private plane to Winston-Salem, where Strat Coyner met them and conveyed them up to Fancy Gap. They had not seen their father since 1951. At first sight he appeared to be an old man lying down with heavy weights on his chest while a black man stood over him. Dick explained to the boys that Fred Johnson was helping strengthen his breathing. In front of them, Dick made an effort to avoid using the oxygen mask. Muriel said hello, then stayed in the background so as not to disturb the reunion. Dick tried to be genial, sat in a chair on the lawn, conversed with them. Michael and Patrick were thrilled just to be with him. He gave the boys quick-developing Polaroid cameras and entertained them by showing how a camera's lens worked; next he set them a competition in painting pictures. Eager to perform well, they did everything he asked. They hovered around him, listening carefully to what he said, hoping that he would like them. After two days he pleaded that he had to have less excitement to properly recover from his illness, but he promised to spend more time with them in the near future. Strat Coyner fetched the boys and put them on a plane home to Marianne.

As Dick and Muriel lived in the cabin that summer, Coyner brought to them two new documents, which they discussed fully and signed. The first, made primarily for tax purposes, put most of Dick's property into a trust that would eventually be transferred to the Sapelo Island Research Foundation. Dick would now draw his income from that, and upon his death the income would go to Muriel. The second document, complement to the first, was Muriel's will, which stated that after her death the income from the trust would go to the research foundation. These two instruments clearly established what Dick wanted to happen to his estate: after bequests to his children, the income would go to Muriel, who would live on it during her lifetime, and then it would be automatically deeded to the foundation.

Despite his close brush with death, Dick hadn't quit smoking. Muriel acquiesced in his habit and even bought cigarettes for him in a nearby town. Once, after such an errand, she came back upset, convinced that there was something wrong with the logo on the packs of Camels. The pyramids had been changed, and she was a believer in the totemic power of pyramids. She nagged at Dick until he dictated a letter expressing his disapproval to John Whitaker, now the head of RJR. Whitaker could reach Dick only on the phone in Muriel's car, but he did so to tell his largest stockholder that RJR was merely making cosmetic changes in the packaging of Camels for the modern era. The company was sound and healthy, Whitaker said, as Dick surely realized, since he was a prime beneficiary of the meteoric rise in its dividends and the price of its stock. Muriel wasn't convinced. She begged Dick to sell his RJR stock. It was at 85, and he'd bought a lot of it at 10. He sold most of his shares and realized a profit of more than $6 million.

About ten days later, on Karl Weiss's day off, the chef took one car into town, and Muriel took the only other one to run some errands. Dick and Fred Johnson were alone. Dick began experiencing difficulty in breathing. The oxygen tank was right at hand, but Fred couldn't locate the cup that delivered the oxygen to the mouth and nose; it wasn't with the bottle. Dick blacked out. Fred frantically tore through everything in the cabin until he finally located the cup, which was buried in a closet under some dirty clothes. He administered the oxygen, and Dick returned to consciousness. Later, when he'd stabilized, Dick came to suspect that Muriel had tried to murder him.

Was he justified in that thought? Or was it a sick man's ramblings? He couldn't know conclusively, but the event and its timing seemed suspicious. He began to be more wary of Muriel.

Sapelo, island of fantasy for Dick Reynolds, now became Sapelo, air-conditioned prison. In the latter part of 1958, Dick was confined mostly to the air-conditioned patio and bedroom, separated from the moist atmosphere of the indoor pool by a glass wall. Outside his sickroom a nurse was stationed; at night, she slept in a room across the hall. For occasions when Dick was well enough to take the sun, an air-conditioned trailer was placed down by the beach.

Muriel felt overly cloistered on the island, and they had frequent fights. She didn't like the nurse, she didn't trust the doctor, the sons were around too much. Further, she told him, she was being so good to him that he couldn't stand it and was turning on her; she was "living in some Edgar Allan Poe story." Dick encouraged her to get away from sickroom duty, and every few weeks she made trips to New York or Palm Beach.

When Muriel was "off island," Dick would have Fred or Cracker Johnson load into a jeep his oxygen bottle and several fifty- to one-hundred-pound bags of dollar-sized gold coins from the wine cellar of South End. They'd go and bury the bags at various secret places around the island. One fifty-pound bag was then worth about ten thousand dollars; Fred counted dozens and dozens of bags. In previous years, Dick had had similar bags of gold transported in the *Aries* to Europe. On coming back to the big house, Dick would ask the men to slip him a package of cigarettes from the closet full of them or to make him an alcoholic drink that the nurse wouldn't see. They did so, willingly. He swore to Fred, "After I'm gone, you won't have anything to worry about. You'll be provided for in your old age."

Michael and Patrick came to Sapelo. It was their first time on the island since they were babies, and they were bursting with excitement at the beautiful place and their freedom to roam it. Patrick brought along the sixteen-millimeter motion picture camera that Dick had sent for his tenth birthday and began enthusiastically "shooting" everything in view. Dick presented the boys with go-carts for use on the paved roads.

On this visit they also met Will, then in his late teens, and John, in his early twenties. Blitz had told her sons to consider Marianne's sons brothers, and the older ones tried to act brotherly. Eventually, the younger boys' constant excitement grated on Dick's nerves, and he asked Will to get them out of the house — somehow.

Will, who was something of a painter, aged with charcoal and lemon juice what seemed to be an ancient map of "Sapeloe" indicating where a pirate's treasure could be found and then stashed it enticingly in an old book. The boys discovered it and spent a day fruitlessly rooting about on the beach. Dick and Will both enjoyed the practical joke; finally Will guided the boys to the right spot, where they unearthed a jar full of copper pennies of recent mint.

After the boys had been reading ghost stories one evening, brother John challenged Pat and Mike to visit the island's Negro cemetery. Dick had told the boys it was off-limits; John said it was a great place for hunting possums. Next evening, after catching several possums, who froze when the glare of a jeep's headlights startled them, the boys and John arrived at the graveyard, a deep grove of rickety tombstones arched over by live oaks with Spanish moss drooping down. The Sapelo blacks believed that a dead person's favorite belongings should be laid atop his grave; in the moonlight Pat and Mike picked up two ancient alarm clocks and crystal glasses, which they took as souvenirs. In the process of scurrying back to the jeep they accidentally knocked over a few tombstones. Dick was furious on two counts: first, because the boys had desecrated the blacks' cemetery; second, because there was a rabies epidemic among the island's possums. Mike and Pat were punished and in addition had to right the tombstones and carefully replace their souvenirs.

Muriel became more brazen in brandishing the small dagger she carried. She was outspoken to the point of rudeness not only to Dick and the servants, but also to the occasional guests. Dick suspected that she was paying or had coerced some of the employees to spy on him. Island manager Tom Durant was routing Dick's mail to her before Dick saw it and may also have been listening in on Dick's phone calls.

Various doctors shuttled back and forth to Sapelo from Atlanta, Savannah, and Winston-Salem. They observed that Dick's health improved when Muriel was not in residence and told him so. A plan began to form in his mind. At Christmas, he wrote out a check to "my dear wife" for $123.28 per day for the next 365 days — $45,000 for the year — and signed it "Old Buck Rabbit." In an accompanying note he hoped this would bring her "happiness . . .

better than jewels." He, too, knew the source of pain and pleasure in the marriage. Secretly, he hoped the money would buy him time to put a desperate plan into action.

===

In early January of 1959, after a frantic call from a nurse at Sapelo, Dr. Harry Evans Rollings flew down from Savannah and found Dick near death — his lungs full of fluid, abdomen extended, heart failing. Only quick measures managed to save his life. Muriel had been away from the island, and when she returned Rollings observed the "obvious tension and hostility" between Dick and Muriel, the air "charged with electricity."

As he struggled to return to health, Dick also tried to trace the cause of his sudden downturn and discovered that his food had been tremendously oversalted: the black woman who prepared it said Mrs. Reynolds had told her to do it that way. The woman's husband was blind and out of work, so Dick let her stay on but transferred her to a different job. Dick also learned from a private detective that on Muriel's most recent trip to Florida she'd had dinner with a man, alone. This last incident convinced Dick that he must somehow get Muriel to take a long trip by herself, during which he could decide whether to divorce her or to make some other arrangement for their future.

He couldn't ask her outright to go away — he was afraid she might kill him; furthermore, getting her off the island without her consent might make things difficult for him legally during a divorce. So he first suggested that Muriel take a trip with Nancy and her fiancé, yachtsman Gilbert Verney. Muriel didn't bite. He tried again, saying that Muriel might like to visit her mother in London.

Suspicious, Muriel told Dick that he could have a divorce if he wanted one, but she would have to be assured of two million dollars; if not, she'd stick to him like glue until he died. Dick protested that he didn't want a divorce but did need peace of mind, and his theme was echoed by doctors Henry Valk and Harry Rollings. The physicians agreed with her that Dick was currently hypersensitive to criticism and was escalating perfectly normal marital differences into full-blown fights — but observed nevertheless that Dick seemed to improve when things were quiet.

As the spring began, Dick reversed his pattern of the past few years and sold no stocks to avoid in 1959 the huge capital gains he had had during 1958. He did this deliberately to lower his income, in case the current impasse should lead to a divorce. Similarly, in order to have no official residence in North Carolina, he instructed Strat Coyner to take the Reynolds name off the offices in Winston-Salem and out of the telephone directory. He didn't tell Strat that this would enable him to sue more easily for divorce as a resident of Georgia. Strat forgot to do as asked.

After months of Dick's blandishments, Muriel seemed persuaded to go alone to Europe for the summer. On the night of June 15, though, she refused to leave the island the next day without a handwritten letter from Dick asking her to go and backup letters from the doctors making this their therapeutic recommendation.

Accordingly, at five-thirty in the morning, "Cross Buck" (Dick) wrote to "Dearest Muriel" that she'd been "isolated with a sick man who is cross and irritable" and had stood it "like a Roman soldier," but that it was time for them both to have a vacation. "I must have peace and not get ferociously mad over trifles that a well man would laugh at." Curiously, he added, "as I grow stronger you become more upset," and so "for our future happiness, I urge you to leave and come back and find your old Buck strong and reasonable."

She left for New York, carrying so much baggage that it required an extra plane to haul it all. She took not only clothes but every piece of her jewelry, as well as hundreds of thousands of dollars in bearer bonds. For years she had been the one who cut the coupons on these bonds, though they belonged to Dick. She thought he wouldn't discover that they were missing for some time, and, indeed, he didn't. Perhaps she was hoping that she'd have a chance to return them before things came to a head; and, if not, she'd simply keep them as insurance — after all, they were payable to the bearer, and Dick would have a hard time claiming that she had stolen them.

In the next several days, Muriel talked with Dick regularly on the telephone. These conversations seem not to have reassured her that all was well, because she then wrote him, with the salutation "Dear Strange One," to reiterate her demand that he set aside money for her or at least agree that none of their property would be sold or transferred without both their signatures: "How strange that you should not desire to give me this sense of security at last."

On her own, she called Strat Coyner, asking him to rewrite her will and not tell Dick about it. What she wanted left out was the part about the property passing to the Sapelo Island Research Foundation after her death; she said it ought to go to her heirs first.

Strat drew up the redraft and sent it to her with a note saying, "While you know I have worked for Dick for a number of years, I would respect your confidence as I feel sure that you would not request of me anything that would put me in an embarrassing position in my relations with him." He didn't tell Dick.

Muriel went to Cartier's and took home a $95,000 diamond and platinum bracelet, got two $20,000 checks from their New York bank, and sent Dick a registered letter enclosing the proper quarterly coupons for the bearer bonds. The notion that this would immediately alert Dick to the fact that the bonds themselves were no longer on Sapelo seems not to have crossed her mind. Only after making these moves did she leave for Europe.

In Paris and Monte Carlo she assumed she was being watched — as, indeed, she was — and behaved carefully, although she did manage to lose $20,000 playing chemin de fer. Dick sent her telegrams, small gifts, and chatty notes with minor news. She replied in similar manner, in one note suggesting that Dick break up the impending marriage of Zach to Linda Lee Tise, whom Muriel thought not good enough for a Reynolds.

That was silly, because Dick was charmed by the unaffected twenty-year-old. Linda Lee showed no signs of being intimidated by Zach's father: when she stopped to see Dick on her way to Florida for a last fling with a girlfriend, she put her tired feet up on a Sapelo table. They talked candidly about Zach. At Merry Acres, he had been going around and around a circular driveway on a motorcycle he wanted to buy from Josh; his speed became so great that he couldn't stop. Rather than hit a brick wall, he crashed through the glass front door and went halfway across the house before halting the machine. Zach was a wild man, but Linda Lee loved him; she was almost the only person with whom he did not stutter. She told Dick that Zach, now in the navy, concealed the fact that he was a Reynolds from his fellow seamen and said that he was a hillbilly moonshiner. Dick recalled his own days as Kid Carolina, his own attempts to escape the Reynolds heritage, his own career in the navy. The Kid Carolina episode was a legendary story at Merry Acres; Linda Lee wondered if Zach was emulating Dick in an effort to be closer to him.

After leaving Sapelo, Linda Lee and her friend were involved in a terrible automobile accident. Linda Lee's leg was nearly severed, and her face was ripped to shreds by glass and metal. Before passing out, she asked the hospital to call Dick, as well as her parents. For several hours, she hovered near death: she later came to believe that she made it through safely because of the strength of her faith. A few days afterward she also learned that it had been due to Dick Reynolds's quick actions. The hospital had been in a quandary about operating since she was underage. By telling the doctors that he'd take responsibility and by getting them instant consultations with his own specialists, Dick allowed them to do the emergency surgery that stanched the blood flow and helped save Linda Lee's leg. Her face was badly scarred, and she wanted to postpone the wedding until she recovered, but Zach wouldn't hear of it.

Dick's attitude toward his sons and their fiancées was not usually so benevolent. In this period, when he suspected his wife of nefarious deeds, the climate of suspicion spread over many other areas of his life. He had private detectives watch his older sons and even a young woman whom one of them was dating. As Dick construed the evidence, none of the sons was gainfully employed or pursuing a career in a mainstream profession, and he didn't like that. The sons realized they were being observed and didn't like *that:* the old man hadn't been a regular guiding presence in their lives, yet he hovered over them and judged them. Being watched brought them no closer to him.

During the summer, while Dick was waiting to see what Muriel would do, Pat and Mike also visited Sapelo. Patrick had become fascinated with the movie camera Dick had given him; he tapped everyone else in the family to play gangsters, vampires, and victims in his movie fantasies. He had also made documentaries of Sapelo and Miami Christmas scenes. Dick seemed pleased by his enthusiasm for cameras.

Patrick observed that Dick was smoking, and the boy couldn't help feeling that the smoking and his father's illness were related. Dick seemed weaker than when they had been here at Easter. He loved them, Patrick was sure, but was unable to do much in the way of demonstrating his feelings. Once, when he and Dick were alone, Patrick asked his father to please "come home, come home" and began to cry. Dick also started to cry, took Patrick in his arms, and told him, "Your mother is a wonderful person, but I can't go back to her. I'm too proud, too proud."

The waiting period came to an abrupt halt when, in short order, the registered letter with the bearer-bond coupons, Muriel's bill from Cartier's, and the statement from the New York bank arrived on Sapelo and were brought to Dick's attention. He was angered but also pleased: now he had evidence that he had understood Muriel's intentions.

He moved immediately into action. He deliberately did not yet open the registered letter, but he did question Strat on the phone and learned about the changed will. Furious, he sent his most trusted private detective, Shelby Williams, to Winston-Salem to see if "Richard J. Reynolds, Jr." had been removed from the office's door and the phone book; it hadn't. Williams also uncovered more about Strat's handling of Dick's affairs than Dick wanted to know. A saddened Dick called his old friend to Sapelo and confronted him. Strat admitted to certain lapses. After thirty-two years, the trust between Dick and Strat was now compromised. Strat was nearing retirement age, so Dick fired him but simultaneously gave him a hundred-thousand-dollar fund as a pension. Ledyard Staples moved down to Sapelo and took over the entire management of Dick's businesses.

Without opening the registered envelope, Dick had deduced that it must contain the coupons for bearer bonds. Trying every avenue to check on what Muriel had done, Dick called Josh in New York and asked if he had taken any bearer bonds. Josh said no and reported that there were none in the safe either. Dick searched the Sapelo house and decided that the bonds must be in Muriel's locked closet.

Before entering the closet, and in the presence of Strat and lawyers Frank Wells and Paul Varner, Dick opened Muriel's registered letter. It contained coupons for $98,000 worth of bonds. With the lawyers' consent, he had men force their way into the locked closet and the interior locked chest. They found some of the bonds but not all: $200,000 of them were still missing.

Also in the closet were witchcraft and voodoo trappings, statuettes of Buddha — and some of Muriel's diaries. Long after the others had gone to bed, Dick sat up reading the little handwritten books, which dated back to 1937. To his chagrin, they were the private notes of a woman who had slept with many men and cadged money from them at every turn. Her allegiance was more to the Indian maharajah than it had been to any of her husbands. The diaries revealed that in recent years, when Muriel had told Dick that she was visiting her mother, she had actually been out with some of her lovers.

By morning, Dick was physically and mentally exhausted. Once again, he felt betrayed. He dispatched Frank Wells to Paris. There, days later, in a room at the Biarritz Hotel, the lawyer handed Muriel a letter containing an outline of what Shelby Williams had turned up about the shadiness of her divorce from Greenough, the unauthorized Cartier's bracelet, the evidence from her diaries, the missing bonds, and the attempt to alter her will to gut the pact she had made with Dick in 1958. Dick's note said he was suing her for divorce and advised her to stay out of the country; in case she came back, he was enjoining her from setting foot on Sapelo.

Chapter Sixteen

Seeking Peace: Annemarie

IN NEW YORK, in the fall of 1959, Muriel consulted famed trial attorney Louis Nizer, who had earlier handled Marianne's divorce from Dick. Muriel was determined to fight for what she believed Dick owed her: $6 million outright or a payment of $200,000 per year. Since the proceedings were going to be contested in the South, not in New York, Nizer recommended that she hire E. Smythe Gambrell of Atlanta. She did. This meant that once again during a divorce, Dick would be opposed by an enemy, for Gambrell was general counsel of Eastern Airlines; Dick had pulled his money out of Eastern and was a $3-million stockholder in rival Delta.

Dick could have negotiated a settlement but chose to fight, principally because he now hated Muriel. He even paid for an old friend of Muriel's to come over from England, let the man read the diaries — which destroyed his previous image of Muriel — then gave him $500 and a return ticket.

Dick also took steps to ready himself financially for a fight, for example, donating the *Aries* to the Woods Hole research laboratory in Massachusetts in exchange for a large tax deduction and setting up the successor to the Georgia Agricultural Research Foundation as the Sapelo Island Research Foundation. He then donated to SIRF a big chunk of the island, along with a block of RJR stock and various scattered real estate parcels that he expected SIRF to sell for additional cash.

He was contrary with Zach and Linda Lee when they visited him on their honeymoon. The young couple was indebted to Dick for helping Linda Lee during her accident and for having used his pull with the navy to get Zach an extended furlough so he could stay near her while she was hospitalized. In an unguarded moment, Zach asked his father if he could buy a jeep from Dick's dealership, at cost. Dick blew up, accusing Zach of trying to take financial advantage of him, just as Muriel had done. He banished Zach and said he'd never speak to him again. Then he turned right around and asked Linda Lee to stay and talk with him; she demurred, pleading that her place was with her husband. He agreed that this was proper and calmed down. However, the couple soon left Sapelo.

Dick thought he had the divorce proceedings leaning his way. In pretrial maneuvering, when Gambrell let it be known that he would try to introduce evidence of Dick's heavy drinking, Dick's lawyers threatened in return to destroy Muriel's credibility by bringing in her diaries. Newspapers reported that "international society" was worried over what might be in those diaries. Gambrell tried to get the trial shifted away from Darien, Georgia, arguing that because Reynolds was the county's most prominent citizen, his wife could not get a fair trial there. He pointed out that in recent months Dick had financed Sheriff Tom Poppell's reelection campaign and paid for an American Legion building in Darien, a gymnasium for a black school, and a community swimming pool. The local judge, offended, ruled that Dick could get a fair trial in Darien.

Two court-appointed physicians came to Sapelo to ascertain Dick's medical fitness to testify at the trial. He angrily raved at them, then invited them to lunch. They reported to the judge that Dick was too ill to appear in court but that he could give a deposition from Sapelo.

The trial began in May 1960 in a small, sweltering courtroom in Darien, before a jury of twelve white men. Most of the gallery, reporters noted, was female. In his two previous divorces, Dick had settled out of court, partly in the hope of avoiding the public display of the dirty laundry of his marriages. This time he was too angry with Muriel to do that, and the result was several weeks of testimony that gave the world a glimpse of the vitriol in the millionaire's life. The prenuptial agreement was shown to the court, but Gambrell argued that it was out-of-date and didn't reflect the couple's current level of spending — and, besides, Dick had tricked Muriel off the island, which invalidated the "contract." Muriel's lawyers went to great lengths to buttress the image of Dick as a drunk who couldn't be trusted. His lawyers, in turn, made a great deal of Muriel's having carried a dagger, of her demand for two million dollars before she would leave Sapelo, the changing of her will, the purloining of the bearer bonds. The diaries were mentioned but were not entered in evidence. Dick tried to show that his wife was a liar, citing the fact that no stillbirth with his or her name as parent had been recorded in New York City in the months immediately after the date on which she'd claimed to have had a miscarriage.

Evidence was introduced of Muriel's attempts to fight back against Dick in the period just before the trial. His attorneys read into the court record some letters she had written to Nancy Bagley, to one of Dick's nurses, and to his various doctors, accusing one and all of conspiring against her. It had been foolish of her to write letters to people who were so obviously sympathetic to Dick and who turned them over to him.

It was even more foolish of her to have written "anonymous" notes to the nurse who had attended Dick during the past year and whom Murial accused of trying to steal Dick from her. The nurse turned these over to Dick, too, and something about them jogged his memory. He called Marianne, and she confirmed that during the 1952 divorce she had received poison-pen letters; the typewriting and handwriting on her letters matched those on the new batch, and the depth of Muriel's hatred became clear.

Dick's call to Marianne started a series of telephone conversations that sometimes lasted for hours, in which the two began a renewed friendship. In one conversation, Dick offered Marianne one million dollars for custody of Patrick; she refused the deal. He agreed to pay a bit more for the boys' schooling. During another call, Marianne told Dick she'd heard about his difficulties in a letter from Tom Durant, which recounted a confessional conversation Dick had had with a visiting Catholic monsignor.

Dick confronted his manager with this evidence of disloyalty. Already ill, Durant was discharged and told to leave the island. Dick couldn't bear to have around anyone who had betrayed him; however, he didn't want Durant to suffer and paid the expenses during the remaining few months of Durant's life. In an echo of his earlier decision about accountant Grey Staples, Dick upgraded Tom's brother Frank Durant to island manager.

For all the fire, it was a relatively short trial. After two weeks the jury decided that Muriel's lawyers had not demonstrated that the prenuptial agreement had been invalidated by anything that happened during the marriage. They granted Dick a divorce. Muriel was awarded the settlement agreed to in 1952 — $15,000 per year. Muriel let it be known that she would not accept nor spend this pittance, and she filed an appeal.

Dick was elated. He was free of Muriel, and getting rid of his third wife hadn't cost very much. Doctors informed him that he had perhaps five years to live. Maybe now he could enjoy them. Before the trial had begun, sister Nancy had convinced Dick that he must go on a long trip when it was over. Nancy had recently remarried, to Gilbert Verney, a businessman involved in various phases of the textile and paper industries and a keen yachtsman. She and Dick pooled $200,000 to jointly charter the big air-conditioned yacht *Natalie* for a summer in Europe. Dick flew to London with a doctor recently out of medical school and with Gunther Lehmann, who had been in his employ for years, as mate on a yacht, personal secretary, bodyguard. They boarded the *Natalie* in England. During the early part of the voyage, in Scandinavian waters, Dick stayed aboard even when the boat was in port, except for one automobile ride around Stockholm with Nancy.

At various points in the cruise, old friends of Dick's came aboard. One of them was Christian Nissen, who brought not only his wife but also a German doctor named Hans Lindemann. Lindemann ran a clinic specifically devoted to people with lung problems such as emphysema.

Dick agreed to take the Lindemann cure and went for six weeks to a small hostel in Bad Harzburg. From the outside it looked like an ordinary, possibly even a seedy, resting place for tired people of modest means. It was not a plush resort but an old-fashioned, somewhat Spartan place where a great deal of attention was paid to exercise, diet, healing waters, and extra vitamins. The physicians and staff had degrees at which American doctors later looked askance — but Dick was in a frame of mind to take risks if they offered some hope of extending his life or, at least, his capacity to enjoy what little time remained to him.

In fact, at Bad Harzburg Dick managed to lose weight and quit smoking and drinking, things that his physicians had long told him were desirable but that heretofore he had not been able to accomplish. The spa's regimen may have helped bring about these changes, but the real inspiration came from Dick's meeting there a young female friend of the Lindemanns'. Annemarie Schmitt was thirty-one, spoke English quite well, and was extremely cultured. She held a doctoral degree in English (she had met Mrs. Lindemann when they were both students) and was currently employed in the personnel department of a chemical firm. A working woman who seemed also to be familiar with nursing, Annemarie was just what the doctor might have ordered: intelligent, independent, mature, and nonthreatening. She was a reason to get well, a potential companion who could join him on the last steps of his life's journey.

In Annemarie's presence Dick experienced a new influx of energy. They took walks together; he was able to exercise for longer periods without continually inhaling oxygen. He asked her to vacation aboard the yacht. On one of their stops Annemarie seemed interested in a series of sixteenth-century illuminated manuscripts. No previous wife or lover of Dick's had ever been cultured enough to appreciate such things. Dick bought them for her. He didn't really understand their finer points himself, but he respected Annemarie's knowledge and taste.

Although she seemed uninterested in his money, he pressed on her jewelry, a fur coat, and some money — about $200,000 in gifts. At the conclusion of the voyage, Dick invited Annemarie to join him in the United States. This would mean her giving up her job, but Dick evidently was able to convince her that his intentions were honorable and that her financial future would be safe in his hands.

Honorable indeed: in the second half of his life, Dick seemed to believe that if he paid passionate court to a woman and was estranged from his current wife, he ought to marry the new woman, whether or not it made sense when evaluated in rational terms. The same pattern was operating here. However, if in going from Marianne to Muriel Dick had jumped headlong from the frying pan into the fire, this time he was escaping in what seemed to be a far more reasonable direction.

Dick and Annemarie traveled from Sapelo to the American West under false names and in transportation purchased for them by friends and employees — principally to avoid detection by Muriel, whom Dick expected to try something untoward. He made only one mistake: the bill for Annemarie's fur coat was accidentally sent to Muriel, and she deduced that Dick was seeing another woman.

Believing that he was divorced and that Muriel's appeal of the court's decision would fail, Dick proposed to Annemarie, who accepted but didn't set an immediate wedding date. They spent Christmas at Sapelo. Annemarie was not as taken with the island as Dick had been in the past. She saw that the black employees made it too easy for Dick to slide back into the old habits that exacerbated his medical difficulties. Also, Sapelo was costing a fortune to keep up, and Dick, because of his condition, was not really able to appreciate and use its beauty.

In early 1961 they flew to London and boarded the *Rotterdam* for a round-the-world cruise. They reached Hong Kong at the beginning of March. Dick cabled his lawyer, Aaron Kravitch, and asked if there were any reason he should not now complete his remarriage; Kravitch assured him that the Supreme Court of Georgia would not rule against him in its review of the divorce.

At the end of World War II, in these waters of the South China Sea, Dick had dreamed of a plantation high above the banks of the Yangtze, of a woman who would succor him. He told the captain of the *Rotterdam* that "for sentimental reasons" he'd like to be married here. On March 15, 1961, in international waters, in a ceremony presided over by the ship's captain, Dick and Annemarie were married. Gunther Lehmann and the Lindemanns were aboard as witnesses.

The new Reynoldses bought a cooperative apartment in Muralto, Switzerland, and began to plan a villa on a mountainside overlooking Lake Lucerne. They purchased parts of several farms so that no one else could block their view and began to build a modest home to accommodate Dick's needs, with central air-conditioning and very few stairs.

During the summer they visited Sapelo. Dr. Harry Rollings found Dick improved but was not impressed with the medical advice given by Dr. Lindemann, who accompanied Dick. Rollings pleaded with Dick not to return to Europe. The blacks slipped Dick a few smokes and drinks, as of old. Shortly before the couple left again for Switzerland, many of these long-term Sapelo employees were summarily fired. The residents of Hog Hammock were stunned — this was not expected behavior from the man who had been so kind to them for nearly thirty years. They blamed Annemarie.

Dick and Annemarie were in Switzerland in September, living as husband and wife, when they learned of the Supreme Court of Georgia's decision. On appeal, the divorce from Muriel was overturned because of a great many errors on the part of the trial judge. The most glaring mistake: the proceedings had taken place while Dick was not in the courtroom. The court also ruled that the prenuptial agreement should never have been placed before the jurors and said that the amount of alimony awarded — which echoed the dollar figure of the prenuptial agreement — was obviously not commensurate with the style in which Muriel previously had been maintained.

The divorce was canceled. Muriel was still legally Dick's wife. He was in danger of being charged with bigamy and would have to go through another divorce. This time, Muriel could accuse him of adultery with Annemarie. Dick was infuriated: he had, he believed, only a short time to live — and would now spend some of it in a courtroom, doing battle with a woman he hated.

=

Blitz and Linda Lee, Zach's wife, sat down one day at Merry Acres, lit cigarettes, and talked about everything. Linda Lee thought it funny that Blitz smoked Viceroys, a non-RJR brand, but put them in a pack that had contained Winstons, RJR's best-selling cigarettes. After Blitz's father died in 1960, Blitz took over the management of his two companies and was doing rather well with them. Her problems were more personal: her sons, now all over twenty-one, seemed to have left her behind. Josh was traveling in Mexico. John had married an employee of Golden Isles Airways, without telling her. Zach was very involved in motorcycles, which she hated. After all her zealous attempts to keep them on the right path, they were drifting!

"You can complain and be mad all you want, but it won't get you anywhere," Linda Lee told her. Blitz accepted this logic and tried to blunt her previously tough criticism of her sons. She loved the boys and knew this might be her last chance to make amends, for doctors had recently diagnosed a colon problem. She took a house in Myrtle Beach, South Carolina, for the summer, made a special point of inviting John and his wife, and made overtures to all of her children and their spouses. She felt better when she reached out to them.

Blitz was duck hunting in November when she became ill and had to be hospitalized. She died of colon cancer in December 1961 at age fifty-two. Her sons buried Blitz on the highest point at Devotion and erected a columned monument. Will wrote a poem for her and had it set in the stone.

Devotion was divided. The main lodge was shared by Josh and Will; John and Zach had other homes on the property. The acreage of Merry Acres was similarly quartered — but none of the sons lived there. They sold off lots and deeded the house itself to Wake Forest University, which didn't seem to know what to do with the mansion. It succumbed to rain and weather damage and was later torn down.

After Blitz's death, the life-style of Zach and Linda Lee changed, and it altered still further with the birth of their daughter, Lee. With part of Zach's inheritance they built a showplace home in Winston-Salem, always kept immaculate; if a picture frame was out of line, Zach would become upset. When a motorcycle crash put Zach in a hospital for a week, Linda Lee pleaded with him to stop racing. To appease her, he no longer announced when he was competing. Soon he had his friends, she had hers, and their circles seldom meshed.

Zach's collection of vintage cars grew, and so did the number of garages adjacent to the Winston house. He began to assemble in the house what soon became the world's most powerful amateur radio operation; the transmitter in his backyard, Zach boasted, was more powerful than the one in northern Virginia used by the Voice of America. He was in touch with fellow hams all over the globe at all hours of the day and night. Linda Lee thought that Zach was now able to broadcast successfully because, since getting married, he'd ceased stuttering.

She also noted that once their house had been completed — and Blitz was dead — Zach began to womanize. Earlier in his life, Linda Lee felt, Zach had been repressed by Blitz, and his wildness had been channeled into motorcycle racing. Now, newly come into money, motherless, and virtually fatherless, he was conducting affairs discreetly but not carefully. In going through Zach's clothes before putting them into the wash, Linda Lee came upon notes with phone numbers and girls' names. She decided to ignore these and hope that he would stop his philandering.

The second divorce trial of Dick and Muriel began in May 1962, almost precisely two years after the first, and in the same venue. Darien was a small shrimping town on the banks of a marshy river. The courthouse was Darien's largest building, and it wasn't very big; beyond that, one or two places laid claim to being restaurants, and there were two gas stations and as many supermarkets. Now the whole town became a circus focused on the courtroom. Dick's lawyers took one motel in Darien, and Muriel's the other, causing a shortage of lodgings for all the press, who came from as far away as New York. Dispatches to a dozen papers were filed daily, and there was radio and even some television coverage. Interest was much greater than the first time around because of the strictures placed on this new trial by the Supreme Court of Georgia ruling.

In the sweltering Darien courtroom, a different, more controlling judge told the more broadly based jury flat out that if they found Dick had committed adultery with Annemarie, or if they decided that Dick had tricked Muriel off the island in 1959, they were to grant the divorce to Muriel, not to Dick, and were to require him to pay a substantial alimony.

The prenuptial agreement wasn't even allowed to be introduced into the proceedings. Another important difference: Dick was present in the courtroom every day, brought in by wheelchair. He took oxygen at five-minute intervals, assisted by a nurse who never left his side. To friends who hadn't seen Dick for a while, he looked seriously deteriorated — a man of fifty-six who appeared twenty years older. Annemarie did not attend; she remained on Sapelo, and Dick traveled back and forth daily.

E. Smythe Gambrell produced more and more evidence of Dick's wealth until both parties agreed to estimate it at $25 million — a figure that was surely too low. For example, a Gilbert Stuart portrait of George Washington hanging at Sapelo, carried on the books at $12,000, was worth twenty times that amount, and there was a similar undervaluation of a set of Audubon bird prints pressed in the nineteenth century. Sapelo's land was listed at $25 per acre of high ground. That was the price paid in the mid-1930s; now farmers in coastal areas of Georgia's McIntosh County were getting hundreds of dollars per acre for high ground.

Muriel's tactics were to paint as horrible a picture of Dick's behavior as possible. Toward that end, Gambrell obtained a deposition from Strat Coyner about his being fired, introduced evidence of Dick's dismissal of Tom Durant, and had doctors come from overseas to testify about Dick's habitual state of inebriation in the fifties and his refusal to heed their advice to stop smoking and drinking. The evidence that Dick had conspired to push Muriel off the island was quite strong, and the Supreme Court of Georgia had ruled that what might have been counterbalancing evidence — of the parties seeming to have agreed orally that Dick would assure Muriel of $2 million to leave — was not admissible. Dick and his legal team decided there was no way around it: the millionaire had to take the stand.

He hobbled through a hushed courtroom to the witness chair, and under the gentle questioning of his attorneys he told how it felt to have emphysema and gasp for breath: "It's like a drowning man that's sinking and it's terrifying to you and you get terrified and you can't breathe." Dick related how he had met Muriel ("She said she'd just lost all her money, gambling"), how she had threatened and hurt him, how she detested young Pat and Mike and treated them badly when they came to visit. Dick's lawyers elicited testimony about Muriel's misrepresentation about her divorce and past affairs; her threats to Marianne, the nurse, doctors, and employees; and her cupidity in the matters of jewelry, bearer bonds, and his estate.

Then came Gambrell's turn. It was already clear to spectators and reporters that Dick and Gambrell hated one another and were out for blood — as well as money. This confrontation was what everyone awaited, and it did not lack for vituperation. They started with the note Dick had written Muriel that night before she left the island. Dick had testified that Muriel had practically dictated it to him.

"You didn't let a stenographer write it for you, did you?" Gambrell asked.

"No."

"You put it in Dick Reynolds's own pen and ink, didn't you?"

"Certainly, yes."

"All by yourself?"

"Sure."

"That's a really nice letter, don't you think?"

"I overdid it, but other than that it was a nice letter."

"And on the strength of it she went, didn't she?"

"Yes, uh-huh."

Dick constantly had to halt his answers to take oxygen. Gambrell tried to catch him in inconsistencies. About the notes written to Muriel after she had gone to Europe in 1959, he asked, "You were sharing in a wholehearted way the nice things that husbands and wives share together, isn't that right?"

"No, sir," Dick replied. "I didn't want her to be coming back over here and molesting me so I was keeping her satisfied . . . I . . . often keep unpleasant things from people."

"How are we going to know when you please to speak frankly and truthfully and when you don't?"

"I'm under oath, here, and I have never told a lie in my life under oath."

Having elicited that statement, Gambrell asked whether Dick hadn't committed adultery with Annemarie. Dick said he was

> embarrassed to have to answer this question, but speaking in legal terms, my marriage [to Annemarie] has never been consummated as a marriage between man and wife. I have been rather ill and I've been looking forward to the time that I might be graced with some peace and quietness to recover my strength and the marriage has never been consummated.

The silence in the courtroom following this admission was a clear indication that few believed him. Legally, though, there was no way to disprove Dick's statement.

Now the tide turned, and Dick started to score some points. When Gambrell hammered at him about inflated medical expenses, Dick offered to take his false teeth out and make them an exhibit. He suggested that if he thought he'd been generous to Annemarie, Gambrell should add up what he'd given Muriel per month and year. Dick also made sure the jury learned that he'd paid Muriel's expenses after their separation — until she started running up a bill of $4,000 for one month's meals at El Morocco. He estimated her jewelry to be worth a half million, the RJR stock that he'd given her at almost $3 million; and since she had also kept the proceeds from the sales of homes in Manhattan and Oyster Bay, she certainly wasn't penniless.

Dick needled Gambrell by describing the debacle of having been persuaded by Muriel to sell some RJR stock. Since 1958, these shares had gone up in price from 85 to 300; he reckoned that he would have been $25 million richer had he kept them. Gambrell was quite involved in Eastern Airlines, rival to Delta, and the rivalry spilled over into the questioning as well. Dick ridiculed Gambrell for chartering an Eastern plane to fly down to Sapelo to take Dick's deposition; Dick had had his own lawyer take a bus and a ferry rather than charter a Delta plane for that trip. To Dick, it was obvious that Gambrell had taken a charter in order to stick him with the inflated expense.

After two weeks of testimony, both sides rested, and the judge reiterated his charge to the jury — if Reynolds tricked his wife off the island, or if he committed adultery, the jury must find for

Muriel. Deliberations took only hours. The jury awarded a divorce to Dick, stating that he did not have to pay a cent of alimony to Muriel, not even the amount stipulated in the 1952 prenuptial agreement. It was a complete victory for Dick.

On Sapelo, Dick learned that Muriel's lawyers had told the press that they'd be filing endless appeals to keep him in court for years to come. Dick knew they could do it; in fact, he felt that the court system was being used against him. He'd played by the rules and won, but Muriel was still attacking him. This feeling added to his general impression of disdain for his homeland.

By this point, Dick was fed up with his life in America. He had insulated himself, and his money had isolated him. He was almost without real friends. The character witnesses he'd called during the trial were all dependent on his favor in one way or another, politicians and university men who courted him for his own money or that of the foundations he controlled. With each divorce he'd cut himself off from those he'd seen socially with his former wife, be it Blitz or Marianne or Muriel. Also, he'd developed the habit of buying the companionship of pals — here with a berth on a yacht, there with a public relations sinecure, elsewhere with a timely loan. He was increasingly critical of his sons and suspicious of their affections. He might complain that no one loved him for himself, but he had worked assiduously to ensure that he would end up in that position.

Dick prepared to leave the United States and take up residence in Europe. He called his four eldest sons to the island for a conference. They were instructed to bring the Joshua Coin and the pilot's license signed by Orville Wright. The legend said that whosoever possessed the coin without also being a son whose names included Joshua would experience bad luck. Blitz had held it, and her early death seemed more evidence of the coin's totemic power.

Josh, John, Zach, and Will now ranged in age from twenty-eight to twenty-two. All had completed or left their formal education and had come into some money. If they were expecting a celebration party amid Sapelo's lush late-spring foliage, they were mistaken. They handed over the coin but said that the pilot's license couldn't be found. Dick was incensed to see the quarter-carat diamond that Blitz had placed in a hole in the middle of the Joshua Coin. In the presence of his sons he ripped out the diamond, drove to the beach, and threw the diamond into the surf. Then he sat the young men down together and told them he was moving to Switzerland and deeding more of the island to the Sapelo Island Research Foundation. He expressed disappointment that they all were living on their incomes and weren't out working.

In his harshness he had forgotten that when he was in his twenties he'd done the same thing — that is, lived on dividends and looked for investments. Dick also refused to acknowledge that by skipping out on them in 1942 and seeing them only occasionally since the mid-1950s, he had failed to provide his sons with guidance or restraint and had contributed to their way of life, which he now deemed undesirable.

After the group diatribe, Dick called in each son individually for a private talk. He asked the youngest, Will, whether he was "all right" financially. Will replied that he had enough and told his father bluntly that he didn't seek any more money from him but believed that the bulk of Dick's estate should go to help the people of North Carolina. Dick agreed that this was what he had in mind.

The sons went back to North Carolina, and Dick proceeded to burn his bridges. Most of the land on Sapelo, with the exception of the southern portion, which included South End, was deeded to SIRF. Dick sold off many of his American assets, such as the Andrew Johnson Hotel, and, family members came to believe, took payment in gold, delivered to him later in Europe. He wrote off as finally uncollectible the old loans to Tony Marston, Abe Attell, and others. Emory Flinn took over his seat on the Delta board and also had charge of a number of Dick's financial operations. Only one more thing remained to be done.

One night in June he took Fred and Cracker Johnson, as well as several other blacks whom he trusted, and with them dug up the last of the bags of gold from their hiding places in the wilder sections of Sapelo. Though ill, Dick directed the operation, compartmentalizing it so that none of those involved — the blacks, his German aides, the crew of the freighter into whose hold the bags eventually went — knew all the details. The freighter may have been the one owned by Dick that usually was employed carrying frozen food to the Virgin Islands.

Once again, Dick told the Johnsons that if he should die shortly they would have no worries at all, implying that he had provided individually for them. Ledyard Staples, he said, would continue to run his office, and the big house was to be kept open to accommodate visitors he would send there from time to time. Then, with

his treasure, his oxygen bottles, his fourth wife, his German retainers, and his memories, Richard Joshua Reynolds, Jr., sailed for
the last time to Europe.

=

While their villa at Emmetten, by Lake Lucerne, was being constructed, Dick and Annemarie lived in apartments in secluded towns
or took over suites in spas. They kept their dwelling places secret,
in part to prevent Muriel from learning their whereabouts; Dick
believed Muriel would kill him if she had the opportunity and was
convinced that she had connections in the underworld. Dick also
insisted that his sons communicate only by sending letters to his
office, which would then be forwarded to him.

Marianne, seeing a Gosport, England, postmark on one of Dick's
infrequent letters to Patrick, assumed that Dick was in this coastal
town building a new yacht; his medical condition precluded travel
on any open yachts, so Marianne was certain that others were
controlling Dick's spending. That was her interpretation. For Patrick, though, there was no mistaking the tone of the note inside:
his father's letters were usually cold and remote.

From boarding school, fourteen-year-old Patrick wrote to his
father boasting that he was the editor of the school magazine and
first lead in the school play, asking for Dick to pay for a skiing trip
to Gstaad, expressing his anger ("How dare you sell Sapelo?"), and
demanding in response a handwritten letter.

In March of 1963 Dick dictated a stiff reply to Patrick over the
telephone to a secretary in Gosport and had her sign it for him. In
it, Dick said that for years his method of writing had been to call
in letters this way or to mail recorder belts to secretaries. He chas-
tized Patrick for bad manners, reminding him that his father was
paying for boarding school and ought not to be presumptuously
commanded to do anything. Generally deprecatory of Patrick's
achievements and attitude, Dick expressed interest in what "Mr.
Smarty-Pants" would have to say in answer to this slap in the face.

Though the letter was insulting, Patrick kept it; after all, it was
one of the few from the man who, present or absent, had a tremendous influence on his life. Patrick longed to talk intimately with
his father. He would have told him about his passion, making films.
With the movie camera that Dick had given him, Patrick filmed
The Madman, an extravaganza starring Michael as a deranged sci-

entist. In his underground laboratory, constructed out of old chemistry sets and Christmas lights, a scientist drinks a smoky potion and goes mad, a state of mind indicated by the sudden appearance of Marianne's wig on his head. Thus attired, he pulls a lever to end the world. In Patrick's own screen-acting debut, he appears on a television set as a frantic, cigarette-smoking newscaster who demolishes his office while reading reports of the world in flames — reports complete with inserts of a model cardboard city as it blows up and burns. Both characters limned well the chaos lying just beneath the surface of the boys' lives at the time. A lingering pan of the ruins of the underground laboratory comes to rest on the scientist, who, as he dies, at last realizes that in destroying the world he has also destroyed himself.

Dick's negotiations with Muriel's lawyers culminated on April 26, 1963, in a settlement of $2,142,624 that also allowed Muriel and her mother to draw $32,000 a year from the trust he had set up for them in 1952. He further agreed to pay her attorneys' second trial fee of $500,000. Muriel was outraged at this because, in addition to receiving this money from Dick, her lawyers had sold her home in Palm Beach and applied the proceeds to the bill for her first divorce trial.

In early July 1963, Dick registered with the Swiss government a document in which Annemarie forfeited all rights to his estate other than a settlement of $300,000 previously given to her, plus the Muralto apartment. On July 10, a registrar was called to the Muralto apartment to remarry Dick and Annemarie. He was used to making marriages, but the scene in the apartment was a bit unusual. He thought he would lead a happy couple in a ceremony, have them sign the papers, be offered a glass of champagne, and go. Miss Schmitt was much in evidence, but he never did get to see the bridegroom directly. He only caught sight of the back of a man sitting at a desk in another room, signing the appropriate documents. In the ten minutes that the registrar was in the apartment, there was no champagne, no kissing of the bride, virtually no acknowledgment of his presence.

On August 14, 1963, Dick wrote a will that left the bulk of his estate to Annemarie and to SIRF but that included bequests to his sons. Evidently, the previous document had been a sort of last litmus test for Annemarie. Once she had signed it without protest and they were married, he could unveil the plan that after his death would leave her comfortable and let her oversee the transfer of the bulk of his estate to SIRF.

In the next year, he had few visitors. Nancy was one. Then there was Emory Flinn, who came to discuss Delta and other business. Dick's American doctor, Harry Rollings, flew over occasionally to examine him and didn't change his mind about Dr. Lindemann, Dick's on-site physician. Hans Lindemann was not listed in the German medical directory, and to Rollings he was clearly not a pulmonary specialist. Similarly, Gunther Lehmann was not a trained nurse, though he was devoted to Dick's well-being. Lehmann and Sergio Amati, an oxygen therapist, were with Dick all the time, while Lindemann made periodic visits.

Dick Reynolds's search for unusual, possibly unhelpful treatment of his irreversible emphysema was not only typical conduct for many rich invalids but also a symbol of his larger, more complex problem. A man of great wealth, he was in this last phase of his life a victim of his circumstances, at the mercy of those who could promise him something his money could not buy: the staving off of death for a few more years. It was the culminating irony of a life spent as the quintessential heir.

As he often boasted, Dick had lived more in the past fifty-eight years than most people. During his comparatively short life he had been playboy, capitalist, investor, yachtsman, politician, and philanthropist. He had done much good and often spent and donated his money wisely — but, on balance, his life was a series of unfulfilled opportunities. In nearly every instance, he had embarked on a venture that had excellent potential — aviation in the twenties, a solid family life in the thirties, politics and shipping in the early forties — only to become discouraged by setbacks. Other men might have considered these difficulties to be temporary or surmountable, but Dick construed them as great obstacles and, time after time, both in work and in love, gave up one promising enterprise and turned his energy and resources to another. He looked to woman after woman with the hope that the next marriage would be perfect and would smooth over the wounds of the previous one — and then was surprised when the same faults and pressures compromised them in their turn. His vast fortune had sustained not only a playboy's excesses but, more important, a playboy's attitude toward work, marriage, achievement, and fatherhood. Unfortunately, his experience was typical: in a study of American multimillionaires of the last hundred years, Frederick Cople Jahrer suggests that most heirs of Dick's generation "fled individual achievement or responsibility and damaged themselves and their fortunes through extravagance, drinking . . . promiscuity and disastrous marriage."

Chief among these failures at the end of Dick's life was his inadequacy as a father. Some rich families (the Rockefellers, Vanderbilts, and Astors, among others) had come to understand that a principal task facing the fathers — a task poorer men didn't have — was to give their children some understanding of how to bear the burdens of wealth. Dick had removed himself from his sons' lives at critical stages of their development and seemed unwilling or unable to provide guidance. This was devastating to the sons; it was also understandable, for Dick had had precious little guidance himself. As Jahrer suggests, many second-generation heirs faced emotional problems throughout life: "Deprived of warmth and affection in their own childhoods, they had difficulty in giving love and support to their sons." Dick interpreted his responsibility to his sons as fiscal rather than emotional nurturance. After his divorces from Blitz and Marianne, he felt that he'd done his duty as a father by paying the boys' mothers to take care of them.

Jahrer also points out that many heirs "traveled productive and destructive routes [at once], assuming different roles or going through various stages in a lifelong search for inner peace or basic survival." Dick had traveled exactly those routes, and, in what he knew to be his last years — months, really — he devoted himself entirely to achieving peace.

Patrick, trying to make amends for his earlier gaffes, wrote Dick about his academic progress. Dick softened and sent him a letter directly from Switzerland at the end of April 1964; he was "very proud of your efforts in journalism as well as your other activities." He said he'd received all of Patrick's letters, "though sometimes I do not feel well enough to answer right away." He reported that Patrick's mother, Marianne, had written, "telling me how poor she is, etc. She demanded a conference with me, but I could not face that as even her letter left me upset for several days." He had asked a young Georgia attorney to talk with Patrick concerning his future education because "I have led such a secluded life for these many years of illness that I would not be in a better position to advise you than [the lawyer]." The letter waxed philosophical. Dick described his early experience toiling six days a week at the cigarette factory to buttress the letter's main point:

> You and Mike, I sincerely hope, will try to make your own mark and contribution toward our present-day life. I have been deeply disappointed that the . . . older brothers have taken the money that I gave them and are living on that without working. They are contributing absolutely nothing to mankind. This deprives them of the privilege of satisfaction they would have if they earned their own way and made their own contribution.

Knowing that he was near death, more than ever Dick's concern was with what he saw as the deleterious effects produced by the family fortune. The money twisted, if it did not directly pervert, everything and everyone it touched: certainly it could be said to have helped kill his brother, Smith, and to have had a drastic impact on his own four attempts at marital happiness. Now, he evidently believed, it was sapping the lives of his sons.

There was a further complication. Dick's policy of keeping the sons from direct contact with him aroused their suspicion and distrust. They wondered why he was in Switzerland, high up in the cold, snowy Alps, when a man with emphysema should have been in a dry, sea-level place like Arizona. Was Annemarie influencing him to stay out of contact with the sons? Had the Germans taken over his mind? Was he being held prisoner against his will?

In July 1964, after spending several months in Europe, one of the older sons located Dick's co-op apartment in Muralto and tried to contact his father. He was told that Mr. Reynolds was not in residence. Next day, Dick called and grilled the son about how he had found the number, lambasted him — "Why don't you work, you worthless bastard?" — and refused to see him.

Shortly afterward, Dick and Annemarie, together with Lehmann, the oxygen therapist, and several other staff people, moved into the completed villa in Emmetten — just as in 1917 R. J. Reynolds, already dying of cancer, had moved his family and retainers into Reynolda. Nestled above Lake Lucerne on the mountainside opposite the famous Burgenstock resort, this final villa, though smaller than Dick's previous residences, had a spectacular view of the lake and the Alps. It was built mostly on one level so that Dick would not have to climb steps. It was also climate-controlled and had central panels that worked the lights; saving electricity still gave Dick satisfaction. Christian Nissen, Dr. Lindemann, and their wives were seen to go in and out a lot. Dick was not glimpsed outside the villa. Annemarie or members of the staff did the shopping; otherwise, observers noted little traffic to and from the mountainside home.

On August 15, 1964, Dick wrote out in longhand a new last will, revoking all others. It said that his estate should be governed by the laws of North Carolina, and it left everything to "my dear Wife Annemarie Reynolds born Schmitt" and named her as executor. Though it did not mention his children, the effect of the will was to completely disinherit his six sons.

In the fall, Nancy Verney came to visit, bearing with her the first draft of a history of the Z. Smith Reynolds Foundation, written by Bryan Haislip. Dick read it and composed a foreword whose language indicates his state of mind at the time:

> Time has a variable quality. The child feels the year will never pass, while the adult thinks how fast it flies. Thirty years is a brief span for a Foundation . . . [but] for a man, it is close to half of his Biblically allotted three score and ten. . . . When only memory is the guide, it is difficult or impossible to assess the achievements of either men or corporate bodies. When enterprises of significant impact upon society are involved, and there is no attempt made to gather and preserve the record, history is poorer. Then, indeed, time has been a thief for the generations to come. . . .

Among the things Nancy discussed with Dick was the part ZSRF was taking in the recently formed North Carolina Fund. In the spirit of President John Kennedy and the war on poverty declared by his successor, Lyndon Johnson, this fund had been set up to make seed money available for antipoverty projects that might eventually serve the federal government's interests. In wholeheartedly putting the foundation he controlled behind the North Carolina Fund, it seemed that Dick Reynolds was still concerned with his native state. When Nancy left Switzerland, she had with her Dick's resignation as ZSRF president. She was soon elected to that post.

At the beginning of December 1964, Marianne cabled Dick. Fed up with the meager amount of support he was giving to Michael and Patrick, she said she was flying over with the boys and would shortly dump them on his doorstep.

As Marianne was packing to make the trip, on December 14, 1964, Dick was rushed from the villa at Emmetten to the emergency ward of the St. Anna Clinic in Lucerne. It appeared that too much oxygen had reached Dick's brain — a danger always present when oxygen is being inhaled directly and one that Dick had often spoken of to friends and relatives. The clinic was small and well equipped, but there was nothing the staff or its machinery could do. The oxygen had literally exploded Dick's brain. A specialist came, but he was too late. Within minutes of Dick's reaching the clinic, he was dead.

Chapter Seventeen

Zach and Patrick

A GREAT DEAL seemed to happen in the week following Dick Reynolds's death. Thirty-six hours after he died, Annemarie gave birth to Irene Sabine Reynolds. On Sapelo, many of Dick's financial and personal records were burned, as were some in Winston-Salem by Strat Coyner, even though he'd been out of Dick's direct employ for several years. Within three days of the death, a lawyer filed in a Swiss court copies of nine wills, including the last, handwritten, unwitnessed document of August 15, 1964.

A telegram from family members in the United States, threatening legal action, averted cremation; however, when two of the older sons arrived in Lucerne they were incensed to find that they were unable to look inside the casket and verify that the dead man was, in fact, their father. Suspicions arose that the body might not be Dick's or that Dick had actually died months earlier and was being buried only after the birth of Irene.

It was another shock for them to learn that Annemarie had been pregnant, for they had had no knowledge of this. Now they received a third surprise — Dick's last will. They were amazed to be disinherited; had Dick's estate been donated entirely to charity, they might have understood, but it was a tremendous blow to know that their father had left it all to Annemarie, whom he had known only four years.

These shocks were followed by a curious peace initiative. On behalf of Annemarie and herself, Nancy offered $500,000, tax-prepaid, to each elder son and $1 million to Marianne for Michael and Patrick if they would agree not to contest the will or the paternity of Irene and, further, would refrain from public discussion of Dick's death and the disbursement of his estate. (Shades of Libby

Holman, Anne Cannon, and the whole mess following Smith's death.)

This offer was anathema to two of the older sons. However, if all did not sign, none would receive any money, so, badgered into it by concern for one another, all four older sons signed. Marianne also hated the offer. She even flew to Switzerland to investigate the possibilities of contesting the will. There were several seemingly suspicious circumstances. Both the will and the birth certificate had been filed in one of the few Swiss jurisdictions where unwitnessed documents could be legally registered. The will voiced a demand that the estate be considered under North Carolina law, which allowed disinheriting of minor children — whereas only two short years earlier Dick had specifically disavowed residence in North Carolina to be advantageously divorced in Georgia. However, Marianne decided that litigation would be lengthy and costly and might not obtain more than what Nancy had offered. Further, if her decision not to sign were to be the one that kept the other sons from receiving anything, later on this might cause the older sons to resent Pat and Mike. She, too, signed, putting the money in trust for her sons when they reached adulthood.

The "gifts" stilled public comment, but in private the questions and the pain continued. Some of the sons resented their father's generosity to the foundation. They respected his urge to be philanthropic but felt that underlying it was an implicit admission that the giver had failed as a parent — failed at the task of preparing his children to take over the management of the family wealth. Beyond the emotional anguish, there was the actual matter of the value of the estate. It was now estimated at between $10 million and $12 million, about half of what the sons thought it was worth. They based their notion on the fact that its value had remained constant through thirty years, three divorces, the building of Devotion and Merry Acres, the enlargement of Sapelo, and the outfitting of residences in New York, Miami Beach, and Palm Beach. Dick had had $28 million in 1934, and in 1962 his own lawyers stipulated that his fortune was $25 million. Where had between $13 million and $15 million gone in the past two years?

Some money could be traced. Several million had been assumed to be Dick's because he received the income from it while alive — but now that he was dead, his portion of the Katharine Smith Reynolds Johnston trust actually belonged to his children. To divorce Muriel had cost him about $3.25 million in settlements and lawyers' fees. The only other major recent expense had been the $600,000 villa at Emmetten. Dick had spent a million or so per year, but in the good times that amount had maintained several lordly residences; his expenses in his last two years could have been no higher than in his freewheeling days. Some members of the family revised their total but had to conclude, conservatively, that between $5 million and $10 million had vanished.

Zach believed the unaccounted-for money was in gold, illegally transported by Dick to Switzerland and hidden there, unreported. However, he and his brothers were constrained by the document they had signed and could do nothing. It fell to Muriel to become obsessed with trying to find out what had "really" happened to her late husband's fortune. Hers was not an easy quest; unable to get a Swiss lawyer to handle the case, she hired private detectives, made several trips to Switzerland herself, and over the next decade turned up many curious facts.

She learned, for instance, that there were no extant documents signed by a doctor or a nurse attesting to the birth of Irene. On the other hand, she obtained a note from a doctor in London who had tested Dick's sperm in 1957 and had determined it to be inactive. These things led her to cast doubt on Irene's paternity. The clerk who'd performed the remarriage ceremony in 1963 admitted to Muriel's representatives that he hadn't really seen Dick; this left open the possibility that a stand-in had been used and that the marriage to Annemarie had never taken place. Dr. Hans Lindemann, in whose care Dick had been assumed to be, denied having been at Emmetten in the weeks preceding Dick's death but said that Gunther Lehmann had all the answers to the mysteries surrounding that death; since the case was not being pursued in a court of law, Lehmann wouldn't talk and couldn't be coerced legally to do so.

Muriel hired a handwriting expert who was willing to testify that the penmanship on the holographic will was not the same as on Dick's letters of just a few years earlier. Grammarians found many word-usage mistakes in the will — Annemarie, for example, was identified as "born Schmitt" — which no American would have made. Muriel concluded that at best, Dick's hand had been forced, and at worst, the will had been forged; she suspected the latter because she remembered that Dick's longtime associate Christian Nissen had often boasted to her of having been a master forger for the Nazis. One of the tantalizing possibilities, though as unprovable as the rest, was that Dick might have written the will under duress and left in the errors as a signal that he was being coerced.

In the lobbies and tearooms of grand hotels in Miami, New York, London, and Monte Carlo, Muriel and Marianne would meet for lunch or drinks. Muriel grew thin to the point of asceticism and affected the appearance of a black-garbed, turbaned soothsayer; Marianne, becoming portly, still favored brightly colored gowns and flamboyance. Sister Dorothy was scandalized by Marianne's lunches with Muriel and would say to her, "How can you see that woman? She broke up your marriage!" Nevertheless, the two Mrs. R. J. Reynoldses continued to commiserate and to believe that Annemarie was somehow involved in Dick's seemingly premature death — though they thought they'd never be able to prove it. By the late 1960s, they had something more to discuss: in 1964, they'd estimated between $5 million and $10 million of Dick's estate missing and presumed it to be in gold, but when President Nixon took the United States off the gold standard, the price of an ounce shot up from $35 to $350 — which meant the "missing" portion was now worth between $50 million and $100 million!

The two ex-wives joined forces to attack the estate. Muriel aimed at proving that her divorce and Dick's subsequent marriage were invalid. Marianne based a claim to Sapelo on the napkin on which Dick had deeded her the entire island as an engagement present. Both spent tens of thousands to bring suit and appeals, and Marianne's went all the way to the United States Supreme Court. Various courts told them that their rights to any part of the estate had been extinguished when each of them had spent the first penny of their divorce settlements. Court losses notwithstanding, the two women became so close that Muriel named Marianne as a beneficiary in her will. And, as the years went by, none of the questions they'd raised about Dick's death, Irene's paternity, or the legitimacy of the will was ever legally resolved.

=

By 1970, Nancy Verney had shed her second husband and changed her name back to Nancy Reynolds. That spring, she was the moving force behind an extensive family reunion. First stop for the several hundred Reynolds, Cox, and Smith relatives was cocktails at Reynolda House. After the death of Charles Babcock, Reynolda had metamorphosed into a showplace for nineteenth-century American art, which was displayed among memorabilia of the R. J. era and furnishings from when the Babcocks were in residence. One crowd pleaser was the Gilbert Stuart portrait of George Washington, transferred from Sapelo and on loan from its current owner, the University of Georgia. To prevent crowds from entering the sleeping porch where the Smith Reynolds tragedy had taken place, the room had been made the site of the museum director's office. It wouldn't do to have visitors peering at the location of a still compelling mystery; Reynolda House's focus was art.

After the stop at Reynolda, buses and limousines took family members on the several-hour ride to the main focus of the reunion, R. J.'s birthplace, at Rock Spring, Virginia. In the late 1960s Nannie C. Terry, wife of the principal of the Hardin Reynolds Memorial School at Critz, had interested Nancy in the fate of the old plantation. It had been falling apart because Harbour's heirs could not afford the upkeep. Of the original furniture, only Nancy Jane Cox Reynolds's beautiful piano remained on the premises. Nancy Reynolds bought Rock Spring to preserve and enshrine the family's early history.

Family members now visiting the birthplace saw a restoration of the old home, which again appeared substantially as it had in R. J.'s youth. Twentieth-century additions had been stripped away. Many items had been found and returned, among them the rifle that R. J. had discovered in the yard after the Yankees had gone, the marital bed, and the convertible lap desk and storage box that Hardin had used, in which Nancy had discovered documents from the nineteenth century.

Those papers of Hardin's, and the memoirs of Abram Reynolds, which also turned up during the reunion preparations, became the core of a family history that Nancy commissioned from tobacco historian Nannie Mae Tilley. In the late fifties and early sixties, Tilley had researched and written a history of the R. J. Reynolds Tobacco Company for RJR; it was completed in 1965, but publication had been held up by the company. During preparations for the reunion, Tilley wrote to Nancy that she wasn't sure of all the reasons for the delay of her book by RJR but believed it had something to do with her crediting of R. J., rather than the later, twentieth-century management, with the ideas and techniques that had made the company prosperous. Nancy had Tilley's history of the family privately printed for the guests at the reunion.

Patrick and his brothers mingled with relatives. They wandered through the small rooms, peered at the stones in the graveyard and at exhibits of the cookhouse and other outbuildings, listened to speeches, and endured the media covering the event. Rock Spring seemed a very modest starting place for two separate fortunes.

The net worth of the people assembled here was in the hundreds of millions of dollars. Most were stockholders of RJR, which was currently paying about 21 percent on equity — better than IBM — and had seen its stock price rise nearly 50 percent in the past two years. In the previous decade RJR had acquired Hawaiian Punch, Chun King and College Inn foods, Filmco Packaging, the Sea-Land transportation company, and an oil company.

There was also the Reynolds Aluminum company. Abram's descendants not only held its stock but also were still its principals: R. S. Reynolds, Jr., was the CEO, and other of his sons were the major officers of Reynolds Aluminum, which in 1969, for the first time, reached the billion-dollar mark in sales. To Patrick, the sons of R. S. and his brothers seemed stable. Maybe that was because they'd had fathers who helped raise them and brought them into a family-owned business. The sons of Dick Reynolds hadn't had those advantages. They were heirs, but of a different sort.

"We are all slaves," Jay Gould had said of himself and other robber barons, "and the man who has one million dollars is the greatest slave of all, except it be he who has two million." But Frederick Jahrer's research concludes that the conflicted nature of the founders paled "in contrast to the anguish of their heirs." The six sons of Dick Reynolds lacked a family business in which to test themselves and accomplish feats from which they could take real pride. Furthermore, they had to contend with two larger-than-life models; it was unlikely that they would be able to match or better the fortune-making accomplishment of grandfather R. J., and it was equally unlikely they would exceed the boundaries of high living and emotional upheaval that defined Dick's days. Although they carried the Reynolds name, they had not inherited enough money to make truly significant impacts in philanthropy or business. What was left for them to do? How were Dick's sons to cope with, perhaps even to overcome, this legacy? If they failed, that would hurt them as badly as failure had hurt Dick and Smith.

Josh, John, and Will had all begun to settle down to quiet existences. Josh had recently married Marie Mallouk, who was very interested in horses. The R. J. Reynoldses bought a small farm on which to train horses for competition and sale; shortly, Marie had the first of several champions that would win many regional contests and national awards at Madison Square Garden. John and Will, also married, turned their attention to computers and real estate.

Zach was the brother most affected by the upheavals of the 1960s. In 1964, he'd been turned on to drugs while on the Isle of Man, in the Irish Sea, for an annual motorcycle racing tournament. When he came back to North Carolina, he took to wearing jumpsuits, long hair, and other badges of the counterculture. By the time of the reunion, Zach was well known in the Winston-Salem area as a backwoods rebel, a local character. As the number of his cars and motorcycles expanded, he built a fourteen-car garage for them next to his new home in Winston-Salem. When out racing, he was a wild man. Linda Lee tolerated the vehicles, and Zach made sure they did not enter the living quarters of the house.

During the summer, at Dick and Blitz's old place at Roaring Gap, Zach plunged into community activities, shepherded the children in swimming and climbing greased poles. In Winston at Halloween he would don costumes and trick-or-treat with his daughter, Lee, and the neighborhood kids.

Chronically without pocket money, he nevertheless bought a motorcycle for one friend at Christmas and paid expenses for others when they got into trouble. Linda Lee wanted him to use his capital to make money; he couldn't be bothered. "There are hardly enough hours in the day," he told her, "to do all the things I have to do." Once, when she nagged at him to change out of good clothes to race his cycles, he ripped up every piece of clothing in his closet and said, "Now I have *no* good clothes."

In the late sixties Zach took up aerobatic flying and worked at it obsessively. Qualifying for a pilot's license, he then added planes to his collection of cars and cycles. Within two years of climbing into a plane for his first lesson, he won first prize in his division at a national aerobatic championship. His maneuvers were dangerous. Just after takeoff, when the plane had cleared the ground, he'd turn completely over, then angle aloft while upside down. He'd also fly toward the runway upside down and pull a handkerchief out of a bottle on the ground. Or he'd push the plane into a free-fall, plunging toward the earth and pulling out of the dive at the last possible second. In another favorite stunt Zach would sit in the stands, dressed as a woman, then leap out of the crowd, cross the runway in high-heeled shoes and balloon breasts, jump into his plane, and pretend to be unable to fly it properly, eliciting scared shrieks from the audience.

Zach often used the excuse of going to air shows to visit his many girlfriends. Or, wearing a black cape and high on LSD, he would sometimes take a local girl out on a midnight motorcycle ride to Devotion. He'd kneel silently before the moonlit tomb of his mother, insisting melodramatically that he, too, would be buried here (and soon) in a pyramid, together with his favorite cycle. There was hardly a young country girl for a hundred miles around who could resist him in such a setting.

Zach's antics appealed to a constituency of cyclists, hangers-on, and adolescent boys and girls who retold and upgraded his every exploit and eccentricity until they were accorded the status of legend. He invented machinery but didn't patent it, owned cars but didn't drive them on the roads, shot guns for sport but wouldn't kill an animal, slept with women but didn't have to marry them, courted death but mocked it. He was able to do things they fantasized about but were afraid to attempt because they didn't have enough money or strength of character. To Zach's audience his abhorrence of cultural pursuits, his refusal to turn his talents to making money, his profligacy, deception of his wife, drug taking, embrace of the occult, and rejection of straight society were evidence that he was the ultimate "good old boy."

This backwoods rebel knew many of the people at the reunion. But long-haired hippie Patrick, recently turned twenty-one, brought up in Miami and New England prep schools, knew only a few. Around the nation, people Patrick's age were horrified at the killing of students at Kent State; however, the conversation under the Rock Spring party tent never touched upon that volatile topic. That contributed to Patrick's feelings of ambivalence toward his more distant relatives, who in years past had completely ignored him. Here was Smith Bagley, Nancy's son, who was running for public office and was already well known in Washington; here was R. S.'s grandson Julian Sargeant Reynolds, at age thirty-four the youngest lieutenant governor in the history of Virginia. These young men had great wealth, solid families, a base in the region. He had none of these things.

Patrick had deeply conflicting emotions about both his money and his less tangible family legacy. When he'd attended the Hotchkiss School — one of the most demanding, academically, in the entire country — he was plagued with feelings of alienation and inadequacy. He'd entered the University of California at Berkeley in the fall of 1967, when the university was at the center of the revolution in student life sweeping the country. He joined the TKE fraternity and made the rowing team — but was soon won over by the blandishments of the counterculture. He smoked pot, investigated free love, grew his hair long, and wore his denims fringed. A young woman in a communally shared house in Berkeley introduced him to concepts of Eastern religions and spiritual awakening. What with listening to rock albums, going to concerts at the Avalon and the Fillmore, and having stoned picnics in the park, in his sophomore year Patrick let his grades drop slightly, and he didn't go out for crew.

On his twenty-first birthday, in 1969, Patrick came into a two-million-dollar legacy from his long-dead grandmother. The Associated Press learned of it and photographed Patrick in his hippie outfit, while a reporter maneuvered him into admitting that "money is beautiful." The picture, headline, and quote were turned into a dig at the masses that Patrick hadn't intended. He felt angry, embarrassed, and used.

He continued to live at the TKE house and spend on the same scale as before but was deluged with letters begging for handouts or insisting that he invest in unlikely schemes or inventions. There were several hate letters, too. People assumed that he had unlimited money, yet because they knew he hadn't earned it accorded him more envy than respect. With groups in a restaurant, he vacillated between dividing checks to the penny and taking the easy way out, simply paying for everyone himself. He soon learned that doing someone a monetary favor invariably tainted a friendship and caused resentment.

The hedonistic compensations of having money allowed him to cruise through the Age of Aquarius until one day, deep in marijuana smoke, a short art-film fantasy played in his head — and he became uncomfortably aware that he'd be unable to make that film until the effects of the pot had worn off. Overwhelmed with the feeling that he'd been wasting his time and life, he left drugs behind and began to make his own experimental short films. Berkeley professor Albert Johnson, director of the San Francisco Film Festival, suggested that Patrick make a documentary about their town. Patrick filmed the controversies over Peoples Park and the Third World Liberation Front. *Berkeley* was good enough to win a prize at the Cannes Film Festival.

By the time of the reunion, then, he was a young filmmaker. That was more important to him than his vexatious Reynolds identity. He bore the family name but only a small fraction of the money; he was Dick's son but had been disinherited and so, along with his brothers, was somewhat ostracized at this gathering. Patrick lifted his movie camera to his eye and recorded the reunion; it was a wonderful way to be present and distanced at the same time.

Among the reasons for Patrick's alienation was his growing awareness that the circumstances surrounding his father's death and last will were too fantastic to be accepted at face value. In recent months Muriel had been in direct contact with Patrick, and her obsession had come to focus on him. Because the agreement with Nancy and Annemarie had been signed when Patrick was a minor, it could be considered not binding, allowing him, in Muriel's view, to get the grave opened and the body examined and entitling him to one sixth of Dick's estate if the death and the last will could be shown to be improper. With this on his mind it was hard to face Aunt Nancy and Annemarie. Patrick panned the camera across the crowd. He wanted to reject the idea of a conspiracy that had done away with his father and his father's millions — but, in these circumstances, it was hard to do.

=

Back in Hollywood after the Reynolds family reunion, without the discipline of being forced to earn his own living, Patrick went after his career goal inefficiently. He didn't seek the sort of jobs other aspiring young filmmakers wanted, such as working as assistants in production companies. Instead, he attended film festivals around the world and took courses at UCLA and then at USC. He spent endless hours in an editing room perfecting his own short films. Lacking confidence in his abilities, he felt uneasy about the money that set him apart from the other struggling young filmmakers.

As did many heirs, he tried to surpass his father by attempting to make a lot of money all at once. He plunged $400,000 into silver bullion and had the satisfaction of seeing the price rise. But he lost money on a prototype electric car, a mobile phone in a briefcase, a bank in the Bahamas, an executive-search company. Often he agreed to deals with a handshake, wrote checks to business partners without consulting attorneys or experts, and in other ways fell victim to associates whose enthusiasm far outweighed their credentials.

He was delighted when his old mentor, Albert Johnson, rescued him from the doldrums with an invitation to join other San Francisco Film Festival people in a tour of the Soviet Union. They met Soviet film stars and directors, were welcomed to their larger-than-usual apartments and special dachas. To Patrick, it was a revelation that in a communist country, where all were supposed to be equal, a few lived much more comfortably than everyone else. Perhaps it was indeed the natural order of things that some were more fortunate than others.

Believing this, he soon concluded that he wasn't a bad (or a good) person for having a lot when others had very little; it was just the luck of the draw. He began to be more relaxed about his inherited wealth and decided there was nothing wrong with spending some of his money on himself. He rented a hilltop castle-estate in the Hollywood Hills. Wolf's Lair was grand and fake at the same time — many rooms, a hideaway pool, a panoramic view of the Los Angeles basin, and another over the Lake Hollywood reservoir. It also had a bridge over a plastic waterfall with an illuminated paper moon above it and a silly throne carved out of stone. These last features concealed a rear view of the famous Hollywood sign.

Actress Shelley Duvall was just emerging from an early marriage and was researching a role in Robert Altman's *Nashville* when Patrick met her at the Starwood discotheque. Sweet and soft-spoken, a bit shy, she was almost the precise opposite of his mother, Marianne. Soon Shelley and he were lovers, and she moved into Wolf's Lair. They became hosts for frequent parties at which the usual guests were a small coterie of young actors and actresses, most of whom appeared in Altman's films.

Visiting Shelley on the set of *Nashville*, Patrick was cast by Altman in a walk-on — and was bitten by the acting bug. Being a film director now seemed to be an unattainable goal; acting was more approachable. He began to study it with coaches Lee Strasberg, Milton Katselas, and Peggy Feurey.

The bit in Altman's movie led to a speaking role in a television production of F. Scott Fitzgerald's short story "Bernice Bobs Her Hair," in which Shelley starred. This production had concluded, and in a few weeks Patrick was scheduled to act in Altman's *Buffalo Bill and the Indians* when a letter from Aunt Nancy arrived.

The missive announced that the Sapelo Island Research Foundation was offering to sell the South End mansion's furnishings to the brothers before holding a general auction. Although others might have found the letter innocuous, it riled Patrick. He was insulted by being asked to bid on what he believed should have been part of his inheritance. After considering it, though, he decided that attending the auction might be his last opportunity to see Sapelo. So he went.

The magnificence and emptiness of Sapelo, conjuring up in his mind's eye both the wonderful and the terrible scenes that had occurred there, produced in Patrick a profound sadness. As the day on Sapelo went on and Nancy continued to be reluctant to speak about matters of any consequence, Patrick was emboldened to ask, "Are you sure that my father really wanted all of us to be entirely cut out of his estate?"

"That's what the last will says, Patrick."

"What about at least letting us visit Sapelo on a regular basis? We'd pay for a cottage. Would that be possible?"

"That would be up to the foundation."

"But you control the foundation!" Patrick replied angrily. She said she didn't and retreated to stoniness.

Later, Patrick learned that Nancy's son, Smith Bagley, the would-be politician who'd been twice defeated in running for Congress, was giving parties on Sapelo for former Georgia governor and presidential candidate Jimmy Carter. So much for Nancy's silence.

Patrick was quite depressed when he returned to Hollywood. In a journal, he poured out all that he knew of his father's and family's life, all the suspicions kept boiling by Muriel and Marianne, everything he could figure out about his fiscal and familial inheritance. The writing was therapy. In the course of it, Patrick tried to stop loathing Dick and struggled to understand him: "Ignoring his children was only part of [Dick's] larger pattern. To successfully cope with the magnitude of his endowments in wealth, genius and physical stamina, he would have needed an equally extreme self-discipline, which he was never inspired or did not choose to cultivate." Patrick wrote that he himself hoped to have that discipline.

He decided to put the past behind him forever, to bury and forget it. He also told Muriel that he would not press her goals of opening up his father's coffin and challenging the estate. He had his own future in films on which to concentrate. He planned to change his last name to Byrne, his mother's real maiden name.

As Zach's notoriety grew, in the early 1970s, he spent less time at home and more experimenting with combinations of mind-altering drugs. There were stories of his piloting his plane while high on LSD.

Zach told cycling friends that Linda Lee was a wet blanket. To him, she seemed overly interested in Winston society. She didn't care for his practical jokes — putting stink bombs in public rest rooms, feigning a heart attack to get a petrified friend to take the controls of his plane. Actually, her main concern was his philandering, which grew steadily. One day Linda Lee was readying a pair of Zach's pants for the laundry and found in them a receipt for a motel room registered to Mr. and Mrs. Zach Reynolds. This was too much: she confronted Zach. He made no apologies for his behavior, nor did he deny having had an affair; he acted as if it were not her place to question what he did with his time.

At Linda Lee's insistence, they went to a marriage counselor, but Zach had little to say. The counselor told them both that Zach's chasing after women was juvenile and a sort of disease. Zach didn't promise to stop. He went on a trip to Florida. Linda Lee had him followed and obtained unmistakable evidence of another affair. She filed for divorce.

Zach was hurt and incredulous that she would take any action against him. There was no hope of reconciliation. A settlement was reached that gave Linda Lee and her daughter trust funds but that left Zach with his cycles, guns, cars, planes, ham radio — and a good portion of his money.

Released from the constraints of matrimony, Zach became more eccentric. He wore only jumpsuits. Kept a coffin in a secret chamber in his new home. Predicted he would die in a plane crash at forty or forty-one. Painted his planes and cycles with astrological symbols and labels such as "Cigarette City Flash" and "Dr. Cancer." In a concealed place he affixed to a dart board slips that showed the names and numbers of his female conquests.

When Zach's divorce became final in 1972, his "tail" board held more than a hundred names. Now thirty-four, he proposed to Dorothy Sides, a woman with whom he'd been keeping company for several years. On their honeymoon, they flew in one of Zach's planes, but shortly thereafter Zach forswore flying altogether.

Henceforth he would travel only on the ground. Friends speculated that he'd had a bad LSD flashback while at the controls of his plane and didn't want it ever to happen again.

Zach adopted Dorothy's daughter from an earlier marriage, and they all lived in the mansion that Linda Lee had vacated. Now he had motorcycles inside as well as outside. A cycling magazine celebrated him as the "unfettered, unrestrained and hopelessly enthusiastic" owner of the world's largest collection of dirt and street bikes. To protect his fiefdom, Zach had a twenty-two-television-set security system installed and wired to an elaborate wall bank in the master bedroom. If he didn't wish visitors to see the system, he could pull a red velvet drape to cover the monitors.

At the homes of Jack Nicholson or Julie Christie, where there were parties to which Patrick would accompany Shelley Duvall, the stars would talk to Shelley and condescend to him as if he were some rich fish she had reeled in. Patrick wondered if Smith Reynolds had ever felt that way around Libby Holman.

He was cast in a new musical by the authors of *Hair* and went to rehearse with it in New York; meanwhile, Shelley was on location making another film. They kept in touch by long-distance, and at the end of one call, their relationship was over. The musical closed, too, after three performances. Patrick returned to Wolf's Lair; without Shelley, the mansion seemed empty. He found an even more majestic estate, in the Holmby Hills. This was Brooklawn, built in the 1920s by one of the founders of Twentieth Century Fox, Winifred Sheehan, for his wife, opera star Maria Juretza. It had enormous public rooms with fourteen-foot ceilings; there was a ballroom with a balcony that would have fit cozily into a grand hotel. Moreover, its dimensions and amenities seemed perfect for the life Patrick believed he had been cheated out of — the style of his father, which he wanted desperately to understand. With profits from silver bullion he paid cash for Brooklawn. Just as Dick had resorted to living well after setbacks in politics and in his first marriage, now Patrick would take the same revenge on Shelley and on Hollywood itself.

He gave two large parties a year, held private acting workshops in the ballroom, dated actresses and models. He went to court and had his name legally changed back to Reynolds. With a partner, he optioned some screenplays and properties but was not able to persuade the studios to put any of them into production. At what seemed to him to be the last moment, he lost many potential starring roles in films. The beauty of Brooklawn was a constant source of pleasure, but at times its enormous, empty rooms only amplified Patrick's growing feelings of failure and despair.

At the end of 1978 Patrick visited Zach. Dorothy had given birth to a daughter, Katherine, in 1977. Zach spent much of his time talking on the ham radio apparatus, working with other hams to locate organs for emergency transplants. In other ways, however, as he reached forty his wildness hadn't been tempered much. In some sessions recorded at this time by ham radio operators, Zach was only occasionally lucid.

Zach boasted to Patrick, with the intensity of a man who'd seen a vision, "They gon' make a movie 'bout me." Both brothers were addicted smokers. In quieter moments Zach confided that he was deeply ashamed that the source of his family's money was cigarettes, a product that caused cancer. Elvis Presley had recently died, at the age of forty-two, and Zach was approaching that same age. He repeated earlier prophecies that he would probably not outlive the king of rock and roll. Dorothy thought seriously about filing for conservatorship of his money.

At the steeplechase at Tanglewood, an annual event in Forsyth County, many of the Reynoldses turned out — Zach, Will, and Aunt Nancy, in addition to Patrick. It seemed they covered all topics of conversation but carefully avoided bringing up Zach's dissipation or the difficulties of Nancy's son, Smith Bagley. Nancy had allowed Jimmy Carter to use Musgrove Plantation after the election as a site for interviewing prospective cabinet members; Smith had been set for a subcabinet job in the administration. Then, however, some old business dealings had come back to haunt him. At the moment, he was under indictment for stock manipulation and other illegal practices; he was expected to be found innocent, but the Carter White House had long since put on the shelf the idea of a high post for Smith Bagley.

At the steeplechase, Zach's drugged condition caused him to collapse. He had to be taken home.

On September 3, 1979, Hurricane David devastated the Carolinas and Georgia. The next day, a nineteen-year-old neighbor of Zach's, who had long been an admirer, asked Zach to go up in the air with him. The young man had just received his pilot's license and wanted to take up his brother and a pal, along with Zach. Zach hadn't flown in a half-dozen years. Despite protests from friends, he agreed to go. He told one buddy to bring some codeine along on the trip, since, he said, he was addicted to that. The friend declined to provide the drug — or to fly.

In midafternoon the plane took off from the Z. Smith Reynolds Airport. The weather was mostly clear, but a pilot at the flying service adjacent to the terminal wondered why somebody who had as much experience as Zach would go aloft when there was residual hurricane turbulence in the air. Several minutes after takeoff, and several miles north, the plane flew parallel to a large highway where a driver saw it nose up, evidently on some sort of maneuver, and then, in the same balletlike manner, nose straight down in a dive.

During the dive, knowing that the plane was in serious trouble, Zach evidently reached over the shoulders of the pilot and put his hands on the controls. There they remained as the plane crashed and burned in woods not far from the highway. Zach and the three teenage boys aboard were all killed.

The precise cause was never pinpointed. It was, perhaps, a botched attempt at a stunt that the pilot was not skilled enough to accomplish. Some friends speculated that Zach had been trying to accelerate and to pull the plane out of its dive but didn't make it. Others believed Zach had quickly realized that a crash was inevitable and, in a manic moment, drove the plane into the ground as a semiconscious form of suicide, fulfilling his own prophecies that his life would become a legend.

Visibly shaken and saddened, all the brothers gathered in Winston-Salem for Zach's funeral. Zach was not buried, as he had requested, in a pyramid by his mother's side and surrounded by his cycles and radio equipment, but Dorothy's solution was near enough. She chose an aboveground sarcophagus sited in full view of her Devotion home; it was covered with bas-reliefs of a handgun, a cycle, a Porsche, a stunt plane, and a large radio antenna. As he had done with Blitz, brother Will wrote an inscription: set into the stone were the words "Dr. Zach: May Your Spirit Be Carried on the Wings of God."

No matter that Zach's death wish had been joked about for years; his death was a shock, an event as sobering for the third generation as the demise of Z. Smith Reynolds had been for his siblings in 1932 — and one that, similarly, left many unanswered questions. Was it suicide? An accident that could have been prevented? Had

Zach been under the influence of drugs? Was his early death inevitable?

Rather than dying young and romantically, as Smith had done, Zach had lived into early middle age. To some he seemed a hero, to others a victim of his circumstances, the embodiment of what Dick Reynolds had feared for his sons, the spoiled rebel who made no contributions to society.

Epilogue

AFTER ZACH'S DEATH, Patrick felt more than ever that the direction of his life was not satisfactory. He needed to get beyond where he was but was unsure of how to do so. He sold all of his RJR stock. It had bothered him that so much of his income came from a company that made cigarettes. More and more information cited cigarettes as a cause of cancer and lung and heart diseases. He had learned that R. J. had begun to manufacture cigarettes only after being convinced that they posed no health hazards. Since that time, though, the evidence had changed. Patrick couldn't alter the source of his family's wealth, but selling all his RJR stock brought him a little satisfaction.

Despite having had roles in eleven films and a half-dozen television shows, Patrick had not seen his acting career take off. Every other important cast member in the television production *Bernice Bobs Her Hair* had now starred in a film. When his starring role didn't materialize, and the studios didn't want to produce the scripts he'd developed, he put show business on a back burner. He had a moment of triumph, however, when he sold Brooklawn at a 400 percent profit.

As he stood in the great hall of Brooklawn, his possessions packed into boxes around him, the conviction came to Patrick that he must write something about his family. It was imperative to explore his own past, to come to know his father and the source of the family's wealth. He began talking to people, gathering materials, looking at things with a new eye.

In 1981, he was introduced to Regine Wahl, daughter of a West German transportation magnate, an aspiring interior decorator. Soon Patrick was thinking about marriage. He and Regine had international jet set friends in common and seemed compatible; a wife and children were just what he needed as a center to his life.

Their 1983 wedding in a small town in Bavaria was an exercise in fantasy. Patrick invited guests from every phase of his life: his mother, Aunt Dorothy, two of Marianne's buddies, Regine's relatives, actor Robin Williams, and a number of jet-setters. His best man was Mohamed Khashoggi, eldest son of billionaire Adnan Khashoggi. All rode in twelve horse-drawn carriages to a church where they were greeted by rose-petal-throwing villagers in traditional peasant garb.

Newly united, the couple was serenaded by brass bands and zithers; then came a night-long party culminating in brunch the following morning, after which Patrick and Regine began a honeymoon in Monte Carlo. The elder Khashoggi's annual birthday celebration was also being held there, and the newlyweds were swept up in it. In the projection room of the Khashoggis' three-hundred-foot yacht, *Nabila*, guests were treated alternately to videotapes of the wedding and clips of the yacht being used in the James Bond film *Never Say Never Again*.

It was a moment that could not last. Patrick didn't have the money to keep up with the Khashoggis; the lavish celebration underlined his realization that living in the grand style was not only unreachable for him financially but also did not answer the fundamental problem of what to do with his life.

He and Regine moved to Beverly Hills and a home smaller than Brooklawn. Patrick went into business with the Wahls; he learned German, took training in European bus factories, and opened a branch of the family's tourist bus business in Phoenix.

In 1984, after numerous tries, Patrick finally quit smoking. A bit perversely, he tried for a seat on the RJR board, although he didn't let board members know his secret goal was to persuade the company to get out of making cigarettes. RJR wasn't interested in his services.

In this time of trying for a fresh start, he also made overtures to Aunt Nancy and Annemarie. After all, Regine, like Annemarie, was German, and she had taken a degree in English. They chatted amiably when Patrick and Regine visited Annemarie and Irene in Switzerland. At Musgrove and Quarry Farm, Nancy's residences, Patrick and Regine paid calls on R. J.'s last surviving child. Nancy had lost a lung to cancer and was now confined by emphysema to a wheelchair. With Annemarie and Nancy, Patrick attempted to find out more about his father, without ruffling feathers. When he mentioned that he wanted to write a book about his family, neither was pleased. Neither woman would sit for interviews, though they did continue to see him socially. When he applied to Reynolda House to look at the papers of his grandfather and great-grandfather, he was refused permission.

Patrick received an unexpected call from his old agent, asking him to audition for a starring role in a spoof of science fiction and adventure films. He won the part, but the production kept getting delayed, and he wondered if it would ever begin.

In early January of 1985, Nancy died. Obituaries called her the most generous child of R. J. Reynolds, one who had contributed millions personally to causes ranging from Planned Parenthood to research into the disposal of toxic wastes and the root causes of poverty and who had directed the Z. Smith Reynolds Foundation in some very productive years.

By this time Nancy's son, Smith Bagley, had been exonerated of the charges against him and was a leading philanthropist in Winston-Salem and Washington. Even after Nancy's death, Patrick found that his cousins and others who controlled access to family records now fifty to one hundred years old continued to refuse permission to consult them, not only to Patrick but to researchers on other projects. It seemed the family did not want anyone to know anything about the past that hadn't been sanitized.

Ironically, Nannie Mae Tilley's long-suppressed but now official history of the RJR Company was finally published in 1985, with an apologetic note saying research had been completed in the 1960s. Tilley's monumental work arrived in bookstores at about the same time that RJR merged with Nabisco to form one of the largest consumer-goods marketers in the world, with annual sales of fifteen billion dollars. Eighty million times a day, company literature boasted, consumers in 160 countries purchased an RJR Nabisco item — cookies, candies, cereals, dog food, Del Monte canned fruits and vegetables, Heublein packaged cocktails, and, of course, tobacco products.

Stock market analysts applauded the merger as a further step by RJR in lessening its dependence on selling cigarettes. Unfortunately, cigarettes were more highly profitable per unit of sales than most other products; it was hard to stop selling an item that accounted for one third of RJR's gross sales and one half of its profits. But, a business magazine concluded, with public health officials attributing 350,000 deaths per year to cigarette smoking, "each death is a potential liability for cigarette makers."

While in North Carolina for Nancy's funeral, Patrick made a point of seeing the old mansions. The estate at Devotion was in decline. Parts of the dams had crumbled. Roofs of ancillary structures had fallen in. Some rooms in the main buildings had not been entered for years. One brother had sold his quarter, and although the other two and Zach's widow, Dorothy, maintained nice residences there, they could not afford to keep up the big buildings, the farm, or the overall property of Devotion as their father or even Blitz had done. In the Depression, employees worked for eighteen cents an hour; now the staff was minimal, and it showed.

Patrick also visited Sapelo. State employees told him that Georgia had obtained Sapelo for what had been virtually a token payment. But, they said — and he saw — the magnificent South End mansion was falling apart, due to skimpy budgets passed by the state legislature, and South End was now in danger of being so weather-beaten as to be uninhabitable. The Sapelo Island Research Foundation estimated the building needed between $5 million and $6 million for major repairs.

The Georgia Department of Natural Resources, owner of the northern half of the island, was suggesting that to make better use of Sapelo (and generate money for repairs) it must be developed to attract more tourists; there was talk of a convention center, and of condominiums along the pristine beach.

Hog Hammock was the worst shock. Patrick interviewed most of the now retired residents while they huddled about ancient stoves in old homes that had become dilapidated. Such people as Fred and Cracker Johnson, and their wives, who had cared for Dick in his time on the island — and especially when he was sick — were now near-destitute. They related how they discovered to their horror that the destruction of Dick Reynolds's records in 1964 had made it next to impossible to prove they had been employed by Dick and therefore ought to be receiving Social Security payments for the years they spent working for him. SIRF, which gave grants of $500,000 annually, earmarked only $25,000 per year for Hog Hammock assistance. The Johnsons, whom Dick had trusted so far as to have them help him bury bags of gold on the island, now felt that his promises to them had been betrayed.

Patrick had journeyed to the funeral and the mansions alone because his marriage had begun to disintegrate. It had been a mistake; he and Regine were not compatible after all. Perhaps, as had Marianne and Dick, he had been trying to realize an unworkable fantasy. Patrick and Regine separated.

Then, almost out of the blue, the producers of the science fiction spoof received their funding, and Patrick began preparing to star as a half-man, half-robot "mandroid." In the early summer, as he was about to go to Spain for the shooting, his mother, Marianne, died unexpectedly. The moment was doubly hard for Patrick since he had to leave for the filming immediately after the funeral. Once in Spain, he concealed grief and threw himself into the work.

As a scheduled six weeks of filming stretched into a hundred grueling days and nights on rivers, in semi-jungle and desert settings, there was no time for Patrick to be confused about his task. Some days, the heat inside his costume — which took hours to put on — reached 130 degrees Fahrenheit. For months, fully engaged in the filmmaking, Patrick regarded himself and was regarded by his colleagues as an actor working his head off, not as a Reynolds heir. When he finished, he didn't know whether the film would be a box-office smash or a flop — those judgments were beyond his control — but he knew that he'd given it his energy and time, that he had enjoyed doing so, and that it was the best thing that could have happened to him.

Patrick had had no single moment of epiphany; rather, the realization had grown in him that a solution to his search for a role in life was achievable, if not yet at hand. For too many years, his wealth and identity as a Reynolds heir had overpowered everything else. The family legacy had smothered him, had distorted his view of the world and the way people lived in it. Behind his struggle to develop an acting career, to make high-paying investments, to be a film producer, was the dream of breaking free from being forever identified as a Reynolds heir. His relationship with his money had led to periods of riotous excess interspersed with episodes of trying to get rid of it; there had been times when he'd felt guilty about his wealth or inadequate to its demands, both blessed and cursed with the money. That was something hard for less "fortunate" people to understand, because they believed that if they were rich they'd be happy and would have no need to work. Knowing otherwise, Patrick could now make some resolutions: he must not permit his wealth to insulate and protect him from failure or success — as wealth had done to his father. And he must not allow it to prevent him from ever growing up — as it had done to Smith Reynolds and, more tragically and recently, to Zach.

In the late spring of 1986, almost by chance, an opportunity and a direction beckoned.

A businessman friend interested in politics had persuaded Patrick to go to Washington together with a group of potential contributors. The group was treated to private briefings and teas with such senior cabinet officials and powerful figures as Secretary of Defense Caspar Weinberger and Federal Reserve Board Chairman Paul Volcker. Senator Robert Packwood of Oregon, then head of a Senate committee on tax reform, told the group that the Senate would vote that afternoon on whether or not to extend the federal excise tax on cigarettes. Patrick identified himself to the senator as a grandson of R. J. Reynolds and told Packwood that in his travels he'd noticed that cigarettes were taxed much more heavily in Europe than they were in the United States. Those taxes were designed to cut into cigarette consumption, and the monies collected were put into research on medical problems caused by smoking. Packwood asked him his views on smoking, and Patrick replied that he would be in favor of greatly increased cigarette taxes and that he thought such a tax would be popular since most Americans now didn't smoke. Packwood challenged Patrick, saying that if he was truly on the antismoking side, he would come right down to the hearing room and testify about it that afternoon.

Patrick told the senator he'd have to think it over. Though he had long believed that smoking posed many dangerous health risks, he was not sure he ought to make his views public. To do so could possibly alienate his brothers and other relatives. He would be accused of biting the hand that had fed him. Moreover, *Eliminators* was about to be released in videocassette — it had had a brief run in theaters — and people would say he was taking a stance now just to publicize his acting career and the writing of this book, which had already begun.

But as he thought about it, the idea grew on him. His father's ugly last years and death had had a tremendous impact on his life. Marianne's heart disease had been aggravated by her smoking. Beyond those deaths, there were the others in the Reynolds family: Grandfather R. J. Reynolds had died from cancer of the pancreas, perhaps tied to his lifelong habit of chewing tobacco; Aunt Nancy had smoked throughout life and succumbed to emphysema; Aunt Mary died of abdominal cancer at forty-four after a lifetime of smoking. Perhaps if Patrick spoke out publicly, a few more people would be moved to quit, a few more families might be spared the terrible early death of a relative from smoking. At length he came to the conviction that as a Reynolds he had an obligation to speak out — because on this issue his words would bear weight and might have some influence.

Patrick sought out representatives of the American Lung Association and was amazed to learn of the extent of the pernicious effects of cigarettes: in the past thirty years, ten million Americans had died prematurely from smoking, and a thousand people a day were being added to that list. Hundreds and hundreds of separate studies reliably linked smoking to heart disease, lung disease, and cancer. Cigarettes were the most heavily advertised product in America, and RJR spent more on advertising than any other tobacco maker. The idea of testifying in public took on in his mind the force of inevitability.

Patrick went to North Carolina and talked face-to-face with each of his brothers. All were against the idea of his speaking out. It was clear that if Patrick did so, his brothers would not second him. All owned considerable blocks of RJR Nabisco stock; moreover, most were residents of Winston-Salem, a city whose fortunes were still deeply interwoven with those of the Reynolds company. They lived in Cigarette City and would have to face friends' and neighbors' dismay at Patrick's "betrayal." Nonetheless, Patrick was their brother, and they were all bound together by the extraordinary circumstances of their birth, wealth, and family history. After heated discussions, Patrick and his brothers "agreed to disagree."

On July 18, 1986, nervous and highly charged, Patrick testified before the House of Representatives' Energy and Commerce Committee's Subcommittee on Health and Environment. Reading a statement as reporters and television cameras focused on him, he began by saying that his father had died from emphysema caused by cigarette smoking. He went on to say, "When my grandfather began making cigarettes he did not know that they cause heart disease, lung disease and cancer. . . . Am I biting the hand that feeds me? If the hand that once fed me is the tobacco industry, then that same hand has killed millions of people and may kill millions more." He pledged to help accomplish Surgeon General C. Everett Koop's goal of a "smoke-free society by the year 2000."

Nearly every major news medium in the United States excerpted Patrick's testimony; CBS News called him an "electrifying witness against the very product that made his family fortune." During the next several days, he repeated the gist of his testimony on a dizzying round of national interview programs. The notion of a Reynolds speaking out against the tobacco industry caught the public's fancy. Requests for him to speak and to be a talk-show guest flooded in.

In the eighteen months following his testimony, he crisscrossed the country on behalf of the American Lung Association and other groups, appearing at rallies boosting antismoking ordinances, on local television and radio interview programs, in educational forums. Audiences said that he spouted the grim statistics as well as any lecturer, but to them what distinguished Patrick's message was his raft of personal stories — about the sight of his father with sandbags on his chest, struggling to strengthen his damaged lungs; of hearing from his mother how Dick had grown angry at her when she began smoking, calling cigarettes a "dirty, disgusting habit." All his life experience and training as an actor seemed to relate to the task of becoming an antismoking advocate. Patrick started audiences laughing with him as he described the secret satisfactions of learning to smoke as a rebellious teenager at Hotchkiss, sitting at a window with mouthwash and room deodorizer at the ready, or the embarrassment of failing several times in attempts to quit before actually being able to stop. He used these personal stories to get audiences' attention so he could convince people of the need to ban all cigarette advertising, raise taxes on cigarettes, and support legislation for clean indoor air.

To one newspaper he was "a controversial new crusader," while to another he was "the latest media star of the anti-smoking movement." Critics pointed out that while Patrick had sold his RJR stock, he hadn't given up the money from his tobacco-born inheritance. Diligent reporters located and sounded out his brothers for comment. "Our father and grandfather are probably spinning in their graves. It's the damndest thing I ever heard," said his brother John. Will responded with his own slogan: "If you don't smoke, don't start, but if you do smoke, smoke a Reynolds product." Only Michael humorously pointed out that despite Patrick's activities, the price of RJR Nabisco's stock was climbing.

The company itself refused to comment on Patrick's efforts, except to say that he was entitled to his opinions. The tobacco industry continued to maintain, as it had for a quarter of a century, that the link between smoking and cancer had not been conclusively shown to exist. Even so, there were industry rumors that all the tobacco giants were seeking for insurance reasons to spin off or divest themselves of their cigarette-making divisions.

Shortly after Patrick's campaign had begun — though certainly not as a consequence of it — RJR Nabisco announced that the company was pulling its corporate headquarters out of Winston-Salem and relocating to Atlanta. When asked why this move was being made, Chief Executive Officer F. Ross Johnson replied that Winston-Salem was too "bucolic" a place to be the home base of his international conglomerate. Many in Winston-Salem, the town that R. J. Reynolds had done so much to put on the map, were outraged by Johnson's comment. It was estimated that several hundred of Winston's managerial-level families would have to move away, tearing the social and economic fabric of Forsyth County.

Visiting in Winston-Salem after the start of his involvement with the crusade against cigarette smoking, and having done a great deal of research for this book, Patrick was continually struck by echoes of the past. In the center of town, the faint, sweet odor of tobacco was omnipresent and inescapable; residents evidently no longer noticed it. Tobacco City was still that, redolent of the world of R. J., the raw youth who had come to build an empire and whose name was prominently displayed — on the statue that Patrick so uncannily resembled, on the high school that sat on the hill, on various buildings and churches. The image of Uncle Will, R. J.'s brother, was now a cartoonlike, pipe-smoking silhouette showing motorists the way to Tanglewood, the public park that had once been his home. The benevolent, paternal image did not sit comfortably with what Patrick now knew about Will's failure to rein in the profligate sons of R. J. in the years after the deaths of their parents.

It was too bad that so little of his father, Dick Reynolds, seemed to remain in the town. The Fifth Street house where he was born was gone now, replaced by a library. Inquiries there revealed that few knew what had stood on the property before the present building was erected; there were no copies of *The Three Cent Pup* in the library's collection, either. At Wake Forest, Dick was a minor presence in a few entries at the library; only old friends seemed to remember that he had been the moving force in the foundation that brought the university to Winston-Salem. At Reynolda, among the examples of nineteenth- and twentieth-century art and the Babcocks' furnishings, there wasn't even a whisper of him, although Patrick was sure that Dick's room was the one with the furniture from the downtown home. Where had Aunt Mary sat when she took Dick's phone call and refused to see him and Marianne? He imagined Smith draped over the magnificent balcony, shooting out the crystals of the chandelier with a pistol; was it the same gun that had later killed him?

In many ways, the lives of his uncle and father had both been tragic — Smith's the more obviously so, but Dick's the more painful for being longer and drawn out. To be an heir on the scale of those two was not something to be easily escaped; the Reynolds legacy had haunted them. Even Zach, Patrick's brother who had been named for Smith, seemed to have been somehow enveloped by the aura of wildness and courting of disaster that followed the line of R. J. Only now, when Patrick was in his mid-thirties, had researched his family history and begun to try to deal with the money generated by it, was he beginning to get out from under its spell. And the process, he felt, was not yet complete.

In 1987 Patrick stepped up his antismoking campaign. Now his speeches stressed the power of the tobacco lobby and the marketing of U.S. brands in Third World countries. Surgeon General Koop wrote that Patrick had "distinguished himself as one of the nation's most influential advocates of a smoke-free America." In early 1988, the World Health Organization, an agency of the United Nations, honored Patrick by giving him an award for furthering the health of the world community.

As a natural outgrowth of his involvement in the fight against smoking, Patrick was asked to become a principal in a commercial venture aimed at helping people to get off cigarettes. He saw in the venture a way to cross-finance his campaign against smoking, and even though it meant a big risk both in financial terms and in personal ones, he believed he now had to take such risks. Patrick plunged a portion of his financial resources, as well as his time and energy, into the Reynolds Stop Smoking Program. If the enterprise succeeded, he'd have a thriving business; if not, he'd be a less wealthy man — but that didn't matter, because he had made a commitment and was taking a risk in a venture that was of a piece with his main focus, the antismoking campaign that was an expression of who he was, where he'd come from, what he believed.

The commercial venture failed to meet expectations and was

closed down, at a loss; however, it brought Patrick to the attention of the nation's largest producer of motivational audiocassettes. This firm asked him to become the public spokesman and to be otherwise affiliated with a stop-smoking program developed by a Yale University doctor and introduced in 1988 during the "Great American Smokeout," an event sponsored annually by the American Cancer Society and the Heart and Lung Associations. Patrick also threw himself into the forefront of the struggle to pass California's Proposition 99, a ballot initiative aimed at collecting an extra twenty-five cents per pack of cigarettes and applying the monies to health research, medical services for the indigent, and education to discourage smoking. Patrick was also on the front lines in an Oregon ballot measure that proposed a ban on smoking in almost every indoor public space in that state.

The fight for Proposition 99 put him, for the first time, into direct confrontation with the RJR Company, one of a consortium of manufacturers who spent an estimated $15 million to try to defeat the California measure. Ads featuring Patrick and actor Jack Klugman battled those of the cigarette manufacturers, and for some time the fate of the initiative was in doubt.

During the last weeks of these campaigns, in October and early November of 1988, RJR Nabisco executives, led by CEO F. Ross Johnson, announced plans for a $17 billion leveraged buyout of the company, one that would net Johnson and a handful of other top executives more than $100 million each. The insiders' bid would later be topped, at $25 billion, by the buyout firm of Kohlberg, Kravis, Roberts & Company, which would acquire RJR Nabisco in early December in the largest corporate takeover in history. Patrick's brothers smiled as the price of their RJR stock climbed — but news of the impending buyout only intensified Patrick's resolve to help get Proposition 99 passed.

As he traveled around the country, speaking about the roots of his concern with smoking, Patrick had daily to consider the history of his family, which had brought him both the inherited wealth that had influenced much of his early life and the motivation for his antismoking crusade.

The story of the tobacco Reynoldses had been a classic American saga. First there was Hardin, that stern, religious man who provided so strong an entrepreneurial and behavioral model that his sons emulated him all their lives. R. J., founder of the RJR Company, had been a genius typical of his times, an innovator and risk taker

records of land transfers. Both books acknowledge Nancy Susan Reynolds as publication sponsor. Perspective on Abram Reynolds's recollections comes from historical and contemporary accounts, such as William Couper's *One Hundred Years at V.M.I.*, John Sergeant Wise's *End of an Era*, R. E. Withers's *Autobiography of an Octogenarian*, and *The Official Records of the Civil War* and *The Record of Virginia Soldiers in War*. The tobacco business and life in the South before and during the Civil War are documented in J. C. Robert's *Tobacco Kingdom*, Avery Craven's *Growth of Southern Nationalism*, E. Merton Coulter's *Confederate States of America*, Bertram Wyatt-Brown's *Southern Honor*, Bell Irwin Wiley's *Life of Billy Yank* and *The Life of Johnny Reb*, Wilbur Cash's *Mind of the South*, and Glenn Davis's *Childhood and History in America*.

CHAPTER TWO: R. J. AND ABRAM

Comments on the history of Reconstruction have been drawn from Crandall A. Shifflett's *Patronage and Poverty in the Tobacco South*, C. Vann Woodward's *Origins of the New South*, James L. Roark's *Masters Without Slaves*, Dwight B. Billings, Jr.'s, *Planters and the Making of a "New South,"* and Nannie Mae Tilley's *Bright Tobacco Industry, 1860–1929* and *The R. J. Reynolds Tobacco Company*.

The educational histories of Abram and R. J. Reynolds have been fleshed out by information from an article about Warren H. Sadler in a Baltimore directory of 1879; by George James Stevenson's *Increase in Excellence: A History of Emory and Henry College*; and through a compendium article on dyslexia by David Holzman.

Abram has been less extensively studied than his brother R. J. His early days in Bristol are detailed in his son R. S. Reynolds's unfinished memoir, *The Marble King of Bristol*, and in Robert S. Loving's *Double Destiny*. Religious revivals, Prohibitionism, and other of Abram's passions are evoked in Charles A. Johnson's *Frontier Camp Meeting;* W. E. Hesseltine's article "Methodism and Reconstruction in East Tennessee"; and Paul E. Isaac's *Prohibition and Politics*. Family legend says that Abram ran for national office on the Prohibition ticket. No evidence of this could be found in an encyclopedic history of the movement.

CHAPTER THREE: ON THE RISE

The main sources for this chapter are the contemporary newspapers of Winston and Bristol and Nannie Mae Tilley's book on RJR. Adelaide Fries's compendium on the history of Forsyth County provided many details, and Henry Foltz's remembrances furnished others about Winston in the 1870s. R. J. Reynolds's moonshining is documented in letters in the Duke University library. His sexual forays are, as one might imagine, less well documented, but they live on in people's memories; even in the

1980s, black visitors at R. J.'s birthplace have made inquiries to determine whether R. J. might have been the father of their lines.

The Mind of the Millionaire, Albert Atwood's 1926 study, incorporates F. W. Taussig's theories as well as many earlier sources and published material.

Abram Reynolds's pamphlet on Bristol has been recently reprinted by the town's historical society and is a wonderful find. The Archives of Appalachia at East Tennessee University provide some documentation on the boom in Bristol and Abram's holdings in it.

CHAPTER FOUR: PLUG WARS

Three books document the Duke family; the most exhaustive is Robert F. Durden's *Dukes of Durham*, but James K. Winkler's earlier book, *Tobacco Tycoon*, provides more personal details. Josephus Daniels's many volumes of autobiography chart his relationship with the Dukes and with R. J. Reynolds. Harbour Reynolds's difficulties with the law are recorded in the Forsyth County courthouse. The description of R. J.'s Victorian "fantasy" is Fambrough Brownlee's.

CHAPTER FIVE: UNDER THE TRUST

Details about Winston at the turn of the century come from the nostalgia columns of the short-lived newspaper *Thursday*. R. S. Reynolds left an uncompleted memoir, *The Marble King of Bristol*, recently printed by a member of the family.

Information on Katharine Smith, later Katharine Reynolds, is skimpy; a major source is Margaret Supplee Smith's article entitled "Reynolda: A Rural Vision in an Industrializing South," which she kindly allowed us to see in manuscript. Other sources include several newspaper interviews of people who knew her or who have read some of her correspondence. Further publications about Reynolda are a series of articles in contemporary magazines and a thesis by Alonzo T. Stephens, Jr.

The comparative lists of millionaires in 1892 and 1902 have drawn comment from several sociologists and historians. The quote from a British social analyst about contemporary greed and the statistical comparisons come from Gustavus Myers's seminal work, *The Ending of the Hereditary American Fortunes*. John Quentin Feller, Jr.'s, thesis on the breakup of the trusts is particularly insightful.

CHAPTER SIX: KING OF TOBACCO

The Archives of Appalachia provide new details on Abram Reynolds's landholdings and the operation of the cleanser business. A file of old issues of *The Three Cent Pup* was turned up by Mrs. Bill Sharpe and provided to us. The circumstances surrounding R. J. Reynolds's last-minute adjustments to his will are related in various court challenges filed against the estate and its guardians by Dick Reynolds in later years. Nancy Reynolds's recollections are quoted in various articles, such as that in the December 1971 issue of *Forbes*.

CHAPTER SEVEN: KATHARINE AND ED

Material on Katharine and Ed Johnston has been obtained from interviews, alumni journals of Davidson College, and court records. Some of the children's early letters, and the one from Bum to Katharine, are in the Nancy Susan Reynolds Papers. Reynolds High yearbooks provide glimpses of the 1920s. Stephen Kern's article on the psychodynamics of Victorian and post-Victorian families puts the upbringing of the Reynolds children in context.

CHAPTER EIGHT: FLY-BOYS

Frederick Cople Jahrer's study of American millionaires of the past hundred years is unsurpassed in its mining of the literature and primary sources; we have taken quotations by Henry Ford and William Vanderbilt from it.

The life-styles pursued by the Reynolds heirs in the 1920s are revealed in the guardianship records filed in Forsyth County. An equally important source is Mary Reynolds's letters to Nancy Reynolds, preserved in her papers. Smith's "suicide" notes were incorporated into the inquest held after his death. Both Smith Reynolds's and Dick Reynolds's involvement in aviation are traced by other family members in a civil suit filed against Smith's estate by Mary Babcock in 1940. Another helpful source on the Reynoldses' flying is Barry Alan Lawing's thesis on the aviation history of Winston-Salem.

R. S. Reynolds's poetry is collected in a small volume, *War Enthroned*. Today, family legend places the beginning of the Reynolds brokerage at 1931, which would make its inception dependent upon Charles Babcock's entry into the firm, but contemporary business references document incorporation and profits data for the brokerage in 1928.

CHAPTER NINE: SMITH AND LIBBY
and
CHAPTER TEN: THE MYSTERY

The best book about the tragedy of Smith Reynolds and Libby Holman is the late Jon Bradshaw's *Dreams That Money Can Buy*; we were fortunate to be able to trade information with Bradshaw during the writing of his book. We have tried to correct some errors that all the books make in regard to various Reynolds family members.

In addition, we have gathered information from the inquest, private records, and interviews, and some from Mary Babcock's letters to her sister, Nancy Reynolds. Unfortunately, in the letters available at the Wake

Forest University library, the series from Mary to Nancy stops abruptly in early 1932 and then resumes in the 1940s; whether there were no letters during the thirties or whether Nancy destroyed some from this period before giving her papers to the archive is not known. Smith Reynolds's log of his "round-the-world" journey was published after his death by Nancy, and, as she acknowledges in her introduction, it has been cleaned up for public consumption. The sanitizing of things connected to Smith is also obvious in the record of the public relations effort commissioned by the Reynolds family after Smith's death, which was provided to us by Linda Lee Reynolds.

Some people whom we interviewed about Smith and Libby preferred to give their information anonymously. The late Peter Wilson knew all the participants and spoke candidly about them just before his death.

CHAPTER ELEVEN: DICK AND BLITZ

Aubrey Brooks's memoir, *A Southern Lawyer*, provides insight into the maneuvering to carve up Smith Reynolds's estate. Bryan Haislip has documented the early years of the Z. Smith Reynolds Foundation. Uncle Will Reynolds's harness-racing career awaits a chronicler, but glimpses are provided by articles in *The Harness Horse*. Unlike the building of Reynolda, the erection of Devotion was the subject of no articles; our information comes from observation, conversation with family members, and interviews with such long-term employees as Edgar Blevins. Some details come from Surry County genealogical books.

Nancy Reynolds's Quarry Farm is the subject of a recent pamphlet in which her early diary is quoted. The Babcocks' alterations to Reynolda are covered in the Alonzo Stephens thesis. In the thirties, in an article about wealthy women, *Esquire* seems to have interviewed both Mary Babcock and Nancy but does not quote them directly. A history of the development of Sea Island, by Harold Martin, contains a report on Dick Reynolds's purchase of Sapelo; our estimate of Dick's having paid 10 percent of actual value for Sapelo and the *Zapala* is based on surrounding land values and known 1920s costs of yachts more than 100 feet long. Material on the *Zapala* itself comes from the files of the Sea Island Company. E. Merton Coulter has written the best book on the island's history — *Thomas Spalding of Sapelo* — and the fauna and flora are unforgettably evoked by the naturalist team of Mildred and John Teal, who worked there. Descriptions of Dick's investments dating to the 1930s come from records of his divorce suits in the 1960s, through income tax statements that list stocks by date of purchase. The country club fracas is related in the pages of the Winston papers, and the yachting is detailed in the *New York Times* and *San Francisco Chronicle*.

CHAPTER TWELVE: POLITICS

Dick Reynolds's public years have been exhaustively researched especially for this book by James Vickers. Dick's public career is described in the pages of North Carolina newspapers, in the letters and papers of some of the participants in political duels (such as O. Max Gardner and Clyde Hoey), and in the remembrances of Marshall Kurfees and other of Dick's friends and co-workers. Because editor Bill Sharpe was a long-term intimate of Dick's, another important source is the pages of *Thursday*, which also document the increasing distance between Dick and Blitz, as do comments in Mary Babcock's letters.

Tom Davis's memoir recalls the start of Piedmont Airlines. There is very little about the flap over Winston-Salem and the Z. Smith Reynolds Airport in the "official" biography of Eastern Airlines, by Robert Serling, but some information has been obtained from interviews and Barry Alan Lawing's thesis on aviation in Winston-Salem.

Dick's connection with the Democratic National Committee is documented in the files of the Franklin Delano Roosevelt Library at Hyde Park. Unfortunately, Ed Flynn's autobiography, *You're the Boss*, was published at the time when Dick's loans had become a point of controversy, and Flynn does not talk much about Dick; however, in letters Dick wrote to Marianne O'Brien in 1944–45 he claims Flynn as one of his best friends. These wartime letters are also the source for Dick's view of his attempts to join the armed services and of FDR's request for him to delay his resignation until a successor could be found.

CHAPTER THIRTEEN: GOING TO WAR

Mary Babcock's letters to Nancy Reynolds and Dick Reynolds's letters to Marianne O'Brien form the basis of this chapter. Dick's correspondence to Admiral O. B. Hardison provides other details, as do the guardianship papers filed by Blitz in 1945. Other sources are interviews with Dorothy Cook, Nettie Allen, Warren Ritchie, Janey Dorsey, and Dean Murphy.

CHAPTER FOURTEEN: STARTING OVER: MARIANNE

The rival divorce motions of Dick and Blitz Reynolds reflect many details about the pair's behavior and feelings during this period. Mary Babcock's letters are also full of information. R. S. Reynolds's unfinished memoir tells of the "opportunity" in aluminum and must be read in the context of the story of the industry as a whole, told in "Aluminum Reborn," *Fortune*, May 1946.

The relationship between Dick and President Truman emerges from several interviews, but not much documentation exists in the files of the

Truman Library. The Sapelo Island brochure provides background on the formation of the foundation there.

A great deal of basic material on the years 1952–62 comes from the extensive files on the two divorce trials involving Dick and Muriel Reynolds, which are in storage at the courthouse in Darien, Georgia. These records also offer data on the participants going back many years earlier. This information was supplemented by papers supplied to us by Muriel before her death in 1983 and by an extended interview with her longtime friend "Hutch" Hutchins. Material on Porfirio Rubirosa is scarce, but most of it is summarized in a *New York Times* obituary.

CHAPTER FIFTEEN: IN DANGER: MURIEL
and
CHAPTER SIXTEEN: SEEKING PEACE: ANNEMARIE

As mentioned previously, the best source for information about 1952–62 is the voluminous records of the divorce trials in 1960 and 1962. In an effort to document the couple's life-style, Muriel Reynolds's lawyers wrung long depositions and many important papers from Dick Reynolds, Stratton Coyner, and other of Dick's advisers.

Interviews with Linda Lee Reynolds and several of Zach Reynolds's friends buttress impressions of his life in the 1950s and 1960s. Fred Johnson and his relatives have told us about moving the hoard of gold, confirming suspicions of many outsiders.

Sources on Dick's last years are scant, but some documents, including several "last wills," were procured by Muriel after his death and passed on to us. Letters from Dick to Patrick Reynolds in 1963 and 1964 have been preserved. Further impressions came from conversations with Nancy Reynolds before her death and with other family members.

CHAPTER SEVENTEEN: ZACH AND PATRICK

Both Marianne and Muriel Reynolds have left documents about their attempts to question Dick Reynolds's last will. Muriel's files, for instance, contain such things as the record of the examination of Dick's sperm count, as well as the opinions of the handwriting and syntax experts she commissioned to look at the last will.

Zach Reynolds's life emerges from interviews with Linda Lee Reynolds, Robert Whitman, Ted Hill, Bob Cranor, and others. His separation agreement and divorce settlement are on record in Forsyth County, as are the suits and countersuits filed after his death (and later withdrawn) by Linda Lee and Dorothy Reynolds. Interviewee David Cannon provides an eyewitness view of the fatal plane crash.

The 1970 reunion is the subject of a file in Nancy Reynolds's papers, which also contains letters from Nannie Mae Tilley written in connection with shaping the *Reynolds Homestead* book. Nannie C. Terry told us the background of the rejuvenation of Rock Spring. The RJR Company's status in 1970 was examined in several articles in 1971; other articles depicted Reynolds Metals at the same point in time. Smith Bagley's difficulties became public in the late 1970s. The problems of Sapelo have surfaced and been written about in various newspapers in the 1980s. Patrick Reynolds's correspondence with Nancy and Annemarie Reynolds has been preserved, though his letters to Nancy have not been found in her papers. Insight into the activities of heirs in the modern era is provided by Lewis Lapham's *Money and Class in America* and John Sedgwick's *Rich Kids*.

EPILOGUE

Patrick Reynolds's antismoking campaign has received full treatment in an AP article by Tom Minehart (*San Francisco Chronicle*, August 27, 1986) and ones by Leslie Bennetts (*New York Times*, October 25, 1986), James Kindall (*New York Newsday*, April 22, 1988), Jon Anderson (*Chicago Tribune*, May 18, 1988), and Steve Marshall (*USA Today*, May 19, 1988).

Bibliography

Books and Pamphlets

Ashe, Samuel E., Stephen B. Weeks, and Charles L. Van Noppen, eds. *Biographical History of North Carolina*. 8 vols. Greensboro, N.C.: N.p., 1905–1917.

Atwood, Albert W. *The Mind of the Millionaire*. New York: Harper & Bros., 1926.

Babcock, Mary Reynolds. *First Aid for Flowers*. New York: Farrar, Straus, 1954.

Beatty, Jerome, Jr. *Our 100th Anniversary, 1875–1975*. Winston-Salem, N.C.: Privately printed by R. J. Reynolds Industries, Inc., 1975.

Billings, Dwight B., Jr. *Planters and the Making of a "New South."* Chapel Hill: University of North Carolina Press, 1979.

Bilstein, Roger E. *Flight Patterns: Trends of Aeronautical Development in the United States, 1918–1929*. Athens: University of Georgia Press, 1983.

Blythe, LeGette. *Reynolda House*. Winston-Salem, N.C.: Privately printed, n.d.

Bradshaw, Jon. *Dreams That Money Can Buy*. New York: William Morrow, 1985.

Bristol Virginia Tennessee, A Pictorial History. Bristol, Tenn.-Va.: Bristol Historical Association, 1985.

Brooks, Aubrey. *A Southern Lawyer*. Chapel Hill: University of North Carolina Press, 1950.

Brownlee, Fambrough. *Winston-Salem: A Pictorial History*. Norfolk, Va.: Donning Co., 1977.

Burgess, George C., and Miles C. Kennedy. *Centennial History of the Pennsylvania Railroad Company, 1846–1946*. Philadelphia: Pennsylvania Railroad, 1949.

Case, Earl C. *The Valley of East Tennessee*. Nashville: Tennessee State Division of Geology Bulletin no. 36, 1925.

Cash, Wilbur J. *The Mind of the South*. New York: Alfred A. Knopf, 1941.

Chase, Reverend B. W. *Tobacco: Its Physical Moral and Social Influences*. New York: William B. Mucklow, 1878.

Cherrington, Everett H., ed. *Standard Encyclopedia of the Alcohol Problem*, vol. 5. Westerville, Oh.: N.p., 1929.

Clase, Pablo, hijo. *Rubi: La vida de Porfirio Rubirosa*. Santo Domingo, Dominican Republic: Publicaciones America, 1983.

[Coffin, Howard Earle?] *Sapeloe Island*. Privately printed, 1933.

Costello, John. *The Pacific War, 1941–1945*. New York: Rawson, Wade, 1981.

Coulter, E. Merton. *The Confederate States of America*. Vol. 7 of *History of the South*. Baton Rouge: Louisiana State University Press, 1950.

————. *The South During Reconstruction, 1865–1877*. Vol. 8 of *History of the South*. Baton Rouge: Louisiana State University Press, 1947.

————. *Thomas Spalding of Sapelo*. Baton Rouge: Louisiana State University Press, 1940.

Couper, William. *One Hundred Years at V.M.I.*, vol. 2. Richmond, Va.: Garrett & Massie, 1939.

Craven, Avery. *The Growth of Southern Nationalism*. Vol. 6 of *History of the South*. Baton Rouge: Louisiana State University Press, 1950.

Daniels, Jonathan. *Tar Heels: A Portrait of North Carolina*. New York: Dodd, Mead, 1941.

Daniels, Josephus. *Editor in Politics*. Chapel Hill: University of North Carolina Press, 1941.

————. *Tar Heel Editor*. Chapel Hill: University of North Carolina Press, 1939.

————. *The Wilson Era — Years of Peace, 1910–1917*. Chapel Hill: University of North Carolina Press, 1944.

————. *The Wilson Era — Years of War and After*. Chapel Hill: University of North Carolina Press, 1946.

Davidson College Bulletin. *The Alumni Journal*. Charlotte, N.C., November 1951.

Davis, Glenn. *Childhood and History in America*. New York: Psychohistory Press, 1976.

Davis, Thomas H. *The History of Piedmont*. Exton, Penn.: Newcomen Society in North America, 1982.

Davis, William. *The Rich*. London: Sidgwick & Jackson, 1982.

Dozier, Howard Douglas. *History of the Atlantic Coast Line Railroad*. Cambridge, Mass.: Houghton Mifflin, 1920.

Durden, Robert F. *The Dukes of Durham, 1865–1929*. Durham, N.C.: Duke University Press, 1975.

Famous Brands from RJR Nabisco. Winston-Salem, N.C.: RJR Nabisco, Inc., 1986.

Flynn, Ed. *You're the Boss*. New York: Viking, 1947.

Friedel, Frank. *FDR and the South*. Baton Rouge: Louisiana State University Press, 1965.

Fries, Adelaide L. *Historical Sketch of Salem Female Academy*. Salem, N.C.: Privately printed, 1902.

Fries, Adelaide L., Stuart T. Wright, and J. E. Hendricks. *Forsyth: The History of a County on the March*. Chapel Hill: University of North Carolina Press, 1976.

Gilbert, Price, Jr. *The Escort Carriers in Action*. Atlanta: Privately printed by R. J. Reynolds, Jr., 1945.

Green, R. Edwin. *St. Simons Island*. Westmoreland, N.Y.: Arner Publications, 1982.

Griffin, Frances. *Old Salem: An Adventure in Historic Preservation*. Winston-Salem, N.C.: Old Salem, Inc., 1970.

Haislip, Bryan. *A History of the Z. Smith Reynolds Foundation*. Winston-Salem, N.C.: John F. Blair, 1967.

Hall, William James, and Helen Johnson McMurray. *Tanglewood: Historic Gem of Forsyth County, North Carolina*. Winston-Salem, N.C.: Hunter Publishing, 1979.

Harkrader, J. C. *Witness to an Epoch*. Kingsport, Tenn.: Kingsport Press, 1965.

Isaac, Paul E. *Prohibition and Politics: Turbulent Decades in Tennessee, 1885–1920*. Knoxville: University of Tennessee Press, 1965.

Jahrer, Frederick Cople. "The Gilded Elite: American Multimillionaires, 1865 to the Present." In *Wealth and the Wealthy in the Modern World*, edited by W. D. Rubinstein. London: Croom Helm, 1980.

Johnson, Charles A. *The Frontier Camp Meeting*. Dallas: Southern Methodist University Press, 1955.

Kern, Stephen. "Explosive Intimacy: Psychodynamics of the Victorian Family." In *The New Psychohistory*, edited by Lloyd De Mause. New York: Psychohistory Press, 1976.

Kinsey, Barbara, and the University of Georgia Marine Institute. *A Sapelo Island Handbook*. Sapelo Island, Ga.: Privately printed, n.d.

Kolko, Gabriel. *Railroads and Regulation, 1877–1916*. Princeton, N.J.: Princeton University Press, 1965.

Lapham, Lewis. *Money and Class in America*. New York: Weidenfeld & Nicolson, 1988.

Lassiter, Barbara B. *Reynolda House: American Paintings*. Winston-Salem, N.C.: Reynolda House, 1971.

Lingle, Thomas Wilson, ed. *Davidson College Alumni Catalogue, 1837–1924*. Charlotte, N.C.: Presbyterian Standard Publishing Co., 1924.

Linn, Jo White. *The Gray Family and Allied Lines*. Salisbury, N.C.: Privately printed, 1976.

———. *People Named Hanes*. Salisbury, N.C.: Privately printed, 1980.

Loving, Robert S. *Double Destiny: The Story of Bristol Tennessee-Virginia*. Bristol, Tenn.-Va.: King Printing, 1955.

Lundberg, Ferdinand. *America's Sixty Families*. New York: Vanguard Press, 1937.

Machlin, Milt. *Libby*. New York: Tower Books, 1980.

Martin, Frederick T. *The Passing of the Idle Rich*. New York: Doubleday Doran, 1911.

Martin, Harold H. *This Happy Isle: The Story of Sea Island and the Cloister*. Sea Island, Ga.: Sea Island Co., 1978.

Mary Reynolds Babcock Foundation. *Annual Report 1983*. Winston-Salem, N.C., 1983.

Morrison, Joseph L. *Governor O. Max Gardner*. Chapel Hill: University of North Carolina Press, 1974.

———. *Josephus Daniels, Small-d Democrat.* Chapel Hill: University of North Carolina Press, 1966.

Myers, Gustavus. *The Ending of the Hereditary American Fortunes.* New York: Julian Messner, 1939.

Noel, Mrs. Henry, and Mr. and Mrs. Jackson D. Wilson, Jr. *Roaring Gap.* Winston-Salem, N.C.: Excalibur Enterprises, 1976.

Official Records of the Civil War, Series I, vol. 37, Pt. I. *The War of the Rebellion.* U.S. War Department. Washington, D.C.: 1880–1901.

Pedigo, Virginia G., and Lewis G. Pedigo. *History of Patrick and Henry Counties, Virginia.* Roanoke, Va.: Privately printed, 1933.

Perry, Hamilton Darby. *Libby Holman, Body and Soul.* Boston: Little, Brown, 1983.

Powell, William S. *North Carolina, a Bicentennial History.* New York: Norton, 1977.

[Reynolds, Abram D.?] *Bristol Tennessee and Virginia.* Bristol, Tenn.-Va.: Bristol Land and Improvement Co., 1889. Reprint. Bristol, Tenn.-Va.: Bristol Historical Society, 1985.

Reynolds, Patrick. *Journal.* Miami: Privately printed, 1975.

Reynolds, Richard S., Jr. "Opportunity in Crisis," *The Reynolds Metal Story.* New York: Newcomen Society in North America, 1956.

———. *Stories About the Reynolds Family.* Privately printed, 1970.

Reynolds, Richard S., Sr. *Crucible.* New York: Fine Editions Press, 1950.

———. *The Marble King of Bristol.* Privately printed by Bill Reynolds, 1981.

———. *War Enthroned and Other Poems.* New York: Georgian Press, 1934.

Reynolds, Z. Smith. *Log of Aeroplane NR-898W.* New York: Privately printed by Nancy Bagley, 1932.

Reynolds High School Yearbook. *The Black and the Gold.* Winston-Salem, N.C.: 1926.

Robert, Joseph Clark. *The Tobacco Kingdom: Plantation, Market and Factory in Virginia and North Carolina, 1800–1860.* Durham, N.C.: Duke University Press, 1958.

Robertson, Jack. *Quarry Farm Gardener's Notes,* ed. Emily Herring Wilson. Quarry Farm, Conn.: Privately printed, 1985.

Robertson, Stewart, Jr. *My Friend Marshall.* Charlotte, N.C.: Heritage Printers, 1978.

Rondthaler, Edward. *The Memorabilia of Fifty Years, 1877–1927.* Raleigh, N.C.: Edwards & Broughton, 1928.

Ross, Walter S. *The Last Hero: Charles A. Lindbergh.* New York: Harper & Row, 1976.

Sadler, Warren H. "Warren H. Sadler." In *The Biographical Cyclopedia of Representative Men of Maryland and District of Columbia.* Baltimore: National Biographical Publishing Co., 1879.

Sapelo Island Research Foundation Report. Washington, D.C.: Sapelo Island Research Foundation, 1983.

Sedgwick, John. *Rich Kids.* New York: William Morrow, 1985.

Serling, Robert J. *From the Captain to the Colonel: An Informal History of Eastern Airlines.* New York: Dial Press, 1980.

Shifflett, Crandall A. *Patronage and Poverty in the Tobacco South*. Knoxville: University of Tennessee Press, 1982.

Sitterson, J. Carlyle. "Business Leaders in Post–Civil War North Carolina, 1865–1900." In *Studies in Southern History*, edited by J. Carlyle Sitterson. Chapel Hill: University of North Carolina Press, 1957.

Sorokin, Pitirim A. *American Millionaires and Multimillionaires*. Reprint. *Journal of Social Forces*, vol. 3, no. 4, May 1925.

Stevenson, George James. *Increase in Excellence: A History of Emory and Henry College*. New York: Appleton Century Croft, 1963.

Stover, John. *The Railroads of the South*. Chapel Hill: University of North Carolina Press, 1955.

Taylor, Oliver. *Historic Sullivan*. Bristol, Tenn.-Va.: Le Roi Press, 1909.

Teal, Mildred, and John Teal. *Portrait of an Island*. New York: Atheneum, 1964.

Tilley, Nannie M. *The Bright Tobacco Industry, 1860–1929*. Chapel Hill: University of North Carolina Press, 1948.

———. *Reynolds Homestead, 1814–1970*. Richmond, Va.: Robert Kilne, 1970.

———. *The R. J. Reynolds Tobacco Company*. Chapel Hill: University of North Carolina Press, 1985.

Tyler, James Hoge. *The Hoge Family*. Greensboro, N.C.: Privately printed, 1929.

Tyler, Lyon G. *Men of Mark in Virginia*, vol. 4. Washington, D.C.: Men of Mark Publishing Co., 1908.

Vanstory, Burnette. *Howard Earle Coffin*. Sea Island, Ga.: Privately printed, 1969.

Walker, Guy Morrison. *The Things That Are Caesar's*. New York: Al Fowle, 1922.

Wecter, Dixon. *Saga of American Society, 1607–1937*. New York: Scribner's, 1937.

Wellman, Manly Wade, ed. *Winston-Salem in History*. 13 vols. Winston-Salem, N.C.: Historic Winston, 1966–1976.

White, Larry C. *Merchants of Death: The American Tobacco Industry*. New York: William Morrow, 1988.

Wight, J. B. *Tobacco: Its Use and Abuse*. Nashville, Tenn.: Privately printed, 1889.

Wiley, Bell Irwin. *The Life of Billy Yank* and *The Life of Johnny Reb*. 2 vols. New York: Doubleday, 1971.

Winkler, James K. *Tobacco Tycoon*. New York: Random House, 1942.

Wise, John Sergeant. *The End of an Era*. Boston: Houghton Mifflin, 1899. Reprint. Baton Rouge: Louisiana State University Press, 1978.

Withers, Robert Enoch. *Autobiography of an Octogenarian*. Roanoke, Va.: Stone Printing, 1907.

Woodward, C. Vann. *Origins of the New South, 1877–1913*. Vol. 9 of *History of the South*. Baton Rouge: Louisiana State University Press, 1951.

Wyatt-Brown, Bertram. *Southern Honor*. New York: Oxford University Press, 1982.

Newspaper Articles

The following newspapers have been consulted extensively: Atlanta — *Constitution, Journal*; Bristol, Tennessee-Virginia — *Courier, Herald-Courier, News*;

London — *Times*; New York — *Daily News, Post, Times*; North Carolina — *Durham Morning Herald, Greensboro Daily News, Mount Airy News, Raleigh News and Observer*; Winston and Winston-Salem — *Daily Pilot, Elite, Evening Star, Journal, Leader, People's Press, Sentinel, Thursday*.

Callahan, Eileen. "Reynolds Millions Are Moving Around." *New York Sunday News*, June 30, 1946.

Davis, Chester, "Reynolda Estate: A Woman's Vision." *Winston-Salem Journal and Sentinel*, June 11, 1967.

Foltz, Henry. "Winston Fifty Years Ago." *Winston-Salem Journal*, January 30, 1926.

Jackson, O. Kay. "Official Explains University's Position in Dispute over Sapelo." *Brunswick* (Georgia) *News*, December 31, 1986.

Morris, Merrill. "UGA Marine Institute in Danger." *Athens* (Georgia) *Observer*, January 15, 1987.

"Nabisco Executives to Take Huge Gains in Their Buyout." *New York Times*, November 5, 1988.

Pasley, Fred. "Has Justice Been Done in the Reynolds Case?" *New York Sunday News*, December 11, 1932.

"Renegade Tobacco Heir Denounces Industry's Fight Against Prop. 99." *San Diego Union*, October 29, 1988.

Rivers, Reita. "For the Sake of All Georgia, Keep Sapelo Island Pristine." *Atlanta Journal and Constitution*, January 25, 1987.

Steadman, Tom. "Residents Say Life Without Reynolds Just Isn't the Same." *Greensboro News and Record*, July 12, 1987.

Thompson, Liz. "Katharine Reynolds." *Winston-Salem Journal*, February 25, 1986.

———. "A Deep Compassion Marked Her Life." *Winston-Salem Journal*, August 7, 1983.

Magazine Articles

"Aluminum and the Emergency." *Fortune*, May 1941.

"Aluminum Reborn." *Fortune*, May 1946.

Barnfather, Maurice. "Tar Wars?" *Forbes*, November 10, 1980.

Bassett, Preston. "Island's Part in World Aviation." *Long Island Forum* 13 (January 1950).

Bechtel, Stefan. "Anatomy of an Inquest." *Greensboro Magazine*, 1978.

Burns, Malcolm R. "Economies of Scale in Tobacco Manufacture, 1887–1910." *Journal of Economic History* 43 (June 1983).

———. "Outside Intervention in Monopolistic Price Warfare: The Case of the 'Plug War' and the Union Tobacco Company." *Business History Review* 56 (Spring 1982).

Erwin, Robert. "Dick Reynolds." *The Uplift* 39 (August 23, 1941).

"$57,000,000 Worth of Whizz and Whoozle." *Fortune*, August 1938.

Gahagan, Tom. "W. N. Reynolds." *The Harness Horse*, June 1940.

Hennessee, W. E. "Reynolds: Family Coat of Arms." *The State*, June 29, 1946.

Hesseltine, W. B. "Methodism and Reconstruction in East Tennessee." *East Tennessee Historical Society Publications* 3 (January 1931).

Holzman, David. "Getting on Right Side of the Brain." *Insight* (October 6, 1986).

Hurst, Tricia. "Growing Up at the Stork." *Interview*, December 1986.

Kuhn, I. C. "Rubi's Back and Zsa Zsa's Got Him." *American Mercury* 79 (August 1954).

MacArthur, Charles. "Personality Differences Between Middle and Upper Classes." *Journal of Abnormal and Social Psychology* 50 (March 1955).

Martin, Richard. "Pressure Rises to Go Smokeless." *Insight* (May 19, 1986).

Moore, W. R. "The Golden Isles of Guale." *National Geographic*, February 1934.

Myers, Ed. "Restoration of the R.J.R. Birthplace." *The State*, September 1, 1970.

"Return of Anne Cannon's Old Love." *American Weekly*, September 28, 1947.

"Richest U.S. Women." *Fortune*, November 1936.

Smith, Margaret Supplee. "Reynolda: A Rural Vision in an Industrializing South." *North Carolina Historical Review*, in press, 1988.

Stone, Michael H., and Clarice Vestenbaum. "Maternal Deprivation in Children of the Wealthy." *History of Childhood Quarterly* (Summer 1974).

Stubbs, Barbara Joyce. "The Story of Roosevelt Field: Forty Years of Flight, 1911–1951." *Nassau County Historical Society Journal* 24 (Summer 1963).

"The Great Aluminum Farce." *Fortune*, July 1951.

"Voyage into the Unknown." *Forbes*, December 1, 1971.

"William N. Reynolds Dies." *The Harness Horse*, September 12, 1951.

Unpublished Materials

Bagley, Dudley Warren. Papers. Southern Historical Collection of the University of North Carolina Library, University of North Carolina, Chapel Hill.

Barrow & Beck letter from Richard J. Reynolds about purchase of brandy. Manuscript Department, William R. Perkins Library, Duke University, Durham, North Carolina.

Carolina, Clinchfield and Ohio Railway Collection. Archives of Appalachia, Sherrod Library, East Tennessee State University, Johnson City.

Critz, Wesley. Papers. Southern Historical Collection of the University of North Carolina Library, University of North Carolina, Chapel Hill.

Duke Company records. Manuscript Department, William R. Perkins Library, Duke University, Durham, North Carolina.

Feller, John Quentin, Jr. "TR, the Department of Justice and the Trust Problem." Ph.D. diss., Catholic University, 1968.

Graham, Frank Porter. Papers. Southern Historical Collection of the University of North Carolina Library, University of North Carolina, Chapel Hill.

Gray, Gordon. Papers. Southern Historical Collection of the University of North Carolina Library, University of North Carolina, Chapel Hill.

Hardison, O. B. Papers. Southern Historical Collection of the University of North Carolina Library, University of North Carolina, Chapel Hill.

J. B. Duke Letterpress Book 1909–1911. Manuscript Department, William R. Perkins Library, Duke University, Durham, North Carolina.

Lawing, Barry Alan. "A History of Aviation of Winston-Salem." Master's thesis, Wake Forest University, 1984.

Martin, John Sanford. Papers. Manuscript Department, William R. Perkins Library, Duke University, Durham, North Carolina.

Moore, John T. Papers. Manuscript Department, William R. Perkins Library, Duke University, Durham, North Carolina.

Nancy Susan Reynolds Papers. Letters relating to 1970 reunion; letters from Mary Reynolds Babcock to Nancy Susan Reynolds, 1917–53; index to Reynolds Family Papers. Baptist Collection, Wake Forest University, Winston-Salem, North Carolina.

North Carolina Collection Clipping File, University of North Carolina, Chapel Hill, North Carolina.

Reines, Philip. "A Cultural History of the City of Winston-Salem, North Carolina, 1766–1966." Master's thesis, University of Denver, 1970.

Reynolds, Patrick. Correspondence with Marianne Reynolds, Muriel Reynolds, Nancy Susan Reynolds, and Richard J. Reynolds, Jr., 1963–85.

Reynolds, Richard J. Letter to Wade H. Bynum, 1896. Manuscript Division, University of Virginia Library, Charlottesville, Virginia.

Reynolds, Richard J., Jr. Democratic National Committee records on Richard J. Reynolds, Jr. (PPF 3730 and OF 300). Franklin Delano Roosevelt Library, Hyde Park, New York.

Reynolds, Richard J., Jr. Files on Richard J. Reynolds, Jr., courtesy of Muriel Reynolds.

Reynolds, Richard J., Jr. Letters to Marianne O'Brien, 1944–46, courtesy of Dorothy Cook.

Reynolds, Z. Smith. Public relations report on Z. Smith Reynolds, H. A. Bruno–R. R. Blythe and Associates, courtesy of Linda Lee Reynolds.

Sea Island Company files about Sapelo Island and Howard G. Coffin, Sea Island, Georgia.

Stephens, Alonzo Theodore, Jr. "The Making of Reynolda House." Master's thesis, Wake Forest University, 1978.

The Three Cent Pup, issues, courtesy of Mrs. Bill Sharpe.

University of North Carolina Alumni Association files, Chapel Hill, North Carolina.

Virginia Iron, Coal and Coke Company Records, ca. 1870–1920. Archives of Appalachia, Sherrod Library, East Tennessee State University, Johnson City.

Warren, Lindsay C. Papers. Southern Historical Collection of the University of North Carolina Library, University of North Carolina, Chapel Hill.

Withers, Robert E. Papers. Manuscript Department, William R. Perkins Library, Duke University, Durham, North Carolina.

Court Papers

Bristol, Tennessee-Virginia, court records.

Commissioner-alderman records, 1874–1942, Winston-Salem, North Carolina, in Forsyth County Courthouse.

Criminal judgment dockets, 1875–1925. Forsyth County records.

Divorce motions and papers, Richard J. Reynolds, Jr., and Elizabeth D. Reynolds, 1946. Forsyth County records.

Divorce trials of Richard J. Reynolds, Jr., and Muriel Reynolds, 1960 and 1962, Darien, Georgia. McIntosh County Courthouse records.

Guardianship records, 1920s (children of R. J. Reynolds). Forsyth County records. Guardianship records, 1940s (children of Richard J. Reynolds, Jr.). Forsyth County records.

Helvering v. Reynolds (Richard J., Jr.), 313 U.S. 428 (May 26, 1941).

Inquest in the matter of the death of Zachary Smith Reynolds, 1932. Forsyth County records.

Reynolds v. *Safe Deposit and Trust Company of Baltimore, et al.*, 1930–31. Forsyth County records.

Suit by Mary Reynolds Babcock against the estate of Zachary Smith Reynolds, 1940. Forsyth County records.

Suits by Linda Lee Reynolds and Dorothy Sides Reynolds, 1980. Forsyth County records.

Wills: Abram David Reynolds, Kate Bitting Reynolds, Katharine Smith Reynolds Johnston, R. J. Reynolds, Walter Reynolds, William Neal Reynolds. Forsyth County records.

List of Interviewees

Formal interviews were conducted from 1983 through 1988. These include: James Banks, Sapelo Island; Edgar Blevins, near Devotion; David Cannon; Dorothy Cook, New York City; Stratton Coyner, Winston-Salem; R. H. Cranor, Winston-Salem; Robert Fox, Winston-Salem; Curly Harris, New York City; Ted Hill, W. H. Hutchins, Atlanta; Emmett, Fred, and Ronnister Johnson, Sapelo Island; Bud and Caroline Johnston, Raleigh; Mabel and Marshall Kurfees, Winston-Salem; Dean Murphy, Miami; Linda Lee Reynolds, Winston-Salem; Marianne Reynolds, New York City; Michael Reynolds, Winston-Salem; Muriel Reynolds, New York City (before 1983); Warren Ritchie, Los Angeles; Nannie C. Terry, Rock Spring; Nettie Allen Voges, Winston-Salem; Robert Whitman; Peter Wilson, Winston-Salem.

We also interviewed many people who generously provided information but who preferred to remain anonymous.

Acknowledgments

In addition to the interviewees cited on p. 338, we would like to thank several other individuals for their contributions. Chief among these is Jim Vickers, whose research and tireless endeavors in the middle 1980s made much of this book possible. Tony Lalor and Kymberly Frolich also labored mightily in the closing phases of research. We would like to give special thanks to the late Jon Bradshaw, who shared with us his interviews and research into the Smith-and-Libby episode.

For their excellent editorial guidance and support, we also would like to thank our manuscript editor, Perdita Burlingame, our copyeditor, Debbie Jacobs, and the executive editor and associate publisher of Little, Brown, Fredrica Friedman.

The authors and researchers received a great deal of assistance from the following libraries and institutions: the Bobst Library of New York University; the Bristol Historical Society; McIntosh County Courthouse; several divisions at Duke University and at the University of North Carolina at Chapel Hill; the Enoch Pratt Free Library of Baltimore; the archives of the F.B.I.; Forsyth County Courthouse; the Franklin Delano Roosevelt Library at Hyde Park; branches of the New York Public Library; the archives of Sea Island, Inc.; the Sherrod Library of East Tennessee State University; Wake Forest University Library; and the Widener Library of Harvard University.

Finally, we would like to thank staff members and volunteers at Rock Spring, Reynolda, and on Sapelo for their assistance and to salute family members for their hospitality during our visits to the South. All of the above people's and institutions' assistance notwithstanding, any errors in the book remain ours.

— *Patrick Reynolds and Tom Shachtman, November 1988*

Index